EITHER/OR

Søren Kierkegaard

VOLUME II

Translated by Walter Lowrie
with revisions and a foreword
by Howard A. Johnson

PRINCETON UNIVERSITY PRESS

PRINCETON, NEW JERSEY

FOREWORD BY THE REVISER

In the case of a book entitled *Either/Or*, says Kierkegaard, "one must either read it entire or not read it at all" (*Papirer*, IV B 24).

This is to appraise you of the fact, in case you had not noticed it before, that what you now have in your hands is Part II of a two-part work. Part I is also available as a paperback and should be read first—unless, like the author of Part I, you are so arbitrary as to go to see the middle of a play and read the third part of a book and by this means would "insure yourself a very different kind of enjoyment from that which the author had been so kind as to plan for you."

Anyone who tries to read this second volume without having read the first will certainly find himself in the dark much of the time. For the pseudonymous author of Volume II is a civil magistrate, Judge William by name, who, as a solid citizen and ethical idealist, undertakes to "Dutch uncle" the melancholy young man, a romanticist, who is the supposed author of Volume I. The lengthy letters addressed by Judge William to the young man, by which the judge would rescue him from the "path of perdition," lose their point and make little sense if we have not first of all made acquaintance with the younger romanticist by meeting him in Volume I. We know not his name, but we can come to know him by reading the Papers of A [i.e., Volume I]. They provide the foil for Judge William, author of the Papers of B [i.e., Volume II]. Although the Papers of A nowhere mention B, the outlook of B is constantly in mind and is constantly protested against. In this way, B is present, though hidden, in A's papers, and A is present in every page that B has written. It is this double debate that gives to *Either/Or* its unity—and its tremendous disjunctive power.

For a better preface than this I refer you, in the first instance, to the Foreword which stands at the beginning of

Volume I. For prefaces better still, consult the "Translator's Preface" written by Mrs. Swenson to introduce Volume I and the "Translator's Preface and Introduction"
which Dr. Lowrie provided for Volume II. For the best
preface of all, see what Kierkegaard himself has written,
at the beginning of the first volume, under the pen name
of Victor Eremita.

A word about the Notes which accompany both volumes: Mrs. Swenson and Dr. Lowrie have both transmitted to the reader a translation of some of the Notes
compiled (over many years and with the help of many
readers) by the Danish editors of Kierkegaard's *Samlede
Værker* (*Collected Works*). From that source the translators took up such notes as they felt to be useful, dis-
carded some they felt to be superfluous, and added some
they felt to be needful. It is the Danish notes thus modi-
fied which, for the most part, have been retained in the
present edition. However, I have felt the same need to
select, reject, and amplify. In so doing I have often had
occasion to be grateful to Professor F. J. Billeskov Jansen
of the University of Copenhagen whose lectures on
Either/Or I had the pleasure of hearing in the academic
year 1947–48. Much of the information and insight I
there derived has found its way into print in his four-
volume anthology of Kierkegaard, *Værker i Udvalg*
(Gyldendalske Boghandel, Nordisk Forlag, Copenhagen,
1950) and in his *Studier i Søren Kierkegaards Litterære
Kunst* (Rosenkilde og Bagger, Copenhagen, 1951). And
some of this, though not nearly enough, has found its way
into the Notes prepared for this current Princeton paperback edition.

Were it not for the fact that even cats may look at
kings, I would not have dared to lay a critical hand on any
translation produced by that famous Knight of *Dannebrog*
who is the subject of a book called *Dr. Lowrie of Princeton & Rome*. Actually I found so little needing revision in
this second volume of *Either/Or* that my name hardly
deserves a place on the title page. Yet I was told that it
must go there—as an act of kindness to librarians!—so as

to bring the title page of Volume II into consistency with that of Volume I. For the situation is already as confusing as can be imagined, since we are dealing with an actual author called Kierkegaard, purported authors styled A and B, a supposed editor named Victor Eremita, *three* different translators, and finally a tinkerer who introduces emendations! Solely, therefore, out of consideration for librarians, whose duties are difficult enough without my compounding them, I have allowed my name to stand.

I am glad to have opportunity here to acknowledge with gratitude that in preparing the manuscript of this revised translation I have had invaluable help from Miss Edith Neftel, Miss Carolyn S. Joy, and the Reverend Richard Reid, all of them esteemed colleagues here at the Cathedral Church of St. John the Divine.

Howard A. Johnson

New York
August 1958

TRANSLATOR'S PREFACE

Only because it is an opportunity, perhaps the last chance I shall have, to express my affectionate veneration for Professor David F. Swenson, have I undertaken to translate this volume. For I learned to my surprise after Dr. Swenson's death that he had translated something, and in some instances a good deal, from most of the eight parts of the first volume of *Either/Or;* and as Mrs. Swenson, wishing to salvage these precious fragments, undertook to complete the translation of that volume, I could do no less than translate the second—for obviously the "Either" could not be published without the "Or." In spite of the fact that S.K. published the second edition of *Either/Or* in one volume, it is too big a book for that, and now when the responsibility for the English translation is divided between two persons, it is convenient that it should be clearly divided by publishing the book, as originally it was published, in two volumes.

Although it is unusual, perhaps unique, to provide a preface for the second volume of a literary work, yet I had to say as much as I have said above. And having said that, I would say moreover that for me this task was not altogether an agreeable one. It is rather ironical that I, who had proposed to translate only S.K.'s latest and most definitely religious works, being interested profoundly only in them, should have found myself obliged, by the fact that no other proficient laborers volunteered, to *proceed backward* and translate several of the "aesthetic" works, ending here with the first literary work which S.K. produced. Although *Either/Or* (especially the part contained in the first volume) is undoubtedly a work of genius, and a work such as no man but S.K. could have produced, yet my experience as a translator who proceeds backward reveals a great discrepancy between this work and the works of S.K.'s maturity, with respect not only to the felicity and exactness of his expression, but also to the sheer weight and value of his thought. Having been accustomed to weighing his golden thoughts by troy measure, I find that avoirdupois scales are good enough for use here. In translating the last works I never ventured to think that I could improve upon S.K.'s careful choice of expression; but here there are many passages, especially in Judge William's first letter, which could easily be improved by a mediocre translator. I go even so far as to say that the book would be improved by leaving out many passages, which not only are badly expressed but often are examples, and tedious examples, of argument for argument's sake, which is the essence of sophistry. Of course I have not omitted any of them, neither have I yielded to the temptation of bettering them. But I protest here that, if in some instances the translation appears stupid or even incomprehensible, the original is no better. Inasmuch as I have been regarded by supercilious critics as an undiscriminating eulogist of S.K., I am not sorry to have an opportunity of saying this here. But I would say at the same time that this big book was written in such an incredibly short time, and in part under such unfavorable conditions, that we have no cause to wonder at its defects. That it was written in eleven months was S.K.'s boast—a very questionable boast. When we reflect how much else he was doing and suffering at that time this feat seems the more difficult and incredible. "Would to God it had been impossible"—as Dr. Johnson said when he heard a soprano praised for reaching the most difficult notes.

This is all I need to say by way of a preface. But I confess to a special liking for prefaces—at least for writing them. The author, having finished his serious labor, can breathe freely, write the preface at his ease, and talk familiarly to the reader. As for the translator, it is the only opportunity he has of writing in his own person. I can speak from experience—for have I not written twenty-six prefaces? Collected, they would make a tidy little volume. S.K.'s most amusing book was entitled *Prefaces*. It will never be translated, for it deals in a free and easy way with allusions to contemporary affairs which cannot be explained without pedantry. In the preface to the *Prefaces* the pseudonymous author, Nicholas Notabene, confides to the reader that he is not permitted to write a *book* because his wife is jealous of his preoccupation with such work, and hence he resorts to the expedient of writing a volume of *prefaces*. But there are other good reasons for writing a sequence of prefaces, although one never sees it done except when public demand has required one or more successive editions—"enlarged and improved," as the Germans say. Then the original preface is commonly preserved, and an indefinite number of prefaces follows it. Alas, I have never had this good fortune. But I have reflected that even without this popular demand for new editions there might be good reasons for accompanying a book with several prefaces.

Perhaps others besides me are accustomed to write a preface before a book is started in order to prescribe the aim —and then of course a very different one after the book is finished. If both were published, we should have an illuminating demonstration of the disparity between purpose and accomplishment. If only one preface is published, it ought to be for the convenience of the reviewers, seeing that they cannot always be expected to find time to read the book. To this end it ought of course to be laudatory. The blurb on the dust cover is usually made out of that, and it is astonishing how the reviewers lap it up. It is perhaps for this reason I have commonly had a *succès d'estime* —which unfortunately has led to no other success. But in addition to this there surely ought to be a preface meant for the readers, and perhaps a special preface addressed, as are all of the prefaces to S.K.'s *Edifying Discourses*, "to that single individual . . . my reader." One might well add a chatty autobiographical preface with a portrait of the author, containing just what the public demands, which generally it gets less authentically, and perhaps less flatteringly, from the reviewer. Another preface might be devoted to the prospective critic, seeking to disarm him in advance. Indeed there is no end to the prefaces which might appropriately accompany every book. Since I am only a translator it would not be seemly for me to try out this experiment here. But precisely as the translator I must follow this with an introduction, which applies of course principally to this volume.

Walter Lowrie

May 11, 1942
Princeton

INTRODUCTION BY THE TRANSLATOR

In his *Journal* (IV A 43) S.K. expresses his "judgment upon *Either/Or*"—and it is not a modest one: "There was a youth, richly gifted as an Alcibiades. He went astray in the world. In his distress he looked about for a Socrates, but among his contemporaries he found him not. Then he begged the gods to transform him into one. And, lo, he who had been so proud of being an Alcibiades became so shamefaced and humbled by the grace of the gods that when he had received just what might properly have made him proud he felt himself inferior to all."

Either/Or is undoubtedly a work of genius, but it is a very uneven work. It is by no means one of S.K.'s greatest books, although in some respects it is perhaps the most interesting, because of the great variety of its contents and its many purple patches. On the other hand, this very variety may be regarded as a defect, and the lack of variety in the second volume makes it tedious, the only spice it has being the interjections of the "young friend," which hark back to S.K.'s aesthetic stage. In the Preface I have already remarked upon the serious defects in Judge William's first letter exalting the aesthetic validity of marriage. A certain dullness in both letters is accounted for only in part by the consideration that the Judge (and perhaps the worthy P. V. Jacobsen who stood as the model for this character) may have been a prosy person, as moralists commonly are, and that S.K. took pains to draw this figure true to type. It was difficult for S.K. to impersonate with great enthusiasm the ethical stage as such, for he himself was well beyond this sphere, having leaped at once into the religious, and he never was of the opinion that the ethical could stand alone, or could stand securely with no other support than the vague religiousness which Judge William evinced.

S.K. says expressly that the last part of *Either/Or* (i.e., the second volume) was written first. That implies that this

volume was written in part at least before he fled to Berlin
from the scandal of his broken engagement, therefore during the two months of agony when he was employed in
trying to induce Regina to "break it off," pretending that
he was a scoundrel. But at that time he was also preoccupied with the completion of his Master's dissertation on
The Concept of Irony and with the public defense of it.
He does not tell us which part of the volume was written
at that time, but there can be no doubt that it was the
first letter dealing with marriage. For us there is an ad-
ditional pathos in this defense of the aesthetic character of
marriage when we reflect that he was depicting in glowing
terms the beauty of marriage just at the time when he felt
compelled to renounce this happiness. And the defects of
this letter are explained, if they are not excused, by the
tragic preoccupations of that time. There was, it is true,
an objective reason for beginning the "Or" with the consideration of marriage; for, as S.K. remarked in his *Journal*
(IV A 234), "marriage is the deepest form of life's revelation," and "it is the duty of every man to be married." The
aesthetic young man, S.K. says, was never revealed: in the
first part only his casual moods were revealed; in the second only his external semblance whereby he would deceive
people. S.K. also remarks (IV A 213) that the aesthetic life
described in the first part came to grief upon time, and
that for this reason the significance of time is stressed in
the second part; also that the first part contains melancholy ("for imagination is always melancholy") and despair, and for this reason the second part teaches despair
as a thing one must will, and teaches one to choose oneself
—the way to overcome melancholy and despair. He explains
too that "to choose oneself" is only another expression for
the Socratic injunction "to know oneself."

We have to suppose then that the second letter was written during the four months he spent in Berlin. It gives evidence of the metaphysical interests, particularly the refuta-
tion of Hegelianism, by which he was absorbed at that
time. But a letter he wrote from Berlin to his friend Emil
Boesen shows how multifarious and distracting were his oc-
cupations there: "This winter in Berlin will always have

great significance for me. I have got a great deal accomplished. When you consider that I have heard from three to four lectures daily, have a language lesson daily, and that I have got so much written [of *Either/Or*] (and this in spite of the fact that at first I had to spend so much time writing out Schelling's lectures, which I did in a fair copy), and got a great deal read—so one cannot complain. And on top of that, all my pains and all my monologues [about Regina]. I have a feeling that I have not long to live, but I am living for a brief term and so much the more intensely."

In spite of all these distractions the Judge's second letter is a solid contribution to modern thought. It deals in a novel way with many important themes which were to find more adequate expression in his later writings, especially in the *Postscript*. The Judge uses the phrase "either/or" with solemn significance, whereas the young friend, who has these words more frequently in his mouth, frivolously takes them in vain. To the Judge they signify the vital importance of disjunction and choice. In this "passion for disjunction" he is in perfect agreement with S.K., who recognized that he was fitly called Either/Or, even if it was annoying to hear this name shouted after him by urchins in the street, and who at the end of his life wrote enthusiastically in one of the numbers of the *Instant* (xiv, p. 106), "Either/Or is the key of heaven." It is the exact opposite, he says, not only of "both—and," but of Hegelian mediation.

Evidently S.K. was himself sharply aware of the defects of the letter in which the Judge defended marriage, for he seized the opportunity presented in the *Stages* to present this argument more fully, and he gave the Judge a chance to redeem himself. Yet when the Judge had said all he knew how to say, it is not to be supposed that he said just what S.K. would have said had he been writing under his own name. For S.K. had something more to say, and something different (cf. my Introduction to the *Stages*, p. 6). But for all that, the Judge says a great deal about marriage, and a great deal that is very valuable, much that no one else has ever thought of saying; and in our day when, owing to the dissolution of our *mores*, this subject is necessarily much discussed, both by serious and by frivolous people, one might profitably turn to Judge William for instruction. I, as a minister of the Gospel with the obligation of talking seriously to every couple that comes to me to be married, being myself well instructed by Judge William, am prepared to talk to them hours on end—and to talk interestingly.

Only after S.K. had returned to Copenhagen early in March 1842 was he completely free to devote himself to *Either/Or,* and presumably the whole of the first volume was written then, in about five months. The whole manuscript had to be copied by a scribe in order to preserve the secret of his authorship, and the time required for this was doubtless not included in the eleven months. The book was published on February 20, 1843. It was "accompanied" by *Two Edifying Discourses,* published under his own name on May 16—the first of the series of religious discourses with which he accompanied all his pseudonymous works.

S.K. protested indignantly against the assumption that this book (especially the first volume) was made up of a lot of essays he had lying ready in his desk. We must take him at his word. And yet it is hard to resist the impression that, even if hardly anything except a few of the *Diapsalmata* had been written out beforehand, the various essays incorporated thoughts which had already occupied his lively imagination in his "aesthetic" days and needed only to be spun out.

Of the many and various reasons S.K. alleges for writing this book—a metaphysical interest, a religious purpose, as a "good deed" to Regina to "clarify her out of the engagement," as "a necessary evacuation"—only the last accounts adequately for most of the matter in the first volume. He needed to get these things off his chest, or, as he said, to "expectorate" them. The religious, moral and metaphysical interests were expressed here and there, but principally they were expressed by the title of the book, which in a way is more important than the book itself. S.K. affirmed that the title is so essential that the book "is not only *called* Either/ Or, but it *is* Either/Or," and that if no title had been printed on it, the reader could have supplied it (IV B 59, p. 217). This in a way the public understood, though they were unable to perceive how the book illustrated this in detail. And even we who are so much better informed about S.K.'s purpose do not find it any too easy to see how, as he affirmed, it "has one plan from the first word to the last, from the first *Diapsalm* to the conclusion of the Sermon" (IV A 214, 216). For his contemporaries it was the more difficult to detect a pervading plan and purpose, because (as he acknowledged in *The Point of View*) this book was "a deceit," even if it was meant, like the method of Socrates, to deceive people into the truth.

Although *Either/Or* produced a great sensation in Copenhagen, nobody was capable of understanding its subtle purpose, and so no one could adequately review it. The reviewers dwelt upon the immense size of the book, the amazing variety of its contents, and above all upon the mystery of its authorship. For this misunderstanding, or rather lack of understanding, S.K. was himself to blame, and yet he was furious. Furious especially at J. L. Heiberg, the *arbiter elegantiarum,* who wrote a long review in his *Intelligensblade.* Heiberg was scandalized by the size of the book and by the too great variety of its contents. Strangely enough, Heiberg, although he if any man was an aesthete, found the aesthetic part offensive and disgusting. It did not occur to him that it drew such an unfavorable picture of the aesthetic life and its consequences of melancholy and despair in order to warn men against it—to warn *him* personally of the end to which he was tending—and to throw the aestheticists into the arms of the ethicist. But it appears to me still more strange that he was profoundly attracted by the ethical part. He imagines a hypothetical reader: "One thinks, 'Have I the time to read a book like that? One may just as well leap into it as creep.' With that one literally *leaps* into the book, reads a little here and there to get a taste of it. One stumbles upon many piquant reflections, some of them perhaps are even profound, one doesn't know for certain, for when one believes one has seen a point one is again disoriented. . . . One hastens on to 'The Diary of the Seducer,' for the title already gives a hint that this production must be more creative than critical. And in a way one does not find oneself disappointed in this expectation, but one is disgusted, offended and indignant, and one asks oneself, not whether it is possible that anyone can be like this seducer, but whether it is possible that the individuality of an author can be so constituted as to find pleasure in putting itself in the place of that character and elaborating it in its most secret thoughts. A glance at the book, and this possibility is substantiated. One closes the book and says, '*Basta!* I have enough of the *Either,* I want to have nothing of the *Or.*' However, one hears the *Or* enthusiastically discussed, and since on every page to which one chances to turn one sees lightning flashes of thought which suddenly illuminate whole spheres of existence, the readers have a presentiment that there must be an organizing power which makes of it all a veritable whole, they feel themselves incessantly under the influence of a rare and highly gifted mind which from a deep speculative spring draws up before their eyes the most beautiful ethical points of view, they are so captivated by this volume that they are unable to lay it down till they have finished it. . . . But the serious reader of whom I have been speaking will, out of respect for an author who has written such an *Or,* take up again the *Either* and carefully read it through."

I confess that if a reviewer were to say something like this about a book of mine, I should not be "furious." Perhaps not many readers in our age will speak so enthusiastically about the second part of *Either/Or.* I confess that the first part is more interesting to me. I am sure that many will find the second part dull, as they did the *Stages,* which has far fewer defects. I was not surprised to hear people say that they found "Quidam's Diary" tedious, but I wondered that they expressed no enthusiasm for "The Banquet." Did not Brandes say that it could hold its own with Plato's *Symposium?* But, after all, I have to reflect that not many people in our day read the *Symposium,* and that those who do would perhaps pronounce it dull if they dared. After all, taste changes from age to age, and the tempo of our time is different.

Incidentally this volume has a singular interest for one who desires to know what sort of man S.K. was in his aesthetic stage, which corresponded precisely with his first seven years in the university. For he is graphically depicted in the descriptions Judge William gives of his "young friend" and in the lines which he ascribes to him. To that extent the second volume of *Either/Or* is autobiographical, almost in the same degree as the first. It is the self-portrait of a great artist; but it is the portrait which he painted of himself after he had ceased to be what he was. In a short while, because of his tragic experience as a lover, he had changed so much that he had to paint from memory, not by looking in a mirror; and, having resolutely chosen the "or," he is now addressing his earlier self through the mouth of Judge William, without by any means identifying himself with this amiable moralist.

In conclusion, I must speak of the Sermon with which the book ends. It is described as an *Ultimatum*. That means not merely a conclusion but a challenging conclusion. Evidently S.K. felt that for the sake of completeness he must make mention of the third stage, the religious. But lugged in as it was by the sermon it was barely mentioned as an addendum. Hence he could say later that *"Either/Or* goes no further than the ethical"—though we can see that the Judge was evidently a "Christian," in the vague sort of way that most people are. One of the reasons for writing the *Stages* was to give due prominence to the religious stage —although in that book the ethical stage has almost dropped out, and the religious stage is not depicted but suggested when we are shown the young man undergoing the metamorphosis which will evidently result in attaining the wings of faith. S.K. says of this sermon, as he might say of any good sermon, that "the aim of the sermon is not to lull, not to win a metaphysical view, but to clear for action"; and he said of himself, "This is what I am able to do at all times."

CONTENTS

EITHER/OR

A Fragment of Life

EDITED BY

VICTOR EREMITA

———

PART II

Containing the papers of B

Letters to A

———

*Les grandes passions sont solitaires, et les trans-
porter au désert, c'est les rendre à leur empire.*
CHATEAUBRIAND[1]

———

Copenhagen, 1843

Can be purchased from the
University Bookseller C. A. Reitzel
Printed at Bianco Luno's Press

[Translation of the original title page]

AESTHETIC VALIDITY
OF MARRIAGE

My Friend,

The lines upon which your eye first falls were written last. The aim of them is to make still one more attempt to force into the form of a letter the copious inquiry which is remitted to you herewith. Thus these lines correspond with the concluding lines and along with them constitute an envelope, apprising you in an external way, as will many proofs of an internal character, that what you read is a letter. The thought that I was writing you a letter I was not willing to relinquish, partly because the time at my disposal does not permit the more careful composition which a dissertation demands, and partly because I was reluctant to let slip the opportunity of addressing you in the tone of earnest admonition which the form of a letter allows. You are so expert in the art of talking in perfectly general terms about everything without letting yourself be moved by it, that I am not tempted to set in motion your dialectical powers. You know well how the Prophet Nathan behaved with King David when the king was willing enough to understand the parable the prophet set forth but was not willing to understand that it applied to him. So to make the application plain Nathan said, "Thou, O King, art the man." Thus I too have constantly sought to remind you that what is said is about you, that to you it is addressed. Therefore, I have no doubt that in reading this you will constantly get the impression that it is a letter you are reading, even though you might be distracted from this thought by the fact that the form of the paper is not appropriate to a letter. As a public functionary I am accustomed to write upon a large sheet of paper. Perhaps this may be advantageous if in your eyes it should contribute to give my epistle a certain official character. The letter which you receive herewith is a rather big one. If it were to be estimated by the scales of the post office, it would be a precious letter; by the troy weight of a subtle criticism it would perhaps turn out to be insignificant. I would therefore beg you not to employ either of these scales: not that of the post office, for you do not receive it in order to forward it; not that of criticism, for I should be loath to see you render yourself guilty of a misunderstanding so gross and unsympathetic.

In case any man but you were to get sight of this investigation, it would certainly strike him as exceedingly strange and superfluous; perhaps if he were a married man he would exclaim with the joviality of a paterfamilias, "Yes, marriage is the aesthetic side of life"; if he were a young man he would perhaps chime in rather confusedly and unreflectively, "Yes, love, thou art the aesthetic side of life"; but both of them would be unable to conceive how it could occur to me to wish to save the aesthetic repute of marriage. Indeed, instead of making myself meritorious in the eyes of actual or prospective husbands, I should presumably incur their suspicion, for a defense is an indictment. And I should have you to thank for this, for I on my part have never doubted—and you, in spite of all your bizarre qualities, I love as a son, as a brother, as a friend; I love with an aesthetic love because some day you will perhaps succeed in finding a center for your eccentric movements; I love you for the sake of your impetuosity, for the sake of your passions, for the sake of your foibles; I love you with the fear and trembling of a religious love because I see the devious paths you are treading, and because to me you are something quite other than a phenomenon. Yea, when I see you make a side spring, when I see you rear like a wild horse, throwing yourself on your haunches and then again plunging forward, I then—well, I refrain from all useless pedagogical intervention, but I think of an unbroken horse, and see also the hand that holds the reins, see the whip of fate raised menacingly over your head. And yet when this investigation finally comes to hand you will perhaps say, "Yes, this is undeniably an immense task he has undertaken, but let us see then how he has resolved it."

Perhaps I speak to you too mildly, perhaps I put up with too much from you, I ought perhaps to have availed myself more of the authority which in spite of your pride I actually exercise over you, or perhaps I ought not to have taken up this subject with you, for in many ways you are after all a terrible person, and the more one has to do with you the worse it is. You are not really an enemy of marriage, but you abuse your gifts for irony and sarcasm by making mock of it. I am ready to concede that in this respect you are not sparring with the air, that you strike a sure blow, and that you have much observation at your disposal, but at the same time I would say that this perhaps is your defect. Your life is wholly given over to preliminary runs. Presumably you will reply that at any rate this is always better than traveling on the railway of triviality and losing oneself atomistically in life's social throng. As I have remarked, one cannot say that you hate marriage, for doubtless your thought has never yet got to that subject, at least not without being scandalized by it, and so you must forgive me for assuming that you have never thought the matter through. What you have a predilection for is the first sensation of falling in love. You know how to submerge yourself in a dreamy and glowing clairvoyance of love. About your entire person you spin as it were a cobweb and then lie in wait. But you are not a child, a consciousness just awakening,[1] and therefore your glance has a very different significance, but you are content with that. You love the accidental. A smile from a pretty girl in a situation which is interesting, a glance which you entrap, that is what you are on the lookout for, that is a theme for your idle imagination. You who always plume yourself upon being an observer must put up with it if you yourself become an object of observation. I will remind you of an instance which I observed. A pretty young girl who accidentally was seated beside you at table was too prim to bestow a glance upon you. It needs to be emphasized that the situation was accidental: you did not know her position, her name, her age, etc. For an instant you were puzzled as to whether this was merely prudery, or whether there was not mixed with it a little embarrassment which under the proper illumination might make an interesting situation. She sat opposite a mirror in which you could see her; she cast a shy glance at it without guessing that your eye had already taken up its abode there; she blushed when your eye met hers. Such sights you preserve as accurately and register as quickly as a daguerreotype, which as you know needs only half a minute even in the worst weather.

Ah! you are indeed a strange being, at one moment a child, at another an old man, at one moment you are thinking with prodigious seriousness about the loftiest scientific problems, proposing to sacrifice your life to them, the next moment you are an amorous fool. From marriage, however, you are a long way off, and I hope that your good genius will keep you from getting into bad ways, for sometimes I sense in you a trace of wanting to play at being a little Zeus.[2] With your love you feel yourself so superior that doubtless you imagine every girl might count herself fortunate to be your sweetheart for a week. Your amorous studies you then for the time being carry on in conjunction with studies aesthetical, ethical, metaphysical, cosmopolitical, etc. One cannot really become angry with you. Evil has in you, as it had in the medieval conception, a certain seasoning of good nature and childishness. With regard to marriage you have always behaved merely as an observer. There is something treacherous in wishing to be merely an observer. How often—yes, I am willing to admit it—how often you have diverted me, but how often you have tormented me too with your tales of how you have wormed yourself into the confidence now of this and now of another husband in order to see how deeply he was stuck in the marriage bog. To worm your way into the confidence of people—for that you really have great gifts, that I will not deny, nor will I deny that it is quite entertaining to hear you relate the results of it and to witness your exuberant joy every time you are in a position to announce a really fresh observation. But, honestly speaking, your psychological interest lacks seriousness and is rather a hypochondriac curiosity.

Now for the matter in hand. There are two things I must especially regard as my task: to show the aesthetic significance of marriage; and to show how the aesthetic element in it may be held fast in spite of the manifold obstacles of actual life. In order, however, that you may abandon yourself with the more security to the edification which this little treatise may possibly procure you, I will let a little polemical prelude precede my discussions, and in it take due account of your sarcastic observations. But with that I hope also that I shall have paid due tribute to the piratical states and can then calmly pursue my calling; for after all I am within my calling when I who am a married man fight in behalf of marriage—*pro aris et focis*.[3] I assure you I take this matter so much to heart that I, who ordinarily do not feel tempted to write books, might actually be tempted to do so, if only I might hope to save a single marriage from the hell into which perhaps it has precipitated itself, or to render a few people more capable of realizing the most beautiful task proposed to men.

As a precautionary measure I will occasionally allude to my wife and my relation to her—not as though I presumed to represent our marriage as the normative example, but partly because the poetical descriptions which are purely fanciful have no very special convincing power, and partly because I count it of importance to show that even in commonplace situations it is possible to preserve the aesthetical. You have known me for many years, you have known my wife for five, you find her quite pretty, or rather attractive, and so do I; and yet I know very well that she is not so pretty by day as in the evening, that a certain sad, almost ailing trait vanishes only in the course of the day, and that it is forgotten when in the evening she can really lay claim to be charming. I know very well that her nose is not the perfection of beauty, that it is too small; but it turns itself saucily to the world, and I know that this little nose has given occasion to so much pleasant banter that, if it were within my jurisdiction, I would never wish for her a more beautiful one. This is a much deeper appreciation of the significance of the accidental in life than that about which you are so enthusiastic. I thank God for all this good and forget the weak points.

This, however, is of minor importance. But there is one thing for which I thank God with my whole soul, namely, that she is the only one I have ever loved, the first one; and there is one thing for which I pray God with my whole heart, that He will give me strength never to want to love any other. This is a family prayer in which she too takes part; for every feeling, every mood, acquires for me a higher significance for the fact that I make her a partaker of it. All feeling, even the highest religious emotions, are able to assume an easy air when people always agree in them. In her presence I am at once priest and congregation. And if sometimes I might be unkind enough not to be mindful of this good and ungrateful enough not to give thanks for it, she will then remind me of it. Look you, my young friend, this is not the coquetry of the first days of love-making; it is not an essay in experimental eroticism, as when in the period of his engagement pretty much every man has proposed to himself and to his fiancée the question whether she has been in love before, or whether he himself has loved anyone before; but this is the downright seriousness of life, and yet it is not cold, uncomely, unerotic, unpoetic. And truly I take it very much to heart that she really loves me and that I really love her—not as though in the course of years our marriage might not attain as much solidity as most others, but the point with me is to renew constantly the first love, and this again in such a way that for me it has just as much religious as aesthetic significance; for to me God has not become so supermundane that He might not concern Himself about the covenant He himself has established betwixt man and woman, and I have not become too spiritual to feel also the significance of the worldly side of life. And all the beauty inherent in the pagan erotic has validity also in Christianity, in so far as it can be combined with marriage. This renewal of our first love is not merely a sad reflection or a poetic recollection of something that has been experienced whereby one at length deludes oneself—that sort of thing produces fatigue, but this is action. Generally, the moment comes soon enough when one has to be content with recollection. One ought as long as possible to keep life's fresh spring open.

You, on the contrary, are actually living by robbery. You sneak up to people unobserved, steal their happiest moment from them, thrust this shadowgraph into your pocket, like the tall man in the story of Peter Schlemihl,[4] and take it out when you wish to. You say maybe that the persons concerned lose nothing by this, that they perhaps often do not themselves know which is their most beautiful moment. You think, on the contrary, that they ought to be obliged to you because by your study of illumination and by your incantations you have let them appear transfigured at the decisive moment into a supernatural size. Perhaps they do in fact lose nothing by this, and yet the question remains whether it is not conceivable that they retained a recollection of it which always remained painful. But you lose: you lose your time—your peace of mind—your patience with life. For you know very well how impatient you are. You once wrote to me that patience to bear life's burdens must be an extraordinary virtue, that for your part you did not even have patience to want to live. Your life resolves itself completely into interesting particulars of this sort. And in case one might venture to believe that the energy with which at such moments you are inflamed might acquire consistency and be spread evenly over your whole life, something great would surely come of you, for at such moments you are transfigured. There is an unrest within you, above which, nevertheless, consciousness soars clearly and lucidly; your whole soul is concentrated upon this sole point, your understanding devises a hundred plans for the attack; it fails in one direction; instantly your almost diabolical dialectic is capable of explaining the previous failure in such a way that it must be serviceable for the new plan of operations. You are constantly hovering over yourself, and however decisive every step may be, you retain a possibility of interpretation which with one word is able to alter everything. And then with that the exaltation of your mood: your eyes sparkle, or rather they shoot out, as it were, a hundred spying eyes; an evanescent blush flits across your face; you rely confidently upon your calculations, and yet you wait with a terrible impatience—I verily believe, my dear friend, that in the end you delude yourself, that with all this talk about catching a man in his happiest moment it is only your overwrought mood you grasp. You are so potentiated that you are creative. It was for this reason I expressed the opinion that this was not so very harmful to others—to you, however, it is absolutely harmful.

And after all, at the bottom of this is there not something prodigiously faithless? Indeed, you say that men do not concern you, that on the other hand it is they that must thank you for the fact that by your contact with them you do not, like Circe, transform them into swine but from swine to heroes. You say that it would be an entirely different matter if there were a man who really confided in you; but such a man you have never yet encountered. Your heart is touched, you melt with inward emotion at the thought of sacrificing everything for such a man. I would not deny that you have a good-natured readiness to help, that the way you succor the needy, for example, is really beautiful, that the gentleness you sometimes display has something noble about it; but in spite of this I believe that here again there is concealed a certain haughtiness. I will not recall to you certain eccentric expressions of this; it would be a shame to throw into the shade by this all the good that may be in you. However, I would remind you of a little incident in your life which it will do you no harm to remember. You once recounted to me that on one of your promenades you were walking behind two old women. My description of the incident has not perhaps at this moment the liveliness it had when you came rushing up to me with your mind full of this thought. They were two women from the poorhouse. Perhaps they had seen better days; but all that was forgotten, and the poorhouse is not exactly the place for nourishing a hope. While one woman was taking a pinch of snuff and offering it to the other she said, "If a body had five dollars." Perhaps she herself was surprised at this daring wish, which echoed across the glaciers like a prayer unanswered. You approached her, after having concealed a five dollar bill in your sketch book before you took the decisive step, in order that the situation might retain a befitting elasticity and that she might not too soon suspect something. You approached her with an almost subservient politeness, as beseemed a ministering spirit; you gave her the five dollars and vanished. You enjoyed then thinking of the impression this would make upon her, wondering whether she would see in it a divine dispensation, or whether her mind, which by reason of many sufferings had perhaps developed a certain defiance, would not rather turn almost with contempt against the divine providence which in this case assumed the character of fortuitousness.

You told me that this prompted you to reflect whether the entirely fortuitous fulfillment of a wish fortuitously expressed might not bring a person actually to desperation, because thereby the reality of life was negated in its deepest root. So what you wanted was to play the part of fate; what you really enjoyed were the multifarious reflections which could be spun from this. I am ready to admit that you are well fitted to play the part of fate, inasmuch as with this word one associates the notion of the most unstable and capricious of all things. For my part, I am disposed to content myself with a less eminent position in life. Moreover, in this instance you have an example wherein you can see to what degree it is true that your experiments have no harmful effect upon people. It looks as if you had the advantage on your side: you have given five dollars to a poor woman, you have fulfilled her highest wish; and yet you yourself admit that this might just as well have the effect upon her that she, as Job's wife counselled him to do, might curse God. You will say, maybe, that these consequences are not under your control, that if one were thus to reckon the consequences, one could not act at all. But I would reply, "Yes, indeed, one can act. In case I had had five dollars, I too perhaps would have given them to her, but at the same time I should have been conscious that I was not behaving experimentally; I should be conscious that divine providence, whose lowly instrument I felt myself to be at that moment, would surely dispose everything for the best, and that I had nothing for which I need reproach myself." How insecure and hovering your life is you can also convince yourself by the consideration that you are anything but sure that some day it may not weigh heavily upon your mind that your hypochondriacal acumen and subtility are capable of bewitching you into a circle of consequences from which you will seek in vain to extricate yourself, that you will be setting heaven and earth in commotion to find again the poor woman for the sake of observing what impression this has made upon her and "in

what way she can best be influenced"; for you always stay
the same, never grow wiser. With your passionate nature
it might well be possible for you to forget your great plans,
your studies, in short that everything might become indifferent to you in comparison with the thought of finding that
poor woman, who perhaps was dead and gone long ago.
In that way you seek to make amends for what you have
done amiss, and thus your life task becomes in itself so conflicting that you want to be at once fate and our Lord God
—a task which even God Himself is unable to realize, for
He is but one of these two.

The zeal you display may be quite praiseworthy, but do
you not see how it becomes clearer and clearer that what
you lack, and lack entirely, is faith? Instead of saving your
soul by entrusting everything to the hand of God, instead of
striking into this short cut, you prefer the endless detour
which perhaps will never bring you to the goal. You presumably will now say, "Well, in that way there is no need
of doing anything." I would reply, "Certainly there is, when
you know that you have a place in the world which is yours,
upon which you ought to concentrate all your activity; but
to act as you do borders upon insanity." You will say that
even if you were to fold your hands idly and let God take
care of her; the woman perhaps would not be helped
thereby. I would reply, "Quite possibly; but you would be
helped—and the woman would too if she likewise were to
put her trust in God. And do you not see that if you really
were to put on your traveling boots and journey out into
the world and waste your time and your strength, you
would be neglecting all your other endeavors and subsequently perhaps would be tormented in turn by this
thought?" But, as I have said, is not this capricious existence faithlessness? It may seem as if by wandering all
around the world to find the poor woman you showed an
extraordinary, an unexampled degree of faithfulness; for
there was not the least egoistical motive, it was not like a
lover who journeys afar to find the loved one; no, it was
pure sympathy. I would reply, "You are right enough in
denying that it is egoism, but it is your usual impudent
spirit of revolt." Everything that is established by divine

and human law you despise, and to liberate yourself from it you grasp at the accidental, as in this case at the poor woman who is unknown to you. And as for your sympathy, it was perhaps pure sympathy . . . for your experiment. You are always forgetting that your existence in the world cannot, after all, be intended merely for the accidental, and the moment you make this the chief thing, you forget entirely what you owe to those next door to you. I know very well that you do not lack sophistical shrewdness for palliating your conduct nor ironical suppleness for underbidding the adversary. You therefore will answer, "I am not so grand as to imagine that I am the one who is able to work for the whole, I leave that to preëminent persons; if only I can work for some particular end, I am satisfied." But this is a monstrous lie; for you are not willing to work at all, you want to experiment, and you contemplate everything from this point of view, often with much insolence; and activity is always an object of your derision—as once you expressed yourself about a man who had come to his end in a ludicrous way, which gave you amusement for many a day, saying that "though in other respects nothing was known of this man's significance for the whole and in a great sense, yet now one can affirm that he verily has not lived in vain."

As I have said, what you want is . . . to be fate. Now pause an instant. I do not mean to preach to you; but there is an earnestness for which I know you have an uncommonly deep respect, and everyone who has the power of evoking it in you, or confidence enough in you to let it appear, will see in you, I know, an entirely different man. Imagine for a moment—to take the very highest instance—imagine that the Almighty Origin of all things, that God in heaven, were thus to propose himself merely as a riddle for men, were to let the whole human race hover in this horrible uncertainty—would there not be something in your inmost being which would revolt against this, would you be able for a single instant to endure the torment, or would you for an instant be able to make your thought hold this horror fast? And yet He most of all, if I dare say so, might use this proud expression, "What matter men to me?" But therefore this is not true; and when I declare that God is incomprehensible I raise my soul to the highest pitch; it is precisely in the most blissful moment I make this declaration; He is incomprehensible because His love is incomprehensible, incomprehensible because His love surpasses all understanding. When this is said of God it denotes the highest excellence; when one is compelled to say it of a man it denotes a fault, sometimes a sin. And Christ did not count it robbery to be equal with God but humbled Himself—and you would account the spiritual gifts bestowed upon you as robbery. But do reflect; your life is passing away, some day for you too the time will come when your life is drawing to a close, when no longer is there any expedient that can prolong it, when memories alone are left, but not in the sense in which you love them, this mingling of poetry and truth, but the serious and faithful memory of conscience; beware lest it unroll before you a list, not properly of crimes, to be sure, but of possibilities wasted, phantoms which it will be impossible for you to drive away. You are still young, the intellectual suppleness you possess clads youth becomingly and delights the eye for a season. One is struck by seeing a clown whose joints are so limber that all necessity for maintaining the human gait and posture is done away. Such are you in an intellectual sense, you can just as well stand on your head as on your feet, everything is possible for you, and by this possibility you can astonish others and yourself; but it is unwholesome, and for the sake of your own tranquility I beg you to see to it that what is your advantage does not end by being a curse. A man who has a conviction cannot at his pleasure turn topsy-turvy upon himself and all things. I warn you, therefore, not against the world but against yourself, and I warn the world against you.

This much is certain, that in case I had a daughter of an age when there could be any question of her being influenced by you, I would warn her most solemnly, and especially if she were also intellectually gifted. And would there not be good ground for giving warning against you when I who imagine, nevertheless, that I am a match for you, if not in suppleness, at least in firmness and balance, if not in variableness and brilliancy, at least in steadiness—when even I sometimes feel with a certain indignation that you infect me, that I am letting myself be carried away by your exuberant mirth, by the apparently good-humored wit with which you make mock of everything, am letting myself be carried away into the same aesthetic-intellectual intoxication in which you live? With you, therefore, I have a certain feeling of insecurity, being now too severe, and now too indulgent. This, after all, is not so strange, for you are an epitome of every possibility, and so at one time I can see in you the possibility of perdition, at another of salvation. Every mood, every thought, good or bad, cheerful or sad, you pursue to its utmost limit, yet in such a way that this comes to pass rather *in abstracto* than *in concreto;* in such a way that this pursuit itself is little more than a mood from which nothing results but a knowledge of it, not even so much that the next time it becomes harder or easier for you to indulge in the same mood, for you constantly retain a possibility of it. Hence, one can reproach you almost for everything and for nothing, because it is and is not chargeable to you. According to circumstances you acknowledge or you do not acknowledge that you have had such a mood; but you are inaccessible to any calculation; what you care about is to have had the mood, completely and pathetically true.

But it was with the aesthetic validity of marriage I proposed to deal. This might seem a superfluous investigation, something which everyone is willing to concede, since it has been pointed out often enough. For through many centuries have not knights and adventurers undergone incredible pains and trouble in order to come to harbor in the quiet peace of a happy marriage? Have not novelists and novel readers worked their way through one volume after another in order to stop with a happy marriage? And has not one generation after another endured the troubles and complications of four acts if only there was some likelihood of a happy marriage in the fifth? However, by these prodigious efforts very little has been accomplished for the glorification of marriage, and I doubt very much if by the reading of such works any man has been made capable of performing the task he set himself or has felt oriented in life. For this precisely is the pernicious, the unwholesome feature of such works, that they end where they ought to begin. After the many fates they have overcome the lovers finally sink into one another's arms. The curtain falls, the book ends, but the reader is none the wiser. For truly (assuming that the first flame of love is present) it requires no great art to have courage and shrewdness enough to fight with all one's might for possession of the good which one regards as the only good; but on the other hand it surely requires discretion, wisdom and patience to overcome the lassitude which often is wont to follow upon a wish fulfilled. It is natural that to love in its first outflaming it seems as if it could not suffer enough hardships in acquiring possession of the beloved object, yea, that in case there are no dangers present it is disposed to provide them in order to overcome them. Upon this the whole attention is directed in plays of this sort, and as soon as the dangers are overcome the scenery shifter knows well what he has to do. Hence, it is rather rare to see a wedding on the stage or to read of one, except in case the opera or the ballet holds in reserve this factor, which may well furnish an occasion for some sort of dramatic galimatias, for a gorgeous procession, for the significant gesticulations and the heavenly glance of a ballet dancer, for the exchange of rings, etc. The truth in this whole exposition, the real aesthetic element, consists in the fact that love is represented as a striving, that this feeling is seen fighting its way through opposition. The fault is that this struggle, this dialectic, is entirely external, and that love comes out of this fight quite as abstract as when it entered into it. When once there awakens an apprehension of love's proper dialectic, an apprehension of its pathological struggle, of its relation to the ethical, to the religious, verily one will not have need of hard-hearted fathers or ladies' bowers or enchanted princesses or ogres and monsters in order to give love plenty to do. In our age one rarely encounters such cruel fathers or such frightful monsters, and in so far as modern literature has fashioned itself in conformity with the antique, money has become essentially the opposition medium through which love moves, and again we sit patiently through the four acts if there is a reasonable prospect of a rich uncle dying in the fifth.

However, it is rather seldom one sees such productions, and generally speaking, modern literature is fully occupied with making fun of the abstract conception of immediate love which was the subject of the romantic novelists. For example, when we review Scribe's activity as a playwright we see that one of his principal themes is the representation of love as an illusion. Of this, however, I only need to remind you, for with Scribe and his polemic you have only too much sympathy; I believe firmly that you would maintain his position against the whole world, even though you would reserve chivalric love for yourself. For so far are you from being destitute of sensibility that with regard to this matter you are the most jealous man I know. I remember that you once sent me a little appreciation of Scribe's play, *The First Love*, which was written with an almost desperate enthusiasm.[5] In this you maintained that it was the best thing Scribe had ever written, and that this play, if rightly understood, was sufficient to make him immortal. I would mention another play which in my judgment shows again the inadequacy of the thing which Scribe substitutes for romantic love. The title is, *Forever*. Here he is ironical about what is called a "first love." By the aid of a shrewd mother who at the same time is a fashionable woman of the world there has been fixed up a new love which the mother believes durable; but to the spectator who is not disposed to be satisfied with the poet's perfectly arbitrary way of ending the thing here with a period, it is very evident that a third love might come along just as well. Taking it all in all, it is remarkable how voracious modern poetry is, and for a long time it has been living on nothing else but love. Our age reminds one vividly of the dissolution of the Greek city-state: everything goes on as usual, and yet there is no longer anyone who believes in it. The invisible spiritual bond which gives it validity no longer exists, and so the whole age is at once comic and tragic—tragic because it is perishing, comic because it goes on. For it is always the imperishable which sustains the perishable, the spiritual which sustains the corporal; and if it might be conceived that an exanimate body could for a little while continue to perform its customary functions, it would in the same way be comic and tragic. But only let our age go on consuming —and the more it manages to consume of the substantial value contained in romantic love, with all the more consternation will it some day, when this annihilation no longer gives pleasure, awaken to the consciousness of what it has lost, and despairingly feel its misfortune.

We will now see whether the age which demolished romantic love has succeeded in putting anything better in its place. First, however, I will indicate the marks by which romantic love may be known. One might say in one word that it is immediate: to see her was to love her; or, though she saw him only once through a slit in the shuttered window of her chamber, nevertheless, from this instant she loved him, him alone in the whole world. Here I ought properly, according to agreement, to leave place for a few polemical outbursts in order to promote in you the secretion of bile which is an indispensable condition for the wholesome and profitable appropriation of what I have to say. But for all that, I cannot make up my mind to do so, and for two reasons: partly because this is a rather hackneyed theme in our time (and honestly it is incomprehensible that in this instance you want to go with the current, whereas ordinarily you go against it); and partly because I really have conserved a certain faith in the reality of romantic love, a sort of reverence for it, accompanied by some feeling of sadness. I therefore do no more than refer to the theme of your polemic in this field, the heading of a little article you wrote: "Sentimental and Incomprehensible Sympathies, or the *harmonia praestabilita* of two hearts." Here we have what Goethe with so much art, in his book entitled *Natural Affinity*, first enabled us to divine in the symbolical language of nature in order to show how it was exemplified in the world of spirit, only that Goethe endeavored to render this power of attraction intelligible by protracting it through a succession of moments (perhaps for the sake of showing the difference between the life of spirit and the life of nature) and did not emphasize the speed, the infatuated impatience and assurance with which an affinity seeks its mate. And after all, is it not beautiful to imagine that two beings are meant for one another? How often one has felt the need of reaching out beyond the historical consciousness, a longing, a nostalgia, for the primeval forest which lies behind us. And does not this longing acquire a double significance when with it there is associated the conception of another being which also has its home in these regions. Hence, every marriage, even one which was entered upon after reflective deliberation, feels the need, at least in certain moments, of such a foreground. And how beautiful it is that the God who is spirit loves also the love which is earthly. The fact that among married people there is a great deal of lying in this respect I am very ready to concede to you, and also that your observations in this field have often amused me; but one ought never to forget the truth that is in it. Perhaps one or another man may think that it is better to have complete authority in the choice of "his life's companion," but such an opinion discloses a high degree of narrow-mindedness and silly self-importance, with no inkling of the fact that the inborn quality of romantic love is freedom and that its greatness consists precisely in this quality.

Romantic love shows that it is immediate by the fact that it follows a natural necessity. It is based upon beauty; in part upon sensuous beauty, in part upon the beauty which can be conceived through and with and in the sensuous, yet not as if it came to evidence through a deliberation, but in such a way that it is constantly on the point of expressing itself, peeking out through the sensuous form. In spite of the fact that this love is essentially based upon the sensuous, it is noble, nevertheless, by reason of the consciousness of eternity which it embodies; for what distinguishes all love from lust is the fact that it bears an impress of eternity. The lovers are sincerely convinced that their relationship is in itself a complete whole which never can be altered. But since this assurance is founded only upon a natural determinant, the eternal is thus based upon the temporal and thereby cancels itself. Since this assurance has undergone no test, has found no higher attestation, it shows itself to be an illusion, and for this reason it is so easy to make it ridiculous. People should not, however, be so ready to do this, and it is truly disgusting to see in modern comedy these experienced, intriguing, dissolute women who know that love is an illusion. I know no creature so abominable as such a woman. No debauchery is so loathsome to me, and nothing is so revolting as to see a lovable young girl in the hands of such a woman. Truly this is more terrible than to imagine her in the hands of a club of seducers. It is sad to see a man who has learned to discount every substantial value in life, but to see a woman on this false path is horrible. Romantic love, however, as I have said, presents an analogy to morality by reason of the presumptive eternity which ennobles it and saves it from being mere sensuality. For the sensual is the momentary. The sensual seeks instant satisfaction, and the more refined it is, the better it knows how to make the instant of enjoyment a little eternity. The true eternity in love, as in true morality, delivers it, therefore, first out of the sensual. But in order to produce this true eternity a determination of the will is called for. But of this I shall say more later.

Our age has perceived very clearly the weak points of romantic love, and its ironical polemic against it has sometimes been thoroughly amusing—whether it has remedied its defects, and what it has put in its place, we shall now see. One may say that it has taken two paths, one of which is seen at the first glance to be a false one, that is, an immoral path; the other is more respectable, but to my mind it misses the deeper values of love, for if love is in fact founded upon the sensuous, everyone can easily see that this immediate, chivalrous faithfulness of theirs is foolishness. What wonder then that women want emancipation —one of the many ugly phenomena of our age for which men are responsible. The eternal element in love becomes an object of derision, the temporal element alone is left, but this temporal again is refined into the sensuous eternity, into the eternal instant of the embrace. What I say here applies not only to a seducer here and there who sneaks about in the world like a beast of prey; no, it is appropriate to a numerous chorus of highly gifted men, and it is not only Byron who declares that love is heaven, marriage is hell.[6]

It is very evident that there is in this a reflection, something which romantic love does not have. For romantic love is quite willing to accept marriage too, willing to accept the blessing of the Church as a pretty adjunct to the festivity, without attaching to it any real significance on its own account. By reason of its disposition to reflection the love here in question has with a terrible firmness and induration of mind made up a new definition[7] of what unhappy love is, namely, to be loved when one no longer loves—the opposite of loving without requital. And verily, if this tendency were aware what profundity is implied in these few words, it would itself shrink from it. For apart from all the experience, shrewdness and cunning this definition reveals, it contains also a presentiment that conscience exists. So then the moment remains the principal thing, and how often one has heard these shameless words addressed by such a lover to a poor girl who could love only once: "I do not demand so much, I am content with less; far be it from me to require that you shall continue to love me to all eternity, if only you love me at the instant when I wish it." Such lovers know very well that the sensuous is transient, they know also what is the most beautiful instant, and therewith they are content.

Such a tendency is, of course, absolutely immoral; yet on the path of thought it brings us in a way nearer our goal, for as much as it lodges a formal protest against marriage. In so far as the same tendency seeks to assume a more decent appearance it does not confine itself merely to the single instant but extends this to a longer period, yet in such a way that instead of receiving the eternal into its consciousness it receives the temporal, or it entangles itself in this opposition between the temporal and the eternal by supposing a possible alteration in the course of time. It thinks that for a time one can well enough endure living together, but it would keep open a way of escape, so as to be able to choose if a happier choice might offer itself. This reduces marriage to a civil arrangement; one need only report to the proper magistrate that this marriage is ended and another contracted, just as one reports a change of domicile. Whether this is an advantage to the State I leave undecided—for the individual in question it must truly be a strange relationship. Hence, one does not always see it realized, but the age is continually threatening us with it. And verily it would require a high degree of impudence to carry it out—I do not think this word is too strong to apply to it—just as on the part of the female participant in this association it would betray a frivolity bordering on depravity. There is, however, an entirely different disposition of mind which might easily get a similar notion into its head, and that is a disposition which I would deal with here more especially, since it is very characteristic of our age. For in fact such a plan may originate either in an *egoistic* or in a *sympathetic melancholy.* People have now been talking long enough about the frivolity of this age; I believe it is now high time to talk a little about its melancholy, and I hope that by this everything will be better clarified. Or is not melancholy the defect of our age? Is it not this which resounds even in its frivolous laughter? Is it not melancholy which has deprived us of courage to command, of courage to obey, of power to act, of the confidence necessary to hope? And now when the good philosophers are doing everything to give intensity to the actual, shall we not become so crammed full of it that we are suffocated? Everything is cut out except the present—what wonder then that for the constant dread of forfeiting this, one forfeits it. Well, it is true enough that we ought not to vanish in an evanescent hope, and that this is not the way to become transfigured in the clouds; but in order truly to enjoy one must have air, and not only in moments of sorrow is it important to have the heavens opened, but also in the time of joy to have a free vista and the folding doors thrown open wide. It is true that enjoyment apparently loses by this a certain degree of the intensity it has by the help of such an alarming limitation; but it is not likely that thereby much will be lost, for this intensity has a good deal in common with the intense enjoyment of the Strasbourg geese which costs them their lives. It might perhaps prove rather difficult to make you perceive this; but on the other hand I surely do not need to explain to you the significance of the intensity one attains in a different way. For in this respect you have great virtuosity—you *cui di dederunt formam, divitias, artemque fruendi.*[8]

In case enjoyment were the chief thing in life, I would sit at your feet as a pupil, for in this you are a master. At one moment you are able to make yourself an old man in order to imbibe in slow draughts through recollection what you have experienced;[9] at another moment you are in the first blush of youth, inflamed with hope; now you enjoy in a manly way, now in a womanly; now you enjoy immediately, now you enjoy reflection upon your enjoyment, now reflection upon the enjoyment of others; now you enjoy abstinence from enjoyment; now you devote yourself to enjoyment, your soul is open like a city which has capitulated, reflection is mute, and every step of the foreigner echoes in the empty streets, and yet there always remains a little observant outpost; now your mind is closed, you entrench yourself brusquely and unapproachably. Such is the situation, and at the same time you will see how egoistic your enjoyment is, and that you never give yourself out, never let others enjoy you. You may be right enough in scorning men who by every pleasure are consumed and wasted, for example, the lovelorn men with tattered hearts, since you on the contrary understand capitally the art of being in love in such a way that it throws your own personality into relief. Now you know very well that the most intensive pleasure consists in holding fast to the enjoyment with the consciousness that the next instant it perhaps will vanish. Hence, the last scene in *Don Juan* pleases you so greatly. Pursued by the police, by the whole world, by the living and the dead, alone in a remote chamber, he once again collects all the power of his soul, flourishes the goblet once again, and once again delights his soul with the sound of music.

But I return to my foregoing proposition, that a melancholy which is partly egoistic, partly sympathetic, may give rise to that point of view. The egoistic sort fears, of course, for its own sake, and like all melancholy it is self-indulgent. It has a certain extravagant deference for the thought of an alliance for the whole life, and a secret horror of it. "What can one rely on? Everything is transitory. Perhaps this being whom I now adore may change; perhaps fate may subsequently bring me into association with another being who for the first time would be truly the ideal I had dreamt of." Like all melancholy it is defiant and knows that it is, thinking, "perhaps precisely the fact that I tie myself to one person by an irrevocable bond may make this being whom otherwise I should love with my whole soul intolerable to me; perhaps, perhaps, etc." The sympathetic melancholy is more painful and at the same time rather nobler; it is fearful of itself for the sake of the other. "Who knows so surely that one may not change? Perhaps what I now regard as good in me may vanish; perhaps that by which I now captivate the loved one, and which only for her sake I wish to retain, may be taken from me, and there she stands then, deluded, deceived; perhaps a brilliant prospect opens for her, she is tempted, she does not withstand the temptation. Great God! I should have that upon my conscience! I have nothing to reproach her for, it is I that have changed, I forgive her everything, if only she can forgive me for being so imprudent as to let her take a step so decisive. I know indeed in my heart that so far from talking her into it I rather warned her against me; I know that it was her free resolution, but perhaps it was precisely this warning which tempted her, which let her see in me a better being than I am, etc., etc." It is easy to see that such a way of thinking is no better served by an alliance for five years than by one for ten, or even by an alliance such as Saladin formed with the Christians, for ten years, ten months, ten weeks, ten days, and ten minutes;[10] indeed, is no better served by such an alliance than by one for the whole life. One sees very well that such a way of thinking feels only too deeply the significance of the saying, "Sufficient unto the day is the evil thereof." It is an attempt to live every day as though that day were the decisive one, an attempt to live as though every day were a day of examination. Hence, when one finds in our times a strong disposition to abolish marriage, this is not as in the Middle Ages because the unmarried life is regarded as more perfect, but the reason of it is cowardice and self-indulgence. It is also evident that such marriages as are contracted for a definite time are of no avail, since they involve the same difficulties as those which are contracted for a whole life, and at the same time are so far from bestowing the required strength for living that on the contrary they enervate the inner power of married life, relax the energy of the will, and diminish the blessing of confidence which marriage possesses. It is also clear at this point, and will subsequently become more so, that such associations are not marriages, inasmuch as, though contracted in the sphere of reflection, they have not yet attained the consciousness of the eternal which morality has and without which such an association is not marriage. There is also something upon which you will agree with me entirely, for how often and how surely have your mockery and your irony hit the mark when you were denouncing what you call "fortuitous love affairs" and the "bad infinity" of love—when one is looking with his sweetheart out of the window, and that instant a young girl turns the corner into another street, and it occurs to him, "It is with her I am really in love," but when he would trace her he is again unsettled, etc.

The other expedient, the respectable way, would be the marriage of convenience. The mere mention of it shows that reason intervenes, and that we have entered the sphere of reflection. One person and another, and you among them, have always made a dubious face at the union here implied between immediate love and the calculating understanding; for really, if one were to show respect for linguistic usage, it ought to be called a marriage of common sense. Especially are you accustomed, with an ambiguous use of words, to recommend "respect" as a solid foundation for the marriage relation. It shows how thoroughly reflective this age is, that it must help itself out with such a compromise as a marriage of convenience. In so far as such an association waives all claim to real love, it is at least consistent, but at the same time it thereby shows that it is not a solution of the problem. A marriage of convenience is therefore to be regarded as a sort of capitulation, necessitated by the complications of life. But how pitiful it is that this should be the only comfort that is left to the poetry of our age, the comfort of despairing; for it is evidently despair which

makes such an alliance acceptable. It is contracted, therefore, more likely by persons who no longer are chickens,
and who also have learnt that love is an illusion and its
realization at the most a *pium desiderium*. What it therefore has to do with is life's prose, subsistence and social
standing. In so far as it has neutralized the sensuous factor
in marriage it appears to be moral, but it nevertheless remains a question whether this neutralization is not just as
immoral as it is unaesthetic. Or even though the erotic is
not entirely neutralized, it is nevertheless disheartened by a
cool common-sense consideration that one must be prudent,
not be too quick in sorting and rejecting, that life after
all never presents the ideal, that it is quite a respectable
match, etc. The eternal, which (as has been shown above)
is properly a part of every marriage, is not really present
here; for a common-sense calculation is always temporal.
Such an alliance is therefore at once immoral and fragile.
Such a marriage of convenience may assume a prettier
form when the motive is somewhat higher. In such a case
it is a motive foreign to the marriage which decides the
matter—as, e.g., when a young girl, out of love for her
family, marries a man who is in a position to rescue it. But
precisely this outward teleology shows clearly that we cannot seek here a solution of the problem. At this point I
might perhaps aptly deal with the manifold motives to marriage about which there is a great deal of talk. Such deliberation and debate are perfectly at home in the sphere
of reason. However, I prefer to reserve this subject for another place, where also, if possible, I may be able to make
this talk hold its tongue.

We have now seen how romantic love was built upon an
illusion, and that the eternity it claims was built upon the
temporal, and that although the knight was sincerely convinced of its absolute durability, there nevertheless was no
certainty of this, inasmuch as its trials and temptations have
hitherto been in a medium which was entirely external.
Such being the case, it was able with a pretty piety to
accept marriage along with love, although, after all, this
acquired no very deep significance. We have seen how this
immediate and beautiful but also very naïve love, being

embodied in the consciousness of a reflective age, must become the object of its mockery and of its irony; and we have seen too what such an age was capable of substituting for it. Such an age embodied marriage in its consciousness and in part declared itself on the side of love in such a way as to exclude marriage, in part on the side of marriage in such a way as to exclude love. Hence, in a recent play a sensible little seamstress, speaking of the love of fine gentlemen, makes the shrewd observation, "They love us but they don't marry us; the fine ladies they don't love, but they marry them."

Herewith this little treatise (as I am compelled to call what I am here writing, although at first I thought only of a big letter) has reached the point from which marriage can be viewed in the right light. That marriage belongs essentially to Christianity, that the pagan nations have not brought it to perfection, in spite of the sensuousness of the Orient and all the beauty of Greece, that not even Judaism has been capable of this, in spite of the truly idyllic elements to be found in it—all this you will be ready to concede without compelling me to argue the matter, and this all the more because it is sufficient to remember that the contrast between the sexes has nowhere been made a subject for such deep reflection that the other sex has received complete justice. But within Christianity also love has had to encounter many fates before we learned to see the deep, the beautiful and the true implications of marriage. Since, however, the immediately preceding age was an age of reflection, as is ours also to a certain degree, it is not so easy a matter to prove this, and since in you I have found so great a virtuoso in bringing the weaker sides into prominence, the task of convincing you of the side which I have undertaken to defend is doubly difficult. I owe you, however, the admission that I am much indebted to you for your polemic. When I think of the multifarious expressions of it which I possess in their dispersion, and imagine them gathered into a unity, your polemic is so talented and inventive that it is a good guide for one who would defend the other side. For your attacks are not so superficial that (if only you or another would think them through) they might not contain the truth, even though neither you nor your adversary observe this in the moment of conflict.

Inasmuch as it appeared to be a defect on the part of romantic love that it was not reflective, it might seem reasonable to let true conjugal love begin with a kind of doubt. This might seem all the more necessary in view of the fact that we approach this subject with the prepossessions of a reflective age. I am by no means prepared to deny that a marriage might be artificially accomplished after such a doubt; but the question remains nevertheless whether the nature of marriage is not substantially altered by this, since it presupposes a divorce between love and marriage. The question is whether it is essential to marriage to annihilate the first love because of doubt as to the possibility of realizing it, in order to make conjugal love possible and actual through this annihilation, so that the marriage of Adam and Eve was really the only one in which immediate love was preserved inviolate, and that again chiefly for the reason which Musaeus[11] wittily suggests, that there was no possibility of loving anybody else. The question remains whether immediate love, the first love, would be secured against this scepticism by being assumed in a higher concentric immediacy, so that conjugal love would be in no need of plowing under the beautiful hopes of first love, but conjugal love itself would be first love, seasoned with an admixture of determinants which would not detract from it but would ennoble it. This is a difficult problem to prove, and yet it is of prodigious importance, lest in the ethical sphere we might have such a cleavage as exists in the intellectual sphere between faith and knowledge. And how beautiful it would be, my dear friend—you will not deny it, for after all your heart is susceptible to love, and your head is only too well acquainted with doubt—how beautiful it would be if the Christian might venture to call his God the God of love, in such a way as to think therewith of that unspeakably blissful feeling, the eternal force in the world —earthly love.

In the foregoing discussion I dealt with romantic and reflective love as discursive points of view, but now we are to see to what extent the higher unity is a return to immediate love, and accordingly to what extent (apart from the *more* which it contains) it contains also what was comprised in the first. It is now clear enough that reflective love constantly consumes itself, and that it stops arbitrarily now at this point, now at another; it is clear that it points beyond itself to the higher position, but the question is whether this higher experience cannot come at once into touch with the first love. Now this higher experience is the religious, in which the reflective understanding comes to an end; and just as for God nothing is impossible, so too for the religious individual nothing is impossible. In the religious sphere love finds again the infinity which it vainly sought in the sphere of reflection. But in case the religious, higher though it certainly is than everything earthly, does not stand in an eccentric relation to immediate love but in a concentric relation, unity might be brought about without any necessity for the pain which religion indeed can heal but which, nevertheless, always remains a profound pain. One very rarely sees this matter made the subject of serious deliberation, because those who have feeling for romantic love do not bother much about marriage, and because on the other hand so many marriages unfortunately are contracted without the deeper erotic which is assuredly the most beautiful thing in a purely human existence. Christianity holds firmly to marriage. So in case conjugal love is unable to contain all of the first erotic, Christianity does not represent the highest development of the human race, and without doubt it is a secret dread of such an incongruity which is largely responsible for the despair which permeates modern lyric both in verse and in prose.

So you see what a task I have undertaken in endeavoring to show that romantic love can be united with and can persist in marriage, yea, that marriage is the true transfiguration of romantic love. This is not by any means to cast disparagement upon the marriages which have been rescued from reflection and its shipwreck, nor would I be so unsympathetic as to grudge them my admiration; it is not to be denied that much can be done in this way, nor ought it to be forgotten that the whole tendency of the age often makes such marriages a dolorous necessity. As for this "necessity," however, it must be remembered that every generation, and each individual in the generation, begins life anew to a certain extent, and that for each one severally there is a possibility of escaping this maelstrom, and it must be remembered, too, that one generation should learn from the other, and that hence there is a likelihood that after reflection has made such a sorry spectacle of one generation the successive generation will be more fortunate. And however many painful confusions life may still have in store, I fight for two things: for the prodigious task of showing that marriage is the transfiguration of first love, not its annihilation, that it is its friend, not its enemy; and for the task (which to others is very trivial but to me is all the more important) of showing that my humble marriage has had such a meaning for me, so that from it I derive strength and courage to fulfill constantly this task.

And now when I approach this investigation I cannot but rejoice that it is to you I am writing. Yea, certain as it is that to no other man would I express myself unreservedly about my marriage, just so certain it is that before you I open my mind with confidence and joy. Sometimes when the noise of the conflicting and laboring thoughts, the tremendous machinery you carry about with you, is hushed, there come then quiet moments which indeed by their stillness may be almost alarming but which prove to be truly refreshing. I hope that this essay will encounter you in such a moment; and just as one may unconcernedly confide to you anything one will when the machinery is in motion, for then you hear nothing, so also without jeopardy one can relate to you everything when your soul is still and solemn. I will talk also about her of whom I commonly speak only to deaf nature, wishing only to hear myself, about her to whom I owe so much, including the fact that I dare frank-heartedly defend the cause of first love and marriage. For what would all my love and all my effort avail if she did not come to my aid, and what would I avail if she did not arouse in me the enthusiasm to will? And yet I know very well that if I were to say this to her she would not believe it; yea, I should perhaps be doing wrong to say it to her, it would perhaps disturb and agitate her deep and pure soul.

The first thing then I have to do is to orient myself, and more especially to orient you, in the definitions of what a marriage is. What properly constitutes it, gives it its substantial content, is obviously love. If this is lacking, the life in common is either satisfaction of a carnal lust, or it is an association, a partnership, for the attainment of one aim or another. But love has in it precisely the characteristic of eternity, whether it be the superstitious, romantic, chivalrous love, or the deeper moral and religious love which is filled with a mighty and lively assurance.

Every estate has its traitors, and so also has the estate of matrimony. I, of course, do not mean the seducers, for they have not entered into this holy estate—I hope that this investigation will encounter you in a mood which does not incline you to smile at this expression. I do not mean those who by divorce have left the ranks, for at least they have had courage to be open rebels. No, I mean those who are only rebels in thought, who do not even venture to let the thought express itself in action, those miserable married men who sit and sigh over the fact that love has long ago evaporated out of their marriage; those married men who, as you once said of them, sit like madmen each one in his matrimonial cell and shake the iron bars and rave about the sweetness of engagement and about the bitterness of marriage; those married men who, according to your own correct observation, are the ones who with a certain malicious joy congratulate everyone who becomes engaged. I cannot describe to you how despicable they seem to me, and how much it delights me when such a husband takes you as his confidant, when before you he pours out his sufferings, repeats by rote all his lies about the happy first love, and you with a cunning look say, "Yes, I shall take good care not to get on smooth ice," and it embitters him even more that he cannot manage to drag you with him into a *commune naufragium* [common shipwreck]. It is to these married men you so often allude when you talk about a tender paterfamilias with four blessed children . . . whom he would like to see in Jericho.

If there were actually something in what they say, then there must be a discrepancy between love and marriage of such a sort that love would be relegated to one particular moment in time and marriage to another, but love and marriage would remain incompatible. So one would seek at once to discover what period it was to which love belonged—would find that it was the period of the engagement, "the beautiful period of the engagement." With an agitation and emotion which savors of the burlesque these people know how to prate continually about the joys of the days of their engagement. I must now admit that I have never had much liking for the spoony sweetmeats of the engagement period, and the more one makes of this period, the more it appears to me to resemble the time many men take before jumping into the water, first walking back and forth on the float, sticking now one hand, now one foot into the water, finding it now too cold, now too warm. If it actually was a fact that the engagement is the most beautiful time, truly I fail to see why they get married—or, supposing they are right, why anybody gets married. Nevertheless, they do get married with all possible bourgeois exactness when aunts and cousins and neighbors and friends find the marriage suitable, betraying in this the same drowsiness and apathy as they do in regarding the engagement as the most beautiful period. If worse comes to worst, I am for those rash men who alone take pleasure in springing out into the water, even though the emotion in this case is never so great, the shudder of consciousness never so refreshing, the reaction of the will never so energetic, as when a strong manly arm encompasses the loved one tightly but tenderly, powerfully and yet in such a way that precisely in this embrace she feels free before the face of God to plunge into the sea of existence.

In case such a separation between love and marriage had any validity except in the empty heads of foolish humans or rather unhumans who know as little about love as they do about marriage—it would be a poor outlook, then, for marriage and for my attempt to show that marriage is an aesthetic musical accord. But what grounds might be alleged for such a separation? It might be because, generally speaking, love cannot be maintained. Here we have the same distrust and cowardice which is so often expressed in our age and is characterized by the fact that it regards development as a step backward and as destruction. At this point I willingly concede that such an unmanly and unwomanly love (which you with your usual effrontery would call a four-penny love) would not be capable of resisting a single puff of life's storm; but from this no argument can be drawn with regard to love and marriage if both were in a wholesome and natural state. Or else it might be because the ethical and the religious which are associated with marriage proved to be so heterogeneous with love that for this cause love and marriage cannot be united; whereas love, if it were allowed to repose in itself and rely upon itself, would be perfectly capable of fighting the battle of life through triumphantly. This view, then, would bring the thing back either to the untried pathos of immediate love, or to the whim and caprice of the particular individual who believed that by his own power he was capable of finishing the race. The notion that it might be the ethical and the religious elements in marriage which have a disturbing effect is a view which at the first glance gives evidence of a certain manliness which may easily deceive a cursory observation, and although it is mistaken it has a great deal more sublimity than the other pitiful view of the perishableness of love. I shall return to it later, with all the more reason because my inquisitorial glance greatly deceives me if I do not see in you a heretic infected to a certain degree by this error.

The substantial factor in marriage is love. But which comes first? Is love the first, or is marriage, of which love then is the sequel? This latter view has enjoyed no little esteem on the part of shallow, common-sense people; it has been preached not infrequently by shrewd fathers and by mothers still shrewder who, thinking that they have had experience, would indemnify themselves by insisting that their children shall have it too. This is the wisdom which dove fanciers also have when they shut up in a little cage two doves which have no sympathy for one another and think that they will soon learn to agree. This view is so stupid that I have alluded to it only for the sake of a sort of completeness, and at the same time to remind you of what you have pilloried. So then love comes first. But according to the view alluded to above, love is of a nature so delicate, in spite of nature it is so unnatural and so coddled, that it cannot endure coming into touch with reality. Here again I am at the point touched upon above. Here the engagement seems to acquire a peculiar significance. It is a love which has no reality, which lives only upon the sweet confectionary of possibility. The relationship has not the actuality of the real, its movements are without content, it never gets beyond the same "fatuous, spoony gesticulations." The more unreal the engaged couple themselves are, and the more these merely feigned gesticulations cost them effort and exhaust their strength, all the more need they will feel to shun the serious figure of matrimony. The engagement, having apparently no reality which results necessarily from it, would be a capital compromise for those who have not the courage to get married. They perhaps feel, and in all probability feel extravagantly, a need of seeking the help of a higher power when they want to take the decisive step. Then they fix the matter up with themselves and with the higher power: with themselves by getting engaged on their own responsibility; with the higher power by not evading the blessing of the Church, which with a good deal of superstition they value too highly. Here again we have a schism between love and marriage, in the most cowardly, the most pinchbeck, the most unmanly form. However, such a monstrosity cannot lead one astray; its love is no love, it lacks the sensuous factor which finds its moral expression in marriage, it neutralizes the erotic to such a degree that an engagement of this sort might just as well take place between men. On the other hand, so soon as the sensuous factor gets its due, this falls under the categories already described. Such an engagement then is unbecoming, from whatever side one looks at it; for in a religious respect also it is unbecoming, being an attempt to deceive God, by sneaking into a relationship for which it thinks it does not need His help, and by having recourse to Him only when it feels that the thing can't turn out well otherwise.

So then it is not marriage which is to evoke love; on the contrary, love presupposes that, and it presupposes it not as a past state but as a present. But marriage contains an ethical and religious factor, as love does not; for this reason marriage is based upon resignation, as love is not. Now if one is not ready to assume that every man in the course of his life passes through two movements, first the pagan movement, if I may so call it, in which love has its home, and after that the Christian movement which is expressed in marriage; in short, if one will not say that love must be excluded by Christianity, then it must be shown that love can be united with marriage. It occurs to me, by the way, that if any outsider were to get sight of this paper, he would likely fall into the deepest amazement that such a matter could give me so much bother. Well, the fact is, I write it only for you, and your development has been of such a nature that you fully understand the . . . difficulties.

So first, an investigation of love. I will attach my argument to a term which in spite of your mockery and that of the whole world has always had a significant meaning for me: the first love. (Believe me, I will not yield, and presumably you will not either, and so this situation remains as a strange incongruity in our correspondence.) When I speak of first love I am thinking of the most beautiful thing in life; when you use this word it is the signal for the vedette posts of your observation to open fire all along the line. But for me this word has nothing ludicrous about it, and as I, to speak candidly, put up with your attack only because I ignore it, I may say, also, that for me it has not the sad connotations it may well have for one man or another. This sadness need not be morbid, for the morbid is always the untrue and the mendacious. It is a fine and healthy sign when a man has had ill-luck with his first love, when he has learned to know the pain of it but has yet remained faithful to his first love, has yet preserved faith in "first love"; it is fine if, then, in the course of years he sometimes recalls it vividly; and though his soul has been sound enough to take leave as it were of this kind of life in order

to consecrate itself to something higher, it is fine if he remembers sadly that which, although it was not perfection,
was nevertheless so beautiful. And this sadness is far more
wholesome and beautiful and noble than the prosaic common sense which has finished long ago with such childish
pranks, or than the devilish shrewdness of Basil, the singing master in the play,[12] which plumes itself upon being
healthy but is really the most consuming sickness. For what
does it profit a man to gain the whole world and lose his
own soul? For me this phrase, "the first love," contains no
sadness at all, or at all events only a little seasoning of sad
sweetness; for me it is a battle cry, and although I have
been for several years a married man, I still have the honor
of fighting under the victorious banner of first love.

For you, on the other hand, the conception of "the first,"
the question of its true significance, its under- and over-
valuation, is an enigmatic oscillation. At one moment you
are solely possessed by an enthusiasm for "the first." You
are so impregnated by the energetic concentration implied
in this thought that it is the only thing you wish for. You
are so glowing, so inflamed, so lovingly ardent, so dreamy
and fertile, sunken as low as a cloud surcharged with rain
—in short, you have a lively conception of what it means
that Jupiter in a cloud or in a gentle rain[13] descended upon
the loved one. The past is forgotten, every limitation is
abolished. You expand more and more, you are sensible of a
softness and elasticity, every joint becomes limber, every
bone a pliable sinew—as a gladiator extends and stretches
his body in order to have it entirely in his power, and everyone must think that thereby he divests himself of his might,
and yet this voluptuous torture is precisely the condition
for thoroughly employing his strength. Now then you are
in the condition in which you enjoy the sheer luxury of
complete receptivity. The gentlest touch is enough to thrill
this invisible, widely extended spiritual body through and
through. There is an animal upon which my thought has
dwelt profoundly. It is the jellyfish. Have you ever observed
how this gelatinous mass is able to extend itself like a disk
and then can slowly sink or rise, lies so still and seems so
firm that one might think one could step upon it? Now it

observes that its prey approaches, then it hollows itself and becomes a pouch and with prodigious impetus sinks deeper and deeper, until by this impetus it draws the prey into— not into its pouch, for it has no pouch, but into itself, for it is itself a pouch and nothing else. It is able to contract itself to such a degree that one cannot comprehend how it was possible for it to expand. Such is pretty much the case with you, and you will simply have to forgive me for not having a more beautiful animal to compare you with, and also for the fact that you cannot perhaps quite forbear smiling at yourself when you think of being a mere pouch.

At such moments it is "the first" you are pursuing, that alone is what you want—without suspecting that it is a self-contradiction to want the first to be constantly recurring again, and that, consequently, you either have never yet reached the first, or else you really have had it, and what you see now, what you are enjoying, is merely a reflection of the first. And it also remains to be observed that you are in error when you believe that the first might be completely present in any other but "the first," if only one seeks rightly. And it needs to be said that in so far as you appeal to your professional practice this also is a misunderstanding, since you have never practiced in the right direction. At other times, on the contrary, you are as cold, as sharp and biting as a March wind, as sarcastic as hoar frost, as clear-minded as the air commonly is in springtime, as dry and infertile, as egoistically astringent as it is possible to be. If when you are in such a state of mind it happens that a man to his discomfiture comes to you to talk about "the first," about the beauty implied in this, perhaps even about his first love, then you become positively angry. "The first" now becomes the most ludicrous, the most foolish of all things, one of the lies in which one generation confirms another. You rage like a Herod from one child-murder to another. You are able, then, to talk without end about how cowardly and unmanly it is to cling to the first, asserting that the truth lies in what is acquired, not in what is given. I recall that in this mood you once came to my room. You filled your pipe as usual, stretched yourself in the softest armchair, put your legs on another, rummaged among my

papers (I remember also that I took them from you), and
then you burst forth with an ironical eulogy upon first love
and everything that is "first," including even "the first licking I got in school," declaring in an explanatory note that
you could say this the more emphatically because the
teacher who administered the licking was the only one you
had ever known who could strike with emphasis. Thereupon you concluded by whistling this ditty,[14] kicking to the
other side of the room the chair upon which you had placed
your feet, and off you went.

In vain one seeks to learn from you what lies behind this
mysterious word, "the first," a word which has had and to
all time will have a prodigious significance in the world.
The significance which this word has for the particular individual is definitive for his spiritual situation as a whole,
while the fact that it has no significance for someone shows
that he is not attuned in such a way that he can be touched
by lofty impulses and be set in vibration by their touch.
However, two ways lie open before the man to whom "the
first" is significant. Either "the first" contains promise for
the future, is the forward thrust, the endless impulse. Such
are the fortunate individuals for whom "the first" is simply
the present, but the present is for them the constantly unfolding and rejuvenating "first." Or "the first" does not im-
pel the individual; the power which is in "the first" does
not become the impelling power in the individual but the
repelling power, it becomes that which thrusts away. Such
are the unfortunate individualities who constantly withdraw
more and more from "the first." The latter situation, of
course, cannot come about totally without any fault on the
part of the individual.

With this word, "the first," all who are touched by ideas
associate a notion of solemnity, and only when used of
things belonging to a lower sphere does "the first" mean
the worst. You are prolific with examples of this use of it:
the first printer's proof; the first time a man puts on a new
dress coat, etc. The more probability there is that a thing
may be repeated, the less significance does "the first" acquire; the less the probability of repetition, the greater is
its significance. On the other hand, the more significant that

thing is which for the first time announces itself, the less is the probability of its being repeated. If there is something so important as to be even eternal, all probability that it may be repeated vanishes. Hence, when one has talked with a certain sad seriousness of the first love as of something which could never be repeated, this is no disparagement of love but a lofty eulogy of it as the eternal power. Thus—for the sake of making a little philosophical flourish, not with the pen but with thought—God only once became flesh, and it would be vain to expect this to be repeated. In paganism it could happen oftener, but this was precisely for the reason that it was not a true incarnation. Thus man is born only once, and there is no probability of a repetition. The notion of transmigration of souls fails to appreciate the significance of birth. I will illustrate further what I mean by a few examples. The first green, the first swallow, we hail with a certain solemnity. The ground of this, however, is the idea we associate with it, so that here what is announced by "the first" is something different from the first itself, the one first swallow, for example. There is an engraving which represents Cain murdering Abel. Adam and Eve are seen in the background. Whether it has value as a work of art I am not competent to decide, but the title inscribed beneath it has always interested me: *prima caedes, primi parentes, primus luctus* [the first murder, the first parents, the first sorrow]. Here again "the first" has profound significance, and in this instance what we reflect upon is "the first" itself, but more with relation to time than to content, since one does not see the continuity with which the whole is posited by the first. (The "whole" might, of course, be understood as the sin transmitted to the race. The first sin—if by that we think of the sin of Adam and Eve—would, it is true, lead one to think of continuity, but as it is the nature of evil not to have continuity, you will easily perceive why I do not use this example.) One more illustration. It is well known that several rigorous sects in Christendom wanted to prove the limitation of God's grace from the words in the Epistle to the Hebrews about the impossibility of renewing again to repentance those who once were enlightened and had fallen away. Here, then, "the first" had all of its deep significance. In this first, the deep Christian life as a whole came to evidence, and he then who apprehended it amiss was lost. But in this case the eternal is dragged down too much into temporal determinants. Still, this example may serve to explain how "the first" is the whole, the whole content. But now when what is implied in "the first" rests upon a synthesis of the temporal and the eternal, everything I have set forth above evidently retains its validity. In "the first" the whole is present implicitly, hiddenly. Now again I am not ashamed to mention the word "first love." To the fortunate individuals the first love is at the same time the second, the third, the last; the first love has here the determinants of the eternal. To the unfortunate individuals the first love is a moment, it has the determinants of the temporal. For the fortunate individuals the first love, in the very fact that it is, is the present; for the others, in the very fact that it is, it is the past. Inasmuch as there is reflection also in the fortunate individuals, this when directed toward the eternal in love will be a source of strength for love, whereas reflection upon the temporal will be the demolition of love. Thus, for him who reflects in a temporal way the first kiss, for example, will be a past fact (as Byron has made it in a little poem[15]); for him who reflects in an eternal way it will be an eternal possibility.

All this has to do with the predicate we attach to love when we call it the "first." I now go on to consider more expressly *the first love*. As a preliminary I will beg you to recall the little contradiction we encountered: the first love comprises the whole content, and if such be the case the shrewdest thing would be, it seems, to pluck it and go on to a second first love. But when one takes the first in vain it vanishes and one doesn't get the second. But after all, is not the first love merely the first? Yes, but when we reflect upon the content it is the first only in so far as we remain in it. If one remains in it, does it then become a second love? No, precisely because one remains in it, it remains the first, if one reflects upon eternity.

The Philistines who think that now they have about reached the period of life when it would be suitable for them to look around and listen around for a helpmeet (perhaps by an advertisement in the newspaper) have already excluded themselves once for all from first love, and such a philistine state of mind cannot be regarded as the condition which precedes first love. It is, of course, conceivable that Eros might be compassionate enough to play upon such a man the prank of making him fall in love. I say "compassionate," for after all it is an extraordinary act of compassion to bestow upon a man the highest earthly good, and that first love always is, even though it be unhappy. But this chance always remains an exception, and the man's previous condition affords no explanation of it. If one would believe the priests of music (who in this respect are most like believers), and if in their company one would give heed to Mozart, surely then the condition which precedes first love must be described by recalling the saying that love makes blind. The individual becomes as if blind; one can almost see this by looking at him; he sinks into himself, contemplates in himself his own contemplation, and yet there is a constant effort to look out upon the world. The world has blinded him and yet he stares out at the world. It is this dreamy yet searching state of mind which Mozart has depicted in the person of the Page in *Figaro*, representing it as a condition which is just as sensuous as it is mental. In contrast to this, first love is an absolute alertness, an absolute beholding; and not to do it an injustice, this must be insisted upon. It is directed towards a single, definite and actual object, which alone has existence for it, everything else being nonexistent. This one object does not exist in vague outline but as a definite living being. This first love contains a factor of sensuousness and beauty, yet it is not merely sensuous. The sensuous factor as such comes to evidence only through reflection, but first love lacks reflection and is therefore not simply sensuous. This gives the character of necessity to first love. Like everything eternal it has the double propensity of presupposing itself back into all eternity and forward into all eternity. This is the element of truth in what the poets have often sung so beautifully, to the effect that the lovers even at first sight feel as if they already had loved one another for a long while. This is the element of truth in the inviolable faithfulness of

chivalry, which fears nothing, is not alarmed by the thought
of any disuniting power. But since the essence of all love
is characterized as a unity of freedom and necessity, so it
is in this case. Precisely in the necessity the individual feels
himself free, is sensible in this of his whole individual energy, precisely in this he senses the possession of all that
he is. It is for this reason one can inerrantly observe in every
man whether he truly has been in love. Love involves a
transfiguration, a spiritualization, which lasts his whole life
long. In him there is a union of all the factors which ordinarily are dispersed; he is at the same moment both
younger and older than men commonly are; he is a man
and yet a youth, yea, almost a child; he is strong and yet
so weak; he is a harmony which, as was said, echoes
through his whole life. We will extol this first love as one
of the most beautiful things in the world, but we will not
lack courage to put it to the test.

This, however, is not what immediately concerns us. Already at this point it is possible to think of a doubt of the
same sort as that which will recur in view of the relation
between first love and marriage. A religiously developed
individual is accustomed to relate everything to God, to
penetrate and leaven every finite relationship with the
thought of God, and thereby to sanctify and ennoble it.
(This statement, of course, is to be understood obliquely.)
In view of this it seems precarious to allow such feelings to
arise in consciousness without taking counsel with God; but
by taking counsel with God the relationship is, in fact, altered. In this instance the difficulty is more easily removed,
for it is characteristic of first love to take by surprise, and being the fruit of surprise it is involuntary, so that it is not obvious how such a consultation with God might be possible.
The only thing that could be thought of would be the
question of remaining in this state—but this is the theme
of a subsequent deliberation. But would it not be possible
to anticipate the first love which, as such, recognizes no
relation to God? I may touch in a few words upon the marriages in which the decision rests with another, a person
other than the individual himself, cases in which the individual has not yet got to the point of freedom as a deter-

minant. We encounter the pitiful forms of this, where by sorcery or similar arts, by recourse to nature-magic, the individual seeks to conjure up the object of his love. The nobler forms are those which one might call religious in the stricter sense. (Marriage in the true sense does not, of course, lack the religious factor, but at the same time it has the erotic factor.) Thus, when Isaac in all humility and trustfulness refers it to God's judgment whom he shall choose for a wife, and putting his confidence in God sends his servant, does not himself look about, because he feels his fate secure in God's hand, this is doubtless very pretty, but the erotic, nevertheless, does not get due recognition. Now in this case one must remember that however abstract the God of Judaism was in general, He was deeply interested in everything pertaining to the vital interests of the Jewish nation, and particularly to its elect figures, and that although He was spirit He was not too spiritual to be concerned about earthly things. To a certain degree Isaac therefore might venture to expect confidently that God would choose for him a wife who was young and beautiful and highly regarded by the people and lovable in every way; but for all that, we feel the lack of the erotic element, even if it proved to be the case that he loved this woman of God's election with genuine youthful passion. Freedom was lacking.

In Christianity one sees from time to time an obscure mixture of the erotic and the religious which is attractive by reason of its obscurity and ambiguity, and which has in it just as much roguishness as childish piety. This, naturally, is to be found particularly in Catholicism, and with us among the common people. I ask you to imagine (and I know that you can do it with pleasure, for this surely is a situation)—imagine a little peasant girl, hiding behind her lashes a pair of eyes which are audacious and yet humble, a girl healthy and blooming, with something in her complexion which is not the flush of sickness but the sign of a superior health; imagine her on Christmas Eve; she is alone in her room, midnight is already passed, and yet sleep which usually visits her so faithfully now evades her; she is sensible of an agreeable, sweet disquietude, she opens the

window halfway, she looks out into the infinite space, alone
with the silent stars, a little sigh makes her feel so light,
she shuts the window, and with a seriousness which yet
has constantly the possibility of lapsing into roguishness she
prays:

> Ye Three Kings of Orient wise,
> Disclose a vision to my eyes.
> Who is the man whose board I'll spread,
> Him for whom I shall make the bed?
> What his name is, be it said.
> Show me the man whom I shall wed.

With that she springs joyfully into bed. Honestly, the Three
Kings ought to be ashamed of themselves if they did not
look out for her; and it's no use saying one doesn't know
what man she wishes: one knows that very well, at least if
all the signs of Yuletide do not fail, she knows it pretty
nearly.

We return now to first love. It is the unity of freedom
and necessity. The individual feels drawn to the other individual by an irresistible power, but precisely in this is
sensible of his freedom. It is a unity of the universal and
the particular; it has the universal as it has the particular
up to the limit of the fortuitous. But all this it has, not by
virtue of reflection but immediately. The more definitely
first love has this character, the more wholesome it is, and
the greater is the probability that it is a first love. With an
irresistible power it draws the two together, and yet in this
they enjoy complete freedom. Now I have no hardhearted
fathers at hand, no sphinxes which must first be overcome,
and as I have wealth enough to provide them with a dowry
—and not having assumed the task, like novel writers and
playwrights, of stretching out the time to the torment of
the whole world, the lovers, the readers and the spectators
—then in God's name let them come together. I am playing
the part of the noble father, you see; and truly it is in itself
a very pretty role, if only we had not frequently made it
so ridiculous. You noticed, perhaps, that I interjected as
appropriate to the father the little phrase, "in God's name."
That you can well condone in the old man, who perhaps

has never known what first love is or has long ago forgotten it. But when a younger man who is still enthusiastic about first love takes the liberty of laying emphasis upon this religious phrase you are perhaps surprised.

So first love possesses all the immediate, temperamental assurance; it fears no danger, it defies the whole world, and my only wish for it is that it may always have as easy a time as in the present case, for I place no obstacles in its way. Perhaps by this I do it no service; indeed, when I come to think of it I may even fall into disgrace. In first love the individual is in possession of a prodigious power, and hence it is just as unpleasant for him not to encounter opposition as it would be for a bold knight who had acquired a sword wherewith he could cut stones to find himself in a sandy region where there was not even a blade of grass he could try it on. So first love is confident enough, it needs no prop; "if it should need a prop," the knight would say, "it is no longer first love." This, then, seems clear enough, but it is also evident that I am moving in a circle. In the foregoing discussion we saw that it was the defect of romantic love that it came to a halt with love as an abstract *an-sich*, and that all the dangers it saw or wished to see were outward dangers which were irrelevant to love itself. We also recalled the fact that if dangers came from another quarter, from within, the thing became much more difficult. But to this the knight of course would reply, "Yes . . . if. But how might that be possible? And if it were possible, this would no longer be first love." You see, this matter of first love is not so easy. I might now remind you that it is a misunderstanding to assume that reflection is able only to destroy, for it is just as capable of saving. However, since what I proposed to show was that first love can coexist with marriage, I will emphasize more particularly what I hinted at in the foregoing, that first love can be assumed into a higher concentricity, and that doubt is not necessary for this. Subsequently I shall show that it is essential for first love to be historical, and that the condition for this is precisely marriage; and with this I shall show that romantic first love is unhistorical—even though one might be capable of filling folios with the knight's exploits.

So, then, first love is immediately secure in itself, but at the same time the individuals are religiously developed. I have a right to assume this, indeed I am bound to do so, for I am about to show that first love and marriage can coexist. It is another matter, of course, when an unhappy first love teaches the individuals to flee to God and to seek security in marriage. With this the first love is changed, even if it remains possible to re-establish it. So, then, they are accustomed to refer everything to God. But of course the referring of everything to God can be done in a multiplicity of different ways. Now it is not in time of sorrow they seek God, neither is it fear or dread which impels them to pray; their heart, their whole being, is replete with joy —what more natural than for them to thank God for it? They fear nothing, for outward dangers will have no power over them, and as for inward dangers, first love does not know them at all. But by this expression of thanksgiving first love is not changed, no disturbing reflection has molested it, it is assumed into a higher concentricity. But like all prayer such a thanksgiving is united with a readiness to act, not in an outward but an inward sense, in the present case with the will to hold this love fast. The nature of first love is not changed by this, no reflection molests it, its firm composition has not been dissolved, it still has its blessed self-assurance, it is merely assumed into a higher concentricity. Perhaps in this higher concentricity it does not know at all what it has to fear, it perhaps thinks of no danger, and yet by this good resolution, which also is a kind of first love, it is elevated into the ethical sphere. But here you will object that by using constantly the word concentricity I am guilty of a *petitio principii,* since I ought to start out with the proof that these regions we are dealing with are eccentric. To this I may reply that if I were to start out from eccentricity I should never reach concentricity; but I also beg you to remember that when I start out from the latter I prove at the same time that the other regions are eccentric. So then we have put first love in relation to the ethical and the religious, and it appeared that its nature need not be changed thereby; and it was precisely the ethical and the religious which seemingly made the union of first love and marriage difficult. So everything seems to be all right.

However, I know you too well to venture to hope to "put you off," as you would say, "with that sort of thing." You are acquainted with absolutely all the difficulties in the world. With your swift and piercing mind you have thought with great speed of a multiplicity of scientific tasks, of personal relationships, etc., but everywhere you have halted at the difficulties, and I hardly believe that it will be possible for you in any single instance to get over them. In a certain sense you resemble a pilot, and yet you are the exact opposite. A pilot knows the dangers and conducts the ship safely into the harbor: you know the shoals, and you always run the ship aground. Of course, you do the best you can, and do it, one must concede, with great alacrity and efficiency. You have such a practiced eye for men and for the seaways that you know at once how far out you must go with people in order to run them aground. Neither are you light-minded about it, you do not forget again that the man is stranded out there; you can remember that with a childish maliciousness the next time you see him, and are then careful to ask how he feels and how he got off the shoal. Presumably you would not be embarrassed to find difficulties in this instance. You would likely remind me that I had left it undetermined and vague which God I was referring to, whether it was not a pagan Eros who would so gladly be privy to love's secrets, and whose presence in the last resort would be a reflection of the lovers' own mood —or whether it was the God of the Christians, the God who is Spirit and is jealous of everything which is not spirit. You would remind me that in Christianity beauty and sensuousness are negated; you would incidentally remark that it was therefore indifferent to the Christians whether Christ was ugly or beautiful; you would beg me to hold myself aloof with my orthodoxy from the secret trysts of lovers, and to refrain especially from any attempts at mediation, which to you are even more distasteful than the crassest orthodoxy. "Yes," you would say, "it must be cheering to the young girl, it must be entirely in accord with her mood, to step up before the altar. And the congregation ought surely to look upon her as an imperfect being who was unable to resist the seductions of lust; she ought to stand there as a pupil stands to be reprimanded or to make public confession; and then the priest should read to her the text, and perhaps thereupon lean over the altar rail and secretly confide to her as a little comfort that matrimony after all is an honorable estate well pleasing to God. The only thing of any value in this whole affair is the situation of the priest, and if it was a pretty young girl, I should be glad to be the priest in order to whisper this secret in her ear."

But, my dear young friend! Yes, truly, matrimony is an estate well pleasing to God; on the other hand, I do not know where anything is said in the Scriptures about a special blessing upon bachelors—and that, after all, is the end of your multifarious love affairs. But in dealing with you one has assumed pretty nearly the most difficult task, for you are capable of proving everything whatever, and under your hands every phenomenon becomes anything whatever. Yes, certainly, the God of the Christians is Spirit, and Christianity is spirit, and discord is posited between flesh and spirit; but "the flesh" is not sensuousness, it is selfishness, and in this sense even the intellectual which you call "spiritual" may be sensual; for example, if a man takes in vain his intellectual gifts he is carnal. And I know well that for the Christians it was not necessary that Christ should be an earthly beauty, and for a different reason than that which you adduce this would be very sad; for how ardently, then, the believer must long to see Him—in case beauty were in this instance something essential. But from all this it by no means follows that the sensuous is abolished by Christianity. First love has in it the factor of beauty, and the joy and fullness which is found in the sensuous when it is innocent can well be admitted into Christianity. But let us beware of one thing, namely, of a false path which is more dangerous than that which you would avoid—let us not be too spiritual. One cannot, of course, leave it to your whim how you will conceive of Christianity. If your conception were correct, the best thing for us would be to begin as soon as possible with all the self-inflicted torments and annihilation of the body which we learn about in the excesses of mysticism. Even health would be a suspicious circumstance. I doubt very much, however, if any pious Christian would deny that he may well pray to God to preserve his health, to the God who went about healing the sick. The lepers in that case ought to have declined to be healed, for they were then closest to perfection. The more simple and childlike a person is, the more he can pray for; but since among other things it is a characteristic of first love to be childlike, I cannot see why it too might not venture to pray, or rather (keeping to the foregoing line of thought) why it might not venture to thank God, without its nature being changed thereby.

But perhaps you still have something more on your conscience. You may as well come out with it, the sooner the better. If in view of one expression or another in what follows you should be prompted to say, "But I never expressed myself in that way!" I would reply, "That is perfectly true, but you, my good Mr. Observer, must forgive a poor married man if he has presumed to make you the object of *his* observation." You conceal something within you which you never frankly utter. Hence it is that in every expression of yours there is so much energy, so much elasticity, because it suggests something more which you leave to be guessed, some outburst still more terrible.

So then you have found that after which your soul aspired, which it thought it was about to find in many mistaken trials; you have found a girl in whom your whole being finds repose; and although you might seem to be a little too experienced, this nevertheless is your first love, of that you are convinced. "She is beautiful" (why of course!), "charming" (I have no doubt of it), "and yet her beauty does not find its expression in the normal but in the unity of the manifold, in the accidental, in the self-contradictory. She is soulful" (You don't say so!), "she shows her devotion in a way which makes one's head swim; she is light, she can swing like a bird on a twig, she has *esprit*—enough to illuminate her beauty, but no more." The day has come when you are to assure yourself of the possession of all that you own in the world—a possession, however, of which you are thoroughly sure. You have begged for the privilege of imparting to her an extreme unction. You already have waited a long time in the family dining room; a brisk chambermaid, four or five inquisitive cousins, a venerable aunt, and the hairdresser, have hurried past you several times. You already are half provoked by it. Then the door of the parlor opens softly, you cast thither a fleeting glance and are delighted to see that not a soul is there, that she has had the tact to remove all irrelevant persons from the parlor. She is pretty, prettier than ever, about her there is an inspiration, a harmony, to the vibrations of which she tingles through and through. You are astonished; she even surpasses your dreams; you are transformed, yet your sub-tile reflection instantly conceals your emotion. Your calm-ness has upon her a still more seductive effect and prompts in her soul a longing which makes her beauty interesting. You approach her, feeling that her finery imparts to the situation an unusual character. You have not yet uttered a word; you see, and yet it is as though you saw not, you would not annoy her with spoony behavior, but even her reflection in the mirror is a delight to you. You fasten upon her bosom a trinket which you had presented to her the very first day, the day you kissed her with a passion which now at this moment seeks its confirmation; she has kept it hidden, no one has seen it. You take a little bouquet com-posed of flowers all of one sort, a flower which in itself is entirely insignificant. Always when you sent her flowers there was a little sprig of it, but unobservable, so that none but she suspected it, she alone. Today this flower is to come to honor and dignity; it alone is to adorn her, for she loved it. You hand it to her, a tear trembles in her eye, she gives it back to you, you kiss it and fasten it upon her bosom. A trace of sadness spreads over her. You, too, are moved. She steps back a pace, she looks at her finery half wrath-fully, it is burdensome to her, she throws her arms about your neck. She is unable to tear herself away, she embraces you as vehemently as if there were a hostile power which would tear her away from you. Her delicate finery is crushed, her hair has fallen down, instantly she vanishes.

You are left again to your solitude, which is broken only by a brisk chambermaid, four or five inquisitive cousins, a venerable aunt, and a hairdresser. Then the door of the parlor opens, she enters, and quiet earnestness is legible in her every expression. You press her hand, you leave her, to meet again . . . before God's altar. That you had forgotten. You who have thought upon so many things, upon this contingency among others, in your infatuation you had forgotten it. You had made the best of situations which were conventionally expected, but upon this you had not reflected—and yet you are far too much developed not to see that a wedding is a little more than a ceremony. A dread seizes you. "This girl whose soul is as pure as the light of day, sublime as the vault of heaven, innocent as the sea, this girl before whom I could kneel in adoration, whose love I feel must be able to pluck me out of all aberration and to give me a new birth, her I am to lead to God's altar, she is to stand there like a sinner, it will be said of her and to her that it was Eve who seduced Adam. To her before whom my proud soul submits, the only one to whom it has submitted, to her it will be said that I am to be her master, and that she shall be obedient to the husband. The moment has come, the Church already stretches out its arms for her, and before it gives her back to me it will first impress a nuptial kiss upon her lips—not the nuptial kiss for which I would give all the world. It already stretches out its arms to embrace her, but this embrace will cause all her beauty to fade, and then it will pass her over to me saying, 'Be fruitful and multiply.' What sort of a power is this which dares to intrude between me and my bride, the bride I myself have chosen and who has chosen me? And this power would command her to be faithful to me. Does she then need to be commanded? And would she be true to me only because a third party, which then she would love more than me, commanded it? And it bids me be faithful to her. Do I need any such bidding? I who belong to her with my whole soul! And this power defines our relationship to one another, it says that I am to command and she to obey. But suppose I have no desire to command, that I feel too lowly for that! No, her I will obey, her hint is my commandment, but to a foreign power I will not submit. No, I will flee with her far away while yet there is time, and I will pray the night to cover us and the silent clouds to recount to us fairy tales in bold symbols appropriate to a nuptial night, and under the immense vault of heaven I will intoxicate myself with her charms, alone with her, alone in the whole world, and I will cast myself into the abyss of her love; and my lips are silent for the clouds are my thoughts and my thoughts are clouds; and I will cry out and conjure all powers in heaven and on earth that nothing may disturb my good fortune, and I will put them to the oath and have them swear to this. Yes, far, far away, that my soul may regain its health, that my breast may again be able to draw breath, that I may not be stifled in this stuffy air. Away!" Yes, that I would say too: *procul, o procul este profani* [Avaunt, avaunt, ye uninitiated]. But have you also reflected whether she will follow you on this expedition? "Woman is weak"—no, she is humble, she is much closer to God than man is. Hence it is that love is everything to her, and she will certainly not disdain the blessing and confirmation which God is ready to bestow upon her. It has never occurred to a woman to object to marriage, and it would not occur to her in all eternity if men themselves do not corrupt her. To be sure, to an emancipated woman this notion might occur. The offense always comes from man's side, for man is proud, he would be everything, would have nothing above him.

That the description I have given fits your case pretty exactly you will certainly not deny, and at any rate you will not deny that it applies to the spokesmen of this tendency. I have intentionally altered a little bit the usual forms in which a lover expresses himself in order to characterize expressly your "first love"; for honestly the love here described, however passionate it is, with however much pathos it expresses itself, is far too reflective, far too intimate with love's coquetry, to be called a first love. A first love is humble and therefore rejoices that there is a power higher than it—if only for the reason that it has some one to thank. (It is for this cause one finds a pure first love more rarely in men than in women.) In you, too, analogies to this were to be found; for you said, indeed, that you would conjure all the powers in heaven and on earth, and this expresses your need of seeking a higher source for your love, only that with you this is a fetishism, a most arbitrary fetishism.

The first thing then that scandalized you was that you should be solemnly instated as her lord and master—as if you were not that (and perhaps all too much so), as if your words did not clearly enough bear the stamp of it. But you will not give up this idolatry, this coquetry, of pretending to want to be her slave, although you thoroughly feel yourself her master.

The second thing was that your soul revolted against the thought that your loved one should be declared a sinner. You are an aesthete, and I could be tempted to propose to the deliberation of your idle head whether this factor would not be apt to make a woman even more beautiful: it implies a mystery which casts an interesting light upon her. The character of childish roguishness which sin may have so long as we dare to account it innocence only enhances beauty. You can well conceive that I am not serious in holding this view, since I feel vividly what it implies and shall subsequently explain it; but I mean to say that if it had occurred to you, you perhaps would have become absolutely enthusiastic about this aesthetic observation. You would have made an immense number of aesthetic investigations as to whether it would be best (i.e., most interesting) to prod with it, so to speak, by an infinitely remote suggestion, or to let the innocent young girl fight alone with this obscure power, or with a sort of solemn seriousness to tip her over into the hands of irony, etc. In short, there would be plenty for your hands to do in this line. You would have thought of the tremulous light which in the Gospel itself is shed upon the woman that was a sinner, whose many sins were forgiven her because she loved much. What I would say, however, is, that again it is your arbitrary interpretation that she is to stand there as a sinner. For it is one thing to know sin *in abstracto,* and another to know it *in concreto.* But woman is humble, and it certainly has never occurred to a woman to be truly scandalized by the fact that the earnest word of the Church was addressed to her. Woman is humble and trustful—who like a woman can cast the eyes down, but who like her can lift them up? If, then, any change were to be wrought in her by the solemn declaration of the Church that sin has entered into the world, it must be that she only the more strongly would hold fast to her love. But from this it does not follow that first love is changed; it is only drawn up into a higher concentricity. It would be very difficult to convince a woman that earthly love in general might be sin, since by this affirmation her whole existence is destroyed in its deepest root. The fact is, moreover, that she has not come to God's altar to deliberate whether or no she shall love the man who stands beside her; she loves him, her very life is in it, and woe unto him who awakens doubt in her and would teach her to revolt against her nature and not to be willing to kneel before God but to stand erect. I ought not, perhaps, to have set myself in opposition to you on this point, for since you have now got it fixed in your head that for first love to exist sin must not have come into the world, you must yourself feel that you are beating the air. (By the fact that you want to ignore sin you prove that you are in the stage of reflection.) But since the individuals between whom we imagined a first love were religiously developed, I have no need to go into this question. For sinfulness is not to be attributed to first love as such but to the selfishness in it, but selfishness only makes its appearance the moment it reflects, and with that first love is destroyed.

Finally, it offends you that a third power wants to impose upon you the obligation of being faithful to her and she to you. For the sake of fairness I beg you to remember that this third power does not obtrude itself, but since the individuals we have in mind are religiously developed they themselves have recourse to it, and the question here at issue is whether there is anything in this which constitutes an obstacle to their first love. You will hardly deny that it is natural for first love to seek corroboration in one way or another by making love an obligation which the lovers impose upon themselves before the face of a higher power. The lovers swear fidelity to one another by the moon, by the stars, by their fathers' ashes, by their honor, etc. If to this you reply, "O well, such oaths don't mean anything; they are simply the reflection of the lovers' own mood—for how otherwise could it occur to them to swear by the moon?"—then I would reply, "With this you yourself have altered the nature of first love; for the beautiful thing about it is precisely this, that for it everything acquires reality in virtue of love. Only in the moment of reflection does it appear void of meaning to swear by the moon; in the moment of the oath this has validity." Might then this situation be changed by the fact that they swear by a power which really has validity? Hardly, I think, for it is of the utmost importance to love that the oath have true significance. So when you think that you would like to swear by the clouds and the stars, but it puts you out that you have to swear by God, it is evident that you are caught in reflection. For the fact is your love must have no witnesses—except such as cannot see. Yes, it is true enough that love is mysterious, but your love puts on such airs that not even God in heaven may know anything about it—in spite of the fact that God (to use a rather frivolous expression) is not an embarrassing witness. But the fact that God must not know anything about it is the selfish and reflective element. For God is in one's consciousness, and yet at the same time He must not be there. First love knows nothing about such things.

This need, then, of letting your love become transfigured in a higher sphere you do not feel, or rather (since first love too feels no need of this but does it spontaneously) you feel the need but will not satisfy it. If I were inclined for a moment to return to your feigned first love, I would say that you might perhaps succeed in conjuring all powers—and yet not far from you there grew a mistletoe.[16] It shot up, it fanned you with its coolness, yet it hid within it a deeper warmth, and you both rejoiced in it—but this mistletoe symbolizes the feverish restlessness which is the life principle in your love; it cools and heats, it changes continually, indeed, at the same moment you could wish that you both might have an eternity before you and that this instant were the last; and therefore the death of your love is certain.

We have seen, then, how first love could come into relation with the ethical and the religious without the intervention of a reflection which would alter its nature, since
it was merely drawn up into a higher concentricity, always
in the sphere of immediacy. In a certain sense a change has
been brought about, and it is this which I will now consider as the metamorphosis (so it might be called) of the
lovers into bride and bridegroom. When first love is referred
to God, this comes to pass for the fact that the lovers thank
God for it. With this an ennobling transformation is ef-
fected. The weakness to which the male is most prone is
to imagine that he has made a conquest of the girl he loves.
In this he is sensible of his superiority—but there is nothing
aesthetic in that. In thanking God, however, he humbles
himself under his love; and truly it is far more beautiful
to receive the beloved from God's hand than to have subdued the whole world in order to make a conquest of her.
Moreover, the man who truly loves will not find repose for
his soul before he has thus humbled himself before God,
and in truth the maiden he loves means too much to him
for him to dare to take her as a prey even in the fairest
and noblest sense. And if he might find joy in conquering
and acquiring her, he will know that the daily acquisition
throughout a whole life is more comely than the preternatural force of a brief period of love-making. But this does not
come to pass by reason of a preliminary doubt; it comes
to pass by immediacy. The real life principle in first love
remains intact, but the fusel oil (if I may use this expression), the undesirable ingredient, is taken away. For the
other sex it is rather natural to feel the predominance of
man and to submit to it; and yet, even though the woman
feels joyful and happy in being nothing, she is in the way
of becoming more or less disingenuous. Then, when she
thanks God for the beloved her soul is secured against suffering; by the fact that she thanks God she removes the
man she loves just so far from her that she is able to draw
breath; and this does not come to pass in consequence of
an alarming doubt (for such she does not know) but by
immediacy.

Already I have indicated above that even the illusory

eternity in first love makes it moral. Now when the lovers refer their love to God this act of thanksgiving imparts to it an absolute stamp of eternity, as does also resolute purpose and the sense of obligation; and this eternity will not be founded upon obscure forces but upon the eternal itself. Purpose has at the same time another significance. That is, it implies the possibility of a movement in love, and hence, also, the possibility of liberation from the difficulty attendant upon first love as such, that it is incapable of budging from the spot. The aesthetical aspect of it consists in its infinity, but the unaesthetical in the fact that this infinity cannot become finitized. I will elucidate by a more figurative expression the fact that the addition of religion cannot disturb first love. Indeed, the religious is properly the expression for the conviction that man by God's help is lighter than the whole world, the very same faith which accounts for the fact that a man is able to swim. If, then, there were a swimming belt which could hold one up, one might suppose that a man who had been in mortal danger would always carry it; but one might also suppose that a man who had never been in mortal danger would likewise carry it. The latter supposition corresponds to the relation between first love and the religious. First love girds itself with the religious, even though no painful experience or alarming reflection has gone before. Only I must beg you not to press this analogy too far, as if religion stood in a merely external relation to first love. I have shown in the foregoing that such is not the case.

Let us then cast up the account once for all. You talk so much about the erotic embrace—what is that in comparison with the matrimonial embrace! What richness of modulation in the matrimonial "Mine!" in comparison with the erotic! It re-echoes not only in the seductive eternity of the instant, not only in the illusory eternity of fantasy and imagination, but in the eternity of clear consciousness, in the eternity of eternity. What power there is in the matrimonial "Mine!"—for will, resolution and purpose have a deeper tone. What energy and pliability!—for what is so hard as will, and what so soft? What power of movement! —not merely the confusing enthusiasm of obscure impulses;

for marriage is made in heaven, and duty permeates the whole body of the universe to its utmost limits and prepares the way and gives assurance that to all eternity no obstacle shall be able to unsettle love! So let Don Juan keep the leafy bower, and the knight the starry dome of heaven, if he can see nothing above it; marriage has its heaven still higher up. Such is marriage; and if it is not thus, it is not the fault of God, nor of Christianity, nor of the wedding ceremony; it is not due to cursing nor to blessing, but it is man's own fault. And is it not a sin and a shame that men write books in such a way as to make people perplexed about life, make them tired of it before they begin, instead of teaching them how to live! And this would be a painful truth, even if they were in the right, but in fact, it is a lie. They teach us to sin, and those who have not the courage for that they make equally unhappy in other ways. Unfortunately, I myself am too much influenced by the aesthetic not to know that the word "husband" grates upon your ears. But I don't care. If the word husband has fallen into discredit and almost become laughable, it is high time for one to seek to restore it to honor. And if you say, "Such a sight as this one never sees, although one often enough sees marriages," this does not disquiet me; for the fact that one sees marriages every day entails the consequence that one more rarely sees the greatness in marriage, especially in view of the fact that people do everything to belittle it. For have not you and your sort carried the thing so far that the maiden who gives her hand before the altar is regarded as a more imperfect being than these heroines in your romances with their "first love"?

Now that I have listened patiently to you and your outburst, you perhaps will forgive me for coming forward with my little observations. (Your outbursts, by the way, were perhaps wilder than you were aware; but even though you have not thoroughly understood these emotions within you, yet when marriage comes to meet you as a reality, you will see that within you there will be a raging storm, though presumably you will not again confide in anyone.) A man loves only once in his life—the heart clings to its first love—marriage! Harken and be amazed at the harmonious accord of these different spheres. It is the same thing, except that it is expressed aesthetically, religiously, and ethically. One loves but once. To effect a realization of this, marriage joins in—and in case people who do not love each other take it into their heads to get married, the Church is not responsible. A man loves only once—this refrain is heard from the most various quarters: from the fortunate to whom every new day gives a glad reassurance; and from the unfortunate. Of the latter there are properly only two classes: those who are always aspiring after the ideal; and those who will not stick to it. The last are the real seducers. One meets them rather seldom, because an uncommon aptitude is always requisite for this. I have known one, but he too admitted that a man loves only once; his wild lusts, however, love was unable to tame. "Yes," say these people, "one loves only once, one marries two or three times." Here the two spheres are again united; for aesthetics says, "No," and the Church with ecclesiastical ethics looks with suspicion upon the second marriage. To me this is of the utmost importance; for if it were true that one loves several times, marriage would be a questionable institution; it might seem that the erotic suffered harm from the arbitrary exaction of the religious, which requires as a rule that one should love only once, and disposes of the business of the erotic as cavalierly as though it were to say, "You can marry once, and that's the end of it."

We have now seen how first love came into relation with marriage without being changed by it. The same aesthetic quality which was found in first love must, therefore, be found also in marriage, since the former is contained in the latter; but the aesthetic quality consists in the infinity, the apriority of first love—as we have already seen. In the next place, it consists in the unity of the contradictions exemplified by love: it is sensuous and yet spiritual; it is freedom and yet necessity; it is in the moment, is definitely in the present tense, and yet it has in it an eternity. All this marriage has too: it is sensuous and yet spiritual, but it is more than that, for the word "spiritual" when it is used of first love means rather that it is soulish, that it is sensuousness permeated by spirit; it is freedom and necessity, but it

is also more, for "freedom" as it is applied to first love is no
more than the soulish freedom of an individual not yet clarified from the dregs of natural necessity. But the more freedom, the more complete the abandonment of devotion, and
only he can be lavish of himself who possesses himself. In
the religious the individuals become free—he from false
pride, she from false humility—and between the lovers who
hold one another in such a close embrace the religious
presses in, not to separate them, but in order that she might
surrender herself with a richer devotion than she had before
dreamt of, and that he might not only receive her but surrender himself, and she receive the devotion. Marriage has
within it inward infinity, even more than first love, for the
inward infinity of marriage is an eternal life. It is a unity
of contradictions, even more than first love, for it has one
contradiction the more, the spiritual, and thereby it has the
sensuous in a still more profound opposition—but the further
one is removed from the sensuous the more aesthetic significance it acquires, for otherwise the instinct of the beast
would be the most aesthetic. But the spiritual factor in marriage is higher than in first love, and the higher heaven is
above the marriage bed, the more beautiful this is, the more
aesthetic; and it is not the earthly heaven which arches
over marriage, but the heaven of the spirit. Marriage is in
the moment, it is sound and vigorous, but in a deeper sense
than first love, for the defect of first love precisely is that
it has an abstract character, but in the purpose which marriage expresses is implied the law of movement, the possibility of an inward history. Purpose is resignation in its
richest form, where it does not have in view what is to be
lost, but what is to be gained by holding fast. In the purpose another person is posited, and love is posited in relation to that person, yet not in an outward sense. But the
purpose is not the fruit acquired by doubt, but is the super-
abundance of promise. So beautiful is marriage, and the
sensuous is by no means renounced but is ennobled.

I confess—it is wrong of me perhaps—that often when I
think of my own marriage, the mental picture of it arouses
in me an inexplicable sadness, for the fact that it will come
to an end, that certain as I am that with her to whom I

was united in marriage I shall live in another life, yet there she will be given to me in another way, that the contradiction which was a component in our love will be abolished. Yet it consoles me to know that I shall remember that with her I lived in the most heartfelt, the most beautiful relationship which human life affords. If I have any understanding of the matter, the defect of earthly love is the same thing as its advantageous quality, i.e., its partiality. Spiritual love has no partiality and moves in the opposite direction, constantly abhorring all relativities. Earthly love in its true form takes the opposite path, and at its highest it is love only for one single person in the whole world. This is the element of truth in the saying that a man loves only one and loves only once. Earthly love begins by loving several—these are the preliminary anticipations—and it ends by loving one. Spiritual love is constantly opening itself more and more, ever extending its circle of love to include more and more persons until it reaches its true expression in loving all. So then marriage is sensuous but at the same time spiritual, free and at the same time necessary, absolute in itself and at the same time inwardly pointing beyond itself.

Having this inner harmony, marriage has, of course, its teleology in itself; it exists because it constantly presupposes itself, and hence, every question about its "why" is a misunderstanding, which comes very natural to prosaic common sense; and though generally the definition of what marriage is, is not so bold as that of Basil the singing master, who asserts that "of all ludicrous things marriage is the most ludicrous," yet it may easily tempt not you only but me too to say that if marriage is nothing else but this, it is of all ludicrous things the most ludicrous.

Meanwhile, let us as a diversion look a little more closely at one and another of these answers. Even though between your laughter and mine there is a vast difference, we can very well laugh a little in company. The difference in our laughter will correspond pretty nearly to the diversity of intonation with which we respond to the question what marriage is for by exclaiming, "God only knows!" Moreover, when I say that we will laugh a little in fellowship it must not be forgotten how much I owe in this respect to you for your observations, for which as a married man I thank you cordially. For when people are not willing to perform effectually the most beautiful task, when they want to dance everywhere else but on the Rhodes which is assigned to them as the dancing place,[17] let them become a sacrifice for you and other cunning persons who behind the mask of a confidant know how to make fools of them. But there is one point I would spare, one point at which I never have and never shall permit myself to laugh. You have often said that it might be "a capital thing" to go around and ask every man severally why he had married, and one would find that in most cases it was a very insignificant circumstance which was the determining cause; and so you seek the ludicrous element in the fact that such an immense effect as a marriage with all its consequences can issue from such a small cause. I shall not linger to point out the incorrectness of your argument when you regard the little circumstance quite abstractly, nor to observe that if the little circumstance comes to something it is because it is superadded to a multiplicity of determinants. What I would dwell upon is the beauty in marriages which have as little "why" as possible. The less "why," the more love—that is, when it is genuine. For the frivolous it will of course be evident in the result that it was a little "why"; for the serious man it will to his joy be evident that it was an immense "why." The less "why" the better. Among the lower classes marriage is generally entered into without any very great "why"; but, therefore, these marriages echo far less frequently with so many "hows"—how they are to get along, how they are to provide for their children, etc. Marriage needs nothing more than its own "why," but that is infinite, and therefore in the sense in which I have been using the word it is not a "why." Of this you too will easily be convinced, for if to the "wherefore" alleged by such a philistine husband one were to reply with the true "therefore," he presumably would say like Basil the singing teacher in Heiberg's play,[18] "So let us invent a new lie." You will also perceive why I am neither able nor willing to see the comical side of this lack of a "why," because I fear that with this the true "why" will be lost. The true "why" is only one, but at the same time it has in it an infinity of energy and power which is able to smother all "hows." The finite "why" is an agglomeration, a swarm, from which each takes his own, the one more, the other less, each more foolish than the other; for even if a man could unite all the finite "whys" at the inception of his marriage, he would be precisely the poorest of husbands.

One of the most reputable answers, apparently, to the "Why?" of marriage is that marriage is a school for character; one marries in order to ennoble and improve one's character. I will attach myself to a definite fact which I owe to you. There was a government employe you "had got hold of"—that is your own expression, and it is just like you, for when there is a subject for your observation there is nothing you shrink from, you consider that you are justified by your vocation. Moreover, he was a rather clever fellow and had in particular a good knowledge of languages. The family was gathered around the tea table. He was smoking his pipe. His wife was no beauty, looked rather simple, was old in comparison with him, and in view of all this one might promptly come to the conclusion that there must be a queer "why." At the table sat a newly married woman, young and rather pale, who seemed to know another "why." The wife herself poured tea, a young girl of sixteen, not pretty but plump and lively, passed it around—she appeared not yet to have attained a "why." In that honorable company your unworthiness had also found a place. You, who were present *ex officio,* and already had made your appearance several times in vain, found naturally that this situation was too favorable to be neglected. Just in those days there was talk about a broken engagement. The family had not yet heard this important local news. The case was pleaded from all sides—that is to say, all were prosecuting attorneys. Then the case was adjudicated and the sinner excommunicated. Feeling ran high. You ventured to put in a little word in favor of the condemned man—which, of course, was not calculated to benefit the person in question but to serve as a cue. That did not succeed, so you went on to say, "Perhaps the engagement was too precipitate, perhaps he had not taken into consideration the momentous 'why,' one might almost say the 'but,' which ought to precede such a decisive step—*enfin* why do people marry, why, why do they?" Each of these "whys" was uttered with a different but equally dubitative intonation. That was too much. One "why" would have been quite sufficient, but such a formal challenge, an attack in force upon the enemy's camp, was decisive. The moment had come. With an air of good humor which bore also the stamp of the predominance of common sense the host said, "Well, my good man, I will tell you. A man marries because marriage is a school for character." Now everything was in train. Partly by opposition, partly by approbation, you got him to outdo himself in grotesqueness—not at all to the edification of his wife, to the scandal of the young married woman and to the astonishment of the young girl. I reproved you for your conduct at that time—not out of consideration for the host, but for the sake of the women towards whom you were malicious enough to make the scene as trying and tiresome as possible. The two younger women do not need my defense, and in fact, it was only your usual coquetry which beguiled you to keep your eye on them. But perhaps the man really loved his wife, and it must have been terrible for her to listen to this. Besides, there was something indecorous in the whole situation. For common-sense reflection is so far from making marriage moral that it rather makes it immoral. Sensuous love has only one transfiguration in which it is equally aesthetic, religious and moral—and that is love. Common-sense calculation makes it just as unaesthetic as it is irreligious, because the sensuous element does not receive its due in immediacy. So the man who marries for this and that and the other reason takes a step as unaesthetic as it is irreligious. The goodness of his purpose makes the case no better, for the trouble is precisely that he has a purpose. In case a woman were to marry in order—indeed, the madness I have in mind is not unheard of in the world, a madness which seems to give her marriage a prodigious "why"—let us say, in order to bear a saviour to the world; in this case the marriage would be just as unaesthetic as it is immoral and irreligious. This is something people cannot make clear enough to themselves. There is a certain class of common-sense men who look down with immense contempt upon the aesthetic as trumpery and childishness, imagining that they are raised high above it by their pitiable teleology; but it is exactly the contrary, such men with their common sense are just as immoral as they are unaesthetic. One always does best, therefore, to look at the other sex, which is both the more religious and the more aesthetic. The host's exposition was at all events very trivial, and I do not need to report it. On the other hand, I will conclude this comment by wishing to every such husband a Xanthippe for a wife, and then children as wicked as possible, so that he may hope to be in possession of the conditions requisite for attaining his purpose.

The fact that marriage actually is a school for character, or (in order not to use so philistine an expression) that it is a genesis of character, I am quite ready to admit, though of course I must constantly maintain that everyone who marries for this reason might be assigned to any other school than that of love. Moreover, a man like that will never derive any profit from this schooling. First of all, he deprives himself of the consolidation, the penetrating shudder through all thoughts and joints which marriage is, for after all, it is truly a deed of daring. But that is what it should be; and so far is it from being the right thing to want to calculate it, that such a calculation is precisely an attempt to enervate it. In the second place, he has lost, of course, the immense working capital of love and the humbling effect which the religious element in marriage has. He is, of course, far too super-shrewd not to bring with him a ready-made conception of how he wants to be developed, and this, then, becomes regulative for his marriage and for the unfortunate being he has shamelessly selected to try the thing out on. But let us forget this and remember with gratitude how true it is that marriage educates—in case, that is to say, a man does not want to stand above it but is willing to subordinate himself as one always does when it is a question of education. It ripens the whole soul by the fact that it gives it a feeling of significance and at the same time imposes the weight of a responsibility one cannot so-

phisticate away, because one loves. It ennobles the whole
man by the blush of bashfulness which belongs to woman
but is the corrector of man; for woman is the conscience
of man. It brings melody into man's eccentric movements,
it gives strength and significance to woman's quiet life, but
this only in so far as she seeks it in man, and so it does
not become an unwomanly manliness. His proud wrath is
quelled by the fact that he turns back constantly to her.
Her weakness is made strong by the fact that she leans upon
him.*

* It is marriage, therefore, which first gives a man his positive
freedom, because this relationship is of a sort that extends over
his whole life, over the least things as well as the greatest. It liberates him from a certain natural embarrassment in natural
situations—a liberation which can indeed be acquired in many
other ways, but often at the expense of the good. It liberates from
stagnation in habit by maintaining a fresh current; liberates
him from people precisely by the fact that it binds him to one
person. I have often noticed that unmarried people toil exactly
like slaves. First of all they are slaves to their whims: they can
indulge them freely without rendering and accounting to anybody; but then they become dependent, indeed, slaves to other
people. What a role is often played by a servant, a housekeeper,
etc. In them the master's whims and proclivities are imperson-
ated and expressed in clock time. They know at what time the
master gets up, or rather how early he's to be called, or rather
how long in advance his study must be warmed before they call
him. They know how to lay out for him clean shirts, how to
turn his stockings inside out so that he can pull them on easily,
how to have cold water ready when he has washed in tepid
water, to close the windows when he goes out, to put out the boot-
jack and slippers for him when he comes home, etc., etc. All
this the servants, especially if they are a bit shrewd, know very
well how to do. In spite, then, of the fact that all this is done
punctiliously, such unmarried persons are often not satisfied.
They are able, in fact, to purchase for themselves the satisfaction
of every wish. Once in a while they are ill-tempered and peevish,
then weak and good-natured. A few dollars make it all right.
The servant promptly learns to take advantage of this: it is
enough if at suitable intervals he does something a bit wrong,
lets the master rage, then he is in despair, and thereupon receives
a *douceur*. So the master is captivated by such a personality, he
doesn't know whether he ought to wonder most at his punctuality
or at the sincere repentance he shows when he has done something amiss. Thus such a personality becomes indispensable to
the master and is a perfect despot.

And then all the pettiness marriage brings with it. O yes, here you will be ready enough to agree with me, but at the same time will pray God to deliver you from it. No, there is nothing that educates so much as the petty. There is a period in a man's life when he ought to keep it at a distance; but there is also a period when it is good, and it requires a great soul to save one's soul out of the petty—but one can do this if one will, for the fact of willing makes the great soul, and he who loves also wills. For man this may be especially difficult, and, therefore, in this respect woman will have such great significance for him. She was created to deal with the small, and knows how to give it an importance, a dignity, a beauty, which enchants. Marriage liberates one from habits, from the tyranny of one-sidedness, from the yoke of whims—and how could all such evil get time to assume shape in a matrimonial union which so often and in so many ways calls itself to an accounting? In it no such things can thrive, for "love suffereth long, and is kind; love envieth not; love vaunteth not itself, is not puffed up, doth not behave itself unseemly, seeketh not her own, is not easily provoked, thinketh no evil; rejoiceth not in iniquity, but rejoiceth in the truth; beareth all things, believeth all things, hopeth all things, endureth all things." Think of these beautiful words of the Lord's Apostle, imagine them applied to a whole life, in such a way that one oftentimes did these things easily, oftentimes failed, oftentimes forgot them, yet returned to them again. Imagine that a married couple dare to repeat these words to one another in such a way that the principal impression is joyful—what blessedness is implied in this, what a transfiguration of character! In marriage one gets nowhere with great passions; one cannot pay in advance, by being loving for a month on a great scale one cannot make good the defect of another time; here every day has its trouble, but also its blessing. I know that I have subjected my pride and my hypochondriac restlessness to her love, I have subjected her impetuosity to our love; but I know also that it has cost many days, I know also that there may be many dangers ahead, but my hope is fixed upon victory.

Or one marries . . . to have children, to make one's humble contribution to the propagation of the human race. Imagine he were to have no children—his contribution would then be humble indeed. To be sure, states have presumed to associate this purpose with marriage, putting a premium on marriage and rewarding the man who has the most male children. At certain times Christianity has opposed this by putting a premium on not getting married. Even though this was a misunderstanding, it nevertheless shows a profound respect for personality that to this degree one would not treat the particular individual merely as a moment in a process but as the definitive reality. The more abstractly the State is conceived and the less individuality is able to assert itself, the more natural it is to issue this injunction and to offer this encouragement. In contrast to this, people in our age are sometimes almost inclined to extol a marriage without children. For in our age people find it hard enough to muster up the resignation required for entering into the marriage relation; if a man has exercised self-denial to that degree, he thinks it's enough, and he cannot put up with the annoyance of having a flock of children. Often enough in novels one finds a dislike for children alleged, perhaps quite casually, as the reason why a particular person does not marry; in real life one sees this expressed in the most refined countries by the fact that the children are removed as early as possible from the paternal home and sent to boarding-school, etc. How often you have been diverted by the tragi-comic fathers with four blessed children whom secretly they wished far away. How often you have been amused at the lofty superiority of such fathers when they were mortified by the pettiness which life brings with it, when the children have to be spanked, when they slobber at table, when they cry, when the great man—the father—feels his boldness checked by the thought that his children bind him to the earth. How often with well-merited cruelty you have brought such a father to the highest degree of suppressed rage by occupying yourself exclusively with his children and letting drop a few words about how blessed a thing it is after all to have children.

To marry for the sake of contributing to the propagation of the race might seem a very objective reason and a very natural one. It might seem as though one were taking God's viewpoint and beholding from thence the beauty of maintaining the race; indeed, one might lay special emphasis upon the words, "Increase and multiply and replenish the earth." And yet such a marriage is as unnatural as it is arbitrary, nor has it any support in Holy Scripture. For in the Bible we read that God established marriage because "it is not good for man to be alone," hence, in order to give him company. Although to some scoffers at religion there might seem to be something a bit questionable about the companionship which began by casting man into perdition, that proves nothing; I prefer to appeal to this event as a motto for all marriages; for only after woman had done this was the most hearty comradeship established between them. Then we read these words, that "God blessed them." These words people completely overlook. And when in one place the Apostle Paul admonishes woman with a good deal of severity to "learn in quietness with all subjection" and to "be in quietness," and thereupon, having stopped her mouth, he adds, to humiliate her still more, "she shall be saved through child-bearing," I truly never would have forgiven the Apostle for this base opinion, if he had not made it all right again by adding, "if they (i.e., the children) continue in faith and love and holiness with sobriety."

It occurs to me in this connection that it may seem strange that I, whose duties leave so little time for study and whose studies such as they are generally take a very different direction, should appear to be so well versed in the Holy Scriptures that I could apply for the final examination in theology. An old pagan, Seneca I think it was, affirmed that by the time a man had reached his thirtieth year he ought to be so well acquainted with his constitution that he could be his own physician; and so I, too, am of the opinion that when a man has reached a certain age he ought to be able to be his own priest. Not as though I were by any means inclined to disdain participation in public worship and the instruction which is there offered; but I think that one ought to be clear in one's own mind about the most important relationships of life, about which, by the way, one rather rarely hears anything very definite said

in a sermon. I have an idiosyncrasy against edifying books
and printed sermons, so when I cannot resort to church I
have recourse to the Scriptures. I commonly seek enlightenment from one learned theologian or another, or from some
learned work in which are to be found the most important
passages of Scripture dealing with the subject in question,
and I read them through. Thus I was already married and
had been married for half a year before it occurred to me
to reflect seriously upon what the New Testament teaches
about marriage. I had been present at several weddings before my own, so I was acquainted with the sacred texts
which are recited on that occasion. Nevertheless, I desired
to have a little more complete acquaintance, and therefore
had recourse to my friend Pastor Olufsen, who was here in
town just at that time. Following his instructions I found
the principal passages and read them through in my wife's
hearing. I well remember the impression made upon her by
that passage from St. Paul. This was a singular situation: I
did not know the passages of Scripture I was about to read
to her, and I did not wish to examine them beforehand; I
cannot bear to be prepared for the impression I shall make
upon her—such a thing suggests an unbecoming distrust.
This you might well take to heart. For it is true you are
not married and so have no person to whom in the strictest
sense you are obliged to be candid; but your preparations
really reach the point of being ludicrous. You are well able
to fool people, you can even seem to do everything as casually, as impromptu as possible, and yet I believe that you
are not able to say good-bye without having deliberated
how you will say it.

But to return to marriage and to the married people who
are indefatigable in perpetuating the race. A marriage of
this sort is wont sometimes to hide behind a more aesthetic
screen. There is an ancient noble family of distinction which
is about to die out; there are only two representatives left,
a grandfather and his grandson. It is the only wish of the
venerable old man that his grandson might marry in order
that the race might not be obliterated. Or it is the case of
a man to whose life not so much importance attaches but
who thinks back with a certain sadness, if not to a more

remote time, at least to his parents, and he loves them so dearly that he could desire that this name might not die out but be kept in the grateful memory of living men. Perhaps he pictures to himself how beautiful it would be if he could talk to his children about their grandfather, dead long ago, to fortify their lives by such an ideal picture, to inspire them to everything noble and great by this presentation of him; he will think, perhaps, that he could pay off something of the debt he owes to his parents. Now all this is very well and very pretty, but essentially it is irrelevant to marriage, and a marriage contracted for such reasons alone is as unaesthetic as it is immoral. I may seem harsh in saying this, but it is true. Marriage can only be undertaken with one purpose, by which it becomes in the same degree ethical and aesthetical, but this purpose is immanent; every other purpose separates what belongs together, and thereby reduces both the spiritual and the sensuous factors to finite terms. It may well be that by such talk an individual may win a girl's heart, especially when the feelings above described truly exist in him; but the thing is wrong, and her nature is essentially perverted, and it always is an insult to a girl to want to marry her for any other reason than because one loves her.

Although the analogy of a stud-farm (if I may use your expression) is not properly applicable to any marriage, yet for the man who has not misunderstood the meaning of his marriage the progeny proves to be a blessing. It is a beautiful thing for a person to owe another as much as possible; but the highest thing one person can owe another is . . . life. And yet a child may owe still more to a father; for in fact it does not receive life pure and simple, but it receives it with a definite content, and when it has long enough reposed upon its mother's breast it is laid upon the father's, and he too nourishes it with his own flesh and blood, with the experiences often dearly bought in the course of a stirring life. And what possibility there is in a child! I am very ready to concur with you in hating the idolatry which is practiced with children, the whole family cult in particular, and the circulation of children at the dinner table to exchange the family kiss, with family admiration and family expectations, while the parents self-complacently congratulate one another upon the difficulties already overcome and rejoice in the consummate product of their art. Yes, I admit it, I can wax almost as sarcastic as you against such a nuisance, but I do not allow myself to be disturbed by it further. Children belong to the inmost and most hidden life of the family, and to this dim region of mystery one ought also to direct every serious or God-fearing thought concerning this theme. But there, too, it will be manifest that every child has a halo about its head, and there, too, every father will feel that there is more in the child than it owes to him, yea, he will feel with humility that the child is a trust, and that he is in the most beautiful sense of the word only a stepfather. The father who has not felt this has taken in vain his paternal dignity. Let us be free from all unseasonable fuss, but let us also be free from your wantonness, when like Holberg's Henrik[19] you would pledge yourself to accomplish the impossible.

The child is the greatest and most important thing in the world; it is the most insignificant and the most unimportant—just as one wants to take it—and one has an opportunity to get a deep insight into a man when one learns how he thinks in this respect. A tiny babe may almost produce a comic effect when one thinks of its pretension to be a human being; it may also produce a tragic effect when one reflects that it comes into the world with a cry, that a long time elapses before it forgets to cry, and that no one has explained this baby cry. It may thus produce various effects, but the religious way of regarding it remains the most beautiful and can well be united with the others. And now as for you—you indeed love possibility, and yet the thought of children will certainly not produce a joyous effect upon you, for I have no doubt that your inquisitive and vagabond mind has taken a peep into this world. This distaste is attributable, of course, to the fact that you want to have possibility under your control. You like to be in the same condition as children when they are waiting in the dark room for the revelation of the Christmas tree; but a child is evidently a possibility of a very different sort, and of so serious a sort that you would hardly have patience to put up with it. And nevertheless, children are a blessing. It is right and seemly that a man should think with profound seriousness upon the responsibility he bears for the child, but if he does not sometimes remember that it is not merely an obligation imposed upon him, but that it is also a blessing, and that God in heaven has not forgotten, as even men do not forget, to lay a gift in the cradle, then that man has not opened wide his heart either to aesthetic or to religious feelings. The better a man is able to hold fast to the conviction that children are a blessing, and the fewer conflicts he has to overcome and the less dubious he is in conserving this jewel which is the only thing the infant possesses, and lawfully possesses because God Himself has confirmed to it this right—all the more beautiful, the more aesthetic, the more religious it is. I, too, sometimes saunter about the streets, abandoning myself to my own thoughts and the impressions momentarily made upon me by the surroundings. I have seen a poor woman who carried on a small business, not in a shop, nor in a stall, but in an open place, standing there in rain and wind with a babe in her arms. She was herself clean and neat, and the babe was carefully wrapped. I saw her many times. A fashionable lady came by and almost rebuked her because she did not leave the child at home—all the more because it was only an obstacle to her. And a priest passed by that same way, and he approached her and offered to put the child in an asylum. She thanked him kindly, but you should have seen the glance with which she bent down and looked at the child. If the child had been frozen, this look would have thawed it; if it had been dead and cold, this look would have recalled it to life; if it had been extenuated by hunger and cold, the benediction of this glance would have refreshed it. But the child slept, and not even its smile could reward the mother. Lo, this woman had perceived that the child was a blessing. If I were an artist, I would never paint anything else but this woman. Such a sight is a rarity; it is like a rare flower which is seen only by a happy chance. But the world of spirit is not subjected to vanity; if one has discovered the tree, it blooms perpetually—this woman I have often seen. I showed her to my wife. I assumed no self-importance, I sent her no rich gifts, as though I had plenary divine authority to distribute rewards; I humbled myself under her; verily she stands in no need of gold, or of fashionable ladies, or of asylums and priests, or of a poor assessor in civil law and his wife. She needs absolutely nothing except that the child will one day love her with the same tenderness—not even of this does she feel the need, but it is the reward she has deserved, a blessing which heaven will not fail to give her. That this is pretty, that it moves even your hardened heart, you will not deny. Therefore, for the sake of impressing upon you the fact that a child is a blessing, I employ no terrifying pictures such as people often use when they would frighten the unmarried with the thought of how lonely they some day will be and how unhappy if they are not surrounded by a flock of children. For, in the first place, you presumably would not allow yourself to be terrified, not by me at least, yea, not by the whole world, though when you are alone with yourself in the dark chamber of melancholy thoughts you are sometimes doubtless in dread of yourself. And, in the second place, it always seems to me a suspicious circumstance that in order to convince oneself of the possession of something precious one must alarm others by the thought that they have it not. Mock, then, if you will, utter the word which hovers upon your lips, scoff at the four-seated Holstein wagon; divert yourself, if you will, by the reflection that the excursion is no further than to Frederiksberg; drive past us, if you will, in your matchless Viennese carriage; but beware of indulging often in your mockery, which directed to this theme might perhaps quietly develop an ideal longing in your soul which would be a dear punishment for you to pay.

But in still another sense children are a blessing, because one has so very much to learn from them. I have seen proud men whom no adverse fate could humble, every one of whom was capable of snatching the girl he loved from the family circle to which she belonged, and doing it with an assurance which seemed to say, "Now thou hast me, so that ought to be enough. I am accustomed to defy tempests, and now how much more when the thought of thee will give me enthusiasm, now when I have much more to fight for." I have seen the same men as fathers—a little mishap which befell their children was capable of humbling them, an illness forced their proud lips to pronounce a prayer. I have seen men who almost took pride in despising God in heaven, who were wont to pick out every believer as the target of their mockery—I have seen them as fathers concerned for the welfare of their children take into their service the most pious persons. I have seen girls whose proud glance made Olympus tremble, whose vain mind was fixed only upon pomp and finery—I have seen them as mothers endure every humiliation, begging almost like mendicants what was for the advantage of their children. I think of a particular case. It was that of a very proud lady. Her child fell ill. One of the physicians of the city was called. He refused to come on account of a previous experience with that family. And now she went to him and waited in his antechamber in order to move him to come by her prayers. But what is the use of these striking descriptions which, even if they are true, are not so edifying as the simpler examples which are visible every day for those who have eyes to see!

Moreover, one has much to learn from children in another way. In every child there is something original, and upon that all abstract principles and maxims come to grief. One must start from the beginning, often with much toil and trouble. There is profound significance in the Chinese proverb: "Bring up your child well—thus you will know how much you owe your parents." And then consider the responsibility which is laid upon the father. One consorts with other men, one attempts to convey to them a notion of that which one regards as the right; one perhaps makes several attempts; when this is of no avail one has nothing more to do with them, one washes one's hands. But when comes the moment when a father dares, or rather when a fatherly heart can resolve to give up every further attempt? A man lives over again his whole life in his children, and only now does he understand his own life. To you, however, it is no use talking about all this; there are things of which one can never form a concrete conception without having experienced them, and among these is that of being a father.

And now, finally, about the beautiful way in which a man by means of his children is connected with a past and with a future. Although one may not have quite fourteen noble ancestors and be concerned about producing the fifteenth in the line, yet one has, in reality, a far longer genealogy, and it is truly a cheering thing to see how in families the human race assumes, as it were, distinct types. The unmarried man, too, can, of course, make such reflections, but he will not, to the same degree, feel prompted to do so, nor entitled to, since, to a certain degree, he is encroaching intrusively.

Another case is that when one marries in order to acquire a home. One has become bored at home, one has traveled abroad and been bored, one has come home again and been bored. For company's sake one keeps a remarkably fine water spaniel and a full-blooded mare, but one still feels the lack of something. At the restaurant where one meets with like-minded friends one looks in vain for an acquaintance who for a long time has not turned up. One learns that he has married, one becomes soft-hearted and sentimental about one's old age; one feels that everything is so empty around one, no one is waiting for one when one stays away. The old housekeeper is at bottom a very honest woman, but then she doesn't know in the least how to cheer one up and make things a bit agreeable. One marries. The neighbors clap their hands in approval, they find that he has acted shrewdly and sensibly—and thereupon they go on to talk about the most important factor in housekeeping, the supremest earthly good, an honest and reliable cook whom one can trust to go to the market alone, and a nimble chambermaid who is so smart that one can use her for everything. If only such a bald-headed old hypocrite would be content with marrying a night nurse—but generally that is not the case. The best is not good enough for him, and finally he succeeds in catching a pretty young girl who is manacled to such a galley-slave. Perhaps she has never loved—what a horrible misunderstanding!

You see, I let you have the floor. However, you must admit that among the simpler classes more especially one finds marriages which have been contracted for the pur-

pose of getting a home, and which are quite pretty. It is
the case of men fairly young who without being especially
knocked about in life have earned a sufficient income and
then think of marrying. This is pretty; I know too that it
would never occur to you to direct your mockery against
such marriages. A certain noble simplicity gives them at
once an aesthetic and a religious aspect. For here there is
no egoistic trait in the thought of wanting to have a home;
on the contrary, it is associated with the conception of a
duty, a calling, which is laid upon them, but at the same
time is a duty dear to them.

One only too often hears married people console themselves and alarm the unmarried by saying, "Yes, at least
we have a home, and when we grow older a place of refuge." Sometimes they add with a rare Sunday flourish in
the edifying style, "Our children and children's children will
one day close our eyes and mourn for us." The opposite is
the fate of the unmarried, they imply. They admit with a
certain envy that these have the best of it for a while, when
they are young; they secretly wish that they were not yet
married, but their turn will come. They liken the unmarried
to the rich man in the parable who has his good things in
advance.

All such marriages suffer from the defect that they treat
one single factor in marriage as the purpose of marriage;
and hence they often feel deluded (the first class, of course,
more especially) when they must admit that marriage after
all means a little more than the acquisition of a comfortable,
agreeable and convenient home. But let us ignore the wrong
side in order to see the beautiful and the good. It is not
granted to every man to extend his activity so very far,
and many of those who imagine that they are working for
something great find themselves sooner or later deluded. By
this I by no means intend to refer to you, for you, of course,
are too clever not to scent the illusion at once, and it has
often enough been the target of your mockery. In this respect you have an extraordinary degree of resignation and
have once for all made a total renunciation. You prefer to
divert yourself. You are everywhere a welcome guest. Your
wit, your lightness in conversation, a certain quality of good-

nature, and a bit of maliciousness, have the effect that on seeing you one associates with this sight the impression of an agreeable evening. You have always been and always will be an acceptable guest in my house, partly because I do not fear you greatly, and partly because I have good prospects of not needing to begin to fear you for a long time to come: my eldest daughter is only three years old, and so early as that you surely would not begin your telegraphic signals. You sometimes have half reproached me for retiring more and more from the world—I remember that once you hummed the melody, "Tell me, Jeanette."[20] The reason for it, of course, is, as I then said to you in reply, that I have a home. It is just as difficult to get hold of you in this instance as it is in every other, for you always have other aims in view. If one would wrench people out of their illusions in order to lead them to something truer, there you are at hand as usual, "in every way at your service." You are absolutely indefatigable in ferreting out illusions in order to smash them. You talk so sensibly, so understandingly, that everyone who has no closer acquaintance with you must believe you are a sedate man. However, you have not reached the truth, you have come to a stop with the destruction of illusions, and inasmuch as you have wrought that destruction in all possible and imaginable directions, you have really worked yourself into a new illusion: the illusion that one can stop there. Yes, my friend, you are living in an illusion, and you accomplish nothing. Here I have pronounced the word which has always had such a strange effect upon you. "Accomplished!" you say, "Who has ever accomplished anything? That is precisely one of the most dangerous illusions. I do not busy myself in any way, I divert myself—especially at the expense of those who believe they are accomplishing something. And is it not indescribably comic that a person can believe this? I shall not plague the world by such great pretensions." Whenever you talk on this theme you make an exceedingly disagreeable impression upon me. It revolts me because there is in it an impudent untruth which when delivered with your virtuosity always assures you of victory, or at least always brings the laughter around to your side.

I remember one occasion when you had been listening for a long time to a man who had become indignant at your talk, answering him not a word, but merely goading him by your sarcastic smile, and then, to the universal delight of those present, you replied, "Well, yes, when you add this speech to all the rest you have accomplished, one can at least not blame you for the belief that you truly are accomplishing something in gross and in detail." When you talk like this it pains me, because I feel for you a certain compassion. If you do not restrain yourself, a rich nature will go to ruin in you. It is because of this gift you are dangerous, because of this your outbursts as well as your coolness have a power which I have never known in any other among the many who dabble at the profession of being discontented. You do not belong to this class either; it is the object of your satire, for you have gone much further. You are joyful, so you affirm, and delighted with life; you smile, you walk with a jaunty flourish of your hat, you do not strain yourself with life's sorrows, you have not even allowed your name to be inscribed in any society for triple lamentations. But precisely for this reason your utterances are so dangerous to younger men, for they must be impressed by the mastery you have attained over everything in life. Now I will not say to you that a man should accomplish something, but I will say, if there are particular passages in your life over which you throw an impenetrable veil, might they not be the sort of things you wished to accomplish although your melancholy moans with pain at accomplishing so little? And how entirely different the whole thing appears within you! Is it not there a profound sorrow over the fact that you are able to accomplish nothing? I know at least one situation: you once let fall a few words about it which did not pass unnoticed. Certainly you would give everything to be able to accomplish something. Whether it is your own fault that you cannot, whether it is your pride which must be broken before you can, I do not know, and I shall never press you further. But why will you take side with all the bad elements which rejoice in your power to insure a triumph? Too often, as I have said, one feels how little it is one is able to accomplish in the

world. I do not say this despondently; I have no reason to
reproach myself; I believe I perform the duties of my office
conscientiously and joyfully, and I shall never feel tempted
to mix in things which do not concern me, with the hope
of accomplishing more; but this activity of mine is a very
limited one, and really it is only by faith one possesses assurance that one is actually accomplishing something.

But then, beside this I have my home. With regard to
this I often think of the beautiful words of Jesus the son
of Sirach,[21] which I would beg you also to consider: "He
that getteth a wife entereth upon a possession: a helpmeet
for him and a pillar of repose. Where no hedge is the possession will be laid waste: and he that hath no wife will
mourn as he wandereth up and down. For who will trust a
nimble robber that skippeth from town to town? Even so,
who shall trust a man that hath no nest and lodgeth where-
soever he findeth himself at nightfall." I did not marry in
order to have a home, but I have a home, and it is a great
blessing; I am not, and I believe you would not venture
to call me, "a fool of a husband." I am not my wife's husband in the sense that the Queen of England has a husband; my wife is not a bondwoman in Abraham's house[22]
whom I am free to drive away with the child, but neither
is she a goddess about whom I dance with spoony devotion.
I have a home, and this home is not everything, but I know
that I have been everything to my wife. I know it partly
because in all humility she has believed it, partly because
I know within myself that I have been and shall be, so far
as one can be everything to another. Here I am able to illustrate for you the beauty of the fact that a person can
be everything to another without being reminded of it by
any finite or particular thing whatsoever. Upon this point
I can talk with all the greater assurance because she certainly is not cast into the shade. She stood in no need of
me; it was not a poor girl I married, doing her an act of
charity (as the world says with all possible contempt for
itself); it was not a silly fool whom I married for other reasons and out of whom by my wisdom I have brought forth
something good. She was independent, and more than that,
she was content with so little that she did not need to sell

herself. She was wholesome, more sound than I, although more impetuous. Of course her life could not be so active as mine, nor so reflective; with my experience I could perhaps save her from many errors, but her wholesomeness made that superfluous. In truth, she owes me nothing, and yet I am everything to her. She had no need of me, but for this cause I have not been indifferent; I have watched over her, and like Nehemiah I am armed even in my sleep[23] —to repeat an expression which came to my tongue on a similar occasion, and to show you that I have not forgotten your sarcastic observation that this might be a great embarrassment to my wife. My young friend, I am not troubled by such an observation, as you can see from the fact that I repeat it, and repeat it, I assure you, without wrath. So I have been nothing and yet everything to her. You, on the other hand, have been everything to a multitude of people, and at bottom you have been nothing to them. And suppose also that in the temporary connections you form with men you were able to endow one man with such a treasure of the interesting and to awaken him to so much productivity that he had enough for his whole lifetime (which is to assume the impossible), suppose that he really gained something from you, yet you yourself . . . lost, for after all you had found no single individual to whom you could wish to be everything; and even if this were a mark of your greatness, this greatness is in truth so painful that I will pray God to exempt me.

The notion which one must first of all associate with the home is that of action, in order to get away from every false and contemptible thought of ease. In man's enjoyment even there ought to be an element of action, even if it is not expressed in any external and palpable deed. In this way a man may be active even though he does not seem to be, whereas woman's domestic activity is more apparent.

But in the next place there is associated with the home such a concretion of small details that it is very difficult to say anything about them in general. In this respect every house has its characteristic features, and it might be interesting to compare a variety of such peculiarities. Naturally, every such characteristic ought to permeate the common spirit of the home, and nothing is more abhorrent to me than the separatistic humbug in families which from the very first make a point of showing how special everything is in their house, which sometimes go so far as to speak a language of their own, or one so full of enigmatic allusions that a man does not know what to make of it. The proper thing is for the family to have such a characteristic distinction, but the art is to hide it.

Those who marry in order to have a home are always making loud complaint that there is no one expecting them, no one to welcome them, etc. This shows clearly enough that really they have a home only when they imagine themselves outside. Praise God, I do not have to go out, whether to remember or to forget that I have a home. The feeling has often gripped me most sensibly when I am sitting, nor do I need to go into the parlor or the dining room to ascertain that I have a home. This feeling often grips me when I sit quite alone in my work room. It grips me when the curtain before the glass door of my study is drawn and I see a blithe face at the pane, and the curtain falls back again and there is a gentle knock, and thereupon a head peeps through the door in such a way that one might think it had no body belonging to it, and that instant she stands by my side—and again vanishes. This feeling may grip me when I am sitting there entirely alone far into the night, as in the old days at college. I can then light my lamp and steal quietly into her room to see if she is really asleep. As a matter of course this feeling often grips me when I come home. And then when I ring the bell she knows the hour I am accustomed to come (we poor government employees are hampered also in this respect, that we cannot take our wives by surprise), she knows the way I am accustomed to ring, so when before the door is opened I hear the noise and rumpus made by the children and by her, and she herself appears at the head of the troupe, and she so childlike that she seems to rival the children in jubilation—then I feel that I have a home. And then if I look serious (you talk so much of being a judge of men, but who is such a judge of men as is a woman?) how altered the frolicsome child is; she does not become disconsolate, does not feel dejected, but there is in her a power, not hard but flexible, like the sword which could cut stone and yet was wrapped around the waist. Or when she can see that I am cross (good Lord, that happens too) how indulgent she can be, and yet what superiority there is in this indulgence.

What more I have in mind to say to you with regard to this matter I prefer to say in connection with a phrase which might well be used of you and which you often use: "a stranger and a pilgrim in the world." Young people who have no notion how dearly experience is bought, nor any presentiment of the unspeakable wealth which it is, may easily let themselves be carried away by the same whirlwind; they may perhaps be affected by your talk as by a fresh breeze which lures them out upon the infinite ocean to which you point them; and you yourself may become almost uncontrollably intoxicated by the thought of that infinity which is your element, an element which like the ocean conceals everything which lies upon its changeless floor. Should not you, who are already an experienced navigator in these waters, know how to tell of disasters and distress at sea? Upon this sea, it is true, one does not know a great deal about the other man. One does not equip great ships which are laboriously launched upon the deep; no, they are very small boats, skiffs for only one person; one takes advantage of the instant, one spreads one's sail, one skims along with the infinite speed of restless thoughts, alone upon the infinite ocean, alone under the infinite sky. Dangerous this life is, but one is familiar with the thought of losing it; for precisely in this the enjoyment consists, that one disappears into the infinite in such a way that no more is left of one but just enough to enjoy this disappearance. Seafaring men relate that on the great oceans one sees a kind of sailboat called the Flying Dutchman. It is able to spread a little sail and then with infinite speed to skim over the surface of the sea. Pretty nearly thus it is with your navigation upon the sea of life. Alone in one's kayak, one is sufficient unto oneself, has nothing to do with anybody except at the moment it pleases one. Alone in one's kayak—I cannot quite understand how one is able to fill this void; but as you are the only man I have known of whom it can be said with some truth that you fill the void, I know also that you have one passenger aboard who is able to help you to fill up the time. You ought therefore to say: alone in one's boat, alone with one's care, alone with one's despair, which one prefers cowardly to retain rather than to suffer the pain of being healed. Permit me now to bring to light the sickly aspect of your life—not as though I wanted to terrify you, for I am not posing as a bugaboo, and you are too knowing to be affected by that sort of thing. But I beg you to reflect how painful, how sad, how humiliating it is to be in this sense a stranger and a pilgrim in the world.

The effect I might possibly make upon you I shall not imperil by provoking you with the thought of family clannishness, the herd instinct, which you abhor; but consider family life in its beauty when it is founded upon a deep and heartfelt sense of community, in such a way that the tie which binds everything together is mysteriously concealed, so that one has only a presentiment of it; think of the hidden life of such a family when it is clothed in an outward form so beautiful that one is nowhere offended by the hardness of its joints; and then think of your relation to it. Such a family would be precisely to your taste, and perhaps you would often take delight in entering this circle. With your easy ways you would soon become, as it were, intimate with that family. I say, "as it were," because you do not really become intimate, and it is perfectly clear that one who is a stranger and a pilgrim never can. They would regard you as a welcome guest, they would, perhaps, be kind enough to make everything as agreeable for you as possible, they would be complaisant towards you, yes; they would treat you as a child to whom one is attached. For your part, you would be inexhaustible in your attentions to the family, inventive to delight them in every way. To be sure, this is all very pretty, and in a moment of chagrin over the fact that no real intimacy exists you might be tempted to say that you don't care to see the family in dressing gowns, the daughter in slippers, and the mother in curl papers; and yet the correct behavior of this family in your presence implies, if you will look more closely, a prodigious humiliation for you. Thus every family would have to behave towards you, and you would be humiliated by it. Or do you not believe that the family keeps hidden an entirely different life which is its sanctuary? Do you not believe that every family has its household gods, although they are not put in the vestibule? And in that utterance of your chagrin is there not concealed a very refined weakness? For really I do not believe that, if ever you were married, you could bear to see your wife in negligee, unless this were a fine dress expressly calculated to please you. You think, of course, that you have done much for the family by entertaining them, by shedding upon them a certain aesthetic luster; but suppose that the family cared very little for this in comparison with the inner life it possesses. You will have the same experience in relation to every family, and proud as you are, this is a humiliation. No one shares sorrow with you, no one confides in you. You think indeed that they often do, you have enriched yourself in fact with manifold psychological observations; but this is often a delusion, for people are commonly willing to talk to you superficially, hinting indirectly at an anxiety, because that sets in motion the interesting in you, which in itself has already the agreeable quality which prompts them to desire this medicine when they do not need it. You know that people would rather take communion from a mendicant monk than from their father confessor, and if precisely on account of your isolated position a man were to address himself to you, this could never acquire the true significance of reciprocal confidence, either for you or for him. Not for him, because he would feel how arbitrary it was to pick you out as a confidant; and not for you, because you could not close your eyes to the equivocal character of your competence.

Undeniably you are a good operator, you understand how to penetrate into the most secret recesses of sorrow and grief, yet so shrewdly that you never forget the way back. Well, I assume that you succeeded in healing your patient, but you got out of it no true and deep joy, for the whole thing bore the stamp of arbitrariness, and you had no responsibility. It is only responsibility that bestows a blessing and true joy, and that even though one may not do the thing half as well as you; it often bestows a blessing when one accomplishes nothing. But when one has a home, then one has responsibility, and in itself this responsibility gives assurance and joy. Precisely because you are not willing to have responsibility, you must find it quite natural, though you often complain of it, that people are ungrateful to you. It is rather rare, however, that you meddle with healing; commonly, as I have said, your principal business is that of destroying illusions, and occasionally working people into illusions. When one sees you with one or two young men, sees how with a few exercises you already have helped them thoroughly over their childish illusions, which are, nevertheless, salutary in so many ways, how they then become lighter than reality, how the wings sprout, while you yourself like an old experienced bird give them an exhibition of what it means with a beat of the wings to soar over the whole of existence; or when you undertake a similar course of training with young girls and study the difference in the mode of flight, noting that in the male flight one hears the beat of the wings, whereas the female flight is like a dreamy stroke with the oars—when one sees this, one cannot be angry with you for the art which brings this to pass, but who ought not to be angry with you for the light-mindedness implied in it? You may surely say of your heart as is said in the old verse:

> *Mein Herz ist wie ein Taubenhaus:*
> *Die eine fliegt herein, die Andre fliegt heraus—*

only that in your case one does not so much see that the thoughts fly in as that new ones are constantly flying out. But beautiful as a dovecote is when used as a symbol of a quiet domestic home, it truly should not be used in this way. And is it not painful and sad to let life go past one thus without ever gaining a firm position? Is it not sad, my young friend, that for you life never acquires content? There is something sad in the feeling that one is growing old, but it is a far deeper sadness which grips one when one cannot grow old. I feel precisely at this moment how much justification I have in calling you "my young friend." The distance of seven years between us is not exactly an eternity; I will not boast of mental maturity in comparison with you, but I can boast of a maturer view of life. Yes, I feel that I really have grown older, but you constantly hold fast to youth's first surprise. And when sometimes, though it is rather seldom, I feel weary of the world, this is associated with a feeling of quiet exaltation, I think of the beautiful words, "Blessed are they that rest from their labors." I do not deceive myself by thinking that I have had a great work to do in life, I did not sort it out, it was assigned to me, and even if it was a lowly business, it has been my business to be glad of it in spite of its being lowly. You certainly do not rest from your labors, rest is a curse to you, you can live only in unrest. Rest is your polar opposite, rest makes you more restless. You are like a hungry man whom food makes only more hungry, a thirsty man whom drink makes only more thirsty.

But I return now to the previous theme, the finite aims with which people enter upon marriage. I have mentioned only three because these appear to have something in their favor for the fact that they take into consideration one or another of the real factors in marriage, although for their one-sidedness they are just as ridiculous as they are un-aesthetic and irreligious. I will not dwell upon a multitude of finite aims which are so perfectly paltry that one cannot even laugh at them. As when one marries for money, or from jealousy, or for prospective advantage, because there are good prospects of her dying soon—or that she may live long and prove to be a blessed branch which bears much fruit, so that by her one may sweep into one's pocket the inheritance of a whole series of uncles and aunts. This sort of thing I prefer not to dwell upon.

As an outcome of this investigation I can emphasize here the fact that marriage in order to be aesthetic and religious must, as it was proved, have no finite "why." But this was precisely the aesthetical feature of first love; and so here again marriage is on a level with first love, and the aesthetic feature of marriage is that in itself it conceals a multiplicity of "whys" which life gradually brings to light in all their blessedness.

However, since what I proposed to prove in the first instance is the aesthetic validity of marriage, and since what

distinguishes marriage from first love is the ethical and religious element, which in so far as it seeks to express itself
in a particular form finds this in the wedding ceremony, I
will dwell upon this topic, in order that I may not seem to
treat the question too lightly or give the slightest appearance
of wishing to conceal the schism between first love and marriage which you and others, for different reasons, seek to
establish. You may be right in affirming that, if many people
do not remark upon this schism, it is because they lack the
energy and the culture requisite for thinking clearly over
either of these things.

However, let us examine more closely the wedding ceremony and its formulas. Here again you may perhaps find
me well armed; and I can assure you that I am well armed
without incommoding my wife,[24] for she is glad to see me
hold off such freebooters as you and your kind. Moreover,
I am of the opinion that, just as Christians ought to be always ready to render an account for the faith that is in
them, so too a married man ought to be always ready to
render an account for marriage, not exactly to everyone who
is pleased to require it, but to everyone whom he counts
worthy, or whom he may think it well to enlighten, even
though, as in the present instance, he is unworthy. And
since you, after having laid waste other territories, have begun to ravage the province of matrimony, I feel challenged
to encounter you.

I can assume that you know the marriage service, indeed, that you have made a study of it. As a rule you are
thoroughly well equipped and generally do not begin an
attack before you are as well informed about the case as
are its experienced defenders. It therefore happens at times,
as you complain, that your attack is too strong, that those
who should defend the case are not so well informed about
it as are you who attack it. Now we will see.

However, before we enter into particulars let us see
whether in the marriage service, regarded simply as a ceremony, there is not something disturbing. The wedding, in
fact, is not a thing which the lovers themselves in an exuberant moment have happened to think of, a thing which
they could give up as a matter of course if in the meantime

they should have a different notion. Thus, it is a power which encounters us. But does love then need to recognize any other power but itself? You will, perhaps, admit that when doubt and anxiety have taught a man to pray he will thankfully submit to such a power, but you insist that first love has no need of it. At this point you must remember that we have conceived of the individuals in question as religiously developed. I am not concerned, therefore, to ask how religion can develop in a man, but how it can subsist along with first love; and certain as it is that unhappy love may make a man religious, it is just as certain that religious individuals can love. Religion is not so foreign to human nature that a rupture is necessary in order to awaken it. But if the individuals in question are religious, then the power which encounters them in the wedding ceremony is not foreign to them; and as their love unites them in a higher unity, so does the religious lift them to a still higher plane.

What, then, does the wedding ceremony accomplish? It provides a survey of the genesis of the human race, and therewith it grafts the new marriage upon the great body of the race. Thereby it presents the universal, the essentially human, and evokes it in consciousness. Perhaps this offends you; you say, perhaps, "At the very instant when one is uniting oneself to a person so tenderly that everything else disappears from view, it is distasteful to be reminded that *es ist eine alte Geschichte*,[25] something that has been and is and will be." You would rejoice in that which is peculiar in your love, you would suffer the whole passion of love to glow in you, and you do not wish to be disturbed by the thought that Tom, Dick and Harry have the same experience. "It is exceedingly prosaic," you say, "to be reminded of one's numerical significance: in the year 1750 on such a day at 10 o'clock, Mr. N.N. and the estimable Miss N.N.; the same day at 11 o'clock, Mr. N.N. and Miss N.N." This sounds to you perfectly dreadful, yet in your reasoning there is concealed a reflection which has been disturbing to first love. Love, as we have already observed, is a unity of the universal and the particular; but the wish to enjoy the particular in the sense you propose indicates a reflection which has placed the particular outside the universal. The more the universal and the particular interpenetrate, the more beautiful love is. Greatness, whether in the immediate sense or in a higher sense, does not signify being peculiar, but the possession of the universal in the peculiarity. Therefore, to first love an introduction which recalls the universal cannot be disturbing. Moreover, the marriage service gives more than that, for in pointing to the universal it leads the lovers back to the first parents. It does not stop with the universal *in abstracto* but exhibits it as it was expressed by the first couple in the human race. This is an indication of what every marriage is. Every marriage, like every human life, is at the same time this particular thing and yet the whole, at once an individual and a symbol. Thus it furnishes the lovers with the most beautiful picture of a couple who were not disturbed by reflecting about other people: it says to the individuals, "Thus you also are a couple, it is the same experience which is here repeated in you, you also are now standing here alone in the infinite world, alone before the face of God." So you see that the wedding furnishes what you require, but that at the same time it gives more, that at one and the same time it gives the universal and the particular.

"But the marriage service proclaims that sin has entered into the world, and to be reminded so emphatically of sin is surely discordant at the moment when one feels most pure. In the next place it teaches that sin entered into the world along with marriage, and this hardly seems encouraging to the respective partners. The Church, of course, can wash its hands if anything unfortunate come out of it, for it has not flattered with a vain hope." That the Church does not flatter with a vain hope might of itself seem to be a good thing. Moreover, in saying that sin entered into the world along with marriage, the Church, nevertheless, permits marriage, and it might be a grave question whether it teaches that sin entered by means of marriage. In any case, it proclaims sin merely as man's universal lot, making no definite application to the individual, and least of all does it say, you are about to commit a sin. It is certainly a very difficult thing to expound in what way sin entered in along with marriage. It might seem as if sin and the sensuous were here identified. However, such cannot be the case, inasmuch as the Church permits marriage. "Yes," you would say, "it does so only when it has taken away all the beauty of earthly love." By no means, I would reply. At least, not one word to this effect is to be found in the marriage service.

In the next place the Church proclaims the punishment of sin: that woman shall bear children with pain and be subject unto her husband. But, after all, the first of these consequences is surely of such a nature that, if the Church did not proclaim it, it would proclaim itself. "Yes," you reply, "but the disturbing thing is that this is said to be the consequence of sin." You find it aesthetically beautiful that a child is born with pain, it is a mark of respect for a human being, a symbolic indication of the significance of the fact that a man comes into the world, in contrast to the beasts which, the lower they are in the scale, the more easily they bring forth their young. I may here again lay emphasis upon the consideration that this is proclaimed as the universal lot of mankind; and the statement that a child is born in sin is the profoundest expression for its highest dignity. It is a glorification of human life that all that pertains to it is referred to the category of sin.

In the next place it is said that the wife shall be subject unto her husband. At this point you will perhaps say, "Yes, that is pretty, and it has always pleased me to see a woman who loves her husband as her lord." But it offends you that this is regarded as the consequence of sin, and you feel called upon to be the champion of woman. Whether you thereby are doing her a service I leave undecided, but I believe that you have not comprehended the nature of woman in all its inwardness, for it belongs to her nature to be more perfect and more imperfect than man. If one would indicate the purest and most perfect quality, one says, "a woman"; if one would indicate the weakest, the most feeble thing, one says "a woman"; if one would give a notion of a spiritual quality raised above all sensuousness, one says "a woman"; if one would give a notion of the sensuous, one says "a woman"; if one would indicate innocence in all its lofty greatness, one says "a woman"; if one would point to the depressing feeling of guilt, one says "a woman." In a certain sense, therefore, woman is more perfect than man, and this the Scripture expresses by saying that she has more guilt. If again you will remember that the Church only proclaims the universal lot of woman, I do not think that from this there can proceed anything disquieting to first love, but only to reflection, which does not understand how to cleave to her with this possibility in mind. Furthermore, the Church does not make woman a mere slave. It says, "And God said, I will make for Adam a helpmeet for him," an expression which has just as much aesthetic warmth as truth; and hence the Church teaches, "A man shall leave his father and his mother and shall cleave unto his wife." We would expect it rather to say that woman shall leave her father and her mother and shall cleave unto her husband, for woman is in fact the weaker one. In the Scriptural expression there is a recognition of woman's importance, and no knight could be more gallant toward her.

Finally, as for the curse which fell to man's lot, the circumstance that with the sweat of his brow he shall eat bread does indeed seem with one word to drive him out of the honeymoon of first love. The fact that this curse, like all divine curses, as often has been remarked, conceals in itself a blessing proves nothing here, for as much as the experience of it must always be reserved for a subsequent time. But I would remind you that first love is not cowardly, that it does not fear danger, and that therefore in this curse it will see a difficulty which cannot terrify it.

What then does the wedding accomplish? "It checks the motion of love," you say. Not at all; but rather it causes that which already was in motion to appear outwardly. It insists upon the universal-human, and in this sense also upon sin; but all the dread and anguish which desires that sin might never have come into the world has its ground in a reflection with which first love is unacquainted. To wish to have it that sin might never have come into the world is to carry mankind back to a more imperfect stage. Sin has entered in, but when the individuals have humbled themselves under it they stand higher than they stood before.

Thereupon the Church turns to the individual and puts to him several questions. Thereby it may seem that he is prompted to reflect: "Why such questions? Love has its assurance in itself." But the Church puts the questions not to make one waver but make one firm and to let that which already is firm express itself. Here the difficulty emerges that in its questions the Church seems to take no account at all of the erotic. It asks, "Hast thou taken counsel with God and with thy conscience, and then with friends and acquaintances?" I shall not insist here upon the very obvious advantage of the fact that such questions are asked by the Church with profound seriousness. The Church, to use your own expression, is not a marriage agency. Can the parties concerned be disturbed by that? In fact, they have gratefully referred their love to God and have thus taken counsel with Him, for when I thank God it is a way, though an indirect way, of taking counsel with Him. If the Church does not ask if they love one another, this is by no means because it would nullify earthly love, but because it assumes it.

Thereupon the Church requires a vow. We saw above how splendidly love can be assumed into a kind of higher concentricity. Resolution makes the individual free, but, as has been explained, the more free the individual is, the more aesthetically beautiful is marriage.

It has thus been made clear, I think, that in so far as the aesthetic character of first love is discovered in its present tense as an immediate infinity, marriage may be regarded as a glorification of it and is more beautiful than it is. This, I think, is obvious from the foregoing discussion, and in the immediate context we have seen also that all the talk about the disparagement of love by the Church is utterly unfounded and exists only for him who has taken offense at religion.

But if such is the case, the rest follows of itself. For what remains is the question whether this love can be realized. When you have conceded all that I have urged hitherto, you will perhaps say, "Well, it is just as difficult to realize marriage as to realize first love." To this I reply, No; for in marriage there is the law of motion. First love remains an unreal *an-sich* which never acquires inward content because it moves only in an external medium; in the ethical and religious purpose marital love possesses the possibility of an inner history and is distinguished from first love as the historical from the unhistorical. First love is strong, stronger than the whole world, but the instant doubt occurs to it, it is annihilated, it is like a sleep-walker who with infinite security can walk over the most perilous places, but when one calls his name he plunges down. Marital love is armed; for by the resolution the attention is not directed merely towards the environment, but the will is directed towards itself, towards the inward man. And now I invert everything and say: the aesthetic does not lie in the immediate but in the acquired—but marriage is precisely the immediacy which has mediacy in itself, the infinity which has finiteness in itself, the eternal which has the temporal in itself. Thus marriage proves to be the ideal in a double sense, both in the classical and in the romantic understanding of the word. When I say that the aesthetic lies in the acquired, this is not by any means to affirm that it lies in the effort as such; for this is negative, and the merely negative is never aesthetic.

On the other hand, when there is an effort which has content in itself, a struggle which has victory in itself, then in that duality I have the aesthetic. This I think I ought to call to mind in view of the enthusiasm of despair with which people in our age hear the acquired exalted in contrast to the immediate, as though the whole point were to lay everything waste in order to build anew. It has really alarmed me to hear the jubilation with which younger men, like the men in the Reign of Terror which followed the French Revolution, cry out, *de omnibus dubitandum*.[26] Perhaps this is narrow-mindedness on my part. Nevertheless, I believe that one should distinguish between a personal and a scientific doubt. Personal doubt is an entirely separate thing, and such an enthusiasm for destruction as one often hears talk of leads at the most to the consequence that a great many men venture out upon the deep without possessing the power to doubt and therefore perish, or they fall into a vacillation which likewise is certain destruction.

If, on the other hand, the conflict of doubt develops in a particular individual the power to overcome doubt, such a sight is uplifting, inasmuch as it shows what a man is capable of, but it is not properly beautiful, for to be beautiful it must have immediacy in itself. Such a development brought about by doubt of the extremest sort seeks what one might describe as the transformation of a person into an entirely different one. Beauty, however, consists in acquiring the immediate in and with doubt. This I must emphasize in opposition to the abstract way of conceiving doubt, the idolatry with which it is regarded, the foolhardiness with which people plunge into it, the blind confidence with which they hope for a glorious issue out of it. It may also be remarked that the more spiritual the aim is, the more one can exalt doubt. But love belongs to a province where it is not a question so much of a thing acquired as of a thing given, and of a given thing which is to be acquired. I cannot conceive what kind of doubt might be appropriate in this case. Might it be the proper preparation for a married man that he had had a doleful experience, that he had learned to doubt, and might that be the truly beautiful marriage which came to pass when by virtue of this doubt he resolved with great moral seriousness to get married and as a husband was faithful and constant? We are ready to praise him, but we will not extol his marriage except as an example of what a man is capable of. Or in order to be a thorough doubter should he also be doubtful of her love, of the possibility of retaining the beauty in the relationship —and yet have enough stoicism to will this marriage? I know very well that you false teachers are prompt to extol such a marriage, precisely for the sake of finding readier acceptance of your false doctrine; you praise it when it serves your purpose to do so, and you say, "Behold, that is the true marriage." But you know very well that this praise conceals a censure, and that woman in particular is by no means served by it, and that in this way you are doing everything to tempt her. Hence you make a distinction, following the old rule: *divide et impera.*[27] You extol first love. That, according to your view, remains a moment outside of time, a mysterious something about which one can utter any lie. Marriage cannot hide itself in this way; it takes a year and a day to unfold—how easy it is, then, to find opportunity to tear down or to build up with such treacherous considerations that desperate resignation is needed to put up with it.

This much we have proved: that conjugal love, regarded as a moment, is not only quite as beautiful as first love but far more so, because it contains in its immediacy a unity of more opposites. It is, therefore, not true that marriage is a highly respectable estate but a tiresome one, while love is poetry. No, marriage is properly the poetical thing. And if the world has so often observed with pain that first love could not be carried through, I am ready with my condolence, but at the same time I would remind you that the fault did not lie so much in the subsequent stage as in the fact that they did not begin aright. The fact is that first love lacks the second aesthetic ideal, the historical element. It does not possess in itself the law of motion. If I were to conceive of personal religious faith as pure immediacy, the kind which would correspond to first love is a faith which in virtue of the promise believes it is capable of moving mountains, and then would go about and work miracles. Perhaps it would succeed, but this faith would have no history; for the patter about all its miracles is not its history, whereas the appropriation of faith in the personal life is the history of faith. Conjugal love possesses this movement, for in the resolution the movement is turned inward. In the religious experience it leaves it to God, as it were, to care for the whole world; in the resolve it is ready in union with God to fight for itself, to acquire itself in patience. There is comprised in the consciousness of sin a conception of human frailty, but in the resolution this is regarded as overcome. I cannot sufficiently stress these considerations with reference to conjugal love. I have certainly done full justice to first love, and I believe I am a better eulogist of it than you are; but its fault is to be found in its abstract character.

Conjugal love, therefore, contains something more, as you can see from the fact that it is capable of giving itself up. Suppose that first love cannot be realized; then, in case it was truly a conjugal love, the individuals will be capable of giving it up and yet remain in possession of its sweetness, though in a different way. This can never be done by first love. But it is by no means to be concluded from this that it was a doubt which gave conjugal love its resignation, as though it were a diminished form of first love. If such were the case, this would not be resignation. And yet no one perhaps knows better how sweet love is than he who renounces it while having power to realize it.[28] But this power, again, is just as great when it is a question of holding on to love and realizing it in real life. The same power is exemplified in holding on to love and in giving it up, and the true retention of it is the power of giving it up expressing itself now in holding on, and in this consists the true freedom in holding on, the true and well-assured hovering.

Conjugal love shows itself to be historical by the fact that it represents a process of assimilation which deals with the experience and refers back the experience to itself. Thus, it is not a disinterested witness of what occurs but is essentially a sympathetic participant, in short, it experiences its own development. Romantic love, too, refers to itself what it experiences, as when the knight sends to his beloved the banners won in battle; but even if romantic love could conceive of ever so long a time involved in such conquests, it never could occur to it that love might have a history. The prosaic view goes to the opposite extreme; it can very well conceive that love acquires a history, but commonly it is a very short history, and this history is so homely and so pedestrian that love can soon acquire feet to walk with. Experimental love also acquires a sort of history; but for all that, as it lacks true apriority, so, too, it lacks continuity and depends merely upon the caprice of the experimenting individual, who is at once his own world and in it is his own fate. Experimental love is therefore very prone to inquire about its own state and condition and in this finds a double joy, not only when the result corresponds to the calculations, but also when it appears that something very different is coming out of it. In the latter case it is also well pleased at finding a task for its indefatigable combinations. Conjugal love, on the other hand, has apriority in itself, and, likewise, constancy in itself, and the power in this constancy is the same as the law of motion, i.e., it is the resolution. In the resolution is posited another thing, but at the same time this other is posited as overcome; in the resolution this other is posited as an inward other, inasmuch as even the outward is visible by means of the reflection in the inward experience. The historical factor here consists in the fact that this other comes forth and acquires its validity, but precisely in its validity is seen to be something which ought not to have validity, so that love, tested and purified, issues from this movement and assimilates the experience. How this other comes forth is not dependent upon the power of the individual, who does not behave experimentally; but at the same time love has triumphed over all this without knowing it. Surely somewhere in the New Testament there is the saying: "Every gift is good if it is received with thanksgiving."[29] Most people are ready to be thankful when they receive a good gift, but at the same time they require that it shall be left to them to determine what gift is good. This is evidence of their narrow-mindedness. The broader thankfulness, on the other hand, is truly victorious and apriorical since it is characterized by an eternal health which is not disturbed even by evil gifts—not for the reason that it knows how to keep them at a distance, but because of the boldness, the lofty personal courage, which ventures to give thanks for them. So it is also with love. At this point it could not occur to me to comment upon all the jeremiads which you mischievously have always in readiness for the edification of distressed husbands. I hope that this time you will restrain yourself, since you have to do with a married man who hardly is likely to be disturbed for your amusement.

But while I am thus pursuing the development of love from its hidden cryptogamous stage to its phanerogamous life I stumble upon a difficulty to which you surely will attach no little significance. I assume for the sake of argument that I have succeeded in convincing you that the religious and ethical factors which distinguish conjugal love do by no means detract from it; I assume that in your inmost being you are profoundly convinced of this and would now by no means disdain a religious point of departure. You would therefore be ready, alone with her who is dear to you, to submit yourself and your love humbly to God. You are really deeply touched and affected—but now (attention!) I utter one word, "the congregation," and with that everything vanishes as in the ballad.[30] You will never succeed, I believe, in getting beyond the determinant of inwardness. "The congregation," you say, "the dear congregation, which in spite of its multiplicity is nevertheless a moral person! Would that, along with the tiresome traits which all moral persons have, it possessed this good trait, that it had one head upon a single neck . . . like Caligula I know what I would do."[31] You surely know the story of the crazy man[32] who had the fixed idea that the room in which he lived was full of flies, so that he was in danger of being suffocated by them. With desperate fear and with desperate fury he fought for his existence. So you seem to be fighting for your life against just such an imaginary swarm of flies, against what you call "the congregation." However, the situation is not really so dangerous. But in the first place I will enumerate the most important points of contact with the congregation, merely reminding you, by the way, that first love has no right to reckon it to its credit that it knows no such difficulties, for this is due to the fact that it is kept entirely abstract and comes into no contact with reality. You will know very well how to distinguish between abstract relationships to an environment if it is resolved by an abstraction. You can perfectly well put up with it if you have to pay the priest and the parish clerk and a functionary of the government, for money is a capital means for resolving every personal relationship. Therefore, you initiated me into your plan of never doing anything and never receiving anything, not even the most trifling, without giving or receiving money. Indeed, one might expect that, if ever you were to get married, you would be capable of paying a *douceur* to everybody who comes to witness your joy in taking this step. In that case you need not be surprised that the congregation increases in number or that what the crazy man feared from the flies should in reality happen to you. What you fear is the personal relationship which by polite inquiries, by congratulations, by compliments, yea, even by wedding presents, makes a claim to being a relationship which is incommensurable with money and seeks to display all possible sympathy, in spite of the fact that precisely on this occasion you on your behalf and that of the lady would prefer to dispense with all sympathy. "By the aid of money," you say, "one can liberate oneself from a multitude of ludicrous situations. With money one can stop the mouth of the church trumpeter who otherwise would loudly herald one's nuptials. With money one can be dispensed from being proclaimed before the whole congregation as a husband, a proper husband, in spite of the fact that one would prefer to be such for one person alone." This is not my invention, it is your description. Can you recall how you once raved on the occasion of a church wedding? You suggested that just as at an ordination the whole company of the clergy who are present come forward to lay their hands upon the ordinand, so should the whole tenderly sympathetic fraternity present at the wedding come forward and salute the bride and bridegroom with a congregational kiss. You declared, indeed, that it was impossible for you to utter the words bride and bridegroom without thinking of the significant moment when a dear father or an elderly friend rises with his glass to pronounce with deep emotion the beautiful toast, "Bride and bridegroom." For just as you felt that the whole ecclesiastical ceremony was calculated to quench the erotic, so you thought that the subsequent worldly festivity was indecent in the same degree as the ecclesiastical. "For after all is it not indecent, ridiculous and in bad taste to place such a *quasi* husband and wife together at the dinner table and thereby suggest the false and indelicate reflection whether the decree of the Church had of itself been sufficient to constitute them a married couple?" So you seem to be in favor of a quiet wedding. To that I have no objection, but I take leave to inform you that in this case you would just as clearly be declared a proper husband. Perhaps you can endure this word better when no one else hears it. Moreover, I would remind you that the phrase in the marriage service is not "before the whole congregation," but "before God and this congregation," which neither discomforts one by its narrowness nor does it lack boldness.

As for the further complaints you make against the "congregation," though you make them with your usual exaggeration, I can forgive you more easily because what you attack here is only the social relationship. In that respect I admit that everybody may have his own opinion, and though I am far from approving your *Sprödigkeit*, I shall for all that be as tolerant as possible. On this subject we presumably shall always remain in disagreement. The great thing, as I regard it, is to live in the congregation, to bring something finer out of it, if one is able; at all events to subordinate oneself to it and put up with it if one is unable to better it. I see no danger to love in the publication of the banns from the pulpit, nor do I believe that such publication will do the hearers any such injury as you with your extravagant rigorism once detected when you maintained that the publication of the banns ought to be abolished because so many people, especially women, went to church only to hear them, so that the impression of the sermon was nullified. There is something false at the bottom of your apprehension, as though such trifles might be able to disturb a strong and healthy love. It is by no means my intention to put up a defense for all the mischievous practices which are current. When I adhere to the congregation I do not identify it with a "highly esteemed public" which, to use an expression of Goethe's, "is shameless enough to believe that everything one undertakes to do is done only to supply matter for conversation." Another consideration by which I can explain to myself your great dread of all fuss and publicity is that you are afraid of missing the erotic instant. You understand how to keep your soul as still and apathetic as a bird of prey is still before it plunges down; you know that the instant is not in any man's power and that, nevertheless, the most beautiful experience is comprised in the instant; therefore, you understand how to be on the lookout and do not wish to anticipate anything with the restlessness with which you await the instant. But when such an event is fixed at a definite time which one knows a long while before and of which by the preparations one is constantly reminded, then one runs the danger of "missing the point." From this one sees that you have not comprehended the nature of conjugal love and that you cherish a heretical superstition about first love.

Let us now consider whether this thing of the congregation is in reality so perilous—if, that is to say, it does not assume so terrible a shape as it does at this instant in your sickly brain. Your life has surely brought you not only into touch but into intimate connection with several persons the remembrance of whom does not alarm you, does not disturb the ideal you cherish, whose names you utter aloud to yourself when you would prompt yourself to good deeds, whose presence expands your soul, whose personality is a revelation to you of the noble and the sublime. Might it then disturb you to have such persons as your confidants? That is almost as if in a religious reference a person were to say, "I wish with my inmost heart to maintain my fellowship with God and Christ, but I cannot bear that He should confess me before all the holy angels." On the other hand, your life and your external circumstances have surely brought you into connection with other people the monotony of whose daily lives is rarely broken by joys and noteworthy diversions. Does not every family reckon such persons among its acquaintances, perhaps in its very midst, and is it not a beautiful thing that these persons who are almost deserted in their loneliness find a support in the family? For them a marriage would therefore be an event of importance, a bit of the poetical woof in their humdrum life, something they long look forward to with joy and long afterwards remember. In a family where I visit I often see an old maid who is contemporary with the mistress of the house. She still remembers so vividly her friend's wedding, alas, more vividly perhaps than the wife herself, remembers exactly how the bride was adorned and every little subordinate circumstance. Would you deprive all such people of the opportunity of joy which you could give them? Let us deal lovingly with the weak. There is so many a marriage which was entered upon as secretly as possible in order to enjoy the pleasure of it thoroughly, and time perhaps brought something else, brought so little that one might be tempted to say, "Well, if at least it had had the significance of giving joy to a multitude of people, it might after all have been worth while." As you know, I hate prying into family affairs as much as you do, but on the one hand I know how to keep this at a distance, and on the other hand I know how to rise superior to it; and you with your acrimonious wit, your polemical talent, your artillery, might you not know how to call it to order? You indeed do so, but none the less it disturbs you. I will not prescribe to you any limits. Cast aside whatever disturbs you, but do not forget my principle, do not forget, if it be possible, to realize the still more beautiful ideal, remember that the art is, if it be possible, to save such men, not to defend yourself. I might prescribe this as a prudential maxim, for you know very well that the more one isolates oneself, the more intrusive one makes these ineffectual gossipy people; you know it who so often have made sport of them by whetting their curiosity and then letting the whole thing dissolve into nothing. I might prescribe this as a prudential maxim, but I will not do so, for I have too much respect for the truth of what I say to be willing to degrade it.

Every process of becoming, in the proportion precisely that it is a healthy process, has an element of the polemical. So, too, has every conjugal union, and you know very well that I hate the slipshod behavior in family life, the insipid *communio bonorum* which makes marriage seem as if it were marriage with the whole family. If conjugal love is a genuine first love, it has something hidden about it, it does not wish to display itself, does not devote its life to the ostentation of family visits, does not derive its nutriment from polite congratulations and an exchange of compliments nor from an idolatrous adoration of the family. That you know very well. I have no objection if you let your wit play upon this sort of thing. In many ways I agree with you, and I believe that it would not do you and the good cause any harm if sometimes you would allow me, as the experienced forester, to indicate the decayed trees which ought to be felled, but also to mark others with a cross as a sign that they are to be spared.

I feel no hesitation in affirming that mysteriousness is the absolute requisite for preserving the aesthetic quality in love—not, however, as though one were to make an affectation of it, pursue it as an end, take it in vain, enjoy merely the pleasure of the mysterious. It is one of the pet notions of first love that it would like to flee to an uninhabited island. This has been held up often enough to ridicule: I shall take no part in the iconoclastic savagery of our age. The fault is to be found in the fact that first love believes there is no way in which it can be realized except by flight. This is a misunderstanding due to its unhistoric character. The art is to remain in the multifarious environment and yet preserve mystery. Here again I might insist upon it as a prudential maxim that only by remaining among people does mystery acquire its true energy, only by encountering this opposition does its point bore in more and more deeply. I will not do so, for the same reason as before, and also because I always recognize a relationship to other people as something which has reality. But art is required for this, and conjugal love does not shun such difficulties, rather it preserves and acquires itself in them. Moreover, the conjugal life has so much else to think about that it doesn't get time to wear itself out with a polemic against a particular antagonist.

Inwardly this prime requisite may be expressed by its polar opposite: open-heartedness, candor, publicity on the largest conceivable scale; for this is the life-principle of love, and here in the intimate life secretiveness is its death. However, this is more easily said than done, and truly it requires courage to carry this principle out consistently, for you perceive that by this I am thinking of something more than the jabbering chattiness which prevails in the family-marriage. There can of course be no question of secretiveness where there is publicity, and the more secretiveness there is, the more difficult is the other. It requires courage to be willing to show oneself as one truly is, it requires courage not to be willing to exempt oneself from a little humiliation when one can do so by a certain air of secrecy, not to be willing to acquire a little addition to one's stature when one can do so by being reticent. It requires courage to want to be wholesome and sound, honestly and candidly to will the true.

However, let us begin with something of minor importance. A newly wedded couple who found themselves, as they said, "constrained to limit their love to the narrow confines of three small rooms," furnished the occasion which prompted you to make a little excursion into the realm of imagination—which lies in fact so near to your every-day habitation that one may doubt if it can properly be called an excursion. You thereupon devoted yourself with the greatest possible care and good taste to the decoration of a future such as you might desire for yourself. You know that I sympathize ungrudgingly with a little experiment of this sort; and, praise God, when a princely carriage with four champing steeds passes me by, I still am child enough to be able to imagine that I am sitting in it, am still innocent enough, when I convince myself that such is not the case, to rejoice that another is sitting there, am still sufficiently unspoiled not to wish that the maximum might be to keep one horse, serving at once for riding and for the carriage, because my circumstances only allow me this. So you thought you were married, happily married, had rescued your love inviolate out of all adversities, and were now deliberating how you would arrange everything in your home so that you might retain as long as possible the fragrance of your love. To that end you had need of more than three rooms. On that point I agreed with you, seeing that as an unmarried man you make use of five. It would be distasteful to you if you were compelled to yield one of your rooms to your wife; in that situation you would prefer to give up four of them to her and yourself live in the fifth, rather than share one room in common. After having pondered these difficulties you continued: "I take the above-mentioned three small rooms as my point of departure—not in the philosophical sense of a postulate, for I have no intention of returning to them, but on the contrary, would get as far away from them as possible." Indeed, you felt such an abhorrence for the three small rooms that, if you could not have more, you would prefer as a vagrant to live under the open heaven—which in fact would be so poetic that it would require a large suite of chambers to compensate for it. By reminding you that this was one of the customary unhistoric heresies of first love I sought to call you to order, and then I was very glad to walk with you through the big, cool, high-vaulted halls of your castle in the air, through the mysterious, half-obscure chambers, through the dining rooms illuminated to furthest corners by a multiplicity of lights, pendant lusters and mirrors, through the small room with folding doors opening upon the terrace, where the morning sun penetrated, and where the perfume of flowers which opened only for you and for your love was wafted in.

I will not pursue further your audacious venture as you sprang like a chamois hunter from crag to crag. Only the principle which lay at the basis of your arrangement shall I discuss a little more in detail. Your principle evidently was: mysteriousness, mystification, refined coquetry. Not only the walls of your chambers should be inset with mirrors, but even your world of consciousness must be diversified by similar refractions of light; not only everywhere in the chamber but also in consciousness you would everywhere encounter yourself and her, her and yourself. "But," you say, "in order to accomplish this the wealth of all the world is not sufficient; in addition to that, spirit is requisite, and a wise moderation controlling the powers of the spirit. People must therefore be strangers to one another to such a degree that familiarity becomes interesting, and so familiar that the strangeness becomes a stimulating opposition. The conjugal life must not be a dressing gown in which one makes oneself comfortable, but neither must it be a corset which hampers one's movements; it must not be a labor which requires fatiguing preparation, but neither must it be a dissolute ease; it must bear the stamp of the accidental, and yet one must remotely sense an art; a person is not exactly required to stare herself blind stitching a carpet capable of covering the floor of the great hall, but on the other hand, the most insignificant thing she makes for me may well have a little mysterious sign stitched on the border. One does not exactly need to have a monogram on the cake every time we eat together, and yet there may well be a little telegraphic allusion. The thing is to keep as far off as possible the point where one has a suspicion of movement in a circle, the point where repetition begins; and, since this cannot be kept off completely, the thing is to have so adjusted oneself that a variation is possible. One has only a certain number of texts—if the first Sunday the preacher preaches himself out, he not only has nothing for the year that follows, but even for the first Sunday of the next year he hasn't anything. People ought to remain enigmatic to one another as long as possible, and when in successive stages they reveal themselves this must come about as far as possible by making use of accidental circumstances, so that the revelation becomes relative and can be viewed from many angles. One must be on one's guard against every symptom of satiety and every suggestion of an after-taste."

You then would dwell on the ground floor of the lordly castle, which should be situated in a beautiful region but in the vicinity of the capital. Your wife, your consort, should dwell in the left wing of the first floor. There was one thing you had always envied in princely persons, that husband and wife dwelt apart. What detracts, however, from the aesthetic character of such a court life was, you thought, the ceremonial which claims to be more important than love. One is announced, one waits a moment, one is received. That in itself, you thought, was something not unbeautiful, but it would first acquire its true beauty when it was a playful part in the divine game of love, when it could be allowed to have validity in such a sense that one could just as well deprive it of validity. Love itself might have many boundaries, but every boundary must at the same time be a luxurious temptation to overstep the boundary. So you dwelt on the ground floor, where you had your library, billiard room, audience chamber, and your bedroom. Your wife dwelt on the first floor. Here was also your *toral conjugale,* a large room with two alcoves, one on each side. Nothing must remind you or your wife that you were married, and yet everything must be arranged in such a way as no unmarried people could have it. You were unaware of what your wife was about, and she of what oc-

cupied you. But this by no means in order to be inactive
or to forget one another, but in order that every contact
might be significant, and in order to keep at a distance the
deadly instant when you would look at one another . . .
and, lo, you were bored! So you would not parade in conjugal procession with your wife upon your arm, you would
desire with still youthful passion to follow her course from
the window when she walked in the garden, you would
sharpen your eye to see her better, and be absorbed in the
contemplation of her image when it had vanished from your
sight. You would steal after her, sometimes she would rest
upon your arm, for after all there always is something pretty
in what has come into prescriptive use among men as the
expression of a definite feeling, you would even give her
your arm, half acknowledging the beauty of this custom,
half laughing over the fact that you were promenading like
a regular married couple. But where could I end if I were
to pursue the clever refinements of your ingenious brain in
this Asiatic luxuriance which almost wearies me and makes
me wish myself back in the three small rooms you passed
by so proudly?

Now if there might be anything aesthetically beautiful
in this view, it is to be found partly in the erotic bashfulness you let one suspect, partly in the fact that at no instant
are you willing to possess her as something definitely acquired but steadily continue to acquire her. The latter is
in itself true and right, but the problem is not envisaged
with erotic seriousness, and hence, it is not solved. You were
constantly clinging to a given immediacy as such, to an impulse implanted by nature, and did not dare to allow it to
transform itself into a consciousness common to both of you;
for this is what I meant by the expression sincerity and
candor. You fear that when the enigmatic is over love will
cease; I, on the contrary, think that love begins only when
that is over. You fear that one dare not know entirely what
one loves, you count upon the incommensurable as the absolutely important ingredient; I maintain that only when
one knows what one loves does one truly love. Moreover,
all your good fortune has one lack, it lacks a blessing, for
it lacks adversities. And since this is a fault, it is fortunate,

in case you actually were to guide anyone by your theory, that it is not true to life. Let us turn then to the actual conditions of life. Now when I insist that adversities have their part in matrimony I do not by any means intend to permit you to identify marriage with a catena of adversities. It is indeed already implied in the resignation characteristic of the resolve that it sees adversities as a concomitant, though they have not yet assumed any definite shape and are not alarming because they are seen as already overcome in the act of resolution. Moreover, the adversity is not seen outwardly but inwardly, as it is reflected in the individual and thus belongs to the history which conjugal love has in common. Secretiveness, as was set forth above, becomes a contradiction when it has nothing to hide in its secret depository, and it becomes a childish prank when its deposit amounts to no more than amorous fudge. Only when a man's love has truly opened his heart, has made him eloquent in a far deeper sense than we are accustomed to associate with the word when we say that love makes one eloquent (for that eloquence the seducer too may have), only when he has deposited all in the consciousness they share together, only then does mysteriousness acquire strength, life and significance. But for this a decisive step is required, and hence it requires courage, yet conjugal love sinks into nothing when this does not take place; for only by this does one show that one loves another and not oneself. And how might one show this but by showing that one only is for the other, and how is one only for the other but by the fact that one is not for oneself? But to be for oneself is the most generic expression for the mysteriousness the individual life possesses when it remains in itself. Love is devotion, but devotion is only possible when I go out of myself.

How, then, can this be combined with the lack of frankness which wishes precisely to remain in itself? "One loses," you say, "by thus revealing oneself." Yes, of course, that man always loses who profits by being secretive. But if you would be consistent, you must carry this much further, so that you must not only dissuade from marriage but from every closer approach to people—and I wonder how you could get on with telegraphic communication. The most interesting reading is that in which the reader is to a certain extent productive; the true erotic art would be to make an impression at a distance, which would be exceedingly dangerous to the person concerned, precisely because it would be out of nothing she herself created her object and then fell in love with her own creation. But this is not love, it is the coquetry of the seducer. On the other hand, he who loves has lost himself and forgotten himself in the other; but in losing himself and forgetting himself in the other he is revealed to the other, and in forgetting himself he is remembered in the other. He who loves will not wish to be mistaken for another, whether it be a better or a more lowly man, and he who has not this reverence for himself and for the loved one does not love. Therefore secretiveness generally has its ground in a feeling of inferiority, one would like to add a cubit unto one's stature. He who has not learned to disdain such a thing has never loved; for if he had, he would have felt that even if he were to add ten cubits unto his stature he would still be too lowly. Generally, it is believed that this humility of love belongs only in comedies and romances or must be referred to the conventional lies of the period of courtship. This, however, is by no means the case: this humility is a true and profitable and constant corrector whenever anybody would measure love with anything but love. Though it were the lowliest and most insignificant person in the world who loved the most talented, the latter, if there was truth in him, would feel, nevertheless, that all his gifts were incommensurable with love, and that the only way he could satisfy the claim implied by the other's love was by loving in return.

Let us never forget that one cannot count with heterogeneous quantities. Only the man, therefore, who has truly felt this has loved; but certainly, he has never been afraid of depriving himself of something which as such has no value to him. Only the man who has become poor in the world has gained the true security of possession, and only the man who has lost all has gained all. Therefore, I cry with Fénelon: "Believe in love, it takes all, it gives all." And this truly is a beautiful, an uplifting, an indescribably blissful feeling, to let all the particular thus vanish beneath one, to let it pale and, like the shapes in the mist, flee away before the infinite power of love. This is a mathematical demonstration which at the instant in which it is concluded is just as beautiful as during the successive stages in which one takes delight in putting out one's hand and letting the factors disappear piece by piece; yea, this is the true enthusiasm of destruction characteristic of love, when it could wish for the whole world, not to glory in it, but to let it perish as a pleasantry for the entertainment of love. And verily, as soon as one opens the door for finite considerations it is just as stupid and just as ludicrous, whether one wants to be loved because one has the highest intelligence, the greatest talent, the loftiest artistic genius, or because he cherishes on his lip the most beautiful moustache. However, these assertions and these sentiments, of course, apply just as well to first love, and it is only the wondrous, unsteady attitude you always assume which makes it necessary here to touch upon this point again.

First love can wish with supernatural pathos, but this wishing easily becomes an "in case" which lacks content, and we are not living in such a paradisiacal state that the good Lord is ready to give every married couple the whole world to deal with as they please. Conjugal love knows better, its movements are not outward but inward, and here it observes at once that it has a wide world for itself, but also that every little act of self-repression is very much more commensurable with the infinity of love; and even though it feels pain in recognizing that there may be so much to fight against, it is conscious also of courage for this fight; yea, it has boldness enough to outdo you in paradoxes when it is almost able to rejoice that sin has entered into the world. But in still another sense it has boldness enough to outdo you in paradoxes, for it has the courage to resolve them. For conjugal love, like first love, knows all these obstacles as vanquished in the infinite moment of love, but it knows also (and this precisely is the historical factor in it) that this victory wills to be acquired, and that this acquisition is not merely a game but also a conflict, yet at the same time not merely a conflict but also a game, just as the war in Valhalla was a deadly conflict and yet a game, because the contestants constantly arose again from the dead rejuvenated; and it knows also that this fencing is not an arbitrary duel but a conflict under divine auspices, and it feels no need of loving more than one, but senses the blissfulness of this restriction, and no need of loving more than once, for it senses an eternity in this once. And do you think, then, that this love which has no secrets might miss something beautiful? Or might it be unable to resist time and be blunted necessarily by daily association? Or might tedium overtake it more swiftly?—as though conjugal love did not possess an eternal content of which one never grows tired, an eternal content which now with kiss and jest, now with fear and trembling, it acquires and continues to acquire. "But," you say, "it must renounce all these pretty little surprises." I see no necessity of that; my notion is not that conjugal love must always stand with its mouth open and chatter even in its sleep. On the contrary, all these little surprises acquire their significance precisely when the total open-heartedness has taken place. For this gives a sense of security and confidence in which these interludes show off to the best advantage. If anyone believes, on the other hand, that the essence of love and of true bliss consists in such a train of little surprises, and thinks that the petty effeminacy and uneasiness with which one must every instant be prepared for a little surprise and even think one up is to be considered beautiful, then I will take the liberty of saying that it is very unseemly, and that it is a very suspicious sign when a marriage has no better trophies to display than a desk full of bonbons, bottles of perfume, dried leaves, embroidered slippers, etc.

However, marriages in which the mystery-system is carried out are to be seen from time to time. For my part, I have never seen a happy marriage of this kind; but since my observation might be entirely accidental I shall state the reasons commonly given for such a judgment. This is a matter of considerable importance to me, for the aesthetically beautiful marriage is always a happy marriage, so if a happy marriage could be constructed on this basis, my theory must be amended. I shall not try to avoid the mention of any form in which this system appears, and I shall describe each as justly as I possibly can, dwelling more especially upon a type which in the house where I saw it put into effect was carried out with a virtuosity which really was fascinating.

You will readily concede that the mystery-system generally proceeds from men, and although it is always bad, it is, nevertheless, more tolerable than the intolerable type in which it is the wife who exercises such a *dominium*. The ugliest form is, of course, a pure despotism in which the wife is a slave, a maid of all work in the domestic economy. Such a marriage is never happy, even if the years produce a hebetude which finds itself content with it. A prettier form is the very opposite of this, an ill-advised solicitude. "Woman is weak," it is said, "she is unable to bear troubles and sorrows, one must treat the weak and fragile creature lovingly." Falsehood! Falsehood! Woman is just as strong as man, perhaps stronger. And is she really treated lovingly when you thus humiliate her? Or who gave you leave to humiliate her? Or how can your soul be so blind that you consider yourself a more perfect being than she is? Only confide to her everything! If she is weak, if she is unable to bear it—well, then, she can lean upon you, you have strength and to spare! This, you see, you cannot bear to do; so it is you who lack strength and not she. Perhaps she has more strength than you, perhaps she was ashamed of you—and, lo, this you have not the strength to bear. Or have you not promised to share with her both good and evil? Is it not, then, to withhold from her her just share when you will not initiate her into the evil? Is not this to quench the better part in her? Perhaps she is weak, perhaps her sorrow will make everything harder—*eh bien*, then share with her the evil. But this, in its turn, will save her; and have you a right to deprive her of a way of salvation? Have you a right to conduct her stealthily through the world? And from whence do you derive your strength? Is she not as close to God as you? Will you deprive her of the opportunity of finding God in the deepest and most heartfelt way—through pain and suffering? And do you know so certainly that she has no presentiment of what your mysteri-

ousness conceals? Do you know whether in secret she does
not sorrow and sigh, whether she has not suffered damage
to her soul? Perhaps her weakness is humility, perhaps she
believes it her duty to bear all this. Hereby you have, in
fact, been an occasion of developing strength in her, but it
was not in the way you had intended or promised. Or are
you not treating her (to use the strongest word for it) . . .
like a concubine? For the fact that you have not several
wives is of no help to her. And is it not doubly humiliating
to her when she perceives that you love her, that you treat
her thus, not because you are a proud tyrant, but because
she is a frail being?

For a long while I was accustomed to visit in a house
where I had opportunity to observe the system of silence
carried out in a more artistic and refined fashion. The husband was a fairly young man of unusual talent, with a fine
intelligence and a poetic nature, too indolent to want to
produce anything, but with an extraordinary flair and tact
for making everyday life poetic. His wife was young, not
without intelligence, but with a character very unusual.
This tempted him. It was the most astonishing thing to see
how he was able to arouse and nourish in her every youthful
enthusiasm. Her whole existence, the whole life they shared
together as a married couple, was entirely woven out of
poetic enchantment. Everywhere his eye was present—
when she looked about it was gone; his finger was in everything, but just as invisibly as God's finger is present in
history. Her thought might turn whither it would—he was
already there before her; he understood like Potemkin[33] how
to conjure up landscapes, and just of the sort that after a
little surprise and a little resistance might be most pleasing
to her. His home life was a little act of creation, and just
as in the great creation man is that to which everything
tends, so did she become the center of an enchanted circle,
wherein she enjoyed nevertheless her full liberty. For the
circle would bend in conformity with her movement and
had no boundaries of which it might be said, "Hitherto and
no further"; she might plunge as she would, in whatever
direction she would, the circle yielded, but it remained
there, nevertheless. She walked as in a toddling-basket, but

this was not woven out of osiers, it was braided out of her hopes, dreams, longings, wishes, fears; in short, it was fabricated out of the whole content of her soul. He himself moved with the utmost security in this dream-world; he relinquished nothing of his dignity, claimed and asserted his authority as husband and lord. It would have disquieted her if he had not done so, it would perhaps have awakened in her a fearful apprehension which would lead her to a solution of the mystery. He did not appear in the eyes of the world, nor even in her eyes, to be so extraordinarily attentive, and yet he knew within himself that she had received no impression of him but just that which he wanted to give her, and he knew that he had it in his power by one single word to dissolve the enchantment. Everything that might make a disagreeable impression upon her was kept at a distance. If any such thing were encountered, she received from him, either in response to her searching queries or with open-hearted anticipation of them, and in the form of candid information, an explanation which he himself had drafted, in stronger or weaker terms, according to the impression he wished to make upon her. He was proud, frightfully consistent, he loved her, but he could not relinquish the proud thought of daring to say to himself, either in the profoundest stillness of the night or in an instant which lay outside of time, "She owes everything to me."

You surely have followed with interest this description, however imperfectly I have succeeded in presenting it; for it summons up before your soul a picture with which you sympathize, which perhaps you would one day seek to emulate if you were to become a married man. Was then this marriage a happy marriage? Yes, if you will. Nevertheless, a dark fate hovered over this happiness. Suppose he were to fail in his effort, suppose she suddenly suspected something—I do not believe she could ever forgive him for it. For the fact that he had done it out of love for her— that her proud soul was too proud to let anyone tell her. There is an old-fashioned expression about the relation between married people which I would recall to your attention. (I always take delight in lending support to the revolution, or rather the holy war, by which the plain and simple but true and rich expressions used for legitimate marriage strive to reconquer the realm from which the writers of romance have expelled them.) It is said of married people that they should live in good understanding with one another. One hears most frequently the negative expression, that a couple do not live in good understanding, meaning that they cannot abide one another, that they beat and bite, etc. Take now the positive expression. The married pair above described live in good understanding—yes, so the world would say; but you surely would not, for how can they live in good understanding when they do not understand one another? But is it not an essential part of understanding that the one knows how careful and loving the other is? Or even if he deprived her of nothing else, yet he deprived her of opportunity for that degree of gratitude wherein her soul would first find repose. Is it not a pretty and beautiful and simple expression: to live in good understanding? (These matrimonial terms, you see, know all about this subject and make no great fuss about that which now one must often insist upon precisely.) This expression assumes as a matter of course that people understand one another clearly and explicitly. It assumes this as a matter of course, as one may see from the fact that an adjective is adjoined with marked emphasis; for otherwise it would suffice to say that they should live in understanding. "Good understanding"—what else does that mean but that they should find their joy, peace, repose, their very life in this understanding?

So you see that the mystery-system does not by any means conduce to a happy or even to a beautiful marriage. No, my friend; candor, open-heartedness, revelation, understanding—these constitute the life principle of marriage, without which it fails to be beautiful or even moral; for that which love unites is then separated: the sensuous and the spiritual. Only when the being with whom in the earthly life I live in the most tender association is in a spiritual respect equally close to me, only then is my marriage moral and, therefore, also aesthetically beautiful. And you proud men who perhaps rejoice secretly in this victorious triumph over woman forget in the first place that it is a sorry triumph when one triumphs over the weaker one, and that the husband honors himself in his wife, and he who does not do so despises himself.

So understanding is the life principle in marriage. One often hears people of experience discuss the question in what case one ought to dissuade a person from marrying. Let them discuss these circumstances and ruminate on them as thoroughly as they will; what they generally have to say does not signify much. For my part I will mention only one case,[34] that is, when the individual life is so complicated that it cannot reveal itself. If the history of your inward development possesses an unutterable content, or if your life has made you privy to secrets; in short, if in one way or another you have gulped down a secret which you cannot draw up except at the cost of your life, then never marry. Either you will feel yourself bound to a being who has no presentiment of what is going on within you, and your marriage then becomes an unseemly misalliance; or you bind yourself to a being who observes this with anxious dread and every instant sees the shadow pictures on the wall. She will, perhaps, resolve never to question you closely, she will renounce the curiosity of dread which tempts her, but she will never be happy, nor you either. Whether there actually are such secrets, whether there is any truth in the close reserve which not even love is able to unlock, I will not decide, I am merely carrying out my principle, and so far as I myself am concerned, I have no secrets from my wife. One might believe that it surely never occurred to such a man to marry, seeing that apart from everything else he must undertake he had also the daily avocation of his painful secret. Nevertheless, this sometimes happens, and such a man is perhaps the most dangerous temptation to women.

But having spoken of mystery and understanding as two sides of the same thing, that thing being the chief thing in love, the condition absolutely requisite for preserving the aesthetic character of marriage, I have reason to fear that you will make the objection that I seem to forget the historical character of love, which, as you say, I commonly

insist upon like a refrain of a ditty. You hope, however, to
delude time by your mysteriousness and your shrewdly calculated relative information. "But," as you say, "when married people start in earnest to recount their shorter or longer
story, the instant will soon arrive when as in childish play
they say, 'the boy has the bun, the story is done.'" My
young friend, you do not perceive that if you can make
such an objection it is due to the fact that you are not in
the correct position? By means of your mysteriousness you
have a temporal purpose, and it really is important to delude time; on the other hand, love by self-revelation has an
eternal purpose and so all competition is impossible. Also,
it is an arbitrary misunderstanding to think of the revelation
as obliging married people to spend a fortnight in recount-
ing their careers, which would be followed by the silence
of the grave, broken only once in a while by a repetition
of the story already told. It lies in the historical character
of marriage that this understanding is reached by a con-
tinuous process, not simply once for all. It is just as in the
individual life: when one has attained clarity about oneself,
when one has had courage to will to see oneself, it by no
means follows that now the history is finished, for now it
begins, now for the first time it acquires real significance
for the fact that every individual moment experienced
leads on to this total view. So also in marriage. In this
revelation the immediacy of first love perishes, yet it is not
lost but lifted up into the collective knowledge of conjugal
life; with this the history begins, and to this collective
knowledge the individual is referred, and in this consists
its *blissfulness*—an expression in which, again, the historical
character of marriage is conserved, and which corresponds
to the *joie de vivre* (or what the Germans call *Heiterkeit*)
which is characteristic of first love.

So it is essential to conjugal love that it become historical,
and the individual being then in the right attitude, the
commandment which says, "In the sweat of thy brow shalt
thou eat bread," is not a terrifying commandment, and the
courage and strength of which conjugal love is conscious
corresponds to the true romantic need of knightly love to
perform adventurous exploits. As the knight is fearless, so,

too, is conjugal love, in spite of the fact that the enemies with which it has to contend are often far more dangerous. Here a wide field for reflection is opened, upon which, however, I do not intend to enter. But if the knight has a right to say that the man who does not defy the whole world to save his lady does not know knightly love, the married man too has a right to say the same. Only I must constantly remind you that every victory of this sort which conjugal love wins is more aesthetically beautiful than that which the knight wins, because in winning this victory the married man at the same time wins again his love in a glorified form. Conjugal love fears nothing, not even little mistakes, little amorous affairs; on the contrary, these only serve to nourish the divine and healthy vigor of conjugal love. Even in Goethe's *Elective Affinities* Ottilia, though eventually she goes to the dogs, is regarded as a slender possibility of serious conjugal love; and how much more might a marriage founded upon deep religious and ethical principles find strength for such a view. Indeed, Goethe's *Elective Affinities* shows what secretiveness leads to. The love there described would not have acquired the power it did if it had not been allowed to grow up in silence. If the man had had courage to reveal himself to his wife, this situation would have been prevented, and the whole affair would have become an interlude in the drama of marriage. The fatality consisted in the fact that both Edward and his wife fell in love with other people at the same time—but this again is the fault of silence. The married man who has the courage to confide to his wife that he loves another is saved by that, and the same holds true of the wife. But when he has not this courage he loses confidence in himself, and so what he seeks is forgetfulness in the love of another. Undoubtedly, it often is not so much true love for the other woman which causes a man to yield as it is a feeling of pain at not having resisted in time. He feels that he has lost himself, and when such is the case, strong opiates are needed to blunt this feeling.

About the difficulties with which conjugal love has to contend I will speak only in general terms and only in order to show that from them conjugal love has nothing to fear so far as concerns the preservation of its aesthetic character. The objections commonly originate in a misunderstanding of the aesthetic significance of the historical, or from the fact that, in general, people apply to a romantic experience only the classical ideal and have not the romantic ideal along with it. A great many other objections are attributable to the fact that, while people always like to think of first love as dancing upon roses, they take joy in letting conjugal love contend with the basest and most pitiful difficulties and fall prey to every chicanery. To this we may add that they privately believe these difficulties insurmountable, and thus they make short work of marriage. One must always be a bit cautious when one is dealing with you. I am not talking about any particular marriage, and so I can depict the situation as I will; but though I do not wish to be guilty of any arbitrary procedure, this does not insure that you will forego this pleasure. When, for example, poverty is proposed as a difficulty with which marriage may have to contend, I would answer: "Work—then all obstacles give way." Since now it is an imaginary or poetical world in which we are moving, you will perhaps take advantage of your poetic license and make answer: "They couldn't get any work. The decline in business and in the shipping trade has left a great many people without bread." Or you permit them to get a little work, but it is not sufficient. Then when I say that by wise economy they surely will be able to make both ends meet, you come out with the information that on account of the critical state of the market the price of wheat is so high that it is perfectly impossible to get along with what otherwise might have been sufficient. I know you only too well. You always take delight in maintaining with your poetic license the opposite point of view, and then, when this has amused you long enough, you seize the occasion of some chance remark to tangle your interlocutor, or some other person present, with a prolix patter which has nothing whatever to do with the matter originally in question. You take delight in suddenly transforming a willful poetic invention into a sort of reality, and then expatiating upon it. In case you had been talking to anyone but me in the manner I have described (for generally you are good enough to spare me), you presumably would have used the "high price of wheat" as a pretext for going on to say: "Such a dearth that bread would cost eight shillings a pound." If there happened, luckily, to be somebody present who replied that this was altogether too incredible, you would explain that "during the famine in Olaf's time bread, and bad bread at that, cost eight and a half shillings a pound, in old Danish currency; and when one considers that in those times money was scarce among the people, you can easily see," etc. If with that you had got this man on the go, you would be beside yourself with joy. The man who had begun the conversation would in vain try to bring you back to the point; everything would be reduced to confusion, and you would have made a married couple unhappy . . . in the world of poetry.

It is this that makes it so difficult to deal with you. If I were to venture out upon what might well be called glare-ice for me, and should try to describe in a novelistic manner a marriage which triumphantly held its own in the conflict with a multitude of such adversities, you would calmly reply, "Well, that is merely fiction, and in the world of poetry one can easily make people happy, it's the very least one can do for them." If I were to take your arm and walk about with you in real life and show you a marriage which had fought the good fight, then you, if you were in the humor, would answer, "Yes, that's well enough. The outward aspects of temptation are susceptible of proof, the inward aspects are not. I assume that in this couple temptation has not possessed an inward power, for otherwise it would not have been possible to resist it." Just as though the true significance of temptation were that people should succumb to it! But enough of this. When once you take it into your head to abandon yourself to this demon of willfulness there is no end to it; and as everything you do is done deliberately, so is this willful prank, and you find delight in making every position insecure.

In a general way I can divide these difficulties into external and internal difficulties, constantly keeping in mind the relativity of such a division in the case of marriage, where, if anywhere, all experiences are internal. First, then,

for the external difficulties. I have no hesitation or fear in
mentioning all the most depressing, humiliating and vexa-
tious finite afflictions, in short, all the items which go to
make up a tearful drama. You and your kind are exceedingly arbitrary in this instance, as you are in every other.
If a play of this sort compels you to undertake a journey
through the caverns of misfortune, you say that it is unaesthetic, sniveling, tiresome. And in that you are right—
but why? Because you are indignant that something sublime and noble perishes in the face of such difficulties. On
the other hand, if you turn to the real world and encounter
there a family which has undergone only half the adversities
which this hangman of a playwright with the voluptuous
enjoyment reserved for a tyrant has devised to torture
others, you shudder, and you think, "Good night to all
aesthetic beauty." You feel compassion, you are willing to
help, in order to drive away gloomy thoughts, if for no
other reason; but as for the poor family, you already have
given it up in despair. But if this thing is true in real life,
the poet has a right to represent it and represents it rightly.
When you are sitting in the theater, intoxicated with aesthetic enjoyment, you have the courage to require of the
poet that he shall let the aesthetic triumph over all paltriness. It is the only comfort left, and, what is still more
effeminate, it is you who take comfort in this, you to whom
real life has furnished no occasion to make test of your
strength. You are the poor and unfortunate one, like the
hero and the heroine in the play, but you have also pathos,
courage, an *os rotundum*[35] from which eloquence gushes
in a powerful stream; you conquer; you applaud the actor,
and the actor is yourself, and the applause of the parterre
is for you, for indeed, you yourself are the hero and the
actor. In dreams, in the airy visions of aesthetics, you men
are heroes. I bother myself relatively little about the theater,
and for my part you may be as merry as you please—let
the theatrical heroes perish or let them conquer, let them
sink through the floor or vanish through the ceiling, I am
not much moved by that. But if in real life it is true, as you
teach and proclaim, that far fewer adversities are capable
of reducing a man to the condition of a slave, so that he

walks with his head bent and forgets that he, too, is created in God's image, then please God may it be your just punishment that all playwrights should write nothing else but tearful dramas with every possible dread and terror, which would not permit your effeminacy to find repose in the theater nor you to distill your supernatural perfume, but would perhaps frighten you until you might learn to believe in the reality of that which you believe only in the form of poetry.

I admit gladly that in my marriage I have not met with many adversities of this sort, I cannot, therefore, speak from experience, yet I have the conviction that nothing is capable of crushing out the aesthetic element in man, a conviction so strong, so blissful, so heartfelt, that I render thanks to God for it as for a gift of grace. And when we read in Holy Scripture about many gifts of grace, I really would reckon this among them: the frankness, the confidence, the trust in reality and in the eternal necessity of the triumph of the beautiful, and the bliss implied in the liberty of coming to the aid of God. This conviction is a constituent factor of my make-up, and I do not allow myself to be effeminately and voluptuously moved to shuddering by the artificial stimulus of the theater. The only thing I can do is to thank God for this firmness of my soul, but in doing so I hope that I have set my soul free from the danger of taking it in vain. You know that I hate all experimentation, but nevertheless, it is generally recognized that a man may have in thought experienced much which he never has occasion to experience in reality. There sometimes come despondent moments, and when a person does not evoke them arbitrarily for the sake of trying his hand at such things, that too is a strife, a very serious strife, and in this strife may be acquired an assurance, which, though it has not exactly the same stamp of reality as that which is acquired in real life, has, nevertheless, a good deal of significance. There are certain cases in life when it is a good sign in a man that he is as it were mad, that he has not separated the world of poetry from that of reality but sees the latter *sub specie poeseos*. Luther says somewhere in one of his sermons where he is talking of poverty and want: "One has never heard of a Christian man dying of hunger." Therewith Luther has disposed of the matter and thinks, doubtless with good reason, that he has spoken about it with much unction and to the genuine edification of his hearers.

Inasmuch, then, as marriage has to deal with such external trials, the thing to do, of course, is to make them internal. I say "of course," and I am speaking rather audaciously when I talk on this subject; but you see I am writing only to you, and it is likely that we both have just about the same amount of experience with adversities of this sort. The thing to do, then, is to transform the external trial into an internal one, if one would preserve the aesthetic character of marriage. Or does it vex you that I still make use of the word aesthetic; do you think that it is almost a kind of childishness in me to persist in seeking this quality among the poor and the suffering? Or maybe you have degraded yourself by adopting the shocking division which assigns the aesthetic to the distinguished, the rich, the mighty, the highly educated, and at the most assigns religion to the poor? Well, it seems to me that the poor do not come out badly in this division. And do you not see that the poor in having the religious have also the aesthetic, and that the rich, in so far as they have not the religious, have not the aesthetic either? Moreover, I have spoken only of the extremes, and it is surely not a rare case that people who cannot be reckoned among the poor have to contend with care and anxiety about their daily bread. Besides, there are other cares which are common to all classes: illness, for example. I am convinced, however, of this, that he who has the courage to transform an external trial into an internal one has already as good as overcome it. By faith he undergoes a transubstantiation even in the moment of suffering. The married man who well enough remembers his love, and in the moment of want has courage to say, "The important thing is not first of all where I can get money and at what rate, but first of all it is about my love, that I have kept a pure and faithful covenant of love with her to whom I am united." He who with not too many inward struggles shall compel himself to say this, and with the youthful wholesomeness of first love, or with the assurance acquired by experience, undertakes to perform this movement—he has conquered, has preserved the aesthetic in marriage, even if he had not three small rooms to live in. Now it is not to be denied (as your cunning mind will soon scent out) that changing the external trial into an internal one may make it still harder. But the gods sell nothing great for naught, and just in this experience consists the educative, the idealizing effect of marriage. It is often said that when one stands alone in the world one can bear all such things more easily. True enough, to a certain degree; but in this talk there is often concealed a great untruth. For why is it one can bear the thing more easily? It is because one can the more easily cast oneself away, suffer damage to his soul, without causing concern to anybody else, can forget God, can let the tempest of despair drown out the cry of pain, can become blunted in feeling, can almost take pleasure in living among men as a specter. Everyone ought indeed to take heed to himself, even though he stands alone; but after all, only the man who loves has a right conception of what he is and what he is capable of, and only marriage gives example of the historic fidelity, which is quite as beautiful as the chivalric sort. For in fact, a married man can never behave in this way; and however the world goes against him, even though for an instant he forgets himself and already begins to feel so light because despair is in the way of buoying him up, feels so strong because he has sipped the stupefying drink which is mixed by defiance and self-disdain, by cowardice and pride, feels so free because the bond which binds him to truth and righteousness is, as it were, broken and he experiences the speed which is the transition from good to bad—yet he will soon return to the old guiding control and as a married man [*Ægtemand*] prove himself a genuine man [*ægte Mand*].

This must suffice for the external trials. I express myself briefly, because I do not feel profoundly competent to take part in the discussion of this subject, and also because an adequate treatment would require exorbitant space. But this is the result I reach: if love can be preserved—and that it can, so help me God—then can the aesthetic also be preserved; for love itself is the aesthetic.

The other objections, which have internal trials in view, are due to a misunderstanding of the significance of time and of the aesthetic validity of the historical. They apply to every marriage, and hence, I can speak of them in very general terms. That I shall now do, trying not to overlook in this generic treatment the gist of the attack or the gist of the defense.

The first objection you would mention is custom, "inevitable custom," you would say, "this terrible monotony, the perpetual sameness in the appalling still-life of the domestic regime of married people. I love nature, but I hate second-nature." One must allow that you know how to describe with seductive warmth and pathos the happy time when one still makes discoveries, and to depict with the colors of dread and horror the time when this is over. You know how to paint in ludicrous and disgusting terms a conjugal uniformity which does not find its match even in nature. "For here, after all, as Leibnitz has already showed,[36] nothing is quite identical. Such a uniformity has been reserved for rational creatures, resulting either from their drowsiness or from their pedantry." Now I by no means am disposed to deny that it is a beautiful time, an eternally memorable time (mark well in what sense I can say this), when in the world of love the individual is affected with astonishment and made blissful by that which indeed had long ago been discovered, of which he had often heard and read, but which now for the first time he appropriates to himself with the whole enthusiasm of surprise, with the whole depth of inwardness. It is a beautiful time, from the very first presentiment of love, the first sight of the beloved object, its first disappearance, the first chord of this voice, the first glance, the first hand-shake, the first kiss, unto the first complete assurance of its possession. It is a beautiful time, the first uneasiness, the first longing, the first pain because she failed to put in an appearance, the first joy because she came unexpectedly. A beautiful time—but this is by no means to say that the subsequent time is not just as comely. You who pretend to such a chivalrous way of thinking, test yourself. When you say that the first kiss is the most exquisite, the sweetest, you offend the loved one;

for what gives the kiss absolute value is time and the qualification it bestows.

In order, however, that I may not hurt the cause I am
defending, you must first render me a little accounting. For
in case you would not proceed arbitrarily you must assail
first love in the same way you assail marriage. For if the
former is to survive in real life it must be espoused to the
same fatalities, and is far from having the same resources
to oppose to them that conjugal love has in the ethical and
the religious. To be consistent you must therefore hate all
love which desires to be an eternal love. So you stop with
first love as a transitory moment. However, in order to have
its true significance first love must have in it the naïve eternity. If once you have had the experience that this was an
illusion, you have lost everything—unless you would struggle to fall again into the same illusion, which is a self-
contradiction. Or might your shrewd head have so con-
spired with your lust that you could entirely forget what
you owe to others? Might you think that even though it
never could be repeated exactly like the first time, there
still was a tolerable expedient: one was rejuvenated by ex-
periencing the illusion in others, one relished the infinity
and enjoyment found in the individual whose virginal girdle
of illusion was not yet loosened? Such an attitude evinces
as much desperation as it does depravity, and since it
evinces desperation it will be impossible to find here enlightenment about life.

The first thing I shall protest is your right to use the word
"custom" for the phenomenon of recurrence characteristic
of every life and so, also, of love. The word custom is properly used only of evil, as indicating either a persistence in
something which is in itself evil, or a repetition of something
which is in itself innocent, but a repetition so obstinate that
it becomes evil. Custom, therefore, always indicates something unfree. But just as one cannot perform the good without freedom, so neither can one remain in it without freedom, and, therefore, with reference to the good one can
never talk about custom.

In the next place I must also protest against your disparagement of conjugal uniformity when you state that

such a thing is not to be found even in nature. That affirmation is, in fact, very true, but uniformity may be the expression of something beautiful, and that being the case, man can be proud of being the inventor of it. Thus, in music uniform tact may be very beautiful and produce a great effect.

Finally, I would say that in case such a monotony were unavoidable in conjugal life, you must yourself see, if you were honest, that the task would be to vanquish it, i.e., to preserve love in and through and under it, and not to despair; for despair can never be a serious task; it is a convenience, which, I am willing to admit, only those grasp who see the task.

But let us now consider how it stands with this notorious uniformity. It is not only your fault but your misfortune that everywhere, and so, also, with respect to love, you think too abstractly. You think a little summary of love's factors, you think (as you perhaps yourself would say) the categories of love. In this respect I willingly concede to you an uncommon categorical thoroughness. You think every concrete object in terms of one factor, and this is the poetical way of thinking. Then when alongside of this you think the protracted character of marriage, this seems to you an appalling incongruity. The trouble is that you do not think historically. If a systematic mind were to think the category of reciprocal action and develop it thoroughly and with sound logic, but should say also, "It will go on for an eternity before the world is through with its eternal reciprocal action," you surely will not deny that one would have a right to laugh at him. This is simply the significance of time, and it is the lot of mankind and of individual men to live in it. If, therefore, you have nothing else to say but that this is not to be endured, then you will have to look about for another auditorium. This would be a perfectly sufficient answer; but not to give you opportunity to say, "Substantially you are of the same opinion as I am but consider it best to put up with what you cannot alter," I shall endeavor to show that it not only is best to put up with it, as surely it is also a duty, but that putting up with a thing is truly the best.

But let us begin at a point which may be regarded as a point of contact. The time which precedes the culmination you are not afraid of, on the contrary, you love it, and by a great multiplicity of reflections you often try to make the instants employed in reproducing it even longer than they originally were, and if anyone were to reduce your life to categories, you would be exceedingly exasperated. During that time preceding the culmination it is not only the great and decisive actions which have interest for you, but every little insignificance, and you know then how to talk prettily enough about the secret which was hid from the wise: that the smallest is the greatest. On the other hand, when the culminating point has been reached everything is changed, everything then shrinks to a poverty-stricken and uninviting abbreviation. This, to your way of thinking, is just simply grounded in your nature, which is bent upon conquest but is able to possess nothing. Now in case you are not willful and perverse enough to persist in maintaining that this is simply the way you are made, there will come a moment when you are compelled to conclude an armistice and open the ranks so that I may come and see if this claim is true, and, if it be, how much truth there is in it. If you will not do this, then, without troubling about you, I will picture to myself an individuality exactly like yours and then calmly proceed with my vivisection of it. I hope, nevertheless, that you will have courage enough to submit personally to the operation, courage enough to let yourself—in reality and not merely in effigy—be hanged.

When you insist that you are "simply made that way," you thereby concede that others *might* be different. I can affirm no more than this, for it might be possible that you are the normal man, although the fact that you are so anxious to assert this hardly suggests that you are the normal man. But how do you conceive of the others? When you see a married couple whose union, as it seems to you, drags on in the most dreadful boredom, "with the most insipid repetition," as you say, "of love's holy institutions and sacraments," then truly a conflagration rages within you, a flame which would consume them. And this, indeed, is not an arbitrary passion on your part; you are in the right, you are justified in letting the lightning of irony smite them, in letting the thunder of wrath terrify them. You do not annihilate them for the reason that you take pleasure in it but because they have deserved it. You condemn them —but what else does "condemn" mean but to require something of them, and if you cannot require it, surely it is a contradiction to require the impossible, and so it is a contradiction to condemn them. Surely you have compromised yourself when you hint at a law which you yourself are not willing to recognize and which, nevertheless, you have applied to others. You are not lacking, however, in self-possession; you say: "I do not blame them, I do not reproach them, I do not condemn them—I pity them." But suppose, now, that the couple in question did not find it at all tedious. A self-satisfied smile flits across your face, a happy conceit has come to you as a surprise and surely will surprise the person whom you address: "I pity them, as I have said, for either they feel the whole weight of boredom, and for this I pity them, or they do not notice it, and then too I pity them for the fact that they are in a pitiable illusion." That is about the way you would answer me, and in case there were several persons present your attitude of assurance would not fail to produce an effect. Now, however, there is nobody listening to us, so I can proceed with the examination. You pity them, then, in both cases. Only a third case is possible, that of the man who knows that this is how it is with matrimony and luckily has not entered into it. But this situation is obviously just as pitiable for the man who has felt love and now sees that it cannot be realized; and, finally, the state of the man who has got himself out of this shipwreck by the egoistic expedients above described is also pitiable, for he has assumed the place of the robber and disturber of the peace. It seems, therefore, that although marriage has generally become the expression for a happy ending, yet its own end is not so very joyful. As the result of this whole investigation we have thus reached the point of pitying everybody universally. But such a result is an absurdity. It is as if one were to say that the result of life's development is that one goes backward. You generally are not afraid of chiming in, and in this case perhaps you would say: "Yes, that sometimes occurs too: when a man has the wind dead against him on a slippery path the result of going forward is often a going backward."

I return again, however, to the consideration of your whole spiritual make-up. You say that yours is a nature designed for conquest and not capable of possessing. In saying this you certainly do not think you have said anything to your own disparagement; on the contrary, you are inclined rather to think yourself greater than others. Let us consider this a little more closely. Which requires greater strength, to go uphill or to go downhill? Evidently more strength is required for the latter, if the grade is a steep one. The disposition to go uphill is inborn in almost every man, whereas most people have a certain dread of going down a steep grade. So, too, I believe that there are far more natures formed for conquest than for possession; and when you feel your superiority over a host of married people and "their stupid animal satisfaction," that may be true to a certain degree, but then you feel that you have nothing to learn from those who are beneath you. True art generally takes the opposite direction to the course which nature follows, though without annihilating the process of nature; and so true art will exhibit itself by possessing, not by conquering. The fact is that possession is conquest in an inverse direction. In this expression you can already see how art and nature strive against one another. The man who possesses has also something which results from conquest; indeed, if one were to be strict in the use of terms, one might say that only the man who possesses really conquers. You likely have the notion that you too possess, for in fact you have the instant of possession. But this is no possession, for there is no deeper appropriation. Thus, when I think of a conqueror who has subdued kingdoms and lands, he was also in possession of these oppressed provinces, he had great possessions, and yet such a prince is called a conqueror, not a possessor. Only when by wisdom he governed them to their own best interest did he really possess them. Now this is very rare in a conquering nature; generally he will lack the humility, the religiousness, the true humanity, required for possession. It was for this reason, you see, that in my exposition of the relation of marriage to first love I emphasized especially the religious factor, because this will dethrone the conqueror and let the possessor come to evidence. Therefore, I commended marriage for the fact that it was precisely designed for the highest end, for lasting possession. Here I may remind you of a saying you often utter with a flourish: "The great thing is not the original but the acquired." Now the passion for conquest and the fact that one makes conquests is the original, the primitive factor, but the fact that one possesses and wills to possess is the acquired. Pride is required for conquest, humility for possession; violence is required for conquest, patience for possession; cupidity for conquest, contentment for possession; food and drink for conquest, fasting and prayer for possession. But all the predicates I have used here, and surely have used rightly, to characterize the conquering nature may be applied with absolute propriety to the natural man; but the natural man is not the highest. Possession is not a spiritually inert and invalid "appearance" even though it has legal force, but it is a steady acquisition. Here you see again that the possessive nature has in himself the conquering disposition; for he conquers like the farmer, who does not put himself at the head of his henchmen and drive his neighbor away, but conquers by digging in the earth. True greatness, therefore, is not conquest but possession. Here perhaps you will say, "I will not decide which is the greater, but I am willing to admit that these are two great formations of men. Everyone may decide for himself to which formation he belongs, and must guard against being transformed by this or the other apostle of conversion." By this last expression I see you have your eye fixed upon me triumphantly. Nevertheless, I will make answer: The one is not merely greater than the other, but it has some sense in it, and the other has not. It has both an antecedent and a consequent clause, the other has merely the antecedent, and instead of the consequent clause a suspicious dash, the significance of which I shall explain to you another time, if you do not know it already.

If now you continue to say that you simply are a conquering nature, that is entirely indifferent to me, for you must concede that it is greater to possess than to conquer. When a man conquers he constantly forgets himself, when he possesses he remembers himself, not as a vain diversion but with all possible seriousness. When one is going uphill one has an eye merely upon the other person, when one is going downhill one must keep watch upon oneself, observing the just relation between the support and the center of gravity.

But I go further. You will perhaps concede that it is more difficult to possess than to conquer. You say, however, "If only I am allowed to conquer, I shall not be so stingy as that; on the contrary, I shall be very liberal in my compliments to those who have the patience to possess, especially if they should be found disposed to work hand in hand with me by being willing to possess my conquests. That is the greater, so let it be, but more beautiful it is not; more ethical it may be, but (with all due deference to ethics) it is at the same time less aesthetic." Let us try to come to a better understanding of one another on this point. Among a great many people there doubtless prevails a misunderstanding which confounds what is aesthetically beautiful with the representation of aesthetic beauty. This is readily explained by the fact that the aesthetic satisfaction of which the soul has need is by most people found in reading or in beholding works of art, etc., whereas there are comparatively very few who themselves see the aesthetic as it is in everyday life, who themselves see everyday life in an aesthetic light and do not merely enjoy the poetic representation. But for an aesthetic representation there always is required a concentration in the moment, and the richer this concentration is, the greater is the aesthetic effect. Now it is only by this concentration that the happy, the indescribable moment, the moment of infinite significance, in short, *the* Moment, acquires its true value. This moment is either, as it were, the predestined moment which vibrates through consciousness by awakening the conception of the divinity of existence; or it presupposes a history. In the first case it takes one by surprise; in the second case there is indeed a history, but the artistic representation cannot dwell upon it, at the most it can merely give a hint of it, and then hasten on to the moment. The more it can put into the moment, the more aesthetic it is. Nature, as a philosopher has said, takes the shortest way. One might say that it takes no way, for at one stroke it is present all at once; and when I would lose myself in contemplation of the vaulted heaven I do not have to wait until the innumerable heavenly bodies take shape, for they all are there at once.

The way of history, on the other hand, like that of the law, is very long and toilsome. Then art and poetry step in to shorten the way and delight us with the moment of accomplishment, as they concentrate the extensive in the intensive. But the more significant that thing is which is to come out, the slower is the way of history, but the more significant is, also, this slow course itself, and the more it will be seen that the way is also the goal. As it is related to the individual life, history is of two kinds: external and internal. They are currents of two sorts with opposite movements. The first kind, again, has two sides. In the one case the individual has not that for which he strives, and history is the strife in which he acquires it. In the second case the individual has that for which he strives, yet cannot come into possession of it because there is constantly something external which hinders him from doing so, and history is, then, the strife in which he triumphs over these hindrances. The second kind of history begins with possession, and history is the development through which one acquires possession. Since in the first case history is external and that towards which it strives lies outside, it has not true reality, and the poetic and artistic representation does quite right in shortening history and hastening on to the intensive moment. To stick to the subject which we have more particularly in hand, let us think of romantic love. Imagine, then, a knight who has slain five wild boars, four dragons, and delivered three enchanted princes, brothers of the princess whom he worships. In the romantic chain of reasoning this has complete reality. To the artist and the poet, however, it is of no importance at all whether there are five or only four monsters slain. The artist is, on the whole, more restricted than the poet, but even the latter will not be interested in relating circumstantially how the hero accomplished the destruction of each individual wild boar. He hastens on to the moment. He perhaps reduces the number, concentrates the toils and dangers with poetic intensity, and hastens on to the moment, the moment of possession. To him the whole historical succession is of comparatively little importance.

Where, however, it is a question of internal history, every little moment is of the utmost importance. Internal history is the only true history; but true history contends with that which is the life principle of history, i.e., with time. But when one contends with time, then the temporal and every little moment of it acquires for this fact immense reality. Whenever the internal process of blossoming in the individual has not yet begun and the individual is shut, there can only be external history. On the other hand, as soon as this blossoming, so to speak, springs out, internal history begins. Think now of the theme with which we started, the difference between the conquering and the possessive natures. The conquering nature is constantly outside himself, the possessive nature within himself; hence, the former has external history, the latter has internal history. But since external history is the one kind of history which can without detriment be concentrated, it is natural that art and poetry choose this especially for representation, and hence, choose likewise the unopened individual and everything that has to do with him. It is said, indeed, that love opens the individual, but this is not true when love is conceived as it is in romances. There the individual is merely brought to the point where he will open—with that it ends; or he is about to open but is interrupted. But since external history and the shut individuality will remain more especially the subjects for artistic and poetic representation, so, too, will everything which goes to compose the content of such an individuality be preferred. But substantially this is what belongs to the natural man. Here are a few examples. Pride can very well be represented, for the essential point in pride is not succession but intensity in the moment. Humility is represented with difficulty, because here if anywhere we are dealing with succession, and whereas the beholder needs only to see pride in its culmination, in the other instance he properly requires what poetry and art cannot give, i.e., to see humility in its constant process of being, for it is essential to humility that it constantly remains, and when it is shown in its ideal moment the beholder senses the lack of something, because he feels that its true ideality does not consist in the fact that it is ideal in the moment but that it is constant. Romantic love can very well be represented in the moment, but conjugal love cannot, because an ideal husband is not one who is such once in his life but one who every day is such. If I would represent a hero who conquers kingdoms and lands, it can very well be represented in the moment, but a cross-bearer who every day takes up his cross cannot be represented either in poetry or in art, because the point is that he does it every day. If I would imagine a hero who stakes his life, it can very well be concentrated in the moment, but not the business of dying daily, for here the principal point is that it occurs every day. Courage can very well be concentrated in the moment, but not patience, precisely for the reason that patience strives with time. You will say that after all art has represented Christ as the image of patience, bearing all the sin of the world, and that religious poetry has concentrated all the bitterness of life in one cup and let one individual drain it in one moment. That is true, but it is because this has been almost spatially concentrated. The man, however, who really knows a little about patience knows very well that it does not properly stand opposed to the intensity of suffering (for with that it rather approaches courage) but to time, and that the true patience is that which is seen to be contending with time, or is properly long-suffering. But long-suffering cannot be represented artistically, for the point of it is incommensurable with art; neither can it be poetized, for it requires the long, protracted tedium of time.

Now what I would further say to you here you may regard as the lowly offering which a poor married man makes at the altar of aesthetics, and though you and all the priests of aesthetics should disdain it, I shall, for all that, know how to console myself, and that all the more because the offering I bring is not showbread,[37] which may be eaten only by priests, but homemade bread, which like all domestic cookery is simple and not highly spiced, but wholesome and nourishing.

When one follows, either dialectically or historically, the development of the aesthetically beautiful, one will find that the direction of this movement is away from spatial determinants to those of time, and that the perfection of art depends upon the successive possibility of detaching oneself from space and orienting oneself towards time. In this consists the transition and the significance of the transition from sculpture to painting, as Schelling has recently pointed out.[38] Music has time as its element, but it gains no permanent place in it; its significance lies in its constant vanishing in time; it emits sounds in time, but at once it vanishes and has no permanence. Finally, poetry is the highest of all arts and is therefore the art which knows best how to set off to advantage the significance of time. It does not need to confine itself to the moment the way painting does, neither does it vanish as music does, but nevertheless, it is compelled, as we have seen, to concentrate in the moment. Hence, it has limits, and (as was shown above) it cannot represent that which has its reality in temporal succession. And yet the fact that the significance of time is stressed does not decrease the aesthetic effect; on the contrary, the aesthetic ideal becomes richer and fuller in proportion as the importance of time is duly emphasized. How, then, can the aesthetic be represented, seeing that it is incommensurable even with poetry? Answer: by living it. It thereby acquires a resemblance to music, which *is* merely because it is constantly repeated, existing merely in the instant of execution. For this reason I called attention above to the pernicious confusion of the aesthetic with whatever can be presented in the form of poetic reproduction. For example, everything I am talking about here can of course be presented aesthetically, not, however, in the form of poetic reproduction, but in the fact that one lives it, puts it into effect in real life. It is in this way aesthetics is neutralized and reconciled with life; for though in one sense poetry and art are a reconciliation with life, yet in another sense they are at enmity with it because they reconcile only one side of the soul. Here I have reached the highest concept of the aesthetic. And truly he who has enough humility and courage to let himself be transfigured to this degree; who feels that he is, as it were, a character in the drama which the Deity composes, where the poet and the prompter are not different persons, where the individual, like a practiced actor who has lived himself into his part and into his lines, is not disturbed by the prompter but feels that what is whispered to him is what he himself would say, so that it almost becomes doubtful whether he puts the words in the prompter's mouth or the prompter in his; he who in the deepest sense feels that he is poet and poetized, who at the moment he feels himself to be the poet possesses the primitive pathos of the lines, at the moment he feels himself poetized has the erotic ear which picks up every sound—that man, and that man alone, has realized the highest ideal of aesthetics. But this history which proves to be incommensurable even with poetry is internal history. It has the idea in itself, and precisely for this reason it is aesthetic. It begins, therefore, with possession, as I expressed it, and its progress is the acquisition of this possession. It is an eternity in which the temporal has not vanished like an ideal moment, but in which it is constantly present as a real moment. When patience thus acquires itself in patience we have inward or interior history.

Let us now glance at the relation between romantic and conjugal love—for the relation between the natures made for conquest and for possession offers no difficulty at all. Romantic love remains constantly abstract in itself, and, if it is able to acquire no external history, death already is lying in wait for it, because its eternity is illusory. Conjugal love begins with possession and acquires inward history. It is faithful. So is romantic love—but now note the difference. The faithful romantic lover waits, let us say, for fifteen years—then comes the instant which rewards him. Here poetry sees very rightly that the fifteen years can very well be concentrated. It hastens on, then, to the moment. A married man is faithful for fifteen years, yet during those fifteen years he has had possession, so in that long succession of time he has continuously acquired the faithfulness he possessed, since after all conjugal love contains within itself first love and by the same token the fidelity thereof. But such an ideal marriage cannot be represented, for the point is time in its extension. At the end of the fifteen years he has apparently got no further than he was at the beginning, yet he has lived in a high degree aesthetically. His possession has not been like dead property, but he has constantly been acquiring his possession. He has not fought with lions and ogres, but with the most dangerous enemy: with time. But for him eternity does not come afterwards as in the case of the knight, but he has had eternity in time, has preserved eternity in time. He alone, therefore, has triumphed over time; for one can say of the knight that he has killed time, as indeed a man constantly wishes to kill time when it has no reality for him. But this is never the perfect victory. The married man, being a true conqueror, has not killed time but has saved it and preserved it in eternity. The married man who does this, truly lives poetically. He solves the great riddle of living in eternity and yet hearing the hall clock strike, and hearing it in such a way that the stroke of the hour does not shorten but prolongs his eternity—a contradiction as profound but far more glorious than the situation[39] described in a well-known tale of the Middle Ages which tells of an unhappy man that he awoke in hell and cried out, "What time is it?" and the devil answered, "Eternity." And now even if this is something which cannot be represented in art, let it be your comfort as it is mine that the highest and most beautiful things in life are not to be heard about, nor read about, nor seen, but, if one will, may be lived. When, then, I willingly admit that romantic love lends itself more aptly to artistic representation than does conjugal love, this is not by any means to say that the latter is less aesthetic than the former; on the contrary, it is more aesthetic. In one of the tales of the Romantic School[40] which evinces the greatest genius, there is one character who has no desire to write poetry like the others among whom he lives, because it is a waste of time and deprives him of the true enjoyment—he prefers to live. Now if he had had the right conception of what it is to live, he would have been the man for me.

Conjugal love has its foe in time, its triumph in time, its eternity in time, and so it would have its problems, even if I were to imagine it free from all the so-called external and internal trials. Generally, it has these too; but if one were to interpret them rightly, one must observe two things: that these trials are constantly inward determinants; and that they constantly have in them the determinant of time. It is easy to see that for this reason, too, conjugal love cannot be represented. It constantly drags itself back inwardly, and (to use the expression in a good sense) it constantly drags along in time; but what is to be represented by reproduction must let itself be lured out, and its time must be capable of abbreviation. You may convince yourself of this more thoroughly by considering the predicates commonly applied to conjugal love. It is faithful, constant, humble, patient, long-suffering, indulgent, sincere, contented, vigilant, willing, joyful. All these virtues have the characteristic that they are inward qualifications of the individual. The individual is not fighting with external foes but fights with himself, fights out love from within him. And they have reference to time, for their truth does not consist in being once for all but in being constantly what they are. And by these virtues nothing else is acquired, only they themselves are acquired. Conjugal love, therefore, is not only what you, mockingly, have often called it: an everyday occurrence; but is also, at the same time, the divine (in the Greek sense); and it is the divine by reason of its being an occurrence every day. Conjugal love does not come with any outward sign, like "the rich bird"[41] with whizzing and bluster, but it is the imperishable nature of a quiet spirit.

Of this fact you and all natures born for conquest have no conception. You are never in yourselves, but constantly outside yourselves. Yea, so long as every nerve in you is aquiver, whether when you are stealing softly about, or when you step out boldly and Janizary music within you drowns out your consciousness—then you feel that you are living. But when the battle is won, when the last echo of the last shot has died away, when the swift thoughts, like a staff officer hurrying back to headquarters, report that the victory is yours—then, in fact, you know nothing more, you know not how to begin; for then, for the first time you are at the true beginning.

What you, therefore, under the name of custom abhor as unavoidable in marriage is merely the historical factor in it, which in your perverted eye acquires such a terrifying aspect.

But what is this thing you are accustomed to think of as not merely annihilated but profaned by the "custom" which is inseparable from conjugal love? Generally you think of what you call "the visible sacred symbol of the erotic," which, as you say, "like all signs or tokens, has in itself no importance but depends for its significance upon the energy, the artistic bravura and virtuosity, themselves proofs of inborn genius, with which it is executed." "How disgusting it is," you say, "to see the languor with which such things are performed in married life, how perfunctorily, how sluggishly it is done, almost at the stroke of the clock—pretty much as among the tribe the Jesuits discovered in Paraguay, which was so sluggish that the Jesuits found it necessary to ring a bell at midnight as a welcome notice to all husbands, to remind them thereby of their marital duties. So everything is done on time, as they are trained to do it." Let us at this point agree that in our meditation we shall not let ourselves be disturbed by the fact that there is a great deal to be seen in existence which is ludicrous and preposterous; let us simply see whether it is necessary, and, if so, learn from you the way of salvation. In this respect I dare not expect much from you; for like the Spanish knight of the doleful countenance you are fighting, though in a different sense, for a vanished time. For as you are fighting for the moment against time, you actually are fighting for what has vanished. Let us take an idea, an expression, from your poetic world, or from the real world of first love: "the lovers *look* at one another." You know very well how to underscore this word "look" and to put into it an infinite reality, an eternity. In this sense a married couple who have lived together for ten years and

seen one another daily cannot "look" at one another. But
might they not therefore be able to look lovingly at one
another? Now here we have again your old heresy. You
have got to the point of limiting love to a certain age, and
limiting love for one person to a very short period of time.
Thereupon, like all conquering natures, you seek recruits
in order to carry out your experiment—but this, indeed, is
the very deepest profanation of the eternal power of love.
This, indeed, is despair. However you turn and twist, you
must admit that the gist of the matter is to preserve love
in time. If this is impossible, then love is an impossibility.
Your misfortune is that you recognize love simply and
solely by these visible signs. If they are to be repeated
again and again, and must be accompanied, you are to note,
by a morbid reflection as to whether they continually possess the reality they once had by reason of the accidental
circumstance that it was the first time, it is no wonder you
are alarmed and that you associate these signs and "gesticulations" with things of which one dare not say *decies
repetita placebunt;*[42] for if that which gives them value was
the characteristic qualification "the first time," a repetition
is indeed impossible. But healthy love has an entirely different worth; it is in time it accomplishes its work, and
therefore, it will be capable of rejuvenating itself by means
of these outward signs, and (what to me is the principal
thing) it has an entirely different conception of time and
of the significance of repetition.

I have shown in the foregoing discussion that conjugal
love has its conflict in time, its victory in time, its blessing
in time. I then regarded time merely as simple progression;
now I shall show that it is not merely a simple progression
in which the original datum is preserved, but a growing
progression in which the original datum increases. You with
your great powers of observation will certainly grant that
I am right in making the general observation that men are
divided into two great classes: those who predominantly
live in hope; and those who predominantly live in recollection. Both have a wrong relation to time. The healthy individual lives at once both in hope and in recollection,
and only thereby does his life acquire true and substantial

continuity. So, then, he has hope and does not will, like those who live off of recollection, to return backward in time. What, then, does recollection do for him? For, after all, some influence it surely must have. It sets a cross over the note of the instant—the further back recollection goes, and the more frequent the repetition, the more crosses there are. Thus, if in the present year the individual experiences an erotic moment, this is enhanced by the fact that he recollects one the year before, etc. In a beautiful way this has also found expression in married life. I do not know in what age the world now finds itself, but you know as well as I that people are accustomed to say that first comes the golden age, then the silver age, then the copper age, then the iron age. In marriage this is inverted: first comes the silver wedding, then the golden wedding. Is not recollection really the point of such a wedding? And yet the marriage terminology declares that this is still more beautiful than the first wedding. Now you must not misunderstand this— as you would do, for instance, if you might be pleased to say, "Then it would be best to get married in the cradle in order to begin promptly with one's silver wedding and have hope of being the first inventor of a brand-new term in the vocabulary of married life." You yourself presumably perceive the fallacy of your witticism, and I shall not dwell upon it any further. What I would remind you of, how-ever, is that the individuals are in fact not merely living in hope; they constantly have in the present both the one and the other, both hope and recollection. At the first wedding hope has the same effect that recollection has at the last. Hope hovers over them as the hope of eternity which fills the moment to the brim. You also will perceive the correct-ness of this when you reflect that if one were to marry merely in the hope of a silver wedding, and then hoped and hoped again for twenty-five years, one would be in no state to celebrate the silver wedding when the twenty-fifth year came around, for indeed, one would have noth-ing to recollect, since with all this hoping everything would have fallen apart. Moreover, it has often occurred to me to wonder why, according to the universal usage and way of thinking, the state of single blessedness has no such brilliant prospects, that on the contrary, people rather turn it to ridicule when a bachelor celebrates a jubilee. The reason, doubtless, is that in general it is assumed that the single state never can rightly grasp the true present, which is a unity of hope and recollection, and that therefore, bachelors are for the most part addicted either to hope or to recollection. But this again suggests the correct relation to time which common estimation also attributes to conjugal love.

There is also something else, however, in married life which you characterize by the word custom: "its monotony," you say, "the total lack of events, its everlasting vacuity, which is death and worse than death." You know that there are neurasthenics who may be disturbed by the slightest noise, who are unable to think when someone is walking softly across the floor. Have you observed that there is also another sort of neurasthenia? There are people so weak that they need loud noise and a distracting environment in order to be able to work. Why is this, unless for the fact that they have no command over themselves, except in an inverse sense? When they are alone their thoughts disappear in the indefinite; on the other hand, when there is noise and hubbub around them, this compels them to pit their will against it. It is for this reason you are afraid of peace and quietness and repose. You are within yourself only when there is opposition, but therefore you are never within yourself. That is to say, the moment you assimilate opposition there is quiet again. Therefore, you do not dare to do so. But then you and the opposition remain standing face to face, and so you are not within yourself.

The same thing, of course, applies here which we noted earlier in the case of time. You are outside yourself and therefore cannot dispense with the other as an opposition; you believe that only a restless spirit is alive, and all men of experience think that only a quiet spirit is truly alive; for you, an agitated sea is the image of life, for me it is still deep waters. Often I have sat by a bit of purling water. It is always the same, the same soft melody, the same green plants on its floor, swaying beneath its quiet waves, the same little creatures running about at the bottom, a little fish which glides under the protection of the overhanging flowers, spreading out its fins against the current, hiding under a stone. How monotonous, and yet how rich in change! Such is the home life of marriage: quiet, modest, purling—it has not many *changements,* and yet like that water it purls, yet like that water it has melody, dear to the man who knows it, dear to him above all other sounds because he knows it. It makes no pompous display, and yet sometimes there is shed over it a luster which does not interrupt its customary course, like as when the moonbeams fall upon that water and reveal the instrument upon which it plays its melody. Such is the home life of marriage. But in order to be seen thus and to be lived thus it presupposes the one quality which I shall mention to you. I find it mentioned in a poem by Oehlenschläger[43] upon which, at least in time gone by, I know you set great store. For the sake of completeness I shall transcribe the whole of it:

> How much must come together in the world
> That love's enchantment may be brought to pass!
> First the two hearts which know each other well,
> Then charm which doth accompany them both,
> The moon then casting its bewitching beams
> Through the beech forests in the early spring,
> Then that these two can meet there all alone—
> Then the first kiss—and then . . . their innocence.

You, too, are given to eulogizing love. I will not deprive you of that which is not indeed your property, for it is the property of the poet, but which, nevertheless, you have appropriated; but since I too have appropriated it, let us share it—you get the whole poem, I the last words: "their innocence."

Finally, there is still another side to married life which has often given you occasion for attack. You say, "Conjugal love conceals in itself something quite different. It seems so mild and heartfelt and tender, but as soon as the door is closed behind the married pair, then before you can say Jack Robinson out comes the rod called duty. You may deck out this scepter as much as you will, you can make it into a Shrovetide rod, it still remains a rod."[44] I deal with this

objection here because it also is due essentially to a misunderstanding of the historical factor in conjugal love. You
would have it that either obscure powers or caprice are the
constituent factors of love. As soon as consciousness comes
forward to join them this enchantment vanishes. But this
consciousness is conjugal love. To express it quite crudely
—in place of the baton with which the director of the or-
chestra indicates the tempo for the graceful attitudes assumed in the dance of first love, you show us the unpleasant
stick of the policeman. First of all you must concede to
me that so long as there is no alteration in first love (and
this, we have agreed, is contained in conjugal love) there
can be no question of the strict necessity of duty. So the
fact is you do not believe in the eternity of first love. Here
we are back again at your old heresy: it is you who so
often set yourself up as the knight of first love, and yet you
do not believe in it, yea, you profane it. So because you
do not believe in it you dare not enter into an alliance
which, when you no longer are *volens* may compel you
nolens to remain in it. For you, therefore, love is obviously
not the highest thing, for otherwise you would be glad there
was a power capable of compelling you to remain in it. You
will, perhaps, make answer that this remedy is no remedy;
but to that I will remark that it depends upon how one
looks at the matter.

This is one of the points to which we constantly return
—you, as it seems, against your will and without being quite
clear what it involves, I with full consciousness of its significance: the point, namely, that the illusory or naïve
eternity of first or romantic love cancels itself out, in one
way or another. Just because you try to retain love in this
immediate form, try to make yourself believe that true
freedom consists in being outside oneself, intoxicated by
dreams, therefore you fear the metamorphosis, not regarding it as such but as something altogether heterogeneous
which implies the death of first love, and hence your abhorrence of duty. For, of course, if duty has not already
subsisted as a germ in first love, it is absolutely disturbing
when it makes its appearance. But such is not the case with
conjugal love. Already in the ethical and religious factors

it has duty in it, and when this appears before it, it is not as a stranger, a shameless intruder, who nevertheless has such authority that one dare not by virtue of the mysteriousness of love show him the door. No, duty comes as an old friend, an intimate, a confidant, whom the lovers mutually recognize in the deepest secret of their love. And when he speaks, it is nothing new he has to say; and when he has spoken, the individuals humble themselves under it, but at the same time are uplifted just because they are assured that what he enjoins is what they themselves wish, and that his commanding it is merely a more majestic, a more exalted, a divine way of expressing the fact that their wish can be realized. It would not have been enough if he had encouraged them by saying, "It can be done, love can be preserved," but when he says, "It shall be preserved," there is in that an authority which answers to the heartfelt desire of love. Love drives out fear; but yet when love is for a moment fearful for itself, fearful of its own salvation, duty is the divine nutriment love stands in need of; for it says, "Fear not, you shall conquer," speaking not futuristically, for that only suggests hope, but imperatively, and in this lies an assurance which nothing can shake.

So then you regard duty as the enemy of love; I regard it as its friend. You will, perhaps, be content at hearing this declaration, and with your customary mockery will congratulate me on such an interesting and uncommon friend. I, on the other hand, will by no means be satisfied with this reply but will take the liberty of carrying the war into your own territory. If duty, once it has appeared in consciousness, is an enemy of love, then love must do its best to conquer it; for you, after all, would not think of love as a being so impotent that it cannot vanquish every opposition. On the other hand, you think that when duty makes its appearance it is all over with love, and you think also that duty, early or late, must make its appearance, not merely in conjugal love but also in romantic love; and the truth is that you are afraid of conjugal love because it has in it duty to such a degree that when it makes its appearance you cannot run away from it. In romantic love, on the other hand, you think this is all right, for as soon as the instant arrives when duty is mentioned, love is over, and the arrival of duty is the signal for you, with a very courtly bow, to say farewell. Here you see again what your eulogies of love amount to. If duty is the enemy of love, and if love cannot vanquish this enemy, then love is not the true conqueror. The consequence is that you must leave love in the lurch. When once you have got the desperate idea that duty is the enemy of love, your defeat is certain, and you have done just as much to disparage love and deprive it of its majesty as you have done to show despite of duty, and yet it was only the latter you meant to do. You see, this again is despair, whether you feel the pain of it or seek in despair to forget it. If you cannot reach the point of seeing the aesthetical, the ethical and the religious as three great allies, if you do not know how to conserve the unity of the diverse appearances which everything assumes in these diverse spheres, then life is devoid of meaning, then one must grant that you are justified in maintaining your pet theory that one can say of everything, "Do it or don't do it—you will regret both."

Now I am not, like you, under the tragic necessity of having to begin a campaign against duty which cannot but have an unfortunate ending. For me, duty is not one climate and love another, but for me duty makes love the true temperate climate, and for me love makes duty the true temperate climate, and perfection consists in this unity. However, to make the falsity of your doctrine thoroughly evident, I will pursue this theme a little longer, begging you to reflect upon the various ways in which one might feel that duty is the enemy of love.

Imagine a man who had become a husband without ever having taken seriously into account the ethical factor in marriage. He loved with the whole passion of youth, and then suddenly was moved by an outward occasion to doubt whether it was not possible that she whom he loved, but to whom also he was tied by a bond of duty, might not think that he loved her after all only because it was his duty. You see that he was in a position like that of the man previously mentioned, to him, too, duty seemed to be in opposition to love; but he was in love, and for him love was truly the highest thing, and hence, his effort would be to overcome this enemy. So he would love her, not because duty prescribed it, not in the scant measure of a *quantum satis* which is all that duty can enjoin, but he would love her with all his soul and with all his strength and with all his might, he would love her even at the moment when (if such a thing were possible) duty bade him desist. You can easily see the confusion in his train of thought. What did he do? He loved her with his whole soul—but this, indeed, is just what duty enjoins. For let us not be confused by the talk of those who have the notion that duty is only a congeries of ceremonial prescriptions. Duty is only one: to love truly with the inward movement of the heart; and duty is as protean in its forms as is love itself, and it pronounces everything good when it is of love, and denounces everything, however beautiful and specious it may be, if it is not of love. You see that this man, too, has assumed an incorrect attitude; but just because there was truth in him he does —although not willing to do only that—just what duty enjoins, neither more nor less. In a way he does more, for the fact that he *does* it; for the "more" which I find it possible for me to do is just this, that I am able actually to do what duty enjoins. Duty commands—more than that it cannot do. The "more" which I am capable of doing is to do what it commands, and the instant I do this I can in a certain sense say that I am doing "more." Translate duty from the external to the internal, and with that I am well beyond duty. You see from this what infinite harmony and wisdom and consistency there is in the world of spirit. When a man starts from a definite point and calmly pursues his path with truth and energy, it must always be an illusion when everything else seems to be in contradiction to it; and when someone believes he has thoroughly demonstrated discord, he has demonstrated harmony. Therefore, the husband we spoke about got off easily, and the only punishment he had to suffer was that duty made a bit of fun of him for his "little faith." Duty constantly chimes in with love. If you separate them, as that man did, and make one part the whole, you are constantly in self-contradiction. It is as if in the word "be" a man were to separate "b" and "e" and so would have no "e" but would maintain that "b" was the whole. The moment he pronounces it he utters the "e" along with it. So it is with true love: it is not a dumb and un-utterable letter, but neither is it a soft and inapprehensible indefiniteness. It is an articulate sound, a letter. Is duty hard? *Eh bien,* then love pronounces it, it realizes it, and thereby does more than its duty. Is love by way of becom-ing so soft that it cannot be held fast? Well then, duty im-poses upon it boundaries.

Now if you were in the same case as that man we have been talking about, if your notion that duty is the enemy of love were only an innocent misunderstanding, things would turn out with you as fortunately as they did with him. But your interpretation, though no doubt it is a mis-understanding, is a guilty misunderstanding. Hence it is that you disparage not only duty but also love, hence it is that duty appears to be an insuperable enemy. For duty loves only true love and has a mortal hatred of false love and slays it. The individuals, if they are in the truth, will see in duty merely the eternal expression of the fact that the path into eternity is prepared for them, that the path in which they would gladly walk they not only are per-mitted to take but are commanded to take, and that over this path there watches a divine providence which con-stantly points out to them the prospect and sets up warn-ing signs at all perilous places. The man who loves, why should he be unwilling to accept a divine authorization just because it is expressed divinely and does not say merely, "You may" but "Thou shalt"? By duty the way is cleared for the lovers, and I believe it is for this reason that duty is expressed by the future tense, to suggest its historical implication.

Now I am through with this little exposition. Presumably it has made an impression upon you, you have a feeling that everything is inverted, and you cannot harden yourself against the logical consistency with which I have spoken. If I had said all this to you, however, in a conversation, you would likely have found difficulty in refraining from the sarcastic remark that I am preachifying. But you can-not properly accuse my presentation of suffering from this fault or of being what it perhaps ought to be when one is speaking to such a hardened sinner as you. And as for your effusions, your wisdom, they not too infrequently recall to mind the Book of the Preacher, Ecclesiastes, and really, one might suppose that occasionally you choose your texts from it.

But I will let you provide me with an occasion for illuminating this matter. For the fact is, you do not generally make light of ethics, and one has first to drive you to a certain point before you throw it overboard. As long as you possibly can you keep it on your side. "I by no means despise duty"—in this way your milder effusions commonly begin, the more refined assassination of duty. "Far from it. But above all, let us have pure bread in the bag, as they say: duty is duty, love is love. Period! Above all, no mixing things up. Or is not marriage the only abortion of this kind, with this hermaphroditic ambiguity? All else is either duty or love. I recognize that it is a man's duty to seek a definite profession in life, I regard it as his duty to be faithful to his calling, and, on the other hand, when he violates his duty he suffers well-deserved punishment. Here is duty. I undertake something definite, I can state precisely what it is, I promise to perform it dutifully—if I do not, I am confronted by a power which is able to compel me. On the other hand, if I attach myself closely in friendship to another person, love is everything in this case, I recognize no duty; if love is at an end, then friendship is over. It is reserved for marriage alone to base itself upon such an absurdity. What after all does it mean to pledge oneself to love? Where are the limits? When have I fulfilled my duty? How is my duty exactly defined? To what judicial board shall I appeal in case of doubt? And if I do not fulfil my duty, where is the power which will compel me? The State and the Church, it is true, have established certain limits; but even though I do not overstep them, may I not be a bad husband? Who will punish me? Who will defend her who suffers under it?" The answer is: you yourself.

However, before I go on to resolve the confusion in which you have ensnared yourself and me, I must make one observation. There is often in your statements a certain de-

gree of ambiguity, which to you is essential and characteristic. What you say might be said as well by the most
light-minded and the most heavy-minded of men. You know
this very well, for it is one of the expedients you employ
to swindle people. You say the same thing at various times,
putting the emphasis at different places, and, lo, the whole
thing turns out to be different! If someone objects that you
are saying something different from what you said once before, you calmly reply, "Isn't it word for word the same?"
But enough of this! Let us see how it stands with your
classification. There is a proverbial expression preserved
through the centuries, characterizing the shrewd policy of
the Romans: *divide et impera.* With a far profounder significance one can apply this to the operation of the human
understanding, for its cunning policy is to divide and by
thus dividing to assure itself of the mastery, seeing that the
powers which would be invincible as allies cancel one another when they are separated and hostile. So your notion
is that all the rest of life can be construed under the category of duty, or under its opposite, and that it never has
occurred to anybody to apply a different criterion, marriage
alone being guilty of this contradiction. You adduce professional duty as an example and think that it is an apt example of a relationship in which duty alone is involved.
This, however, is by no means the case. For if a man were
to conceive of his profession as merely the sum total of ap-
pointments he had to keep at definite times and places, he
would debase himself and his calling and his duty. Or do
you think that such a view would make a man a good civil
functionary? What place would be left for the enthusiasm
with which one sanctifies one's calling, what room for the
devotion with which one loves it? Or what judicial forum
could keep check on him? Or is not this love and enthusiasm
required of him precisely as a duty? And would not every
man who assumed an office without these qualities be regarded by the State as a hireling, whose toil and moil it
might indeed use and reward, though in another sense he
was an unworthy official? If the State does not say this expressly, it is because what it demands is something external,
something tangible, and when that is performed, the other

is assumed. On the other hand, the main point in marriage is inwardness, which can neither be seen nor pointed out—but of this the precise expression is love. Hence I see no contradiction in requiring love as a duty; for the fact that no one can check up on it has nothing to do with the case, seeing that the man can keep check on himself. If you continue, then, to demand this external control, it is either because you want to shirk duty, or because you are so fearful for yourself that you would have yourself declared legally incompetent—but that is just as wrong and unacceptable as the other.

If you hold fast what I have set forth in the foregoing treatise, just as I have expounded it, you will easily perceive that in holding fast to the inwardness of duty in love I have not done so with the wild alarm which sometimes is displayed by men in whom prosaic common sense has first annihilated the feelings of immediacy and who, then, in their old age have betaken themselves to duty, men who in their blindness cannot express strongly enough their scorn of the purely natural, nor stupidly enough sing the praise of duty—as though with this it was different from what you call it. Of such a breach between love and duty I, thank God, know nothing; I have not fled with my love into wild regions and deserts where in my loneliness I return to savagery, neither have I asked all my neighbors what I should do. Such isolation and such participation are equally mad. I have constantly had *impressa vestigia* before me, even in the universally valid sphere which is duty. I have also felt that there are instants when the only salvation is to let duty speak, that it is wholesome to let it punish me. I have felt this not with the melancholy effeminacy of a *heautontimoroumenos*,[45] but with all seriousness and emphasis. But I have not been afraid of duty; it has not appeared before me as an enemy which would disturb the bit of happiness and joy I had hoped to preserve through life, rather it has appeared before me as a friend, the first and only confidant of our love. But this power of having constantly a free outlook is the blessing bestowed by duty, whereas romantic love goes astray or comes to an impasse because of its unhistorical character.

Dixi et animam meam liberavi[46]—not as though my soul
had been entangled hitherto, and now in this prolix ex-
pectoration had found vent. No, this is merely a wholesome
respiration in which I have enjoyed my freedom. *Respiration* is a word which indicates the flowing back of that
which first had flowed out. In respiration the organism enjoys its freedom, and so have I in this letter enjoyed my
freedom, the freedom I have every day.

So may you accept with a well-prepared mind the well-
tested gift I offer you. If you should find it far too small a
thing to satisfy you, then see if it might not be possible to
prepare yourself better, see whether you have not forgotten
some precautionary measure. The Serbs have a popular
legend[47] about a prodigious giant who had an appetite
just as prodigious. He came to a poor cottager and wanted
to share his midday meal. The cottager placed on the table
the little his humble house afforded. The giant's greedy eye
had already devoured it all, and had likely made the observation that he would not have been any better fed if he
had actually eaten it up. They seated themselves. It never
occurred to the cottager that there might not be enough
for both. The giant reached for the dish. The cottager
stopped him by saying, "It is the custom in my house to
say a prayer first." The giant submitted to it—and, lo, there
was enough for both.

Dixi et animam meam liberavi—for I have liberated her,
also, whom I love with the youthful enthusiasm of first
love. Not as though she had previously been bound, but
she has rejoiced with me in our freedom.

When you receive my affectionate greetings receive also,
as you commonly do, a greeting from her, as kindly and
cordial as ever.

It is a long time since I have seen you *chez nous*. I can
say this both in a literal and in a figurative sense. For during the fortnight I have employed my evenings *instar
omnium* in writing this letter I have constantly seen you
beside me; yet even in a figurative sense I cannot properly
say that I have seen you *chez nous*, i.e., in my house, in my
room, but rather outside my door where with my reproaches
I have driven you. On my part this has not been a dis-

agreeable task nor unkindly meant, and I am sure you will not take it amiss. However, it will be still more agreeable to me to see you frequently *chez nous*, both in a literal and a figurative sense. I say this with all the pride of a husband who feels himself entitled to use the formula *chez nous;* I say it with all the humane respect which every person may always be sure of encountering *chez nous*. Accept, therefore, an invitation for next Sunday—not a family invitation which reads "forever" and means a whole day—come when you will, sure of being always welcome; stay as long as you will, being always an acceptable guest; leave when you will, always with God's speed.

EQUILIBRIUM
BETWEEN THE AESTHETICAL
AND THE ETHICAL
IN THE COMPOSITION
OF PERSONALITY

My Friend,

What I have so often said to you I say now once again, or rather I shout it: Either/or, *aut/aut*. For a single *aut* adjoined as a rectification does not make the situation clear, since the question here at issue is so important that one cannot rest satisfied with a part of it, and in itself it is too coherent to be possessed partially. There are situations in life where it would be ridiculous or a species of madness to apply an either/or; but also, there are men whose souls are too dissolute (in the etymological sense of the word) to grasp what is implied in such a dilemma, whose personalities lack the energy to say with pathos, Either/or. Upon me these words have always made a deep impression, and they still do, especially when I pronounce them absolutely and without specific reference to any objects, for this use of them suggests the possibility of starting the most dreadful contrasts into action. They affect me like a magic formula of incantation, and my soul becomes exceeding serious, sometimes almost harrowed. I think of my early youth, when without clearly comprehending what it is to make a choice I listened with childish trust to the talk of my elders and the instant of choice was solemn and venerable, although in choosing I was only following the instructions of another person. I think of the occasions in my later life when I stood at the crossways, when my soul was matured in the hour of decision. I think of the many occasions in life less important but by no means indifferent to me, when it was a question of making a choice. For although there is only one situation in which either/or has absolute significance, namely, when truth, righteousness and holiness are lined up on one side, and lust and base propensities and obscure passions and perdition on the other; yet, it is always important to choose rightly, even as between things which one may innocently choose; it is important to test oneself, lest some day one might have to beat a painful retreat to the point from which one started, and might have reason to thank God if one had to reproach oneself for nothing worse than a waste of time. In common parlance I use these words as others use them, and it would indeed be a foolish pedantry to give up using them. But sometimes it occurs, nevertheless, that I become aware of using them with regard to things entirely indifferent. Then they lay aside their humble dress, I forget the insignificant thoughts they discriminated, they advance to meet me with all their dignity, in their official robes. As a magistrate in common life may appear in plain clothes and mingle without distinction in the crowd, so do these words mingle in common speech—when, however, the magistrate steps forward with authority he distinguishes himself from all. Like such a magistrate whom I am accustomed to see only on solemn occasions, these words appear before me, and my soul always becomes serious. And although my life now has to a certain degree its either/or behind it, yet I know well that it may still encounter many a situation where the either/or will have its full significance. I hope, however, that these words may find me in a worthy state of mind when they check me on my path, and I hope that I may be successful in choosing the right course; at all events, I shall endeavor to make the choice with real earnestness, and with that I venture, at least, to hope that I shall the sooner get out of the wrong path.

And now as for you—this phrase is only too often on your lips, it has almost become a byword with you. What significance has it for you? None at all. You, according to your own expression, regard it as a wink of the eye, a snap of the fingers, a *coup de main*, an abracadabra. At every opportunity you know how to introduce it, nor is it without effect; for it affects you as strong drink affects a neurasthenic, you become completely intoxicated by what you call the higher madness. "It is the compendium," you say, "of all practical wisdom, but no one has ever inculcated it so pithily (like a god in the form of a puppet talking to suffering humanity) as that great thinker and true practical philosopher who said to a man who had insulted him by pulling off his hat and throwing it on the floor, 'If you pick it up, you'll get a thrashing; if you don't pick it up, you'll also get a thrashing; now you can choose.'" You take great delight in "comforting" people when they have recourse to you in critical situations. You listen to their exposition of the case and then say, "Yes, I perceive perfectly that there are two possibilities, one can either do this or that. My sincere opinion and my friendly counsel is as follows: Do it/or don't do it—you will regret both." But he who mocks others mocks himself, and your rejoinder is not a mere nothing but a profound mockery of yourself, a sorry proof how limp your soul is, that your whole philosophy of life is concentrated in one single proposition, "I say merely either/or." In case this really were your serious meaning, there would be nothing one could do with you, one must simply put up with you as you are and deplore the fact that melancholy [literally, heavy-mindedness] or light-mindedness had enfeebled your spirit. Now on the contrary, since one knows very well that such is not the case, one is not tempted to pity you but rather to wish that some day the circumstances of your life may tighten upon you the screws in its rack and compel you to come out with what really dwells in you, may begin the sharper inquisition of the rack which cannot be beguiled by nonsense and witticisms. Life is a masquerade, you explain, and for you this is inexhaustible material for amusement; and so far, no one has succeeded in knowing you; for every revelation you make is always an illusion, it is only in this way you are able to breathe and prevent people from pressing importunately upon you and obstructing your respiration. Your occupation consists in preserving your hiding-place, and that you succeed in doing, for your mask is the most enigmatical of all. In fact you are nothing; you are merely a relation to others, and what you are you are by virtue of this relation. To a fond shepherdess you hold out a languishing hand, and instantly you are masked in all possible bucolic sentimentality. A reverend spiritual father you deceive with a brotherly kiss, etc. You yourself are nothing, an enigmatic figure on whose brow is inscribed Either/or—"For this," you say, "is my motto, and these words are not, as the grammarians believe, disjunctive conjunctions; no, they belong inseparably together and therefore ought to be written as one word, inasmuch as in their union they constitute

an interjection which I shout at mankind, just as boys shout
'Hep' after a Jew."

Now although nothing you say in that style has the
slightest effect upon me, or, if it has any effect, it is at the
utmost the effect of arousing a righteous indignation, nevertheless, for your own sake I will reply to you. Do you not
know that there comes a midnight hour when everyone
has to throw off his mask? Do you believe that life will
always let itself be mocked? Do you think you can slip
away a little before midnight in order to avoid this? Or are
you not terrified by it? I have seen men in real life who so
long deceived others that at last their true nature could not
reveal itself; I have seen men who played hide and seek so
long that at last madness through them obtruded disgust-
ingly upon others their secret thoughts which hitherto they
had proudly concealed. Or can you think of anything more
frightful than that it might end with your nature being
resolved into a multiplicity, that you really might become
many, become, like those unhappy demoniacs, a legion,
and you thus would have lost the inmost and holiest thing
of all in a man, the unifying power of personality? Truly,
you should not jest with that which is not only serious but
dreadful. In every man there is something which to a certain degree prevents him from becoming perfectly transparent to himself; and this may be the case in so high a
degree, he may be so inexplicably woven into relationships
of life which extend far beyond himself that he almost cannot reveal himself. But he who cannot reveal himself cannot
love, and he who cannot love is the most unhappy man of
all. Your own tactic is to train yourself in the art of being
enigmatic to everybody. My young friend, suppose there
was no one who troubled himself to guess your riddle—
what joy, then, would you have in it? But above all, for
your own sake, for the sake of your salvation—for I am
acquainted with no condition of soul which can better be
described as perdition—stop this wild flight, this passion of
annihilation which rages in you; for this is what you desire,
you would annihilate everything, you would satiate the
hunger of doubt at the expense of existence. To this end
you cultivate yourself, to this end you harden your temper;

for you are willing to admit that you are good for nothing, the only thing that gives you pleasure is to march seven times around existence and blow the trumpet and thereupon let the whole thing collapse, that your soul may be tranquilized, yea, attuned to sadness, that you may summon Echo forth—for Echo is heard only in emptiness.

However, I am not likely to get further with you along this path; moreover, my head is too weak, if you would put it that way, to be able to hold out, or, as I prefer to say, too strong to take pleasure in seeing everything grow dizzy before my eyes. I will therefore take up the matter from another side. Imagine a young man at the age when life really begins to have significance for him; he is wholesome, pure, joyful, intellectually gifted, himself rich in hope, the hope of everyone who knows him; imagine (yea, it is hard that I have to say this) that he was mistaken in you, that he believed you were a serious, tried and experienced man from whom one could confidently expect enlightenment upon life's riddles; imagine that he turned to you with the charming confidence which is the adornment of youth, with the claim not to be gainsaid which is youth's privilege—what would you answer him? Would you answer, "I say merely either/or"? That you would hardly do. Would you (as you are wont to express it when you would indicate your aversion to having other people vex you with their affairs of the heart), would you stick your head out of the window and say, "Try the next house"? Or would you treat him as you do others who ask your advice or seek information from you, whom you dismiss as you do the collector of tithes by saying that you are only a lodger in life, not a householder and paterfamilias? No, you would not do this either. A young man with intellectual gifts is the sort of thing you prize only too highly. But in the case I suppose, your relation to the youth is not just what you would have wished, it was not an accidental encounter which brought you in contact with him, your irony was not tempted. Although he was the younger, you the older man, it was he, nevertheless, who by the noble quality of his youth made the instant serious. It is true, is it not, that you yourself would like to be young, would feel that there was something beautiful in being young but also something very serious, that it is by no means a matter of indifference how one employs one's youth, but that before one there lies a choice, a real either/or. You would feel that, after all, the important thing is not to cultivate one's mind but to mature one's personality. Your good nature, your sympathy, would be set in motion, in that spirit you would talk to him; you would fortify his soul, confirm him in the confidence he has in the world, you would assure him that there is a power in a man which is able to defy the whole world, you would insist that he take to heart the importance of employing time well. All this you can do, and when you will, you can do it handsomely.

But now mark well what I would say to you, young man —for though you are not young, one is always compelled to address you as such. Now what did you do in this case? You acknowledged, as ordinarily you are not willing to do, the importance of an either/or. And why? Because your soul was moved by love for the young man. And yet in a way you deceived him, for he will, perhaps, encounter you at another time when it by no means suits your convenience to acknowledge this importance. Here you see one of the sorry consequences of the fact that a man's nature cannot harmoniously reveal itself. You thought you were doing the best for him, and yet perhaps you have harmed him; perhaps he would have been better able to maintain himself over against your distrust of life than to find repose in the subjective, deceitful trust you conveyed to him. Imagine that after the lapse of several years you again encountered him; he was lively, witty, intellectual, daring in his thought, bold in his expression, but your ear easily detected doubt in his soul, you conceived a suspicion that he had acquired the questionable wisdom: I say merely either/or. It is true, is it not, that you would be sorry for him, would feel that he had lost something, and something very essential. But for yourself you will not sorrow, you are content with your ambiguous wisdom, yea, proud of it, so proud that you will not suffer another to share it, since you wish to be alone with it. And yet you find it deplorable in another connection, and it is your sincere opinion that it was deplorable for the young man to have reached the same wisdom. What a monstrous contradiction! Your whole nature contradicts itself. But you can only get out of this contradiction by an either/or, and I, who love you more sincerely than you loved this young man, I, who in my life have experienced the significance of choice, I congratulate you upon the fact that you are still so young, that even though you always will be sensible of some loss, yet, if you have, or rather if you will to have the requisite energy, you can win what is the chief thing in life, win yourself, acquire your own self.

Now in case a man were able to maintain himself upon the pinnacle of the instant of choice, in case he could cease to be a man, in case he were in his inmost nature only an airy thought, in case personality meant nothing more than to be a kobold, which takes part, indeed, in the movements but nevertheless remains unchanged; in case such were the situation, it would be foolish to say that it might ever be too late for a man to choose, for in a deeper sense there could be no question of a choice. The choice itself is decisive for the content of the personality, through the choice the personality immerses itself in the thing chosen, and when it does not choose it withers away in consumption. For an instant it is so, for an instant it may seem as if the things between which a choice is to be made lie outside of the chooser, that he stands in no relationship to it, that he can preserve a state of indifference over against it. This is the instant of deliberation, but this, like the Platonic instant,[1] has no existence, least of all in the abstract sense in which you would hold it fast, and the longer one stares at it the less it exists. That which has to be chosen stands in the deepest relationship to the chooser, and when it is a question of a choice involving a life problem the individual must naturally be living in the meantime, and hence, it comes about that the longer he postpones the choice the easier it is for him to alter its character, notwithstanding that he is constantly deliberating and deliberating and believes that thereby he is holding the alternatives distinctly apart. When life's either/or is regarded in this way one is not easily tempted to jest with it. One sees, then, that the inner drift of the personality leaves no time for thought experiments, that it constantly hastens onward and in one way or another posits this alternative or that, making the choice more difficult the next instant because what has thus been posited must be revoked. Think of the captain on his ship at the instant when it has to come about. He will perhaps be able to say, "I can either do this or that"; but in case he is not a pretty poor navigator, he will be aware at the same time that the ship is all the while making its usual headway, and that therefore it is only an instant when it is indifferent whether he does this or that. So it is with a man. If he forgets to take account of the headway, there comes at last an instant when there no longer is any question of an either/or, not because he has chosen but because he has neglected to choose, which is equivalent to saying, because others have chosen for him, because he has lost his self.

You will perceive also in what I have just been saying how essentially my view of choice differs from yours (if you can properly be said to have any view), for yours differs precisely in the fact that it prevents you from choosing. For me the instant of choice is very serious, not so much on account of the rigorous cogitation involved in weighing the alternatives, not on account of the multiplicity of thoughts which attach themselves to every link in the chain, but rather because there is danger afoot, danger that the next instant it may not be equally in my power to choose, that something already has been lived which must be lived over again. For to think that for an instant one can keep one's personality a blank, or that strictly speaking one can break off and bring to a halt the course of the personal life, is a delusion. The personality is already interested in the choice before one chooses, and when the choice is postponed the personality chooses unconsciously, or the choice is made by obscure powers within it. So when at last the choice is made one discovers (unless, as I remarked before, the personality has been completely volatilized) that there is something which must be done over again, something which must be revoked, and this is often very difficult. We read in fairy tales about human beings whom mermaids and mermen enticed into their power by means of demoniac music. In order to break the enchantment it was necessary in the fairy tale[2] for the person who was under the spell to play the same piece of music backwards without making a single mistake. This is very profound, but very difficult to perform, and yet so it is: the errors one has taken into oneself one must eradicate in this way, and every time one makes a mistake one must begin all over. Therefore, it is important to choose and to choose in time. You, on the contrary, have another method—for I know very well that the polemical side you turn towards the world is not your true nature. Yea, if to deliberate were the proper task for a human life, you would be pretty close to perfection. I will adduce an example. To fit your case the contrasts must be bold: either a parson/or an actor. Here is the dilemma. Now all your passionate energy is awakened, reflection with its hundred arms lays hold of the thought of being a parson. You find no repose, day and night you think about it, you read all the books you can lay your hands on, you go to church three times every Sunday, pick up acquaintance with parsons, write sermons yourself, deliver them to yourself; for half a year you are dead to the whole world. You can now talk of the clerical calling with more insight and apparently with more experience than many who have been parsons for twenty years. When you encounter such men it arouses your indignation that they do not know how to get the thing off their chests with more eloquence. "Is this enthusiasm?" you say. "Why I who am not a parson, who have not consecrated myself to this calling, speak with the voice of angels as compared with them." That, perhaps, is true enough, but nevertheless, you have not become a parson. Then you act in the same way with respect to the other task, and your enthusiasm for art almost surpasses your clerical eloquence. Then you are ready to choose. However, one may be sure that in the prodigious thought-production you were engaged in there must have been lots of waste products, many incidental reflections and observations. Hence, the instant you have to choose, life and animation enter into this waste mass, a new either/or presents itself—jurist, perhaps advocate, this has something in common with both the other alternatives. Now you are lost.

For that same moment you are at once advocate enough to be able to prove the reasonableness of taking the third possibility into account. So your life drifts on.

After you have wasted a year and a half on such deliberations, after you have with admirable energy exerted to the utmost the powers of your soul, you have not got one step further. You break the thread of thought, you become impatient, passionate, scolding and storming, and then you continue: "Either hairdresser/or bank teller; I say merely either/or." What wonder, then, that this saying has become for you an offense and foolishness, that it seems, as you say, as if it were like the arms attached to the iron maiden whose embrace was the death penalty. You treat people superciliously, you make sport of them, and what you have become is what you most abhor: a critic, a universal critic in all faculties. Sometimes I cannot help smiling at you, and yet it is pitiful to see how your really excellent intellectual gifts are thus dissipated. But here again there is the same contradiction in your nature; for you see the ludicrous very clearly, and God help him who falls into your hands if his case is similar to yours. And yet the whole difference is that he perhaps becomes downcast and broken, while you on the contrary become light and erect and merrier than ever, making yourself and others blissful with the gospel: *vanitas vanitatum vanitas*, hurrah! But this is no choice, it is what we call in Danish letting it go, or it is mediation like letting five count as an even number. Now you feel yourself free, you say to the world, farewell.

> *So zieh' ich hin in alle Ferne,*
> *Ueber meiner Mütze nur die Sterne.*[3]

Therewith you have chosen . . . not to be sure, as you yourself will admit, the better part. But in reality you have not chosen at all, or it is in an improper sense of the word you have chosen. Your choice is an aesthetic choice, but an aesthetic choice is no choice. The act of choosing is essentially a proper and stringent expression of the ethical. Whenever in a stricter sense there is question of an either/or, one can always be sure that the ethical is involved. The only absolute either/or is the choice between good and evil, but that is also absolutely ethical. The aesthetic choice is either entirely immediate and to that extent no choice, or it loses itself in the multifarious. Thus, when a young girl follows the choice of her heart, this choice, however beautiful it may be, is in the strictest sense no choice, since it is entirely immediate. When a man deliberates aesthetically upon a multitude of life's problems, as you did in the foregoing, he does not easily get one either/or, but a whole multiplicity, because the self-determining factor in the choice is not ethically accentuated, and because when one does not choose absolutely one chooses only for the moment, and therefore can choose something different the next moment. The ethical choice is therefore in a certain sense much easier, much simpler, but in another sense it is infinitely harder. He who would define his life task ethically has ordinarily not so considerable a selection to choose from; on the other hand, the act of choice has far more importance for him. If you will understand me aright, I should like to say that in making a choice it is not so much a question of choosing the right as of the energy, the earnestness, the pathos with which one chooses. Thereby the personality announces its inner infinity, and thereby, in turn, the personality is consolidated. Therefore, even if a man were to choose the wrong, he will nevertheless discover, precisely by reason of the energy with which he chose, that he had chosen the wrong. For the choice being made with the whole inwardness of his personality, his nature is purified and he himself brought into immediate relation to the eternal Power whose omnipresence interpenetrates the whole of existence. This transfiguration, this higher consecration, is never attained by that man who chooses merely aesthetically. The rhythm in that man's soul, in spite of all its passion, is only a *spiritus lenis*.[4]

So, like a Cato I shout at you my either/or, and yet not like a Cato, for my soul has not yet acquired the resigned coldness which he possessed. But I know that only this incantation, if I have the strength for it, will be capable of rousing you, not to an activity of thought, for of that you have no lack, but to earnestness of spirit. Perhaps you will succeed without that in accomplishing much, perhaps even in astonishing the world (for I am not niggardly), and yet you will miss the highest thing, the only thing which truly gives meaning to life; perhaps you will gain the whole world and lose your own self.

What is it, then, that I distinguish in my either/or? Is it good and evil? No, I would only bring you up to the point where the choice between the evil and the good acquires significance for you. Everything hinges upon this. As soon as one can get a man to stand at the crossways in such a position that there is no recourse but to choose, he will choose the right. Hence, if it should chance that, while you are in the course of reading this somewhat lengthy dissertation, which again I send you in the form of a letter, you were to feel that the instant for choice had come, then throw the rest of this away, never concern yourself about it, you have lost nothing—but choose, and you shall see what validity there is in this act, yea, no young girl can be so happy with the choice of her heart as is a man who knows how to choose. So then, one either has to live aesthetically or one has to live ethically. In this alternative, as I have said, there is not yet in the strictest sense any question of a choice; for he who lives aesthetically does not choose, and he who after the ethical has manifested itself to him chooses the aesthetical is not living aesthetically, for he is sinning and is subject to ethical determinants even though his life may be described as unethical. Lo, this is, as it were, a *character indelebilis* impressed upon the ethical, that though it modestly places itself on a level with the aesthetical, it is nevertheless that which makes the choice a choice. And this is the pitiful thing to one who contemplates human life, that so many live on in a quiet state of perdition; they outlive themselves, not in the sense that the content of life is successively unfolding and now is possessed in this expanded state, but they live their lives, as it were, outside of themselves, they vanish like shadows, their immortal soul is blown away, and they are not alarmed by the problem of its immortality, for they are already in a state of dissolution before they die. They do not live aesthetically, but neither has the ethical manifested itself in its entirety, so they have not exactly rejected it either, they therefore are not sinning, except in so far as it is sin not to be either one thing or the other; neither are they ever in doubt about their immortality, for he who deeply and sincerely is in doubt of it on his own behalf will surely find the right. *On his own behalf,* I say, and surely it is high time to utter a warning against the great-hearted, heroic objectivity with which many thinkers think on behalf of others and not on their own behalf. If one would call this which I here require selfishness, I would reply that this comes from the fact that people have no conception of what this "self" is, and that it would be of very little use to a man if he were to gain the whole world and lose himself, and that it must necessarily be a poor proof which does not first of all convince the man who presents it.

My either/or does not in the first instance denote the choice between good and evil; it denotes the choice whereby one chooses good *and* evil/or excludes them. Here the question is under what determinants one would contemplate the whole of existence and would himself live. That the man who chooses good and evil chooses the good is indeed true, but this becomes evident only afterwards; for the aesthetical is not the evil but neutrality, and that is the reason why I affirmed that it is the ethical which constitutes the choice. It is, therefore, not so much a question of choosing between willing the good *or* the evil, as of choosing to will, but by this in turn the good and the evil are posited. He who chooses the ethical chooses the good, but here the good is entirely abstract, only its being is posited, and hence it does not follow by any means that the chooser cannot in turn choose the evil, in spite of the fact that he chose the good. Here you see again how important it is that a choice be made, and that the crucial thing is not deliberation but the baptism of the will which lifts up the choice into the ethical. The longer the time that elapses, the more difficult it is to choose, for the soul is constantly attached to one side of the dilemma, and it becomes more and more difficult, therefore, to tear oneself loose. And yet this is necessary if one is to choose and is therefore of the utmost importance if a choice signifies something, and that it does I shall show later.

You know that I have never pretended to be a philosopher, and least of all when I am conversing with you. Partly to tease you a bit, partly because it really is my dearest and most precious and also in a certain sense my most important position in life, I am accustomed to appear in the role of a married man. I have not sacrificed my life for art and learning, what I have sacrificed myself for is insignificant in comparison with these things; I sacrifice myself for my profession, my wife, my children, or, more properly expressed, I do not sacrifice myself for them, but I find in them my satisfaction and joy. These are insignificant things in comparison with what you live for; and yet, my young friend, take heed lest the greater things for which you really are sacrificing yourself might deceive you. Now although I am not a philosopher, yet I am compelled at this point to venture upon a little philosophic inquiry which I would beg you not so much to criticize as to take to heart. For the polemical result which resounds in all your songs of triumph over life has a strange resemblance to the pet theory of the newer philosophy, that the principle of contradiction is annulled.[5] I know very well that the standpoint you occupy is to philosophy an abomination, and yet it seems to me that philosophy is guilty of the same error, and that the reason why this has not been noticed immediately is that philosophy is not even in as correct a position as you are. Your place is the domain of action, that of philosophy is contemplation. As soon as one would transport philosophy into the practical domain it must reach the same result you reach, even though it does not express itself in the same way. You mediate contradictions in a higher madness, philosophy mediates them in a higher unity. You turn towards the future, for action is always futuristic. You say, "I can either do this or do that, but whichever of the two I do is equally mad, *ergo* I do nothing at all."

Philosophy turns towards the past, towards the whole enacted history of the world, it shows how the discrete factors are fused in a higher unity, it mediates and mediates. On the other hand, it seems to me to give no answer at all to the question I put to it, for I ask about the future. You, after all, do in a way give an answer, even though it is nonsense. Now I assume that philosophy is in the right, that the principle of contradiction really is annulled, or that the philosophers transcend it every instant in the higher unity which exists for thought. This, however, surely cannot hold with respect to the future, for the oppositions must first be in existence before I can mediate them. But if the oppositions are there, then there must be an either/or. The philosopher says, "That's the way it's been hitherto." I ask, "What am I to do if I do not want to be a philosopher?" For if I want to be that, I see clearly enough that I, like the other philosophers, shall soon get to the point of mediating the past. In the first place, there is no answer to my question what I ought to do; for if I were the most gifted philosophic mind that ever has lived in the world, there must be one thing more I have to do besides sitting and contemplating the past. In the second place, I am a married man and by no means a philosophic mind, but I turn with all due respect to the devotees of this science to learn what I ought to do. However, I get no reply, for philosophy mediates the past and has its existence in it, the philosopher hastens back into the past to such a degree that, as a poet says of an antiquarian, "only his coat tails are left behind in the present."

At this point you are united with the philosophers. What unites you is that life comes to a stop. To the philosopher world history is concluded, and he mediates. Hence, in our age as the order of the day we have the disgusting sight of young men who are able to mediate Christianity and paganism, are able to play with the titanic forces of history, and are unable to tell a plain man what he has to do in life, and who do not know any better what they themselves have to do. You are very versatile in expressions for your pet result. I will call attention to one of them because in it you show a striking resemblance to the philosopher, even though his real or assumed seriousness would forbid him to take part in the obligato variation in which you take delight. If you are asked whether you will sign your name to an address to the King, or whether you desire a constitution or the right to impose taxes, or whether you will join this or that benevolent movement, you reply, "My revered contemporary, you misunderstand me, I am not in the game at all, I am outside like a tiny Spanish 's'."[6] So it is, also, with the philosopher, he is outside, he is not in the game, he sits and grows old listening to the songs of long ago, harkening to the harmonies of mediation. I honor science, I respect its devotees, but life, too, has its demands, and although on seeing a single particularly talented pate losing himself onesidedly in the past I should be perplexed how to judge him, doubtful what opinion I should form of him irrespective of the deference I would entertain for his intellectual ability, yet in our age I am not perplexed, since I see a host of young men who could not possibly be all of them philosophic minds losing themselves in the pet [yndling] philosophy of our age, or, as I am tempted to call it, the juvenal [yngling] philosophy. I have a valid claim upon philosophy, as has everyone whom it does not dare show to the door on the ground of a total lack of parts. I am husband of a wife, I have children; what if in their name I were to ask philosophy what a man has to do in life? You will perhaps smile, in any case the philosophic youth will smile at a paterfamilias, and yet I think that it is a tremendous argument against philosophy if it has no answer. Has the course of life been brought to a stop? If the generation that now is can live off of contemplation, what will the following generation live off of? Contemplating the same thing? The foregoing generation has on this hypothesis accomplished nothing, has left nothing behind it to be mediated. Here again I can lump you with the philosophers, and I say to both of you that you miss the highest thing. My position as a married man here comes to my aid and enables me to illustrate the better what I mean. If a married man were to say that the perfect marriage is one where there are no children, he would be guilty of the same misunderstanding as the philosophers. He makes himself the absolute, and yet every married man will feel that this is untrue and unbecoming, and that the fact that he himself becomes a relativity, as he does by means of the child, is far more true.

Perhaps, however, I have already gone too far, have embarked upon investigations which perhaps I ought not to have attempted, partly because I am not a philosopher, partly because it is not at all my purpose to entertain myself with you by discussing one or another phenomenon of this age, but rather to accuse you, to make you feel in every way that you are the accused party. However, since I have in fact gone so far, I will reflect a little more precisely upon the problem of the philosophic mediation of opposites. If what I have to say lacks stringency, it perhaps makes up for that by more earnestness, and it is only on this ground I set it forth. For I have no intention of competing for any philosophic distinction, but once having taken my pen in hand I have a mind to defend with that the cause which ordinarily I defend in other and better ways.

As truly as there is a future, just so truly is there an either/or. The time in which the philosopher lives is not absolute time, it is itself a relative moment, and it always is a suspicious circumstance when philosophy is unfruitful; indeed, this must be regarded as a dishonor, just as in the East unfruitfulness in a woman is regarded as a disgrace. So time itself is a relative moment, and the philosopher is a relative moment in time. Our age therefore will in turn appear to a subsequent age as a discrete factor, and a philosopher of a subsequent age will in turn mediate our age, and so forth. To that extent philosophy is within its rights, and we should only have to regard it as an accidental mistake on the part of the philosophy of our time that it confounded our time with absolute time. However, it is easy to see that the category of mediation has hereby suffered a considerable shock, and that the absolute mediation becomes possible only when history is finished, in other words, that the System is in a constant process of becoming. What philosophy maintains, however, is that there is an absolute mediation. Naturally, this is of the utmost importance to it, for if one gives up mediation, one gives up speculation. On the other hand, it is a precarious thing to concede this, for if we concede mediation, then there is no absolute choice, and if there is nothing of that sort, then there is no absolute either/or. This is the difficulty, yet I believe that it is due partly to the fact that two spheres are confounded with one another, that of thought and that of freedom. The op-

position does not subsist for thought, which goes over to
the other side and thereupon combines both in a higher
unity. For freedom the opposition does subsist, for freedom
excludes the other side. I am by no means confounding
liberum arbitrium with the genuine positive freedom, for
this, too, has to all eternity evil outside itself, even if the
evil be only an impotent possibility, and it does not become
more perfect by more and more absorbing the evil but by
more and more excluding it. But exclusion is precisely the
opposite of mediation. That with this I am not espousing the
notion of a radical evil I shall show later.

The spheres with which philosophy properly deals,
which properly are the spheres for thought, are logic, nature, and history. Here necessity rules, and mediation is
valid. That such is the case with logic and nature nobody
will deny. On the other hand, there is some difficulty about
history, for here, it is said, freedom rules. I believe, however, that history is wrongly conceived, and that the difficulty is due to this. For history is more than the product
of the free actions of free individuals. The individual indeed
acts, but his action passes into the order of things which
sustains the whole of existence. What will be the issue of
it the agent does not really know. But this higher order of
things which digests, so to speak, the free actions and
weaves them into its eternal law is necessity, and this necessity is the dynamic of world history, and hence it is quite
right for philosophy to employ mediation, I mean the relative mediation. If I contemplate a world-historical individual, I can distinguish the works of which the Scripture says
that "they follow him" from the works by which he belongs
to history. With what one might call the inward work philosophy has nothing whatever to do, but the inward work
is the genuine life of freedom. Philosophy regards the outward work, and this it does not see in isolation but as it
is absorbed into and transformed by the world-historical
process. This process is properly the subject matter of philosophy, and this it regards under the category of necessity.
It therefore holds at a distance the reflection which would
suggest that everything might have been different, it regards world history in such a way that there can be no

question of an either/or. That in this way of regarding history much foolish and inept talk is mingled is at least my opinion; that especially the young wizards who wish to conjure up the spirits of history seem to me ridiculous, I do not deny, but I also incline with profound reverence before the grand achievements which our age has to show. As I have said, philosophy views history under the category of necessity, not under that of freedom; for even if one speaks of the historic process as free, that is meant only in the same sense as when one talks of the organizing process in nature. With regard to the historical process there is no question of an either/or, although it has probably never occurred to any philosopher to deny that an either/or presents itself in the case of an individual who must act. Hence, the unconcernedness, the indulgence, with which philosophy contemplates history and its heroes; for it views them under the category of necessity. Hence again its inability to make a man act, its disposition to bring everything to a standstill; for properly it demands that one should act necessarily, which is a contradiction.

Thus, even the humblest individual has a dual existence. He also has a history, and this is not merely a product of his own free actions. The inward work, on the contrary, belongs to him and must belong to him unto all eternity; neither history nor world history can take that from him, it "follows him" either for joy or for sorrow. There rules in this inward world an absolute either/or, but with this world, philosophy has nothing to do. If I picture to myself an elderly man who looks back upon an eventful life, I admit that he can get a mediation out of it, for his history was intertwined with that of time; but in the most inward sense he gets no mediation. An either/or still separates enduringly that which was separated when he chose. If there is to be any talk of mediation, one might say that repentance is such; but repentance is no mediation, it does not look with pleasure upon that which is to be mediated, it consumes it with its wrath—but this resembles exclusion, the opposite of mediation. Here it is evident that I do not assume a radical evil, since I posit the validity of repentance. Repentance, it is true, is an expression for reconciliation, but it is also an absolutely irreconcilable expression.

But all this, perhaps, you concede—you who, nevertheless, in many ways make common cause with the philosophers . . . except in so far as you undertake on your own private account to make game of them. You think perhaps that I as a married man may well be content with this concession and can make use of it in my household economy. Honestly speaking, I ask nothing more, but I should like to know which life is the highest, that of the philosopher, or that of the free man. In case the philosopher is merely a philosopher, completely lost in his profession, without knowing the blessed life of freedom, then he lacks a very important thing, he gains the whole world and loses himself. This never can happen to a man who lives for freedom, even though he were to lose ever so much.

For freedom, therefore, I am fighting (partly in this letter, partly and principally within myself), I am fighting for the future, for either/or. That is the treasure I desire to bequeath to those whom I love in the world; yea, if my little son were at this instant of an age when he could thoroughly understand me, and my last hour had come, I would say to him, "I leave to thee no fortune, no title and dignities, but I know where there lies buried a treasure which suffices to make thee richer than the whole world, and this treasure belongs to thee, and thou shalt not even express thanks to me for it lest thou take hurt to thine own soul by owing everything to another. This treasure is deposited in thine own inner self: there is an either/or which makes a man greater than the angels."

Here I will break off this reflection. It perhaps does not satisfy you, your greedy eye devours it without being satisfied by it, but that is because the eye is the sense which is most insatiable, especially when like you one does not hunger but suffers from a lust of the eye which cannot be satisfied with seeing.

That which is prominent in my either/or is the ethical. It is therefore not yet a question of the choice of something in particular, it is not a question of the reality of the thing chosen, but of the reality of the act of choice. This, however, is the decisive thing, and it is to an apprehension of this I would strive to arouse you. Up to this point one man can be of help to another, but having reached this point the importance one man can have for another becomes more subordinate. In the previous letter I remarked that the experience of having loved imparts to a man's nature a harmony which never is entirely lost; now I would say that the experience of choosing imparts to a man's nature a solemnity, a quiet dignity, which never is entirely lost. There are many who set great store upon having seen one or another distinguished world-historical personality face to face. This impression they never forget, it has given to their souls an ideal picture which ennobles their nature; and yet such an instant, however significant, is nothing in comparison with the instant of choice. So when all has become still around one, as solemn as a starlit night, when the soul is alone in the whole world, then there appears before one, not a distinguished man, but the eternal Power itself. The heavens part, as it were, and the I chooses itself—or rather, receives itself. Then has the soul beheld the loftiest sight that mortal eye can see and which never can be forgotten, then the personality receives the accolade of knighthood which ennobles it for an eternity. He does not become another man than he was before, but he becomes himself, consciousness is unified, and he is himself. As an heir, even though he were heir to the treasure of all the world, nevertheless does not possess his property before he has come of age, so even the richest personality is nothing before he has chosen himself, and on the other hand even what one might call the poorest personality is everything when he has chosen himself; for the great thing is not to be this or that but to be oneself, and this everyone can be if he wills it.

That in a sense it is not a question of the choice of a something, you will see from the fact that what appears as the alternative is the aesthetical, the indifferent. And yet nevertheless there is here question of a choice, yea, of an absolute choice, for only by choosing absolutely can one choose the ethical. By the absolute choice the ethical is posited, but from this it does not follow by any means that the aesthetical is excluded. In the ethical the personality is concentrated in itself, so the aesthetical is absolutely excluded or is excluded as the absolute, but relatively it is still left. In choosing itself the personality chooses itself ethically and excludes absolutely the aesthetical, but since he chooses himself and since he does not become another being by choosing himself but becomes himself, the whole of the aesthetical comes back again in its relativity.

So the either/or I propose is in a sense absolute, for it is a question of choosing or not choosing. But since the choice is an absolute choice, so is the either/or absolute; in another sense, however, it is only by this choice the either/or comes to evidence, for with that [the choice between choosing and not choosing] the choice between good and evil makes its appearance. This choice between good and evil which is posited in and with the first choice need not concern me here; I would merely constrain you to go on to that point where the necessity of choice is manifest, and thereupon would contemplate existence under ethical categories. I am not an ethical rigorist, an enthusiast for a formal, abstract freedom. If only the choice is posited, all of the aesthetical returns again, and you will see that only then does existence become beautiful, that only in this way can a man succeed in saving his soul and gaining the whole world, can succeed in using the world without abusing it.

But what is it to live aesthetically, and what is it to live ethically? What is the aesthetical in a man, and what is the ethical? To this I would reply: the aesthetical in a man is that by which he is immediately what he is; the ethical is that whereby he becomes what he becomes. He who lives in and by and of and for the aesthetical in him lives aesthetically.

It is not my intention to go more particularly into the investigation of all that is implied in this definition of the aesthetical. It also seems to me superfluous to enlighten you about what it is to live aesthetically—you who are such an expert practitioner in this mode of life that I might rather need your help. Nevertheless, I will sketch several of the stages of the aesthetic life in order that we may work ourselves up to the point where you properly belong. This to

my mind is important lest you escape me too soon by one
of your favorite side-leaps. Moreover, I have no doubt that
in many ways I shall be able to enlighten you about what
it is to live aesthetically. Although I would send to you as
the most reliable guide any man who wished to live aesthetically, I would not send him to you if, in a higher sense,
he wished to perceive what it is to live aesthetically, for
about that you could not enlighten him, precisely because
you are enmeshed; only he can do that who stands on a
higher level and lives ethically. For an instant you might
perhaps be tempted to make to me the sophistical rejoinder
that then I am unable to give a reliable elucidation of what
it is to live ethically, since I myself am enmeshed in it.
This, however, would only furnish me with an occasion
for a further elucidation. The reason why the man who
lives aesthetically can in a higher sense explain nothing, is
that he constantly lives in the moment, yet all the time is
conscious only in terms of a certain relativity and within
certain bounds. It is by no means my intention to deny that
to live aesthetically when such a life is at its highest may
call for a multiplicity of intellectual gifts, yea, even that
these must be intensively developed to an uncommon degree; but nevertheless, they are enslaved, and transparency
is lacking to them. Thus one often finds certain species of
animals which possess far sharper and more intense senses
than man, but they are bound to the instinct of the animal.
I would fain take you as an example. I have never denied
that you possess distinguished intellectual gifts, as you can
see also from the fact that I have often reproached you for
abusing them. You are witty, ironical, a close observer, a
dialectician, experienced in pleasure, you know how to calculate the instant, you are sentimental or heartless according to circumstances; but beneath all this you are constantly
only in the moment, and therefore your life dissolves, and
it is impossible for you to explain it. If then a man would
learn the art of enjoyment, he is quite right in going to you;
but if he wishes to understand your life, he goes to the
wrong person. By coming to me perhaps he would sooner
find what he seeks, in spite of the fact that I am by no
means in possession of your intellectual gifts. You are en-

meshed and have, as it were, no time to tear yourself loose; I am not enmeshed, either by my judgment of the aesthetical or by my judgment of the ethical; for in the ethical I am raised above the instant, I am in freedom—but it is a contradiction that one might be enmeshed by being in freedom.

Every man, however lowly his talents are, however subordinate his position in life, naturally feels the need of forming a life view, a conception of life's significance and of its purpose. The man who lives aesthetically does that too, and the universal expression which has been heard from age to age and in all stages is this: one must enjoy life. Naturally, there is great variety corresponding to the different conceptions of enjoyment, but in this expression, that one is to enjoy life, all are agreed. *But he who says that he wants to enjoy life always posits a condition which either lies outside the individual or is in the individual in such a way that it is not posited by the individual himself.* With respect to this last sentence I would beg you to hold fast the expressions I have used, for they are chosen deliberately.

Let us now run through these stages quite briefly in order to press on to the place where you belong. You are already, perhaps, a bit annoyed at the generic expression I formulated for living aesthetically, and yet you will hardly be able to deny that it is correct. Only too often you are heard to scoff at people for not knowing how to enjoy life, believing that you on the other hand have mastered this study. It is quite possible that they do not understand it, but in the expression of their aim they are in entire agreement with you. You perhaps have a presentiment that in this deliberation of mine you will be yoked with the sort of people whom you especially abhor. You think perhaps that I ought to be gallant enough to treat you as an artist and to pass over in silence the bunglers you have trouble enough with in life and with whom you would not have anything in common if you could help it. I cannot help you, however, for you have something in common with them, nevertheless, and something very essential at that, namely, your view of life, and in my eyes the matter in which you differ from them is something unessential. I cannot help laughing at you. You see, my young friend, you are pursued by a curse: the many brothers in your art whom you are entirely unwilling to own. You incur the danger of falling into bad and common company—you who are so haughtily superior. I do not deny that it must be disagreeable to possess a view of life in common with drunken revelers and penny-sportsmen; nor is this exactly your case, for to a certain extent your position lies beyond the aesthetic domain, as I shall show later.

Great as the differences within the aesthetic domain may be, all the stages have this similarity, that spirit is not determined as spirit but is immediately determined. The differences may be extraordinary, all the way from complete stupidity (*Aandløshed*) to the highest degree of cleverness (*Aandrighed*), but even at the stage where cleverness is evident the spirit (*Aanden*) is not determined as spirit but as talent.

I will describe quite briefly each particular stage and will dwell only upon that which in one way or another fits you or which I could wish you would apply to yourself. Personality immediately determined is not spiritual but physical. Here we have a view of life which teaches that health is the most precious good, that on which everything hinges. The same view acquires a more poetic expression when it is said that beauty is the highest. Now beauty is a very fragile good, and therefore, one seldom sees this view carried through. One encounters often enough a young girl (or maybe a young man) who for a brief time prides herself upon her beauty, but soon it deceives her. I remember, however, to have once seen it carried through with rare success. In my student days I sometimes went during the vacation to the residence of a count in one of the provinces. In his younger days the Count had had a diplomatic post, he was now elderly and lived quietly at his countryseat. The Countess had been extraordinarily beautiful as a young girl, as an elderly person she was still the most beautiful woman I have ever seen. The Count in his youth had great success with the fair sex because of his manly beauty. At the Court the handsome young gentleman-in-waiting was still remembered. Old age had not broken him, and a noble, genuinely superior dignity made him still more good-looking. Those who had known them in their earlier days declared that this was the handsomest couple they had ever seen, and I who had the good fortune to learn to know them in their later years, found this perfectly natural, for they were still the handsomest couple one could see. Both the Count and the Countess were highly cultivated, and yet the life view of the Countess was concentrated in the thought that they were the handsomest couple in the whole land. I still remember vividly an occurrence which convinced me of this. It was a Sunday morning, there was a little festival in the church close to the countryseat. The Countess was not feeling quite well enough to venture to attend, but the Count went elegantly dressed in his uniform of gentleman-in-waiting, decorated with his orders. The windows of the great hall looked out on an allée which led up to the church. By one of them stood the Countess. She was dressed in a tasteful morning gown and was really charming. I had enquired of her health and had entered into conversation about a yachting party which was to come off the following day. Then far down the allée the Count was seen. She relapsed into silence, became more beautiful than I had ever seen her, had an expression almost sad, the Count had come so near that he could see the Countess through the window, she threw him a kiss with the utmost grace, then turned to me and said, "Little William, my Detlev is surely the handsomest man in the whole kingdom, is he not? Yes, I can see well enough that he has sunk together a little bit on one side, but no one can see that when I am walking with him, and when we walk together we are surely the handsomest couple in the whole land." No little miss of sixteen years could be more blissfully happy over her fiancé, the handsome page at Court, than was her ladyship over the already aged lord-in-waiting.

Both views of life agree in the principle that one must enjoy life, and that the requisite condition lies in the individual himself, but in such a way that it is not posited by the individual himself.

We go further. We encounter views of life which teach that one must enjoy life but which place the condition for it outside the individual. This is the case with every view of life where wealth, glory, high station, etc., are accounted life's task and its content. In this connection I would also speak of a certain kind of love. If I picture to myself a young girl heart and soul in love, whose eye knew no pleasure but in seeing her lover, whose soul had no thought but him, whose heart had no desire but to belong to him, for whom nothing in heaven or on earth had any significance except him, then here we have again an aesthetic view of life where the condition is located outside the individual. You, of course, regard it as foolishness to be in love in this fashion, you think of it as something which occurs only in romances. Nevertheless, it is a thing that can be thought, and it is certain, at least, that in the eyes of many people such a love would be regarded as something admirable. I shall explain to you later why I cannot approve of it.

We go further. We meet views of life which teach that one must enjoy life, but the conditions for this lie in the individual himself, yet in such a way that they are not posited by him. In this case the personality is generally determined as talent, a mercantile talent, a practical talent, a mechanical talent, a mathematical talent, a poetical talent, an artistic talent, a philosophical talent. Satisfaction in life and enjoyment is sought in the development of this talent. One does not, perhaps, stop with the talent in its immediacy, one cultivates it in all ways, but the condition for satisfaction in life is the talent itself, a condition which is not posited by the individual. The people in whom one finds this view of life often belong to the class which you are accustomed to make sport of for their tireless activity. You think that you yourself are living artistically and you are entirely unwilling to concede that they are. That you have a different view of what it is to enjoy life is undeniable, but this is not the essential thing; the essential thing is that one wants to enjoy life. Your life is far more *vornehm* than theirs, but theirs is far more innocent than yours.

Just as all these views of life have this in common that they are aesthetical, so also they resemble one another in the fact that they have a certain unity, a certain coherence, there is one definite thing upon which they all turn. That upon which they build their life is in itself something simple, and therefore, it is not split up as is the life view of those who build upon what is in itself a multiplicity. The latter is the case with a view of life upon which I shall now dwell at a little more length. Its teaching is, "enjoy life," and it explains it thus: "live for your pleasure." Pleasure, however, is in itself a multiplicity, and so one easily perceives that this life is split into a boundless multiplicity, except in so far as in a particular individual from childhood up pleasure is determined as a particular pleasure, e.g., a lust for fishing or hunting or for keeping horses, etc. Inasmuch as this view is split into a multiplicity one easily perceives that it lies in the sphere of reflection; this reflection, however, is only a finite reflection, and the personality remains in its immediacy. In lust itself the individual is immediate, and however delicate and refined, however crafty it may be, the individual remains immediate in this lust; in the enjoyment of pleasure he is in the moment, and however multifarious he is in this respect, he remains constantly immediate because he is in the moment. To live in order to satisfy one's taste for pleasure implies a proudly superior station in life, and very seldom, God be praised, does one see this view carried through consistently, on account of the troubles of earthly life which give man something else to think about. If such were not the case, I have no doubt we would often be witnesses of this dreadful spectacle, for it is certain, at least, that we often enough hear people complain that they feel themselves hampered by a prosaic life—which unfortunately means, very often, that they only long to enjoy themselves in all the wildness lust may whirl them into. For in order that this view may be carried out the individual must be in possession of a multiplicity of outward conditions, and this good fortune, or rather misfortune, is seldom allotted to a man—this misfortune, for it is certainly not from the gracious but from the angry gods this "fortune" comes.

It is seldom one sees this view of life carried out on any considerable scale, but it is not so rare to see people who bungle at it a little, and when the conditions requisite for it are lacking, are inclined to think that if only they had the conditions under their control they surely would have attained the happiness and joy they longed for in life. However, in history one meets now and then with an example, and as I believe that it may be useful to see where this view of life ends when everything favors it, I will portray such a figure, selecting for this purpose that omnipotent man the Emperor Nero, before whom the whole world made obeisance, who always found himself surrounded by a countless throng of obliging ministers of pleasure. With your habitual audacity you once maintained that one could not blame Nero for burning Rome in order to get a conception of the conflagration of Troy, but one might question whether he was enough of an artist to know how to enjoy it. It is one of your imperial pleasures never to shrink from any thought, never to be dismayed by it. To enjoy that pleasure one has no need of a praetorian guard, nor of silver and gold, nor of the treasures of all the world; one can be quite alone with it and come to a decision in perfect quiet; it is a wiser indulgence, therefore, but not less dismaying. Your intent was surely not to defend Nero, and yet a kind of defense is implied in fixing attention not upon what he did but upon how he did it. I know very well that this audacity of thought is something one often finds in young men, who at such moments try it out, as it were, on the world, and then are easily tempted to make much of it themselves, especially when others are listening to it. I know very well that you as well as I, indeed every man, even Nero himself, would shrink from the thought of such savagery, and yet I never would counsel any man to credit himself in the strictest sense with strength enough not to become a Nero. For note that when I seek to characterize Nero's nature and apply to it a term which in my opinion essentially explains it, it will perhaps seem to you too mild a word, and yet as a judge I am certainly not mild, though in another sense I never judge any man. But believe me, the word is not too mild, it is the true expression, but at the same time it may serve to show how close to a man such an aberration may be; one may say that to every man who does not go through his whole life like a child there comes a moment when he has a presentiment, even if it is a distant one, of this perdition. Nero's nature was *melancholy*. In our age it has become something great to be melancholy. For this reason I can understand that you find this word too mild. I attach myself to an earlier church doctrine[7] which reckoned melancholy among the cardinal sins. If I am right, this is a very unpleasant piece of intelligence for you, for it turns upside down your whole view of life. But to avoid misunderstanding I will remark at once that a man may have sorrow and distress, yea, it may be so great that it pursues him perhaps throughout his whole life, and this may even be beautiful and true, but a man becomes melancholy only by his own fault.

So I picture to myself the imperial voluptuary. Not only when he ascends his throne or marches to the Senate is he surrounded by lictors, but especially when he sallies forth to satisfy his lust, in order that they might clear the way for his predatory raid. I imagine him somewhat older, his youth is past, the light heart has escaped from him, he is already familiar with every conceivable pleasure, satiated with it. But this life, depraved as it may be, has nevertheless matured his soul, and yet in spite of all his understanding of the world, in spite of his experience, he is still a child or a youth. The immediacy of the spirit is unable to break through, and yet it demands a metamorphosis, it demands a higher form of existence. But if this is to come about, an instant will arrive when the splendor of the throne, his might and power, will pale, and for this he has not the courage. Then he grasps after pleasure; all the world's cleverness must devise for him new pleasures, for only in the instant of pleasure does he find repose, and when that is past he gasps with faintness. The spirit constantly desires to break through, but it cannot attain the metamorphosis, it is constantly disappointed, and he would offer it the satiety of pleasure. Then the spirit within him gathers like a dark cloud, its wrath broods over his soul, and it becomes an anguishing dread which ceases not even in the moment of pleasure. Lo, therefore is his eye so lowering that no one can bear to look upon it, his glance so flashing that it terrifies, for behind the eye lies the soul as a gross darkness. They call this glance an imperial glance, and the whole world trembles before it, and yet his inmost nature is anguished dread. A child who looks at him in an unaccustomed way or any casual glance may terrify him, it is as though this person owned him; for the spirit wills to break through, wills that he shall possess himself in his consciousness, but that he is unable to do, and the spirit is repressed and gathers new wrath. He does not possess himself; only when the world trembles before him is he tranquilized, for then there is no one who ventures to lay hold of him.

Hence this dread of men which Nero shares with every personality of this sort. He is as though possessed, in himself unfree, and hence it seems as if every glance would bind him. He, the Roman Emperor, may be afraid of the glance of the most wretched slave. He meets such a glance, his eye consumes the man who thus ventures to look upon him. A ruffian stands by the Emperor's side, comprehends this wild glance of his, and that man is no more. Nero has no murder upon his conscience, but the spirit has a new dread. Only in the moment of pleasure does he find distraction. He burns up half of Rome, but his torment remains the same. Before long such things entertain him no more. There is a still higher pleasure available, he would terrify (*aengste*) men. To himself he is enigmatic, and dread (*Angst*) is his very nature, now he would be a riddle to all and find delight in their dread. Hence this imperial smile which no one can comprehend. People approach his throne, he greets them with a friendly smile, and yet a terrible dread grips them, perhaps the smile is their death sentence, perhaps the floor is opening and they are about to plunge into the abyss. A woman approaches his throne, he smiles graciously upon her, and yet she becomes almost impotent with dread; perhaps this smile already singles her out as a sacrifice to his lust. And this dread delights him. He does not wish to produce awe, he wishes to terrify. He does not step forth with imperial dignity—weak, impotent, he slinks here and there, for this powerlessness is still more disquieting. He looks like a dying man, his breathing is feeble, and yet he is the Emperor of Rome and holds in his hands the lives of men. His soul is faint, only witty sayings and clever conceits are capable for an instant of giving him breath. What a world he has drained! and yet he is unable to breathe if this source of pleasure is dried up. He is capable of having a child cut down before the mother's eyes to see if her despair would give passion a new expression which would entertain him. If he were not Emperor of Rome, he perhaps would end his life with suicide; for in truth it is only another expression for the selfsame thing when Caligula wishes that the heads of all men were set upon one neck so as to be able with one stroke to annihilate the whole world, and when a man puts himself to death.

Whether it was the case with Nero, I do not know, but in such characters one sometimes finds a certain good humor, and if Nero had it, I have no doubt that the people who surrounded him were prompt to call it graciousness. There is something very singular about this, but it furnishes also a new proof of the immediacy which constitutes by its repression genuine melancholy. So it comes about that at the very time when all the treasures of the world and its glory hardly avail to delight him, a single word, a curious little happening, the outward appearance of a man, or some other such insignificant thing, is enough to give him extraordinary joy. A Nero can rejoice over such a thing like a child. Like a child—that is precisely the right expression, for it is the whole immediacy of the child which appears in him unaltered and unexplained. A thoroughly developed character cannot rejoice in this way, for it is true that the man has retained childlike qualities, but he has ceased to be a child. Ordinarily Nero is an old man; occasionally he is a child.

Here I will bring to an end this description, which upon me at least has made a very serious impression. Nero is alarming even after his death, for, depraved as he is, he is, nevertheless, flesh of our flesh and bone of our bone, and even in a monster there is something human after all. I have not set this forth in order to busy your imagination, I am not an author that sues for a reader's favor, least of all for yours, and as you know, I am not an author at all, and I

am writing only for your sake. Neither have I set this forth
in order to give you and me occasion to thank God along
with that Pharisee that we are very different. It awakens
in me other thoughts, though I thank God that my life
has been too uneventful to suggest more than a remote
presentiment of such a horror, and now I am a happy married man. As for you, I rejoice that you are still young
enough to learn something from this. Let each learn what
he can, at least we both can learn that a man's unhappiness
is never due to the fact that he has not the outward conditions in his power, this being the very thing which would
make him unhappy.

What, then, is melancholy?[8] It is hysteria of the spirit.
There comes a moment in a man's life when his immediacy
is, as it were, ripened and the spirit demands a higher form
in which it will apprehend itself as spirit. Man, so long as
he is immediate spirit, coheres with the whole earthly life,
and now the spirit would collect itself, as it were, out of this
dispersion and become in itself transformed, the personality
would be conscious of itself in its eternal validity. If this
does not come to pass, if the movement is checked, if it is
forced back, melancholy ensues. One may do much by way
of inducing forgetfulness, one may work, one may employ
other expedients more innocent than those of Nero, but melancholy remains. There is something inexplicable in melancholy. The man who has sorrow and anxiety knows why
he is sorrowful or anxious. If a melancholy man is asked
what ground he has for it, what it is that weighs upon him,
he will reply, "I know not, I cannot explain it." Herein lies
the infinity of melancholy. This reply is perfectly correct,
for as soon as a man knows the cause, the melancholy is
done away with, whereas, on the contrary, in the case of the
sorrowful the sorrow is not done away when a man knows
why he sorrows. But melancholy is sin, really it is a sin
instar omnium, for not to will deeply and sincerely is sin,
and this is the mother of all sins. This sickness, or rather
this sin, is very common in our age, and so it is under this
all young Germany and France now sighs. I do not wish
to provoke you, I would threaten you as leniently as possible. I am willing to admit that in a way melancholy is

not a bad sign, for as a rule only the most gifted natures
are subject to it. Neither shall I vex you by assuming that
everyone who suffers from indigestion has for this cause
a right to call himself melancholy—a thing often enough to
be seen in our time when to be melancholy is the dignity
to which everybody aspires. But he who would claim to
be more eminently gifted must put up with it when I charge
him with the accountability of being also more guilty than
other men. If he will see this situation rightly, he will not
see in it a disparagement of his personality, though it will
teach him to bow with genuine humility before the eternal
Power. As soon as that movement comes about, melancholy
is essentially done away with, although to the same individual it may well happen that his life has in store many
sorrows and anxieties, and *à propos* of this you know that
I am the last man to teach the wretched commonplace that
sorrow is of no avail, that one must drive sorrow away. I
should be ashamed of myself if with these words I were to
approach a person in sorrow. But even the man in whose
life this movement comes about quietly, peaceably and sea-
sonably, will, nevertheless, always retain a little melancholy;
but this is connected with something far deeper, with
original sin, and it is due to the fact that no man can become perfectly transparent to himself. On the other hand,
the men whose souls are acquainted with no melancholy
are those whose souls have no presentiment of a metamorphosis. With them I have nothing to do here, for I am
writing only to and about you, and to you I believe this
explanation will be satisfactory, for you hardly assume like
many physicians that melancholy is an ailment of the body
—and for all that, strangely enough, the physicians cannot
relieve it. Only spirit can relieve it, for it is a spiritual ailment. And when the spirit finds itself, all the small troubles
vanish, all the causes which according to some people produced melancholy, for example, that one cannot find oneself in the world, that one comes to the world both too late
and too early, that one cannot find one's place in life; for
he who owns his own self eternally can come neither too
early nor too late, and he who possesses himself in his
eternal validity surely finds his significance in this life.

However, this was an episode, for which I hope you will forgive me since it came about essentially for your sake. I return to the view of life which represents that man should live for the satisfaction of pleasure. A shrewd common sense readily perceives that this cannot be carried through and that therefore it is not worth while making a start at it. A refined egoism perceives that it misses the very point in pleasure. So here we have a view of life which teaches one to enjoy life but expresses it thus: "Enjoy yourself, in enjoyment it is yourself you must enjoy." This is a higher reflection, but for all that it does not penetrate to the personality itself, which remains in its accidental immediacy. In this case the condition requisite for enjoyment is after all an outward one which is not within the control of the individual, for although he says he enjoys himself, yet he enjoys himself only in the enjoyment, but the enjoyment is dependent upon an outward condition. So the difference is that he enjoys reflectively, not immediately. To that extent even this Epicureanism is dependent upon a condition over which it has no control. A certain callousness of the understanding then contrives an expedient and teaches: "Enjoy yourself while constantly casting away the conditions." But it follows as a matter of course that he who enjoys himself by casting away the conditions is just as dependent upon them as is he who enjoys them. His reflection constantly turns back to himself, and as his enjoyment consists in providing as little content as possible for enjoyment, he is constantly scooping himself out, as it were, since such a finite reflection is, of course, incapable of opening the personality.

I believe that by these reflections I have now outlined, intelligibly enough at least for you, the territory of the aesthetical views of life. All of the stages have this in common, that what one lives for is that whereby one immediately is what one is; for reflection never grasps so high that it grasps beyond this. It is only a very cursory indication I have furnished, but I had no desire to give more; it was not the various stages which were important to me, but only the movement which is imperatively necessary, as I shall now show, and it is upon that I would beg you to fix your attention.

So I assume that the man who lived for his health was, to use an expression of yours, just as hale when he died as ever he was; that the above-mentioned noble couple danced at their golden wedding, and that a whisper of admiration passed through the hall just as it did when they danced on the day of their nuptials; I assume that the rich man's gold mines were inexhaustible, that honors and dignities followed the happy man's pilgrimage through life; I assume that the young girl got the man she loved, that the man of mercantile talent harnessed with his trade connections all quarters of the globe and held the purses of all the world in his purse, that the mechanical talent succeeded in connecting heaven and earth—I assume that Nero never yawned, but that new pleasures surprised him every instant, that the cunning Epicurean could find delight in himself every instant, that the Cynic constantly had conditions to cast away in order to rejoice in his lightness—this I assume, and so all these people were happy. That, surely, you will not affirm, and the reason for it I shall explain later on; but this you will willingly concede, that many people would think them happy, and that one or another would imagine he said something very clever when he added that what they lacked was that they did not appreciate it. I will now make the opposite movement. Nothing of all this comes to pass. What then? Why, then, they despair. You will do no such thing, you will say perhaps that it is not worth while. Why it is that you will not admit despair I shall explain later on. Here I only require you to acknowledge that a great many men would find it natural to despair. Let us see now why they despair. Is it because they discovered that what they built their life upon was transient? But is that, then, a reason for despairing? Has any essential change occurred in that upon which they built their life? Is it an essential change in the transitory that it shows itself to be transitory? Or is it not rather something accidental and unessential in the case of what is transitory that it does not show itself to be such? Nothing has happened which could occasion a change. So if they despair, it must be because they were in despair beforehand. The only difference is that they did not know it. But this is an entirely fortuitous difference. So it appears that every aesthetic view of life is despair, and that everyone who lives aesthetically is in despair, whether he knows it or not. But when one knows it (and you indeed know it), a higher form of existence is an imperative requirement.

With only a few words I will explain myself further with respect to my judgment about the young girl and her love. You know that in my capacity as a married man it is my custom on every occasion to maintain against you, both orally and in writing, the reality of love, and therefore, to prevent any misunderstanding, I will also give expression to my thought here. Perhaps a man who is shrewd in a finite sense would become a little dubious about such a love, he would perhaps perceive its fragility and in opposing it would express his paltry wisdom by the proverb, "Love me little, love me long"—as if his worldly wisdom were not still more fragile or at least far more paltry than her love! You will easily perceive that I could not express my disapproval of it in that way. It is very repulsive to me to carry on a thought experiment in the domain of love. I have only loved once and am still indescribably happy in this love. It is repulsive to me to think of being loved by any other person than the one to whom I am joined and in any other way than that by which she makes me so happy. But I will make the venture. Suppose, then (however it may have come about), that I have become the object of such a love. It would not make me happy, and I would never accept it—not because I should disdain it, for God knows that I would rather have a murder on my conscience than to have disdained a maiden's love—but for her own sake I would not permit it. So far as in me lieth, I desire to be loved by everybody, by my wife I desire to be loved as dearly as one person can love another and it would pain me if I were not so loved, but I do not desire more, I will not permit anyone to take harm to her soul by loving me; I should love her too truly to permit her to abase herself. To a proud mind there is something seductive in being loved thus, and there are men who understand the art of infatuating a girl so that she forgets everything else but them—let them look to it how they justify this. Such a girl is for the most part punished severely enough, but the despicable thing is to let this occur. Observe that it is for this reason I said and still say that the young girl was equally in despair whether she got the loved one or not, for in fact it was an accidental circumstance if the man she loved was so upright that he would help her out of her heart's delusion; and even though the means he employed to this end were never so hard, I would affirm, nevertheless, that he acted towards her uprightly, sincerely, faithfully, chivalrously.

So the aesthetic view of life has proved itself to be despair. It might therefore seem to be in place to undertake the movement which brings to evidence the ethical. However, there still remains one stage, an aesthetic life view which is the most refined and superior of them all, into which I must inquire with the greatest care, for now it is your turn. You can follow with composure everything I have set forth hitherto, and in a way it is not to you I have been speaking, and it would be of little use to talk in this fashion to you or to explain to you that life is vanity. That you know very well and in your way have sought to adjust yourself. The reason why I have expounded this is that I desire to protect my rear and would prevent you from suddenly leaping back. This last life view is despair itself. It is an aesthetic life view, for the personality remains in its immediacy; it is the last aesthetic life view, for to a certain degree it is conscious of its own nullity. There is a difference, however, between despair and despair. If I imagine an artist, a painter, for example, who becomes blind, he then perhaps will despair if there is nothing deeper in him. He despairs then over this particular thing, and if his sight were restored to him again, his despair would cease. Such is not the case with you, you are far too intellectually gifted for that, and your soul is in a certain sense too deep for this to befall you. Nor in outward respects has any such misfortune happened to you. You still have in your power all the factors requisite for an aesthetic life view, you have wealth and independence, your health is unimpaired, your mind still vigorous, nor have you yet become unhappy for the fact that a girl would not love you. And yet you are in despair. It is not despair about any actual thing but a despair in thought. Your thought has hurried on ahead, you have seen through the vanity of all things, but you have got no further. Occasionally you plunge into pleasure, and every instant you are devoting yourself to it you make the discovery in your consciousness that it is vanity. So you are constantly beyond yourself, that is, in despair. This is the reason why your life lies between two prodigious contradictions; sometimes you have enormous energy, sometimes an indolence just as great.

I have often observed that the more costly the fluid with which a man intoxicates himself, the more difficult it is to cure him, the intoxication being more beautiful and the consequences apparently not so dreadful. The man who gets drunk on gin is at once sensible of the dreadful consequences, and one may have hope of his salvation. He who uses champagne is cured with more difficulty. And you, you who have chosen the most refined means! For no intoxication is so beautiful as despair, so becoming, so attractive, especially in a maiden's eyes (that you know full well), and especially if one possesses the skill to repress the wildest outbursts, to let despair be vaguely sensed like a distant conflagration while only a glimpse of it is visible outwardly. It imparts a light swing to the hat and to the whole body, it gives one a proud and defiant air. The lips smile arrogantly. It gives an indescribable lightness to life and a lordly survey of all things. And now when such a figure approaches a young girl, when this proud head is bowed only before her, before her alone in the whole world, this flatters, and alas, there might be one who was innocent enough to believe in this false bow. Is it not shameful when a man thus . . . but no, I shall not deliver a thundering speech; that would only provoke you, I have other, more powerful expedients. I have that hopeful young man, he is perhaps in love, he comes to you, he is mistaken in you, he believes that you are a trustworthy, upright man, he would take counsel of you. In reality you can shut your door against every such unhappy young man, but your heart you cannot shut; though you do not wish him to be a witness of your humiliation, you shall not be spared it, for you are not so depraved as all that, and when you are alone with yourself you are more good-natured perhaps than anybody believes.

Here, then, I have your view of life, and believe me, much in your life will be explicable to you if with me you regard it as thought-despair. You are a hater of all activity in life. Very reasonably, for before there can be any meaning in activity there must be continuity, and that is what your life lacks. You occupy yourself with your studies, it is true; you are even industrious. But it is only for your own sake, and it is done with as little teleology as possible. For the rest you are idle, like the laborers in the Gospel you stand in the market place, you thrust your hands into your pockets and look on at life. Then you take repose in despair, nothing concerns you, you will not get out of the way of anything, you say, "If one were to throw a tile from the roof, I wouldn't get out of the way." You are like a dying man, you die daily, not in the serious significance usually attached to this word, but life has lost its reality, and, as you say, you always count your days by the number of times notice is served on you to quit your lodging. You let everything pass you by, it makes no impression, but now suddenly there comes something that grips you, an idea, a situation, a smile from a young girl, and then you are "in it." For as there are certain occasions when you are not "in it," so there are others when you are and when you are very much "at your service." Wherever there is something happening you are "in it." You behave in life as you say you are accustomed to do in a crowd, working your way into the thickest group, contriving, if possible, to be pressed up above the others, and when you are up you make yourself as comfortable as possible, and so, also, you let yourself be carried through life.

But when the crowd has dispersed and the event is over you stand again at the street corner and look on at the world. A dying man, as you know, possesses supernatural energy, and so it is also with you. If it is an idea that has to be thought through, a book to be read through, a plan to be carried out, a little romance to be experienced—yes, even a hat that has to be bought, then you take hold of the thing with prodigious strength. According to circumstances,

you work indefatigably for a day, for a month; you take
joy in convincing yourself that you still possess the same
vigor as before, you take no rest, "Satan himself could not
keep up with me," you say. If you work in common with
others, you work them till they are ready to drop. But then
when the month is up, or the half year, which you regard
as the maximum, you break off, saying, "Here the story
ends"; you retire and leave the other party to finish the
work, or if you have worked at it alone, you say nothing
about it to anybody. You then pretend to yourself and to
others that you have lost the inclination and flatter yourself
with the vain thought that you could have continued to
work with the same intensity if you had been inclined to
do so. But this is a prodigious deception. You would have
succeeded as most others do in finishing the work if you
had patiently willed to do so, but at the same time you
also would have learned by experience that it requires an
entirely different sort of perseverance from that which you
have. So in this way you have deluded yourself and have
learnt nothing for your subsequent life. I can serve you here
with a little piece of enlightenment. I am not unaware how
deceitful one's own heart is, how easily one can deceive
oneself—not to speak of a person like you who are in possession of a dialectical power to loose, which not only bestows dispensation for everything but dissolves and oblit-
erates it.

So for my part, when something has confronted me in
life, when I have resolved upon something which I feared
in the course of time might acquire for me a different aspect, when I have done something which I feared in the
course of time I might interpret differently, I have written
down in a few clear words what it was I purposed to do
or what I had done and why. Then when it seems to me I
have need of it, some time when my resolution or my action
did not stand out vividly before me, I take out my charter
and pass judgment upon myself. It seems to you, perhaps,
that this is pedantic, that it is too tedious and not worth
making such a fuss about. I have no reply to make but
this: if you feel no need of it, if your consciousness is always so unfailing and your memory so faithful, then let it

be. But that I do not believe, for the talent your soul lacks
is memory, I do not mean for this and that, not for ideas,
witty sayings, or dialectical quirks—far be it from me to
maintain that—but I mean memory of your own life, of
what you have experienced in it. If you had such memory,
the same phenomenon would not so often repeat itself in
your life, and your life would not exhibit what I would call
half-hour works, and would call them this even if you had
spent half a year on them, seeing that you have not finished
them. But you enjoy deluding yourself and others. If you
were always as strong as you are in the instant of passion,
I do not deny that you would be the strongest man I have
ever known. But that you are not, as you yourself know
right well. Hence, you retire, hiding yourself almost from
yourself, and give yourself up to the repose of indolence.
In my eyes, from whose watchfulness you cannot always
withdraw, you become almost ludicrous by reason of your
momentary zeal and the justification you derive from this
for your derision of others. Once upon a time there were
two Englishmen who went to Arabia to buy horses. They
brought with them several English race horses, wishing to
try their qualities in comparison with the Arabian steeds.
They proposed a race, and the Arabs were willing and left
it to the Englishmen to select what horse they would from
the Arabian steeds, what horse they would race against;
but they were not willing to hold the race at once, they
said that forty days was needed for training. They waited
forty days, the amount of the prize was fixed, the horses
saddled, and then the Arabs asked how long they should
ride. "One hour," was the answer. This surprised the Arab,
and he replied laconically, "I thought we should ride for
three days."

Behold, thus it is with you. If one would run a race with
you for an hour, Satan, as you say, couldn't keep up with
you; a three days' race would be too much for you. I
remember once telling you this story, and I remember your
reply, that it was a ticklish thing to run a race of three days,
there was risk of acquiring such headway that one could
never come to a stop, and that therefore you refrained from
all such violence, "once in a while I ride horseback, but I

neither wish to be a cavalryman nor to pursue any other unflagging activity in life." And to a certain degree this is quite true, for you are always afraid of continuity, principally for the reason that it deprives you of the opportunity of deceiving yourself. The strength you possess is the strength of despair; it is more intense than ordinary human strength, but also it lasts a shorter time.

You are constantly hovering above yourself, but the ether, the fine sublimate into which you are volatilized, is the nullity of despair, and beneath you you behold a multiplicity of subjects for learning, information, study, observation, which for you, indeed, have no reality, but which you capriciously combine and employ to adorn as tastefully as possible the palace of the mind's luxurious delight where occasionally you sojourn. What wonder, then, that for you existence is a fairy tale, that (to use your own words) you are often tempted to begin every speech by saying, "Once upon a time there was a king and a queen who unfortunately had no children," and that thereupon you forget everything else for the sake of the remark that strangely enough this is always the reason given by fairy tales for the sorrow of a king and a queen, whereas in ordinary life we hear rather of the sorrow of having children, as asylums and such like institutions go to prove. Now you have got the notion that "life is a fairy tale." You are capable of spending a whole month reading nothing but fairy tales, you make a profound study of them, you compare and analyze, and your study is not barren of result—but what do you use it for? To divert your mind; you let the whole thing go off in a brilliant display of fireworks.

You are hovering above yourself, and what you behold beneath you is a multiplicity of moods and situations which you employ to find interesting contacts with life. You can be sentimental, heartless, ironical, witty—in this respect one must grant that you are well schooled. Then as soon as anyone is capable of rousing you out of your indolence you throw yourself with your whole passion into your practice, and in your practice you have no lack of art, being only too thoroughly equipped with wit, agility, and all the seductive gifts of the mind. You are (as with self-complacent arro-

gance you express it) never so ungallant as to present yourself without bringing with you a little odorous, freshly-
plucked bouquet of wit. The more one knows you, the more
one is struck by the calculated shrewdness which pervades
all that you do in the short time you are moved by passion.
For passion never blinds you but makes you all the more
clear-sighted. You then have forgotten your despair and
all that commonly weighs upon your soul and thought, the
accidental contact you have established with a person en-
gages your attention absolutely. I will remind you of a little
occurrence which took place in my own house. It is presumably to the two young Swedish girls who were present
I must express my thanks for the prize speech you delivered.
The conversation had taken a rather serious turn and
reached a point where it was not agreeable to you. I had
expressed myself a bit in opposition to the exaggerated respect for intellectual gifts which is so characteristic of our
age, I had insisted that what really matters is something
quite different, an inwardness of the entire being for which
language possesses no other expression but faith. By this
you were, perhaps, placed in a less favorable light, and as
you perceived clearly enough that along the path on which
we had struck out you could get no further, you felt called
upon to try your hand at what you yourself call "higher
madness"[9] in a sentimental key: "What! Am I supposed
not to have faith? Why, I believe that in the inmost depths
of the stillness of the forest, where the trees are reflected in
the dark water, in its mysterious darkness, where even at
midday there is twilight, there lives a being, a nymph, a
maiden; I believe she is more beautiful than any one can
conceive, I believe that in the morning she plaits garlands,
that at midday she bathes in the cool water, that in the
evening she sadly plucks the leaves from the garlands; I
believe that I should be happy, the only man deserving to
be so called, if I could catch her and possess her; I believe
that in my soul there is a longing to search the whole world,
I believe that I should be happy if that longing were satisfied; I believe that after all there is some meaning in the
world if only I could find it—do not say, then, that I am not
strong in faith and fervent in spirit." Perhaps you think that

such a speech might entitle you to become a worthy member of a Greek symposium, for it is to this end among others you are cultivating your talents, and this you would regard as the most beautiful life, to gather together every night with Greek youths, to sit with a garland woven about your hair and deliver panegyrics upon love or upon whatever subject might occur to you; yea, you are willing to devote yourself wholly to delivering panegyrics. To me this speech seems claptrap, however artful it is, and however impressive at the moment, especially when you yourself are permitted to declaim it with your feverish eloquence; and it seems to me, also, an expression of your disturbed mental condition, for it is quite natural that one who believes nothing that other people believe should believe in such imaginary beings, just as it often happens that one who is not afraid of anything in heaven or on earth is afraid of spiders. You smile, you think that I am falling into a trap, that I believed that you believed this which you were further from believing than any other man. That is quite so, for your speech always ends in absolute scepticism, but shrewd and calculating as you are, you cannot deny that for an instant you warm yourself with the morbid heat which lies in such an extravagance. Your intent, perhaps, is to deceive others, and yet there is a moment when without being aware of it you deceive yourself.

What applies to your studies applies to everything you do, you exist in the instant, and for an instant you attain a preternatural size, you sink your whole soul into the thing by an exertion of the will, for at the instant your whole nature is thoroughly under your command. He who sees you only at such an instant is very much deceived, whereas if he waits till the next instant, he may easily manage to exult over you. You remember, perhaps, the familiar fairy tale by Musaeus[10] about the three young squires of Roland. One of them acquired from the old witch they visited in the forest a thimble which rendered him invisible. By means of that he penetrated into the chamber of the beautiful princess Urraca and declared his love to her, making a strong impression upon her since she saw nobody and surmised that it was a fairy prince who honored her with his love. Nevertheless, she required him to reveal himself. Here lay the difficulty: as soon as he showed himself the enchantment might vanish, and yet there was no joy to be had from his love if he could not reveal himself. I have at hand, as it happens, this fairy tale of Musaeus and will transcribe a little passage which I would beg you to read through for the true good of your soul. "He consented unwillingly, as it seemed, and the imagination of the princess thrust before her the picture of the most beautiful man whom she thought with tense expectancy she was about to see. But what a contrast between the original and the ideal, since nothing appeared but a common visage, an ordinary person whose physiognomy betrayed neither genius nor sentiment!" What you wish to attain by these contacts with men, that you do attain, for you are considerably shrewder than that young squire, so you easily perceive that it doesn't pay to become revealed. When you have imposed upon a man an ideal picture of yourself (and here one must concede that you can make yourself appear ideal in any direction whatsoever) you generally withdraw and then enjoy the pleasure of having duped a person. What you attain at the same time is that the coherence in your life view is broken and you have a new element which causes you to begin afresh.

Theoretically you are through with the world, finiteness cannot subsist before your thought; practically you are through with it to a certain degree, that is, in an aesthetic sense. Nevertheless, you have no world view, you have something which resembles a view, and this gives your life a certain composure, which must not, however, be confounded with a secure and refreshing confidence in life. You are composed only in contrast with one who is still pursuing the phantoms of pleasure, *per mare pauperiem fugiens, per saxa, per ignes.*[11] In relation to pleasure you are superbly proud. That is quite natural, for indeed, you are through with finiteness altogether. And yet you are not able to give it up. You are content in comparison with those who are pursuing contentment, but it is in absolute discontent you find contentment. You are not concerned about seeing all the glories of the world, for in thought you are beyond

them, and if they were offered to you, you would likely say
as you commonly do, "Well, one might well devote to them
a whole day." You are not concerned because you have not
become a millionaire, and if this were offered to you, you
would likely answer, "Well, it might be quite interesting to
have been that, and one might well spend a month at it."
And if one were able to offer you the love of the most
beautiful maiden, you would answer, "Well, for half a year
that would not be so bad." I will not here join in the cry of
complaint often raised against you that you are insatiable,
I would say rather that in a certain sense you are right, for
nothing finite, not the whole world, can satisfy the soul of
the man who feels need of the eternal. If one could offer
you dignities and honor, the admiration of your contemporaries (for that is your weak point), you would answer,
"Well, for a short time that would be pretty good." You do
not really desire it, and you would not take one step to
attain it. You would perceive that for this to have any
significance you must actually be so eminently gifted in
mind that this would be truth, and even in this case your
thought sees even the highest degree of intellectual talent
as something transitory. Your polemical temper gives you a
more extreme expression for this when in your exasperation
with life as a whole you could wish you were the most
foolish of all men and yet were admired and adored by
your contemporaries as the wisest of all, for this would be
a far more profound mockery of existence than if the really
clever man were honored as such. You therefore desire
nothing, wish for nothing, the only thing you might wish for
would be a divining twig which could give you everything,
and that you would use to scrape your pipe.

So you are through with life, and, as you say, you have
no need to make a will, for you have nothing to leave. But
you are unable to hold yourself erect on this pinnacle, for
it is true that your thought has taken everything from you,
but it has given you nothing in place of it. The next instant
a little insignificance captivates you. It is true that you
regard it with all the superiority and pride which your arro-
gant thought bestows upon you, you disdain it as a paltry
toy you are almost tired of before you take it in hand, but

it preoccupies you, nevertheless, and though it is not the thing itself which preoccupies you (that is never the case with you), yet you are preoccupied by the fact that you are willing to condescend to it. When you treat persons in this way your nature exhibits a high degree of faithlessness, for which, however, no one can reproach you ethically, for you are situated outside of ethical determinants. Fortunately, you are very little inclined to participate with others, and therefore this defect is not noticed. You often come to my house, and you know that you are always welcome, but you know, too, that it never occurs to me to invite you to participate in the least thing. I would not even take a drive with you in the forest, not because you cannot be very merry and entertaining, but because your participation is always a falsehood, for if you really take pleasure, it is not in something which gives pleasure to the rest of us, or in the drive, but in something you have *in mente;* and if you are not pleased, it is not because something unpleasant occurs which puts you out of sorts (for that might happen to the rest of us), but because already at the instant you are getting into the carriage you have discerned the nullity of this diversion. I am ready to forgive you for this, for your mind is always too active, and it is a true word you often apply to yourself, that you are like a woman in confinement, and when one is in such "interesting" situations it is no wonder that one is a little different from others.

However, the spirit will not let itself be mocked, it revenges itself upon you, it binds you with the chain of melancholy. My young friend, this is the way to become a Nero—if in your soul there were not a pristine seriousness, if in your thought there were not an innate depth, if you had not a spirit of magnanimity . . . and if you had become Emperor in Rome. However, you take another path. Now there appears before you a life view which seems to be the only one able to satisfy you, that is, to immerse your soul in sadness and sorrow. However, your thinking is so sound that this view cannot meet the test; because to such an aesthetic sorrow existence is just as vain as it is to every other aesthetic life view. If a person cannot sorrow more profoundly, I can say with truth that sorrow wears off just as joy does, for all that is merely temporal perishes. And if many find it a comfort that sorrow wears off, it seems to me that this thought is just as comfortless as the observation that joy wears off. So your thought annihilates again this life view; and when one has annihilated sorrow one retains joy; instead of sorrow you choose a joy which is sorrow's changeling. This joy you have now chosen, this laughter of despair. You return again to life, under this illumination existence acquires a new interest for you. Just as you find great joy in talking to a child in such a way that what you say is understood by it very well and easily and naturally, while for you it means something entirely different, so you find joy in deceiving men by your laughter. When you can get people to laugh with you and shout for joy and delight themselves, then you triumph over the world, then you say to yourself, "If only ye knew what ye are laughing at!"

However, the spirit will not suffer itself to be mocked, and the gloom of melancholy grows denser around you, and the lightning flash of a mad wit reveals this to you more strikingly, more dreadfully. And there is nothing that diverts you, all the pleasure of the world possesses no significance for you, and though you envy the simple their foolish enjoyment of life, you do not pursue it. Pleasure does not tempt you; and pitiful as your condition is, it is a mercy it does not. It is not my intention to extol the pride within you which disdains pleasure, but rather to extol the grace which holds your thought fast. For if pleasure tempted you, you would be lost. But the fact that it does not tempt you shows what path you now must take, that you must go forward, not backward. There is another false path not less dreadful, and here again I rely not upon your pride but upon the grace which constantly sustains you. It is true enough that you are proud, and that it is better for a man to be proud than to be vain, it is true that there is a dreadful passion in your thought and that you regard it as a claim you have no intention of relinquishing, that, to use your own words, you prefer to regard yourself as a creditor in the world who has not been paid rather than to annul the claim —and yet all human pride affords but a frail security.

Behold, my young friend, this life of yours is despair.

Hide this if you will from others, from yourself you cannot hide it, it is despair. And yet in another sense this life is not despair. You are too frivolous to despair, and you are too melancholy not to come in touch with despair. You are like a woman in childbirth, and yet you are constantly deferring the moment and remain constantly in pain. If a woman in her travail were to get the idea that she might give birth to a monster, or were to ponder within herself what it really was she would bring forth, her case would be similar to yours. Her effort to check the course of nature would be unavailing, but yours is indeed possible, for that to which a man gives birth in a spiritual sense is a *nisus formativus*[12] of the will, and that is in a man's own power. What is it then you fear? You are not about to give birth to another human being, you are merely to give birth to yourself. And yet, as I know well, there is a seriousness in this which perturbs the whole soul: to become conscious of oneself in one's eternal validity is more significant than everything else in the world. It is as though you were caught and ensnared and could nevermore, either in time or eternity, make your escape, it is as though you lost your own self, as though you ceased to be, it is as though the next instant you would regret it and yet it could not be undone. It is a serious and significant moment when for an eternity one attaches oneself to an eternal power, when one receives oneself as a person whose memory no lapse of time shall efface, when in an eternal and unfailing sense one becomes aware of oneself as the person one is. And yet one can leave it alone!

So here there is an either/or. Let me talk to you as I never would do if anybody else were listening, partly because I can claim no right to speak to you thus, and partly because I am speaking only of future possibilities. If you will not harken to this, if you will continue to divert your soul with the trumpery of wit and the vanity of *esprit*, then do so, leave your home, travel abroad, go to Paris, devote yourself to journalism, sue for the smile of effete women, cool their hot blood with the coldness of your wit, let it be the proud theme of your life's labor to drive away the boredom of an idle woman or the gloomy thoughts of an

enfeebled voluptuary, forget that you were a child, that
there was piety in your soul and innocence in your thought,
silence every higher voice in your breast, doze your life
away in the glittering inanity of the *soirées*, forget that there
is an immortal spirit within you; and when wit grows mute
there is water still in the Seine and gunpowder in the store
and traveling companionship at every hour of the day. But
if you cannot do this, if you will not (and this you neither
can nor will), then collect yourself, quell every rebellious
thought which would presume to commit high treason
against your better nature, despise all the pettiness which
would envy your intellectual gifts and itself desires them in
order to put them to a still worse use, despise the hypocritical virtue which unwillingly bears life's burdens and
yet would be honored because it bears them; but do not
for this cause despise life, respect every honest effort, every
unassuming endeavor which modestly hides itself, and
above all have a little more reverence for woman; believe
me, it is from her comes salvation, as surely as depravity
comes from man. I am a married man and to that extent
I am partial, but it is my conviction that if it was a woman
that ruined man, it was woman also that has fairly and
honestly made reparation and still does so; out of a hundred
men who go astray in the world ninety and nine are saved
by women and one by immediate divine grace. And as I
am also of the opinion that it is the nature of man to go
astray in one way or another, and that to a man it applies
as truly as to a woman that he ought to abide in the pure
and innocent peace of immediacy; you can easily see that
in my opinion woman [when she restores a man to this
state] makes due requital for the harm she has done.

What then must you do? Another perhaps would say,
"Get married. Then you will have something else to think
about." Yes, that you will, but the question remains whether
this will be any advantage to you, and whatever you may
think of the other sex, you think at all events too chivalrously to wish to marry for that reason; and moreover, if
you are unable to sustain yourself, you will hardly get another person who is capable of sustaining you. Or one might
say, "Look for a job, throw yourself into the life of affairs,

that is a distraction, and you will forget your melancholy. Get to work. That's the best thing." Perhaps you will succeed in getting to the point where your melancholy seems as if it were forgotten, but forgotten it is not; occasionally it will break out and will be more dreadful than ever, it will then perhaps be capable of doing what it could never do before, it may take you off your guard. Furthermore, however you may think of life and its affairs, you will nevertheless think too chivalrously of yourself to choose a profession for that reason, for that, after all, is a kind of falsehood, like marrying for the same reason. What then must you do? I have only one answer: despair.

I am a married man, my soul clings firmly and wisely to my wife, to my children, to this life which I shall always extol for its beauty. So when I counsel you to despair, it is not a fantastical youth who would whirl you away in the maelstrom of the passions, nor a mocking demon who shouts this comfort to the shipwrecked, but I shout it to you, not as a comfort, not as a condition in which you are to remain, but as a deed which requires all the power and seriousness and concentration of the soul, just as surely as it is my conviction, my victory over the world, that every man who has not tasted the bitterness of despair has missed the significance of life, however beautiful and joyous his life might be. By despairing you do not defraud the world in which you live, you are not lost to it because you have overcome it, as surely as I can affirm of myself that I am a proper married man, in spite of the fact that I, too, have despaired.

When in this way I look upon your life, I declare you fortunate, for at the instant of despair it is truly of the utmost importance for a man not to be mistaken about life; this is just as dangerous for him as for a woman in travail to go amiss. He who despairs over one particular thing incurs the danger that his despair may not be genuine and profound, that it may be a delusion, a sorrow only for a particular loss. It is not thus you are to despair, for no particular thing has been taken from you, you still possess everything you had. If the despairing man makes a mistake, if he believes that the misfortune lies in his multifarious surroundings, then his despair is not genuine and it will lead him to hate the world and not to love it, for true as it is that the world is a burden to you because it is as if it would be to you something else than it can be, it is also just as true that when in despair you have found yourself you will love the world because it is what it is. If it is a fault or guilt or a troubled conscience which brings a man to despair, he will perhaps have difficulty in regaining his joyfulness. So, then, despair with all your soul and with all your mind; the longer you put it off, the harder the conditions become, and the demand remains the same. I shout this to you, like the woman who offered to sell to Tarquin a collection of books and when he would not give the sum she demanded burned one-third of them and demanded the same sum, and when again he would not give the sum she demanded burned another third of them and demanded the same sum, until finally he gave the original sum for the last third.

It is on beautiful terms despair is offered to you, and yet there are more beautiful terms. Imagine a young man as talented as you are. Let him love a girl, love her as dearly as himself. Let him once ponder in a quiet hour upon what it is he has constructed his life and upon what she can construct hers. Love they have in common, and yet he will feel that there are differences. She possesses, perhaps, the gift of beauty, but this has no importance for him, and after all, it is so fragile; she has, perhaps, the joyful temper of youth, but that joy has no great significance for him, but he possesses the power of the mind and feels the might of it. He desires to love her in truth, and it never occurs to him to attribute this power to her, and her meek soul does not demand it, and yet there is a difference, and he will feel that this must be done away if he is to love her in truth. Then he will let his soul sink into despair. It is not for his own sake he despairs but for hers, and yet it is for his own sake too, for he loves her as dearly as himself. Then will despair devour everything till he finds *himself* in his eternal validity, but then he has also found her, and no knight can return more happily and gladly from the most perilous adventures than does he from this fight with flesh and blood and the vain differences of the finite, for he who despairs finds the eternal man, and in that we are all equal. The foolish thought of wishing to dull his mind or neglect its culture will not occur to him as a way of bringing about equality; he will preserve the gifts of the mind, but in his inmost heart he knows of himself that he who possesses these gifts is one who possesses them not. Or imagine a profoundly religious temperament, a man who from a true and sincere love for mankind cast himself into the ocean of despair till he found the absolute, the point where it is indifferent whether a forehead is squat or is arched as proudly as heaven, the point which is not indifference but absolute validity.

You have sundry good ideas, many whimsical notions, and a great quantity of follies—retain them all if you will, though I do not require you to. But one idea you have which I would beg you to hold fast, an idea which assures me that my mind is akin to yours. You have often said that you would rather be anything but a poet, since as a rule a poet-existence is a human sacrifice. For my part, I would not deny that there have lived poets who had found themselves before they began to write poetry or who found themselves by poetizing, but on the other hand, it is also certain that a poet-existence as such lies in the obscurity which is due to the fact that a beginning of despair was not carried through, that the soul keeps on shivering with despair and the spirit cannot attain its true transformation. The poetic ideal is always a false ideal, for the true ideal is always the real. So when the spirit is not allowed to soar up into the eternal world of spirit it remains midway and rejoices in the pictures reflected in the clouds and weeps that they are so transitory. A poet-existence is therefore, as such, an unhappy existence, it is higher than finiteness and yet not infiniteness. The poet sees the ideals, but he must flee away from the world in order to rejoice in them, he cannot bear about in the midst of life's confusion these divine images within him,[13] cannot tranquilly pursue his course unaffected by the caricatures of these ideals which appear on all sides, not to speak of having strength to clothe himself in them. The poet's life is, therefore, often an object of paltry compassion on the part of men who think themselves secure because they have remained in finiteness. You said once in a moment of despondency that doubtless there were some people who had privately cast up their accounts with you and were willing to be quits on the following terms: you were to be recognized as a clever pate, and in requital for that you were to sink out of sight and be no officious member of society. Yes, it is undeniable, there is such paltriness in the world which would triumph in this way over everything which projects even an inch above the ordinary level. However, do not let it disturb you, do not defy it, do not show your contempt for it—in this instance I would say as you are wont to say, "It's not worth the trouble." But if you do not wish to be a poet, there is no other way for you except that which I have indicated: despair!

So then choose despair, for despair itself is a choice; for one can doubt without choosing to, but one cannot despair without choosing. And when a man despairs he chooses again—and what is it he chooses? He chooses himself, not in his immediacy, not as this fortuitous individual, but he chooses himself in his eternal validity.

This point I shall endeavor to illuminate with application to you. In modern philosophy there has been more than enough talk about speculation beginning with doubt, but on the other hand, as far as I have been able to concern myself occasionally with such reflections, I have sought in vain for illumination upon the point of difference between doubt and despair. I will here attempt to throw light upon this distinction, in the hope that it will serve to orient you and put you in the correct position. I am far from presuming to claim any real competence as a philosopher, I have not your virtuosity in playing with the categories, but what in the deepest sense is the significance of life must be comprehensible also to a simpler man. Doubt is a despair of thought, despair is a doubt of the personality; hence it is I hold so stoutly to the category of choice, which is my solution, the nerve in my life view—and such a thing as a life view I have, even though I do not by any means presume to have a system.[14] Doubt is the inward movement in thought itself, and in doubting I behave as impersonally as possible. Now I assume that thought, by carrying doubt through, finds the absolute and rests in it—rests in it, therefore, not as a consequence of choice but in consequence of the same necessity in consequence of which it doubted. For doubt itself is determined by necessity, and so, likewise, is rest. This is the lofty characteristic of doubt for which it has so often been extolled and praised by people who hardly know what they are saying. But the fact that it is determined by necessity shows that the whole personality is not engaged in the movement. Hence, there is a good deal of truth in it when a man says, "I would willingly believe, but I cannot, I must doubt." Hence, one often sees that a doubter has in himself a positive content which lives apart from all communication with thought, that he may be an exceedingly conscientious person who has no doubt whatever about the validity of duty and the rule for his behavior, no doubt whatever about a multitude of sympathetic feelings and moods. On the other hand, in our age especially, one sees men who have despair in their hearts but yet have conquered doubt. This has struck me particularly in considering certain of the philosophers of Germany. Their thought is tranquilized, the objective logical thought is brought to rest in its corresponding objectivity, and yet they are in despair, even though they find distraction in objective thinking; for a man can find distraction in many ways, and there is hardly any anaesthetic so powerful as abstract thinking, because here it is a question of behaving as impersonally as possible.

Doubt and despair therefore belong in entirely different spheres, different sides of the soul are set in motion. Yet with this I am by no means satisfied, for doubt and despair would then be coordinate, and such is not the case. Despair is a far deeper and more complete expression, its movement much more comprehensive than that of doubt. Despair is precisely an expression for the whole personality, doubt only an expression for thought. The presumptive objectivity of doubt, whereof it is so proud, is precisely an expression for its incompleteness and imperfection. Doubt therefore is related to difference, despair to the absolute.

Talent is requisite for doubting, but no talent at all is requisite for despair; but talent as such is a difference, and that which has need of talent in order to assert itself can never be the absolute, for the absolute as absolute can only be for the absolute. The lowliest, the least talented man, can despair, a young girl who is anything but a thinker can despair, whereas everyone readily feels the foolishness of saying of them that they are doubting souls. The reason why a man's doubt may be tranquilized and he, nevertheless, may be in despair and continue in it, is that in a deeper sense he does not will despair. One cannot despair at all without willing it, but to despair truly one must truly will it, but when one truly wills it one is truly beyond despair; when one has truly willed despair one has truly chosen that which despair chooses, i.e., oneself in one's eternal validity. The personality is tranquilized only in despair, not by necessity, for I never despair by necessity, but by freedom, and only thereby does one win the absolute. In this respect our age, in my opinion, will make progress—if I may venture to have an opinion about our age, seeing that I know it only from my reading of the newspapers and an occasional book or from my conversations with you. The time is not far off when people will learn, perhaps at a dear price, that the true point of departure for finding the absolute is not doubt but despair.

But I return to my category. I have only one, for I am not a logician, but I assure you that it is the choice both of my heart and of my thought, my soul's delight and my bliss—I return to the importance of choosing. So, then, in choosing absolutely I choose despair, and in despair I choose the absolute, for I myself am the absolute, I posit the absolute and I myself am the absolute; but in complete identity with this I can say that I choose the absolute which chooses me, that I posit the absolute which posits me; for if I do not remember that this second expression is equally absolute, my category of choice is false, for the category is precisely the identity of both propositions. That which I choose I do not posit, for in case this were not [already] posited, I could not choose it, and yet if I do not posit it by the fact that I chose it, then I did not choose it. It exists, for in case it were not in existence I could not choose it; it does not exist, for it only comes into being by the fact that I choose it, otherwise my choice would be an illusion.

But what is it I choose? Is it this thing or that? No, for I choose absolutely, and the absoluteness of my choice is expressed precisely by the fact that I have not chosen to choose this or that. I choose the absolute. And what is the absolute? It is I myself in my eternal validity. Anything else but myself I never can choose as the absolute, for if I choose something else, I choose it as a finite thing and so do not choose it absolutely. Even the Jew who chose God did not choose absolutely, for he chose, indeed, the absolute, but did not choose it absolutely, and thereby it ceased to be the absolute and became a finite thing.

But what, then, is this self of mine? If I were required to define this, my first answer would be: It is the most abstract of all things, and yet at the same time it is the most concrete—it is freedom. Permit me at this point to make a little psychological observation. One often hears people give vent to their discontent with life, and often hears them express their wishes. Picture to yourself such a bungler—let us skip over the wishes which illuminate nothing because they have to do with the entirely accidental. He wishes: Would that I had that man's intelligence, or that man's talent, etc.—yea, to go to the extremest point, would that I had that man's firmness. Such wishes one hears frequently, but have you ever heard a man seriously express the wish that he might become another man? This is so far from being the case that it is precisely characteristic of the individuals we call unfortunate that for the most part they cling tightly to their own selves, that in spite of all their sufferings they would not for all the world be anybody else. And the reason for this is that such individuals are very close to the truth and feel the eternal validity of their personality, not in its blessings but in its bane, even though they have refrained from giving voice to this perfectly abstract expression for the gladness of being themselves rather than anybody else. But then, that man of the many wishes thinks constantly that he would remain himself although everything were to be changed. So there is something in him which is absolute in relation to everything else, something whereby he is the man he is, even though the alteration he would accomplish by his wish were the greatest possible. That he is mistaken I shall show later, but here I would merely find the most abstract expression for this "self" which makes him the man he is. And this is nothing other than freedom. It would actually be possible in this way to produce a highly plausible proof for the eternal validity of the personality. Yea, even a suicide does not really desire to do away with his self, he too wishes, he wishes another form for his self, and therefore one may find a suicide who was in the highest degree convinced of the immortality of the soul but whose whole being was so entangled that by this step he expected to find the absolute form for his spirit.

The reason, however, why it seems to an individual as if he might constantly be changed and yet remain the same (as if his inmost nature were an algebraic sign which could signify anything whatever) is to be found in the fact that he is not correctly situated, has not chosen himself, has no conception of such a thing; and yet even in his lack of understanding there is implied a recognition of the eternal validity of the personality. He, on the other hand, who is correctly situated has a different experience. He chooses himself, not in a finite sense (for then this "self" would be something finite along with other things finite), but in an absolute sense; and yet, in fact, he chooses himself and not another. This self which he then chooses is infinitely concrete, for it is in fact himself, and yet it is absolutely distinct from his former self, for he has chosen it absolutely. This self did not exist previously, for it came into existence by means of the choice, and yet it did exist, for it was in fact "himself."

In this case choice performs at one and the same time the two dialectical movements: that which is chosen does not exist and comes into existence with the choice; that which is chosen exists, otherwise there would not be a choice. For in case what I chose did not exist but absolutely came into existence with the choice, I would not be choosing, I

would be creating; but I do not create myself, I choose
myself. Therefore, while nature is created out of nothing,
while I myself as an immediate personality am created
out of nothing, as a free spirit I am born of the principle
of contradiction, or born by the fact that I choose myself.
The man we are speaking of discovers now that the self
he chooses contains an endless multiplicity, inasmuch as it
has a history, a history in which he acknowledges identity
with himself. This history is of various sorts; for in this history he stands in relation to other individuals of the race
and to the race as a whole, and this history contains something painful, and yet he is the man he is only in consequence of this history. Therefore, it requires courage for
a man to choose himself; for at the very time when it seems
that he isolates himself most thoroughly he is most thoroughly absorbed in the root by which he is connected with
the whole. This alarms him, and yet so it must be, for when
the passion of freedom is aroused in him (and it is aroused
by the choice, as also it is presupposed in the choice) he
chooses himself and fights for the possession of this object
as he would for his eternal blessedness; and it is his eternal
blessedness. He cannot relinquish anything in this whole,
not the most painful, not the hardest to bear, and yet the
expression for this fight, for this acquisition is . . . repentance. He repents himself back into himself, back into the
family, back into the race, until he finds himself in God.
Only on these terms can he choose himself, and he wants
no others, for only thus can he absolutely choose himself.
What is a man without love? But there are many sorts of
love: I love a father and a mother differently, likewise my
wife, and every distinct sort of love has its distinct expression; but there is also a love by which I love God, and
there is only one word in the language which expresses it
. . . it is repentance. When I do not love Him thus, I do
not love Him absolutely, do not love Him with my inmost
being, and every other sort of love for the absolute is a misunderstanding, for (to take for example what is usually extolled most highly and which I myself hold in honor) when
thought clings to the absolute with all its love, it is not the
absolute I love, I do not love absolutely, for I love neces-

sarily; as soon as I love freely and love God I repent. And if there might be any other reason why the expression for my love of God is repentance, it would be because He has loved me first. And yet this is an imperfect account of the reason, for only when I choose myself as guilty do I choose myself absolutely, if my absolute choice of myself is to be made in such a way that it is not identical with creating myself; and though it were the iniquity of the father which passed by inheritance to the son, he repents of this as well, for only thus can he choose himself, choose himself absolutely; and though tears were almost to blot out everything, he holds on to repentance, for only thus can he choose himself. His self is, as it were, outside of him, and it has to be acquired, and repentance is his love for this self, because he chooses it absolutely out of the hand of the eternal God.

What I have stated here is not professorial wisdom, it is something every man can state who wills to do so, and which every man can will to do if he will. I have not learned it in lecture rooms, I have learned it in the drawing room, or in the nursery, if you will, for when I see my small son running about the room, so joyful, so happy, I then think, "Who knows if after all I have not had an injurious influence upon him? God knows I take all possible care of him, but this thought does not tranquilize me." Then I say to myself, "There will come a moment in his life when his spirit will be ripened by the instant of choice, then he will choose himself, then also he will repent what guilt of mine may rest upon him. And it is a beautiful thing for a son to repent his father's fault, and yet he will not do this for my sake but because he only thus can choose himself. So come what may, that which one regards as the best may after all have the most injurious consequences for a person, and yet all this is nothing. I can be of much use to him, that I shall endeavor to do, but the highest thing he alone can do for himself." Here is the reason why it is so painful for men to choose themselves, it is because absolute isolation is in this case identical with the profoundest continuity, because so long as one has not chosen oneself there is, as it were, the possibility of being somewhat different either in one way or another.

Here you have my humble opinion about what it is to choose and to repent. It is unseemly to love a young girl as if she were one's mother, or to love one's mother as though she were a young girl. Every kind of love has its distinct characteristic, love for God has its absolute characteristic, its expression is repentance. And what is all other love in comparison with this? It is only childish prattle in this contrast. I am not a fantastic youth who seeks to recommend his theories, I am a married man, I dare let my wife hear me say that all love in comparison with repentance is only childish prattle; and yet I know that I am a proper husband, "I who as a married man still fight under the triumphant banner of first love"; I know that she shares my view, and therefore, I love her even more dearly, and therefore, I would not love that young girl we spoke about, because she did not share this view.

That new paths, devious and dangerous, present themselves at this point, that he who creeps upon the ground is not so much exposed to the danger of falling as is he who climbs to the mountain summit, that he who remains in the chimney corner is less liable to go astray than is he who ventures out into the world, all this I know, but for all that I hold no less confidently to my choice.

Here a theologian will discover a point of departure for manifold reflections. I will not go into them further since I am only a layman. I will only try to illuminate the foregoing discussion by the observation that in Christianity repentance found for the first time its true expression. The pious Jew felt the iniquity of the fathers resting upon him, and yet he did not feel this nearly so deeply as the Christian, for the pious Jew could not repent it, because he could not absolutely choose himself. The guilt of his forefathers weighed upon him, brooded over him, he sank under this burden, he sighed, but he could not lift it; that he only can do who absolutely chooses himself through repentance. The greater the freedom the greater the guilt, and this is one of the secrets of blessedness, and if it be not cowardice, it is at least faint-heartedness not to be willing to repent the guilt of the forefathers; if not paltriness, it is at least pettiness and lack of magnanimity.

So then the choice of despair is "my self"—for though when I despair it is true that, among all the other things I despair of, I despair also of myself, yet this self of which I despair is a finite thing like every other finitude, whereas the self I choose is the absolute self, or myself according to its absolute validity. Such being the case, you will see again in this instance why I said in the foregoing and continue to say that the either/or I posited between living aesthetically and living ethically is not a complete dilemma because it properly has to do with only one object of choice, since in this choice I am not really choosing between good and evil but I choose the good, but in the fact that I choose the good I make *eo ipso* the choice between good and evil. The original choice is constantly present in every subsequent choice.

So, then I bid you despair, and never more will your frivolity cause you to wander like an unquiet spirit, like a ghost, amid the ruins of a world which to you is lost. Despair, and never more will your spirit sigh in melancholy, for again the world will become beautiful to you and joyful, although you see it with different eyes than before, and your liberated spirit will soar up into the world of freedom.

Here I might break off, for I have now brought you to the point where I would have you, that is, if you yourself will to be there. I wanted you to tear yourself loose from the illusions of the aesthetic life and awake from a dream of half despair to the earnestness of the spirit. It is not my intention, however, to break off, for from this point of vantage I would give you a reflection upon life, an ethical life view. It is but a frugal gift I offer you, partly because my talent is not adequate to the task, partly because frugality is a prime characteristic of everything ethical, a characteristic which may seem strange to one who comes from the abundance of the aesthetical. Here it is in point to say, *nil ad ostentationem, omnia ad conscientiam* [Nothing for appearance, everything for conscience]. For still another reason it might seem precarious to break off here, because it might easily appear as if I ended in a sort of quietism where the personality comes to repose with the same necessity as thought comes to repose in the absolute. What, then, would be the advantage of having gained oneself? What is the advantage of procuring a sword which is able to conquer the whole world if one were to make no other use of it but to thrust it into the scabbard?

But before I go on to set forth more in detail such an ethical view of life I would indicate in a few words the danger which lies before a man at the instant of despair, the reef upon which he may run aground and be totally shipwrecked. The Scripture says: "What would it profit a man if he were to gain the whole world and suffer damage to his soul?"[15] What compensation would he have? The converse of this is not expressly stated in the Scripture but it is implied in this sentence. It would read thus: what harm would it do a man if he were to lose the whole world and yet receive no damage to his soul? What compensation would he need? There are expressions which in themselves seem simple and yet fill the soul with an uncanny dread because they become almost more obscure the more one thinks over them. With respect to religion the sin against the Holy Ghost is such an expression. I do not know if the theologians have succeeded in giving a precise explanation of this; I do not count myself capable of doing so, but then I am only a layman. On the other hand, the expression, "suffer damage to one's soul," is an ethical expression, and he who pretends to have an ethical life view must be supposed to have an explanation of it. One often hears this saying used, and yet every man who would understand it must have experienced profound emotions in his soul, yea, he must have been in despair, for it is properly the movements of despair which are described here: on the one side the whole world; on the other side one's own soul. You will easily see that by following up this expression one reaches the same abstract definition of "soul" which was reached earlier as the definition of the "self" when we were considering the fact that wishing does not imply wanting to be another person. For if I may gain the whole world and yet suffer damage to my soul, then the expression "whole world" must comprise all the finite things of which I, as such, am immediately in possession. My soul appears, then, to be indifferent to these things. If I lose the whole world without suffering damage to my soul, then again the expression "whole world" comprises all the determinants which I as such immediately have, and yet my soul is unharmed, and so it is indifferent to them. I may lose my wealth, my honor in the eyes of others, my intellectual powers, and suffer no damage to my soul. I could gain it all and yet suffer damage. What then is my soul? What is this inmost being of mine which can remain unaffected by this loss and suffer damage by this gain?

Before the eyes of the despairing man this movement is manifest, it is no rhetorical expression but the only adequate one, when on the one side he sees the whole world, and on the other side his self, his soul. In the instant of despair this distinction is manifest, and then all depends upon how a man despairs. For, as I have expounded this in a previous passage dealing with every aesthetical view of life, it is despair to gain the whole world, and to gain it in such a way that one suffers damage to one's soul, and yet it is my sincere conviction that it is a man's true salvation to despair. Here again is manifest the importance of willing one's despair, of willing it in an infinite sense, in an absolute sense, for such a willing is identical with the absolute resignation. If, on the other hand, I will in a finite sense, then I suffer damage to my soul, for then my inmost being does not undergo its transformation in despair; on the contrary it shuts itself up, it is hardened, so that finally despair is obduracy, whereas the absolute despair is an experience which infinitizes. So when in my despair I gain the whole world I suffer damage to my soul for the fact that I finitize myself by living for it; when I despair at having lost the whole world I suffer damage to my soul, for I finitize it in quite the same way, since here again I regard my soul as posited by finiteness. That a man by his crimes can gain the whole world and yet suffer damage to his soul goes without saying, but there is a seemingly far more innocent way by which this may come about. Hence, I said that the young girl we spoke about was just as much in despair whether she got the man she loved or not.

Every finite despair is a choice of finiteness, for I choose it just as really when I lose it as when I gain it; whether I shall obtain it does not depend upon my power, but whether I choose it does. The finite despair is, therefore, an unfree despair, it does not really will to be in despair, it wills to possess finitude, but to will this is despair. Upon this narrow point a man may maintain his position, and so long as he holds himself there I cannot quite resolve to venture to declare that he has suffered damage to his soul. He is standing upon an exceedingly dangerous point. Every instant there is a possibility of damage. Despair is there, but it has not yet attacked his inmost being; only when in a finite sense he hardens himself in despair has he suffered damage to his soul. His soul is, as it were, anaesthetized by despair, and only when upon awakening he chooses a finite way out of despair has he suffered damage to his soul, for then he has shut himself up, then his rational soul is smothered and he is transformed into a beast of prey which will shun no expedient because all is self-defense. There is a horrible dread suggested by this thought that a man has suffered damage to his soul, and yet everyone who has despaired will have had a presentiment of this false way, this way of perdition. That a man may thus suffer damage to his soul is certain; how far such is the case with the particular individual can never be determined, and let no man venture on this point to judge another. A man's life may appear strange, and one may be tempted to believe that such is the case with him, and yet he may possess an entirely different interpretation which assures him of the contrary. On the other hand, he may have suffered damage to his soul without anybody suspecting it, for the damage does not lie in the outward semblance, it lies in man's inmost being, it is like the decay which dwells in the heart of the fruit while the outward appearance may be pleasant to look upon, it is like the hollowness of the nut of which the shell gives no intimation.

So when you choose yourself absolutely you easily discover that this self is not an abstraction or a tautology; at the most it may seem so at the moment of orientation in which one is employed in separating until one finds the most abstract expression for the self, and yet for all that it is an illusion to suppose that the self is entirely abstract and empty, for it is not conscious simply of freedom in general, as thought might conceive it, but it was produced by a choice and is conscious of this definite free being who is himself and no other. This self contains a rich concretion, a manifold variety of determinants and characteristics, being the whole aesthetical self which is chosen ethically. Therefore, the deeper down you go into yourself, the more you will feel the significance even of insignificance (not in a finite but in an infinite sense) because it is posited by you, and when a man thus chooses himself in an ethical sense this does not mean merely a reflection about himself, but one might characterize this act by recalling the passage of Scripture which speaks of giving an account for every idle word. For when the passion of freedom is aroused, the self is jealous of itself and will by no means allow it to remain undetermined what belongs to it and what does not. Hence, in the first instant of choice the personality issues forth apparently as naked as does a child from the body of its mother; the next instant it is concrete in itself and only by an arbitrary abstraction can it come to pass that a man is able to remain at this point. He becomes himself, quite the same self he was before, down to the least significant peculiarity, and yet he becomes another, for the choice permeates everything and transforms it. Thus his finite personality is infinitized by the choice whereby he infinitely chooses himself.

Now he is in possession of his self as posited by himself, that is, as chosen by himself, as free; but in the fact that he thus possesses himself there comes to evidence an absolute difference, the difference between good and evil. So long as he has not chosen himself this difference is latent. How is it possible at all that the difference between good and evil emerges? Is it something we can think, that is to say, is it an affair for thought? No. With this I have again reached the point where we were in the foregoing discussion when I raised the question why it could seem as if philosophy had abolished the principle of contradiction[16] when as a matter of fact it had not got so far as that. In the act of thinking, my relation to the thing thought is one of necessity, but precisely for this reason the difference between good and evil does not exist. Think anything you will, think the most abstract of all categories, think the most concrete, you never think under the rubric of good and evil; think the whole of history, and you think the necessary movements of ideas, but you never think under the rubric of good and evil. You are constantly thinking relative differences, never the absolute difference. As I see it, therefore, one can readily concede to philosophy that it cannot think an absolute contradiction, but it by no means follows from this that such a contradiction does not exist. In thinking I infinitize myself too, but not absolutely, for I disappear in the absolute. Only when I absolutely choose myself do I infinitize myself absolutely, for I myself *am* the absolute, for only myself can I choose absolutely, and this absolute choice of myself is my freedom, and only when I have absolutely chosen myself have I posited an absolute difference, the difference, that is to say, between good and evil.

In order to abolish the factor of self-determination in thinking, philosophy says, "The absolute *is* for the fact that I think it," but since philosophy itself perceives that by this way of expressing it free thinking is indicated, not the necessary thinking it is wont to extol, it substitutes in place of this another expression, to wit, that my thinking of the absolute is the self-thinking of the absolute in me. This expression is by no means identical with the foregoing, but it is exceedingly significant, nevertheless. For it represents that my thought is a constituent factor of the absolute, and this implies the necessity of my thinking, it implies the necessity which obliges me to think this thought. Such is not the case with the good. The good *is* for the fact that I will it, and apart from my willing it, it has no existence. This is the expression for freedom. It is so also with evil, it *is* only when I will it. By this the distinctive notes of good and evil are by no means belittled or disparaged as merely subjective distinctions. On the contrary, the absolute validity of these distinctions is affirmed. The good is the *an-und-für-sich-Seiende* posited by the *an-und-für-sich-Seiende* [being in and of itself], and this is freedom.

It might seem as though with doubtful propriety I use the expression, "to choose oneself absolutely," for this might seem to imply that with the same absoluteness I choose both good and evil and that with the same necessity both good and evil belong to me. In order to prevent this misunderstanding I use the expression that I "repent myself out of the whole of existence." For repentance is the expression for the fact that evil belongs to me necessarily, and at the same time the expression for the fact that it does not necessarily belong to me. If the evil in me did not belong to me essentially, I could not choose it, but if there were something in me which I could not choose absolutely, I would not be able to choose myself absolutely at all, so I would not myself be the absolute but only a product.

Here I will bring these reflections to an end in order to show how an ethical view of life regards personality and life and their significance. For regularity's sake I will return to a few observations which were made at an earlier point with regard to the relation between the aesthetical and the ethical. Every aesthetical life view is despair, it was said. This was attributed to the fact that it was built upon what may be and may not be. Such is not the case with the ethical life view, for it builds life upon what essentially belongs to being. The aesthetical, it was said, is that in a man whereby he immediately is the man he is; the ethical is that whereby a man becomes what he becomes. By this I do not intend to say that the man who lives aesthetically does not develop, but he develops by necessity not by freedom, no metamorphosis takes place in him, no infinite movement whereby he reaches the point from whence he becomes what he becomes.

When an individual regards his self aesthetically he becomes conscious of this self as a manifold concretion very variously characterized; but in spite of the inward diversity, all of it taken together is, nevertheless, his nature; each component has just as much right to assert itself, just as much right to demand satisfaction. His soul is like a plot of ground in which all sorts of herbs are planted, all with the same claim to thrive; his self consists of this multifariousness, and he has no self which is higher than this. If, then,

he has the aesthetic seriousness you talk about so often
and a little worldly wisdom, he will see that all cannot possibly thrive equally, so he will choose, and what determines
his choice is a more or less, which is a relative difference.
So let us imagine that a man might live without coming in
contact with the ethical; he would then be able to say, "I
have a bent to be a Don Juan, a Faust, or a robber chieftain;
this bent I must cultivate, for the aesthetical seriousness requires that I become something definite, that I permit the
germ deposited in me to develop completely." Such a view
of the personality and its development would be perfectly
correct aesthetically. You see from this what an aesthetic
development means, it is a development like that of the
plant, and although the individual becomes, he becomes
what he immediately is. He who regards personality
ethically is at once in possession of an absolute difference,
viz., that between good and evil, and if in himself he finds
more of the evil than of the good, this does not mean that
the evil is what is to come forth, but it means that the evil
is to be repressed and the good is to come forth. So when
the individual develops ethically he becomes that which he
becomes; for even when he allows the aesthetical within
him to possess validity (which for him has not at all the
same meaning as for the man who lives aesthetically) it is
nevertheless dethroned.

Even the aesthetic seriousness, like seriousness of every
sort, is profitable to a man, but it can never save him completely. To a certain extent this is true in your case, I believe; for just as the ideal has always done you harm for
the fact that you have stared yourself blind in gazing at it,
so also it has been profitable to you, inasmuch as the bad
ideal has always exercised a repellent effect upon you. Of
course your aesthetic seriousness cannot cure you, for you
never get further than letting the bad alone for the reason
that it cannot be ideally carried out, but you do not let it
alone because it is bad or because you abhor it. You have
not got further than the feeling that you are just as impotent with relation to the good as with relation to the evil.
Moreover, evil never exercises, perhaps, a more seductive
influence than when it makes its appearance in an aesthetic

guise. It requires a very high degree of ethical seriousness never to be willing to construe evil under aesthetical categories. Such a conception of it sneaks cunningly into every man, and the predominant aesthetical culture of our age is in no small measure contributory to this. Hence, one hears not infrequently even a moralizer inveigh against evil in a way which makes it evident that the orator, although he extols the good, takes satisfaction, nevertheless, in the thought that he might have been the most intriguing and crafty of men but had disdained this possibility in comparison with being a good man. Yet this betrays a secret weakness and shows that the difference between good and evil does not stand out clearly before him in all its seriousness. After all, there is so much good left in every man that, while he feels that to be a good man is the highest thing, yet for the sake of having some little mark of distinction from the common herd he demands a high degree of appreciation for the fact that he who had so many qualifications for becoming bad had nevertheless become good. Just as if having many qualifications for becoming bad were a merit, and just as if by dwelling upon these qualifications he did not show a predilection for them.

So, too, one often finds men who really in their inmost heart are good but have not the courage to acknowledge it because they would thereby come under categories which they account too trivial. These men also recognize the good as the highest, but they have not the courage to own that evil is what it is. One also hears people say very often, "That was a poor ending to the story," and as a rule one can be sure that what is in this way hailed and advertised is the ethical. When, in whatever way it may be, a man has become an enigma to other men, and then there is an explanation and it turns out that he was not, as people hoped and delighted to think, a sly and crafty deceiver, but is a good-natured and worthy man, then they say, "Nothing but that! Was that all?" Yes, verily, it requires much ethical courage to acknowledge the good as the highest, because thereby one falls under perfectly general categories. To that people stoutly object, they would like to have for themselves the distinction of difference. For ev-

eryone can be a good man who wills it, but it always requires talent to be bad. Hence, many would like to be philosophers, not Christians, for to be a philosopher talent is
required, to be a Christian humility, and that everyone
can have who wills it. What I say here you are well able
to take to heart, for in your inmost nature you are not a
bad man. Now do not be angry with me; I have no intention of offending you; you know that I have had to make a
virtue of necessity, and as I have not your talents I must
try to hold in some honor the thing of being a good man.

In our time they have sought also in other ways to enervate the ethical view of life. For although they find that
the business of being a good man is a pretty poor career
in life, they nevertheless retain a certain respect for it and
are disquieted when they see its claim asserted. I do not
mean, of course, that a man should make display of his
virtue and flaunt before the eyes of everybody the fact that
he is a good man; but on the other hand, neither should
he take pains to hide it or fear to acknowledge his effort
to be good. If he does acknowledge it, they will at once
raise against him the cry that he wants to make himself
important, wants to make out that he is better than others,
they unite in the same flippant expression: "Let us be men.[17]
Before God we are all miserable sinners." I do not need to
tell you this, but I do need to warn you against far too
much activity into which your mockery often carries you.
It is quite natural, therefore, that in the modern drama the
bad is always represented by the most shining talents; the
good, the upright, by a grocer's clerk.[18] The spectators find
this a matter of course and learn from the play what they
knew beforehand, that it is far beneath their dignity to be
put in the same class with a grocer's clerk. Yes, my young
friend, it requires much ethical courage not to wish to be
distinguished by differences but to be content with the universal. In this respect our age needs a thorough shaking-up
—which also will not tarry, for there surely will come the
instant when our age will have a chance to see how the
individuals most distinguished in an aesthetic sense, being
singled out by differences, are in despair over these differences and want to find the universal. That may be good for

us little people, inasmuch as we, too, sometimes feel embarrassed at not being distinguished by differences because we are too insignificant for that . . . and not because we have been great enough to disdain them.

Every man who lives merely aesthetically has for this reason a secret terror at the thought of despair, for he knows very well that what is brought forth by despair is the universal, and he knows also that it is the differences which make him what he is. The higher an individual stands, the more differences he has annihilated or despaired over, but he always has one difference left which he is not willing to annihilate, that, namely, in which his life consists. It is remarkable how even the simplest men discover with admirable promptitude what might be called their aesthetic difference, however unimportant it may be; and one of the pitiful things in life is the foolish strife commonly carried on to determine which difference is more significant than the other. The aesthetic minds also express their aversion to despair by saying that it is a sudden break. This expression is quite correct on the assumption that life's development ought to consist in the necessary unfolding of the immediate. If this is not the case, despair is no break but a transfiguration. Only the man who despairs over something in particular suffers a break, but that is due precisely to the fact that he does not fully despair. Aestheticists are also afraid that life will lose the diverting multifariousness it possesses as long as it is so conceived that every single individual is living under aesthetic categories. This, again, is a misunderstanding, occasioned, it may be, by various rigoristic theories. By despair nothing is destroyed, all of the aesthetical remains in a man, only it is reduced to a ministering role and thereby precisely is preserved. Yes, it is true that one does not live in it as before, but from this it by no means follows that it has been lost; it may perhaps be employed in a different way, but from this it by no means follows that it is gone. The ethicist simply carries through the despair which the higher aestheticist began but arbitrarily broke off; for however great the differences may be, they are only relative. And when the aestheticist himself admits that even the difference which lends significance to his life is transitory and yet adds that it is always best to take delight in it so long as one has it, this is really cowardice which loves a certain sort of snugness where it is not too high to reach the ceiling, and this is unworthy of a man. It is as though a man were to take delight in a relationship based on a misunderstanding which sooner or later must come to light and had not courage to become conscious of it or to admit it but would enjoy the relationship as long as possible. You, however, are not in this case, but you are like one who has admitted the misunderstanding, broken off the relationship, and yet would now be constantly taking leave of it.

The aesthetic view takes account of the personality in its relation to the environment, and the expression for this relation in its repercussion upon the individual is pleasure. But the aesthetic expression for pleasure in its relation to the individual is mood. In mood the personality is present but only dimly present. For he who lives aesthetically seeks as far as possible to be absorbed in mood, he seeks to hide himself entirely in it, so that there remains nothing in him which cannot be inflected into it; for such a remainder has always a disturbing effect, it is a continuity which would hold him back. The more the personality disappears in the twilight of mood, so much the more is the individual in the moment, and this, again, is the most adequate expression for the aesthetic existence: it is in the moment. Hence the prodigious oscillations to which the man who lives aesthetically is exposed. He, too, who lives ethically experiences mood, but for him this is not the highest experience; because he has infinitely chosen himself he sees the mood below him. The remainder which will not "go into" mood is precisely the continuity which is to him the highest thing. He who lives ethically has (if I may recall an earlier expression) memory of his life—and he who lives aesthetically has not. He who lives ethically does not annihilate mood, he takes it for an instant into consideration, but this instant saves him from living in the moment, this instant gives him mastery over the lust for pleasure, for the art of mastering lust consists not so much in annihilating it, or entirely renouncing it, as in determining the instant. Take whatever lust you will, the secret of it, the power in it, consists in the fact that it is absolutely in the moment. One often hears people say that the only remedy is for one to abstain from it entirely. This is a very wrong method, which also can be successful only for a short time. Imagine a man who is addicted to gambling. Lust awakens with all its passion, it is as if his life were in jeopardy if the lust were not satisfied. If he is capable of saying to himself, "This instant I will not do it, in an hour I will," he is cured. This hour is the continuity which saves him. When a man lives aesthetically his mood is always eccentric because he has his center in the periphery. Personality has its center within itself, and he who has not his self is eccentric. When a man lives ethically his mood is centralized, he is not moody, he is not in a mood, but he has mood and he has mood in himself. What he labors for is continuity, and this is always master over mood. His life does not lack mood, yea, it has a total mood; but this is acquired, it is what one might call *aequale temperamentum*,[19] but this is no aesthetic mood, and no one has it by nature or immediately.

But he who has now infinitely chosen himself—can he say, "Now I possess myself, I require nothing more, and to all the changes of the world I oppose the proud thought: I am the man I am"? By no manner of means! In case a man were to express himself thus he would easily see that he was on a wrong path. The fundamental error would, in that case, too, lie in the fact that in the strictest sense he had not chosen himself. He had chosen himself maybe, but outside himself. He had interpreted quite abstractly what it is to choose and had not grasped himself in his concretion, he had not chosen in such a way that by the choice he became himself, became invested with his self; he had chosen himself from necessity, not with freedom; aesthetically he had taken in vain the ethical choice. The more significant the result which is to issue from the choice, the more dangerous are the byways, and here there appears a dreadful byway. When the individual has grasped himself in his eternal validity this overwhelms him by its fullness. The temporal vanishes from before his eyes. At the first instant this fills him with indescribable bliss and gives him

a sense of absolute security. If then he begins to gaze upon
this bliss, the temporal advances its claim. This is scorned.
What the temporal can give, the more or the less which
now presents itself, is so very unimportant in comparison
with what he eternally possesses. Everything comes with
him to a standstill, he has, as it were, reached eternity before the time. He relapses into contemplation, he gazes at
himself, but this gaze cannot fill up the time. Then it appears to him that time, that the temporal, is his ruin; he
demands a more perfect form of existence, and at this point
there comes to evidence a fatigue, an apathy, which resembles the languor which is the attendant of pleasure. This
apathy may rest so broodingly upon a man that suicide
appears to him the only way of escape. No power can wrest
from him his self, the only power is time, but neither can
that wrest from him his self; it checks him and delays, it
arrests the embrace of the spirit with which he grasps his
self. He has not chosen himself; like Narcissus he has fallen
in love with himself. Such a situation has certainly ended
not infrequently in suicide.

The error lies in the fact that he has not chosen in the
right way, not simply in the sense that he had no eye for his
error, but that he has seen himself under the category of
necessity—himself, this personality, with all these manifold
characteristics, he has seen as part and parcel of the world-
process, he has seen this self confronted by the eternal
Power the fire of which pervades it without consuming it.[20]
But he has not seen himself in his freedom, has not chosen
himself with freedom. If he does that, then the very instant
he chooses himself he is in motion; concrete as his self is,
he has nevertheless chosen himself in accordance with his
possibility, in repentance he has ransomed himself for the
sake of remaining in his freedom, but he can remain in his
freedom only by constantly realizing it. He, therefore, who
has chosen himself is *eo ipso* active.

This perhaps may be the place to mention a life view in
which you take a high degree of pleasure, especially in
your quality as *docent,* sometimes as practitioner. It comes
to nothing less than that sorrow is, after all, the real meaning of life and to be the unhappiest man is to be the hap-

piest.[21] At first glance this view does not seem to be an aesthetic life view, for pleasure can hardly be the solution it offers. Neither is it ethical, however, but it has its place in the perilous transition from the aesthetical to the ethical, when the soul is so easily ensnared by one expression or another of the theory of predestination. You hold many false doctrines; this is nearly the worst, but you know also that it is the most serviceable when it is a question of stealing up to men and sucking them into your power. You can be as heartless as anybody, you can make jest of everything, even of a man's pain. You are not unaware that this is tempting to youth, yet in the end you put yourself by this conduct at a considerable distance from the young, for such behavior is just as repellent as it is attractive. If it is a young woman you would deceive in this way, it does not escape you that a womanly soul has too much depth to be captivated long by such devices; yea, even though for a moment you have engaged her attention, yet it soon will end by her getting tired of the thing and almost conceiving an aversion for you, for her soul does not require such stimulants. Then the method is changed. By random enigmatic outbursts which only she can understand you let it be suspected that the explanation of it all is to be found in a far away melancholy. With her only are you open—but in so cautious a way that she never really gets to know; you leave it to her imagination to picture the deep sadness which you hide profoundly within you. You are shrewd, one cannot deny that, and true it is, as a young girl said of you, that you would end presumably by becoming a Jesuit. The more cunningly you know how to spin the thread which leads deeper and deeper into the secret places of melancholy, the more joyful you are, the more sure of drawing her to you. You do not make long speeches, you do not proclaim your pain by a faithful grasp of the hand, by "a romantic gaze into a kindred soul's romantic eyes"; you are too shrewd for that. You shun witnesses and rarely allow yourself to be taken off your guard. There is an age when no poison is more dangerous to a young girl than sadness; that you know, and in itself this knowledge, like every sort of knowledge, may be all right, but on the other hand, the use you make of it I shall not praise.

Since you have hardened your mind to construe the whole of existence under aesthetic categories, it is a matter of course that sorrow has not escaped your attention, for in itself it is as interesting as joy. The tenacity with which you hold on to the interesting wherever it is to be found gives constant occasion to your companions to misunderstand you and at one moment to regard you as absolutely heartless, at another as a good-natured man, whereas, in fact, you are neither. Such a misunderstanding may even be occasioned by the fact that one quite as often sees you seeking out sorrow as attending upon joy—if, be it noted, there is in sorrow as well as in joy an idea, for only by that is the aesthetic interest awakened. If you could be light-minded enough to make a person unhappy, you might give occasion to the strangest delusion. Unlike others who faithlessly are seeking only for joy, you would not retire then and pursue joy along other paths; no, sorrow exhibited in the same individual would become even more interesting to you than joy, you would remain with the man, you would be absorbed in his sorrow. You have experience, inwardness, the power of words, the pathos of tragedy, you know how to proffer to the afflicted the only assuagement sorrow yearns for—the expression. You delight in seeing how the sorrower finds repose in the string-music of mood when you are the performer; you soon become indispensable to him, for your expressive rendering lifts him up above the dark waves of care. He, on the other hand, is not indispensable to you, and soon you are tired. For to you it is not merely joy which

> Is like a fleeting friend
> One meets upon the road,[22]

but it is sorrow too, since you are a traveler always on the road. So when you have comforted the sorrower, and as a compensation have distilled the interesting out of this experience, you leap into your carriage and shout, "Away!" If the question is asked, "Whither?" you respond like the hero Don Juan, "To pleasure and merriment."[23] For you are weary of sorrow, and your soul craves the opposite.

You do not really behave quite so badly as I have described; I will not deny that you often take a genuine interest in the afflicted person, that you really want to heal him and win him back to joy. Then, as you say, you strain like a mettlesome steed to work him out of the snares of sorrow, you spare neither time nor strength, and once in a while you succeed. Even then I cannot praise you, for under all this something is concealed. In fact, you are jealous of sorrow, you cannot bear to think that anybody else has sorrow, or has a sorrow which it might not be possible to overcome. So when you heal the afflicted you enjoy the satisfaction of saying to yourself, "But my sorrow no one can heal." That is the result. Whether you are seeking the distraction of joy or of sorrow you always keep *in mente*, have firmly fixed in your soul, that there is one sorrow which cannot be relieved.

So I have reached the point where you affirm that the meaning of life is sorrow. The whole more recent development is characterized by the fact that people have a greater inclination to be sorrowful than to be joyful. This is regarded as a higher view of life—and it is too, in the sense that to want to be joyful is natural, the other unnatural. And there is the further consideration that being joyful does, after all, impose upon the individual a certain obligation to be thankful, even if his thoughts are so confused that he doesn't quite know whom to thank; sorrow exempts one from that, and so vanity is all the more content. Our age, moreover, has in so many ways had experience of the vanity of life that it does not believe in joy, and so to have something to believe in, it believes in sorrow. Joy, it says, passes away but sorrow lasts, and therefore, he who constructs his view of life upon this builds upon solid ground.

If we inquire now more expressly what sort of a sorrow it is you talk about, you are shrewd enough to evade the ethical sorrow. It is not repentance you mean; no, it is aesthetic sorrow, especially reflective sorrow. That has its ground not in guilt but in misfortune, in fate, in a sad disposition, in the effect others produce, etc. All of that is what you know very well from romances. If you read it in books, you laugh at it; if you hear others speak of it, you mock them; but when you yourself hold forth on this theme, there is sense in it, you think, and truth.

Now the view which takes sorrow to be the meaning of life might in itself seem sorry enough, yet I cannot refrain from pointing out one aspect which perhaps you did not expect to hear mentioned: that it is a disconsolate view. I say here again, as I said before, that in the same sense that joy passes away, so also does sorrow. This is something I do not need to tell you, for you can learn it from your master Scribe,[24] the famous French playwright, who has often derided the sentimentality which believes in an eternal sorrow. He who says that sorrow is the meaning of life has joy outside him in the same way that he who would be joyful has sorrow outside him. Joy may take him by surprise in exactly the same way that sorrow may take the other by surprise. His life view thus hinges upon a condition which is not in his power, for it is really just as little in a man's power to give up being joyful as to give up being sorrowful. But every life view which hinges upon a condition outside itself is despair. And so, wanting to sorrow is despair in exactly the same sense as wanting to be joyful, since it always is despair to have one's life dependent upon that which may pass away. Be therefore as shrewd and as inventive as you will, frighten joy away by a tearful exterior, or, if you prefer, deceive it by your exterior in order to conceal your sorrow, joy is able nevertheless to take you by surprise; for time devours the children of time,[25] and such a sorrow is one of time's children, and the eternity it falsely pretends to is a deceit.

The deeper the reason for sorrow, the more plausible it may seem that it might be possible to preserve it for a whole lifetime, yea, that one had no need to do anything, but that it would remain as a matter of course. If it is sorrow for a particular occurrence, it will appear indeed very difficult to preserve it. That you perceive clearly enough, and therefore, when you would express yourself about the significance of sorrow for the whole life you think more especially of unfortunate individuals and tragic heroes. The whole disposition of the unfortunate individual is characterized by the fact that he cannot become happy or joyful, there broods over him a fate, as there does over the tragic hero. Here, then, it is quite in place to say that sorrow is the meaning of life, and here we have reached an out and out fatalism, which always has something seductive about it. Here you put forward your pretension which amounts to neither more nor less than that you are the most unfortunate man. And yet it is undeniable that this is the proudest and most defiant thought that can arise in the brain of a man.

Let me make answer to you as you deserve. First of all, you do not sorrow. That you know full well, for it is your favorite expression that the unhappiest man is the happiest. But this is a falsehood more dreadful than any other, it is a falsehood which turns against the eternal Power which governs the world, it is a rebellion against God, like laughing when one ought to weep, and yet there is a despair which is capable of this, there is a defiance which sets at naught even God Himself. But this is also treason against the human race. It is true you too make a distinction, but still you think that there is to be distinguished a sorrow so great that it is impossible to bear it. But if there exists such a sorrow, it is not for you to determine which it is, the one distinction is as good as the other, and you have betrayed man's most sacred right and the grace he relies upon. There is a treason against greatness, a base envy, which affirms substantially that the great men have not been tested by the most perilous temptations, that they have slipped easily into their honors, and that they too would have succumbed if the superhuman temptation you talk about had come upon them. And is it thus you think to honor greatness . . . by belittling it? thus you propose to bear witness to it . . . by denying it?

Now do not misunderstand me. I am not the sort of person who thinks that one has no business to sorrow; I despise that petty common sense, and if I have a vote in this matter, I choose sorrow. No, I am well aware that it is beautiful to sorrow, that there is sense in tears, but I know too that a man should not sorrow as one without hope. Be-

tween us two there is an absolute opposition which cannot
be resolved. I am unable to live under aesthetic determinants, I feel that with this the things I hold most sacred
perish, I require a higher expression, and the ethical gives
me that. And here it is that sorrow receives its true and
profound significance. Be not shocked by what I am about
to say, be not amazed that when I speak of a sorrow which
heroes can scarcely bear I talk of children. It is a mark of
a well-behaved child that it is disposed to ask permission
without taking too much into account whether it may reasonably assume a right to do the thing, and so too it is a
mark of a magnanimous man, of a profound soul, that he is
disposed to repent, that he does not take the matter up
legally with God but repents and loves God in his repentance. Without this his life is nothing, merely froth upon
water. Yea, I assure you that though without fault of mine
my life were so fraught with sorrow and suffering that I
might call myself the greatest tragic hero, take delight in
my pain, and appal the world by reciting it, my choice is
made, I divest myself of the hero's dress and the pathos of
tragedy, I am not the victim who can be proud of his sufferings, I am the humbled man, conscious of my guilt, I have
only one expression for what I suffer . . . guilt, one expression for my pain . . . repentance, one hope before my
eyes . . . forgiveness, and if I find this difficult, ah, I have
only one prayer, I would cast myself upon the ground and
implore of the eternal Power who guides the world one
boon, that sooner or later it might be granted me to repent.
For I know only one sorrow which could bring me to despair and with that hurl down all things, the sorrow of
discovering that repentance was a delusion, not a delusion
with respect to the forgiveness it seeks but with respect to
the accountability forgiveness implies.

And do you think that by treating it thus I do not give
sorrow its due, that I run away from sorrow? By no manner of means! I deposit it in my very being, and therefore,
never forget it. It is nothing but disbelief in the compe-
tency of spirit if I do not dare to believe that I can possess
something within me without looking at it every instant.
Ordinarily what one would treasure most securely one de-

posits in a place where one does not go every day, and so it is too in a spiritual sense. I have sorrow within me, and I know that it will continue to be a part of my being, I know this far more surely than does he who for dread of losing it takes it out every day.

Never has my life been so tumultuous that I have felt tempted by the wish to confound chaotically the whole of existence, but in my everyday life I have often realized how profitable it is to give sorrow an ethical expression—not to obliterate the aesthetical factor in sorrow but to master it ethically. So long as sorrow is quiet and humble I do not fear it; if it becomes vehement and passionate, becomes sophistical and beguiles me into despondency, then I arise, I brook no rebellion, I will not suffer anything in the world to trick me out of that which I have received from God's hand as a gift of grace. I do not chase sorrow away, do not seek to forget it, but I repent. And even if sorrow is of such a sort that I myself am not to blame for it, I repent of letting it acquire power over me, I repent that I did not at once carry it to God, and if this had been done, it would have had no power to beguile me.

Forgive me for speaking here again about children. When a child begins to whimper and is not content with either this or that, then people say, "I will give you something to cry about," and this is accounted an excellent method. So it is with me, for even when one has reached maturity one always retains something of the child. So when I whimper I say to myself, "You will get something to cry about," and then I undergo a transformation. And this I can assure you is very salutary for a man, for the tears an aesthetic sorrower sheds in behalf of himself are hypocritical tears and bear no fruit, but to feel oneself guilty is truly something to cry about, and in the tears of repentance there is an eternal benediction. When the Saviour went up to Jerusalem and wept over the great city that knew not the things which belonged to its peace, it is possible that He might have moved it also to weep with Him; but if it had been aesthetic tears the city shed, it would have been of little avail, and yet surely the world has not seen many tragedies like that which was in store for the chosen people.

If they had been tears of repentance, yes, then there would have been substance in them, and yet in this case it was a question of repenting more than one's own guilt, for it was not the generation then living which alone was guilty, it was the iniquity of the fathers which rested upon them. And here repentance is revealed in its deeper significance, for while in a sense it isolates me, in another way it unites me with the whole race, for my life does not begin in time with nothing, and if I cannot repent the past, freedom is a dream.

You now perceive, perhaps, why I deal with this life view. Personality is here again viewed under the category of necessity, and only so much freedom is left that like a restless dream it is able to keep the individual half awake and lead him astray in the labyrinth of sufferings and fateful dispensations where he everywhere beholds himself and yet cannot come to himself. It is incredible how frivolously one often sees such a problem treated. Even systematic thinkers treat it as a natural phenomenon which they can only describe and have nothing more to say—without ever reflecting that if there were such a natural phenomenon, all the rest of their wisdom is nonsense and illusion. Hence it is that one feels so much more helped by the Christian view than by the wisdom of all philosophers. The Christian view concludes all under sin, a thing which philosophy has not the ethical courage to do, being too aesthetic. And yet this courage is the only thing that can save life and save man—unless a man expects to be helped by breaking off his scepticism capriciously and combining with several like-minded persons to determine what the truth is.

The first form which the choice takes is complete isolation. For in choosing myself I detach myself from the whole world till by this detachment I end in abstract identity. The individual having chosen himself in terms of his freedom, is *eo ipso* active. His action, however, has no relation to any surrounding world, for the individual has reduced this to naught and exists only for himself. The life view here revealed is none the less an ethical view. It found expression in Greece in the effort of the single individual to develop himself into a paragon of virtue.[26] Like the anchorites in

Christendom of a later time he withdrew from the activities of life, not to be absorbed in metaphysical ruminations, but in order to act—not outwardly but in himself. This inward action was at once his task and his satisfaction, for in fact it was not his purpose to cultivate himself for the sake of being able later to serve the state all the better; no, in this self-cultivation he was sufficient unto himself, and he forsook civic life never to return to it. He did not, therefore, in a real and proper sense withdraw from life; on the contrary, he remained in its multifarious relationships because contact with it was pedagogically necessary for his own sake, but civic life as such had no significance for him; by one magic formula or another he had made it innocuous, indifferent, unimportant to him. The virtues he developed were thus not civic virtues (as were the true virtues in paganism, corresponding to the religious virtues in Christendom), they were the personal virtues—courage, valor, temperance, moderation, etc. Naturally one very seldom sees this view of life realized in our age, because everyone is too much affected by the religious to stop with this abstract definition of virtue. The imperfection of this life view is easily seen. The fault lay in the fact that this individual had chosen himself altogether abstractly, and hence the perfection he aspired after and attained was likewise abstract. It was for this reason I emphasized the fact that choosing oneself is identical with repenting oneself; for repentance puts the individual in the most intimate connection and the most exact cohesion with a surrounding world.

There has often been seen, and even in the Christian world one may sometimes see, analogies to this Greek view of life, only that in Christianity by the admixture of mystical and religious elements it becomes fuller and more beautiful. A Greek who developed himself into a perfect compendium of all the personal virtues, by however high a degree of virtuosity, finds his life nevertheless no more immortal than the world whose temptations his virtue overcame, his blessedness is a lonely self-satisfaction, as transient as everything else. The life of a mystic is far deeper. He has chosen himself absolutely. For although one rarely hears a mystic express himself in these terms, although he generally uses the seemingly opposite expression that he has chosen God, yet substantially, as was shown above, this comes to the same thing. For if he has not chosen himself absolutely, he is not in any free relation to God, and precisely in freedom consists the characteristic Christian piety. This free relation is often expressed in the language of the mystic by saying that he is the absolute Thou. The mystic has chosen himself absolutely and so in terms of his freedom, and thus he is *eo ipso* active, but his action is inward action. The mystic chooses himself in his complete isolation; the whole world is for him dead and reduced to naught, and the weary soul chooses God or itself. This expression, "the weary soul," must not be misunderstood, must not be misused to belittle the mystic, as though it were a questionable thing that the soul chose God only when it had become weary of the world. By this expression the mystic doubtless indicates his repentance that he has not chosen God before, and his weariness must not be regarded as identical with being tired of life. You will see already at this point how little the life of the mystic is ethically determined, since it is the highest expression of his repentance to repent that earlier, before he became concrete in the world, while his soul was merely abstractly defined, that is, as a child, he had not chosen God.

The mystic, in the fact that he has made a choice, is *eo ipso* active, but his action is an inward action. Inasmuch as he is active his life has a movement, a development, a history. A development may, however, be metaphysical or aesthetical in such a degree that it is doubtful whether in a proper sense one dare call it a history, since this word implies development in the form of freedom. A movement may be desultory to such a degree that it is doubtful whether one dare call it a development. When such a movement consists in the fact that one experience returns again and again, we have undoubtedly a movement, yea, we may perhaps be able to discover a law for this movement, but we have no development. The repetition in time is without significance, and continuity is lacking. This is true in a high degree of the life of the mystic. It is appalling to read a mystic's lament over the dull moments. Then when the dull moment is past comes the luminous moment, and thus his life is constantly changing, it has movement indeed, but no development. His life lacks continuity. What really supplies the continuity is a feeling, the feeling of longing, whether this longing be directed towards what is past or towards what is to come. But the fact that a feeling fills the intervening space shows precisely that cohesion is lacking. The life of the mystic is determined metaphysically and aesthetically to such a degree that one dare not call it a history except in the sense in which one speaks of the history of a plant. The whole world is a dead world for the mystic, he has fallen in love with God. The development of his life is then the unfolding of this love. As there are instances of lovers who have a certain resemblance to one another, also in their outward appearance, their looks, the shape of the face, so too the mystic is absorbed in the contemplation of the Deity, whose image is more and more reflected in his loving soul, and thus the mystic renews and revives the lost divine image in man. The more he contemplates, the more clearly this image is reflected in him, the more he himself comes to resemble this image. His inward action therefore does not consist in the acquisition of the personal virtues but in the development of the religious or contemplative virtues. But even this is too ethical an expression for his life, and we must say that his real life is prayer. I will not deny that prayer, too, belongs to the ethical life, but the more ethically a man lives the more purposeful is his prayer, so that even in the prayer of thanksgiving there is an element of purpose. It is not so with the prayer of the mystic. Prayer is all the more significant for him the more erotic it is, the more it is inflamed by a burning love. His prayer is the expression of this love, is the only language in which he can address the Deity with whom he is in love. As in earthly life the lovers long for the moment when they can breathe out their love for one another and let their souls fuse in a gentle whisper, so the mystic longs for the moment when he in prayer can, as it were, steal in to the presence of God. As the lovers experience the highest degree of bliss in this whispering when really they have nothing to talk about, so for the mystic his soul is all the more blissful, his love a happier one; the less content his prayer has, the more nearly with his sigh he disappears from before his own eyes.

It might, perhaps, not be amiss to characterize more in detail the falseness of such a life, especially in view of the fact that every deeper personality always feels an attraction to mysticism. Thus you are by no means lacking in the factors which might dispose you, for a time at least, to become a mystic. Here is a field on which the greatest contrasts meet, the purest and most innocent soul with the most culpable, the most talented man and the simplest.

First I will state quite simply what it is that offends me most in such a life. This is my personal judgment. Later I shall seek to show that I correctly indicated the perils, and I shall show too the reasons for them and point out the false paths which lie so near.

In my opinion one cannot acquit the mystic of a certain intrusiveness in his relation to God. Who will deny that a man shall love God with all his heart and with all his mind, yea, that he is not only to do this but that to do it is blessedness itself? From this, however, it by no means follows that the mystic is to disdain the reality of existence to which God has assigned him, for thereby he really disdains God's love or requires a different expression of it from that which God is willing to give. Here applies the serious saying of Samuel, "To obey is better than sacrifice, and to harken than the fat of rams." But this intrusiveness may assume an even more questionable form. As for example when a mystic proves his relationship to God by the fact that he himself is precisely what he is, regarding himself because of some accidental trait or another as the object of the partiality of the Deity. For thereby he degrades the Deity and himself. Degrades himself, for it is always degrading to be distinguished from others by reason of some accidental trait; and degrades God, for he makes of the Deity a false god in whose court he is a favorite.

What in the next place is displeasing to me in the life of a mystic is the softness and weakness of which one cannot acquit him. That a man wishes to be assured in his inmost heart that he loves God in truth and sincerity, that many a time he feels prompted to convince himself thoroughly of this, that he may pray God to let His Spirit bear witness along with his own spirit that he does so love Him— who would deny the beauty and the truth in this? But from this it by no means follows that every instant he will repeat the experiment, will every instant make trial of his love. He will have enough greatness of soul to believe in God's love, and then he will also have the frank-heartedness to believe in his own love and to continue gladly in the situation assigned to him, knowing that this continuance is the surest expression of his love, of his humility.

Finally, the life of the mystic displeases me because I regard it as a deceit against the world in which he lives, against the men to whom he is bound by obligations and with whom he might have come into relationship if he had not been pleased to become a mystic. Generally the mystic chooses the solitary life, but with that the situation is not clear, for the question is whether he has a right to choose it. In choosing the solitary life he practices no deceit upon the others, for thereby he says to them in effect, "I will have no relationship with you"; but the question is whether he has a right to say this, a right to do this. It is especially as a husband, as a father, that I am an enemy of mysticism. My household has also its *aduton*,[27] but in case I were a mystic I must have still another for myself alone, and then I would be a pretty poor husband. Now since in my opinion, which I shall set forth later, it is the duty of every man to marry, and as it cannot possibly be my meaning that a man shall marry in order to become a poor husband, you will easily see that I must have an aversion to all mysticism.

He who devotes himself one-sidedly to the mystical life becomes at last so alien to all men that every relationship, even the tenderest, the most heartfelt, becomes indifferent to him. It is not in this sense one is to love God more dearly than father and mother; God is not so self-loving as that, neither is He a poet who wishes to torment men with the most frightful collisions—and hardly could a more frightful thing be conceived than that there might be a collision between love for God and love for the persons for whom love has been planted by Him in our hearts.

You surely have not forgotten young Ludvig Black-
feldt[28] with whom a few years ago we both of us, and I
especially, were in pretty close touch. He certainly was a
very talented fellow, his misfortune was that he lost himself
in a mysticism which was not so much Christian as Indian.
If he had lived in the Middle Ages, he doubtless would have
found refuge in the cloister. Our age has no such helps. If a
man goes astray, he must necessarily perish if he be not
entirely healed. We have no such relative salvation to offer
him. You know that he ended with suicide. With me he had
a sort of intimacy and to that extent contradicted his pet
theory that one should not put oneself in relationship to any
man but only to God immediately. Hence his intimacy with
me was not great, and he never opened himself to me fully.
During the last half year of his life I was an anxious witness
of his eccentric movements. It is possible that I stopped
him several times. I cannot know this definitely since he
never opened himself to any one. He had an unusual gift
for concealing his psychic condition and for giving to one
passion the semblance of another. Finally he put an end to
his life without anyone being able to explain the reason for
it. His physician expressed the opinion that it was due to
partial insanity. Well, that was a very sensible thing for
him to say. In fact, his mind was unimpaired up to the last
moment. Perhaps you do not know that there exists a letter
which he wrote to his brother, the Councillor of Justice, in
which he informs him of his intention. I enclose herewith
a copy of it. It has harrowing evidence of genuineness and
is a highly objective expression of the last agony of complete isolation.*

* "Honorable Mr. Councillor,
I write to you because in a way you are my nearest of kin, and
yet in another way you are not nearer to me than other men.
When you receive these lines I am no more. Should anyone ask
you the reason, you can say that once there was a princess called
Morning Glory, or something else like that; for so it is I myself
would reply if I had the joy to survive myself. Should anyone
ask you the occasion for it, you can say that it was on the occasion of the great conflagration. Should anyone ask you about
the time, you can say that it was in the month of July, so notable
for me. Should no one ask you any of these questions, you are to
make no reply.

Poor Ludvig was certainly not affected religiously, yet he was affected mystically; for the characteristic of mysticism is not the religious factor but the isolation in which the individual, heedless of every relation with the given reality, would put himself in immediate rapport with the Eternal. The fact that as soon as the word mysticism is mentioned one thinks at once and most naturally of something religious is accounted for by the consideration that religion has a tendency to isolate the individual, as you may be convinced by the simplest observation. You perhaps go to church rather seldom, but you are likely to be all the more observant. Have you not noticed that, though in a sense one gets an impression of a congregation, yet the individual feels isolated? People are as strangers to one another, and it is only by a long detour, as it were, they are again united. And to what is this due but to the fact that one's God-relationship is so strongly felt in all of its inwardness that alongside of this the earthly relationships lose their importance? In the case of a healthy man this instant of isolation will not be long, and such a momentary withdrawal is so far from being an illusion that it rather increases the inwardness of the earthly relationship. But what may be wholesome as a transient factor becomes a very serious sickness when it is one-sidedly developed.

Since I cannot boast of theological culture, I do not feel capable of setting forth more fully the character of religious mysticism. I have regarded it only from my ethical standpoint and therefore I am justified, I believe, in attaching to the word mysticism a much broader meaning than it generally has. I do not doubt that in religious mysticism there

---

I do not regard suicide as a praiseworthy thing. It is not out of vanity I have resolved upon it. On the contrary, I believe in the correctness of the proposition that no man can bear to behold the infinite. That once became evident to me in an intellectual respect, and the expression for this is ignorance.[29] That is to say, ignorance is the negative expression for infinite knowledge. Suicide is the negative expression for infinite freedom. It is a form of the infinite freedom, but the negative form. Hail to him who finds the positive form.

With the highest respect,
I am deferentially yours."

is to be found much that is beautiful, that the many deep and earnest natures who devoted themselves to it have experienced much in their lives and were thereby qualified to give counsels and directions and hints which are of service to others who venture upon that perilous path; but in spite of all that, this path is not only a perilous path but a wrong path. There is always an inconsistency implied. When the mystic has no respect for reality in general it is not obvious why he does not regard with equal distrust that moment in reality when he was affected by the higher experience.

So the fault of the mystic is not that he chooses himself, for in my opinion he does well in doing that, but his fault is that he does not choose rightly, he chooses with freedom, and yet he does not choose ethically; but one can choose oneself with freedom only when one chooses oneself ethically, but one can choose oneself ethically only by repenting oneself, and only by repenting does one become concrete, and only as a concrete individual is one a free individual. The fault of the mystic does not therefore consist in any later phase but in the very first movement. If this first movement is right, then every further withdrawal from life, every ascetic self-torment, is only a further and correct consequence. The fault of the mystic is that by his choice he does not become concrete for himself, nor for God either; he chooses himself abstractly and therefore lacks transparency. For it is a mistake to think that the abstract is the transparent. The abstract is the turbid, the foggy. Therefore, his love for God reaches its highest expression in a feeling, a mood: in the dusk of evening when fogs prevail he melts with vague movements into one with his God. But when one chooses oneself abstractly one does not choose oneself ethically. Only when in his choice a man has assumed himself, is clad in himself, has so totally penetrated himself that every movement is attended by the consciousness of a responsibility for himself, only then has he chosen himself ethically, only then has he repented himself, only then is he concrete, only then is he in his total isolation in absolute continuity with the reality to which he belongs.

I cannot often enough repeat the proposition, however simple it may be in itself, that choosing oneself is identical with repenting oneself. For upon this everything turns. The mystic too repents, but he repents himself out of himself, not into himself; he repents metaphysically, not ethically. To repent aesthetically is detestable because it is effeminate; to repent metaphysically is an untimely superfluity, for the individual did not in fact create the world and so does not need to take it so much to heart if the world really turns out to be vanity. The mystic chooses himself abstractly and so must repent abstractly. This one can see best from the judgment the mystic passes upon existence, the finite reality in which nevertheless he lives. For the mystic teaches that it is vanity, illusion, sin. But every such judgment is a metaphysical judgment and does not define ethically my relation to existence. Even when he says that finiteness is sin he says after all about the same thing as when he calls it vanity. If on the other hand he would hold fast the ethical meaning of the word sin, he does not define his relation to it ethically but metaphysically, for the ethical expression would not be to flee from it but to enter into it, to abolish it or to bear it. Ethical repentance has only two movements: either to abolish its object or to bear it. These two movements indicate also a concrete relationship between the repentant individual and the object of his repentance, whereas fleeing away indicates an abstract relationship.

The mystic chooses himself abstractly. One can therefore say that he constantly chooses himself out of the world. But the consequence is that he is unable to choose himself back again into the world. The truly concrete choice is that wherewith at the very same instant I choose myself out of the world I am choosing myself back into the world. For when I choose myself repentantly I gather myself together in all my finite concretion, and in the fact that I have thus chosen myself out of the finite I am in the most absolute continuity with it.

Since the mystic chooses himself abstractly his misfortune is that he has so much difficulty in starting to move, or rather that this is an impossibility for him. As it is in your case with your earthly first love, so it is in the case of the mystic with his religious first love: he has tasted the whole bliss of it and now has nothing to do but wait to see if it will come again in just as much glory, and of this he can easily be tempted to nourish a doubt which I have so often pointed out when I remark that development is retrogression, a postponement. Reality is for the mystic a delay, indeed a delay of so perilous a sort that he almost incurs the danger that life may deprive him of that which he once possessed. If therefore one were to ask a mystic what is the significance of life, he would perhaps reply, "The significance of life is to learn to know God and become in love with Him." This, however, is not an answer to the question, for here the significance of life is conceived as a moment, not as succession. Hence, if I were to ask him what significance it has for life that life has this significance, or in other words, what is the significance of the temporal as a whole, he has not much to answer, at any rate not much that is cheerful. If he says that the temporal is an enemy which must be overcome, then one could ask him further whether it might have any significance that this enemy was overcome. In fact this is not what the mystic really means, what he wants rather is to be through with the temporal. Consequently, just as he misunderstood reality and construed it metaphysically as vanity, so, too, he misunderstands the historical and construes it metaphysically as unprofitable labor. The highest significance he can ascribe to the temporal is that it is a time of probation in which again and again one is put to the test without anything really resulting from it and without the individual getting further than he was at the beginning. This, however, is a misunderstanding of the temporal, for though it always retains something characteristic of the *ecclesia pressa*,[30] it constitutes at the same time the possibility of the glorification of the finite spirit. It is precisely the beauty of the temporal that in it the infinite Spirit and the finite spirit are separated, and it is precisely the greatness of the finite spirit that the temporal is assigned to it. The temporal therefore, if I may venture to say so, does not exist for God's sake, in order that in it, speaking mystically, He may test and try the loved one, but it exists for man's sake and is the greatest of all the gifts of grace. For man's eternal dignity consists in the fact that he can have a history, the divine element in him consists in the fact that he himself, if he will, can impart to this history continuity, for this it acquires only when it is not the sum of all that has happened to me or befallen me but is my own work, in such a way that even what has befallen me is by me transformed and translated from necessity to freedom. The enviable thing in human life is that one can come to the aid of the Deity, can understand Him, and again the only way of understanding Him which is worthy of a man is by freely appropriating everything which comes to one, both the joyful and the sorrowful. Does it not seem so to you? It does to me, indeed it seems to me as if one had only to say this aloud to a man to make him envious of himself.

The two standpoints here suggested might be regarded as an attempt to realize an ethical view of life. The only reason why this attempt does not succeed is that the individual has chosen himself in his isolation or has chosen himself abstractly. This can also be expressed by saying that the individual has not chosen himself ethically. He is therefore not in connection with reality, and such being the case, no ethical view of life can be consistently carried out. He on the other hand who chooses himself ethically chooses himself concretely as this definite individual, and he attains this concretion by the fact that this act of choice is identical with this act of repentance which sanctions the choice. The individual thus becomes conscious of himself as this definite individual, with these talents, these dispositions, these instincts, these passions, influenced by these definite surroundings, as this definite product of a definite environment. But being conscious of himself in this way, he assumes responsibility for all this. He does not hesitate as to whether he shall include this particular trait or the other, for he knows that he stands to lose something much higher if he does not. Thus at the instant of choice he is in the most complete isolation, for he withdraws from the surroundings; and yet at the same moment he is in absolute continuity, for he chooses himself as product; and this choice is the choice of freedom, so that when he chooses himself as product he can just as well be said to produce himself. Thus at the instant of choice he is at the conclusion, for he concludes himself in a unity, and yet the same instant he is at the beginning, for he chooses himself freely. As product he is pressed into the forms of reality, in the choice he makes himself elastic, transforming all the outwardness into inwardness. He has his place in the world, with freedom he chooses his place, that is, he chooses this very place. He is a definite individual, in the choice he makes himself a definite individual, for he chooses himself.

So the individual chooses himself as a concretion determined in manifold ways, and he chooses himself therefore in accord with his continuity. This concretion is the reality of the individual, but as he chooses it in accord with his freedom one can also say that it is his possibility, or (to avoid an expression so aesthetical) that it is his task. For he who lives aesthetically sees only possibilities everywhere, they constitute for him the content of the future, whereas he who lives ethically sees tasks everywhere. The individual therefore sees this actual concretion of his as his task, his goal, his aim. But the fact that the individual sees his possibility as his task expresses precisely his sovereignty over himself, which he never relinquishes, even though he can find no pleasure in the very embarrassing sovereignty which characterizes a king without a country. This gives the ethical individual a sense of assurance which he who lives merely aesthetically lacks entirely. He who lives aesthetically expects everything from without. Hence, the morbid dread with which many people speak of the appalling experience of not having found one's place in the world. Who will deny that it is a pleasant thing to have been fortunate in this respect? But such a dread always indicates that the individual expects everything from the place, nothing from himself. He, too, who lives ethically will try to choose his place rightly; however, if he notices that he has made a mistake, or that obstacles arise over which he has no control, he does not lose courage, for he never relinquishes the sovereignty over himself. He at once sees his task and is instantly active. In like manner one often sees men who are afraid that if once they were to fall in love they might not get the girl who is exactly the ideal which suits them. Who will deny that it is a pleasant thing to get such a girl? But

nevertheless, it is a superstition to believe that what is outside a man is what is able to make him happy.

He, too, who lives ethically wishes to be fortunate in his
choice; however, if it turns out that the choice was not
completely in accordance with the wish, he does not lose
courage, he at once sees his task and knows that the art is
not to wish but to will. Many, though they have a just conception of what a human life is, wish to be contemporary
with great events, to be involved in important situations.
Who will deny that such things have their validity? But
nevertheless, it is superstition to think that an event or a
situation as such is capable of making a man something.
He who lives ethically knows that it all depends upon what
one sees in every situation, with what energy he regards it,
and that he who thus cultivates himself in the unimportant
situations may experience more than he who has been a
witness to, yea, a part in the most notable events. He
knows that everywhere there is a dancing floor,[31] that even
the lowliest man has his, that his dance, if he will, can be
as beautiful, as graceful, as mimic, as brisk as that of those
who were assigned a place in history. It is this proficiency
of the fencer, this suppleness, which is properly the immortal life of the ethical. To him who lives aesthetically applies
the old saying, "to be/or not to be," and the more he is
allowed to live aesthetically, the more requirements his life
makes, and if merely the least of these is not fulfilled, he is
dead. He who lives ethically has always a way of escape
when everything goes against him; when the storm broods
over him so darkly that his neighbor cannot see him, he
nevertheless has not perished, there is always a point he
holds fast, and that is . . . his self.

Only one thing I would not omit to mention, namely,
that so soon as the gymnastic of the ethicist becomes an
experimentation he has ceased to live ethically. All such
gymnastic experimentation is nothing else but what sophistry is in the realm of knowledge.

Here I would recall the definition I gave a while ago of
the ethical, as that by which a man becomes what he becomes. The ethical then will not change the individual into
another man but makes him himself, it will not annihilate

the aesthetical but transfigures it. It is essential to a man who is to live ethically that he become so radically conscious of himself that no adventitious trait escapes him. This concretion the ethical would not obliterate but it sees in this its task, it sees what it has to build upon and what it has to build. Commonly one regards the ethical quite abstractly and therefore has a secret horror of it. The ethical is thus regarded as something foreign to the personality, and one shrinks from abandoning oneself to it since one cannot be quite certain what it may lead to in the course of time. So it is that many men are afraid also of death because they entertain dark and obscure conceptions of the soul passing over in death to another dispensation where the prevailing laws and conventions differ from those with which they have become acquainted in this world. The reason for such a fear is the reluctance of the individual to become transparent to himself; for, provided one is willing, one easily sees the absurdity of this fear. So it is also with the ethical. When a man is afraid of being transparent he always shuns the ethical, for precisely this is what the ethical wills.

In opposition to an aesthetical view which would enjoy life, one often hears of another view which finds the significance of life in living for the fulfillment of its duties. With this one intends to indicate an ethical life view. However, the expression is very imperfect, and one might almost believe that it was invented in order to bring the ethical into disrepute. At all events, in our age one often hears it used in such a way that one is almost inclined to smile, as for example when Scribe[32] allows this thesis to be expressed with a sort of burlesque seriousness which contrasts very unfavorably with the joy and merriment of pleasure. The fault is that the individual is placed in an outward relation to duty. The ethical is defined as duty, and duty in turn is defined as a congeries of particular propositions, but the individual and duty stand outside of one another. Such a life of duty is of course very uncomely and tiresome, and if the ethical had not a far deeper connection with personality, it would be very difficult to defend it against the aesthetical. I will not deny that there are men who get no further, but that is not due to duty but to the man himself/

It is strange that the word duty can suggest an outward relation, inasmuch as the very derivation of the word [*Pligt*] indicates an inward relation; for what is incumbent upon me, not as this fortuitous individual but in accordance with my true nature, that surely stands in the most inward relation to my self. For duty is not an imposition [*Paalæg*] but something which is incumbent [*paaligger*]. When duty is viewed thus it is a sign that the individual is in himself correctly oriented. For him, therefore, duty will not split up into a congeries of particular definitions, for that is always an indication that he stands in an outward relation to it. He has clad himself in duty, for him it is the expression of his inmost nature. When he has thus oriented himself he has become absorbed in the ethical and will not chase breathlessly after the fulfillment of his duties. The genuine ethical individual therefore possesses calmness and assurance because he has not duties outside himself but in himself. The more profoundly a man has planned his life ethically, the less will he feel the need of talking every instant about duty, of being fearful every instant as to whether he has fulfilled it, of taking counsel every instant with others about what his duty is. When the ethical is rightly viewed it makes the individual infinitely secure in himself, when it is not rightly viewed it makes the individual insecure, and I cannot imagine a more unhappy and agonizing existence than that of a man who manages to put duty outside himself and yet would endeavor to realize it.

If one views the ethical as outside the personality and in an external relation to it, then one has abandoned everything, then one has fallen into despair. The aesthetical as such is despair, the ethical is the abstract and as such it is incapable of producing anything whatever. Therefore, when one sometimes sees men with a certain honest zeal toiling and moiling to realize the ethical which constantly flees like a shadow as soon as they seek to lay hold of it, the sight is at once comic and tragic.

The ethical is the universal and so it is the abstract. In its complete abstraction the ethical is therefore always prohibitive. So it appears as law. Whenever the ethical has the form of a positive command it already contains something of the aesthetical. The Jews were the people of the Law. Hence they understood perfectly most of the commandments in the Laws of Moses, but the commandment they seem not to have understood was that commandment to which Christianity most closely attached itself: "Thou shalt love God with all thy heart." This commandment is not at all negative, neither is it abstract, it is in the highest degree positive and in the highest degree concrete. When the ethical becomes more concrete it passes over into the definition of morals and customs. But so regarded the reality of the ethical consists in the reality of a national individuality, and here the ethical has already appropriated an aesthetical factor. Nevertheless, the ethical is still abstract and cannot be fully realized because it lies outside the individual. Only when the individual himself is the universal is it possible to realize the ethical. This is the secret of conscience, it is the secret which the individual life shares with itself, that it is at once an individual life and at the same time the universal, if not immediately as such, yet according to its possibility. He who regards life ethically sees the universal, and he who lives ethically expresses the universal in his life, he makes himself the universal man, not by divesting himself of his concretion, for then he becomes nothing, but by clothing himself with it and permeating it with the universal. For the universal man is not a phantom, but every man as such is the universal man, that is to say, to every man the way is assigned by which he becomes the universal man. He who lives aesthetically is the accidental man; he believes himself to be the perfect man by reason of the fact that he is the only man. He who lives ethically labors to become the universal man. So for example when a man is aesthetically in love the adventitious plays a prodigious role, and it is a matter of importance to him that no one has loved as he does, with all the nuances. When he who lives ethically marries he realizes the universal. Therefore he does not become a hater of the concrete but has one concrete expression the more, deeper than every aesthetical expression, in the fact that in love he sees a revelation of the universal human. So he who lives ethically has himself as his task. His self in its immediacy is accidentally determined, and the task is to work up together the accidental and the universal.

So the ethical individual has duty not outside him but in him; at the moment of despair it makes its appearance and then works itself out through the aesthetical and in it and with it. One can say of the ethical individual that he is like quiet waters which run deep, whereas he who lives aesthetically is only superficially moved. Hence, when the ethical individual has completed his task, has fought the good fight, he has then reached the point where he has become the one man, that is to say, that there is no other man altogether like him; and at the same time he has become the universal man. To be the one man is not in itself anything so great, for that everybody has in common with every product of nature; but to be that in such a way that he is also the universal man is the true art of living.

So personality has not the ethical outside it but in it, and out of this depth it breaks forth. Then, as I have said, we must take care that it shall not with an abstract and empty tempestuousness reduce the concrete to naught but rather that it shall assimilate it. Since, then, the ethical lies deepest in the soul it is not always visible to the eye, and the man who lives ethically may do exactly the same things as the man who lives aesthetically, so that for a time this may create a deception, but finally there comes an instant when it is evident that he who lives ethically has a limit which the other does not recognize. In this assurance that his life is ethically planned the individual reposes with secure confidence and therefore does not torment himself and others with captious apprehensions about this and that. The fact that the man who lives ethically leaves a large space for the indifferent I find quite natural, and it is indicative of veneration for the ethical that one will not press it into every insignificant affair. The effort to do this always fails and it is to be found only in those who do not possess courage to believe in the ethical and who lack inward confidence in a deeper sense. There are men whose pusillanimity is recognizable precisely in the fact that they are never ready with the sum total because for them this is not single but manifold. But this, too, lies outside the ethical, and there is, of course, no other ground for it but weakness of will, which like all other weakness of mind may be regarded as a sort of insanity. The life of such men is employed in straining at gnats. They have no conception either of the pure and beautiful earnestness of the ethical or of the care-free gladness of the indifferent. But of course for the ethical individual the indifferent is dethroned and every instant he is able to set limits to it. Thus one believes also in the existence of a providence, and the soul reposes securely in this assurance, and yet it would not occur to one to try to permeate every accidental circumstance with this thought or to become convinced of this faith every minute. To will the ethical without being disturbed by the indifferent, to believe in providence without being disturbed by the accidental, represents a condition of sound health which every man can acquire and retain if he will. In this case, too, the point is to see the task, to perceive that when a man has a tendency to be distracted in this way the task is to put up a resistance, to hold fast the infinite and not go on a wild-goose chase.

He who chooses himself ethically has himself as his task, and not as a possibility merely, not as a toy to be played with arbitrarily. He can choose himself ethically only when he chooses himself in continuity, and so he has himself as a task which is manifoldly defined. This manifoldness he does not try to obliterate or to volatilize; on the contrary, he repents himself tightly into it, because this manifoldness is himself and only by being repentantly absorbed in it can he come to himself, since he does not assume that the world begins with him or that he creates himself. Language itself has stamped this last view with contempt, and one always says contemptuously of a man that he is self-made. But when repentantly he chooses himself he is active, not in the direction of isolation but in the direction of continuity.

Let us now for once compare an ethical and an aesthetical individual. The principal difference, and one on which everything hinges, is that the ethical individual is transparent to himself and does not live *ins Blaue hinein* as does the aesthetical individual. This difference states the whole case. He who lives ethically has seen himself, knows himself, penetrates with his consciousness his whole concretion, does not allow indefinite thoughts to potter about within him, nor tempting possibilities to distract him with their jugglery; he is not like a witch's letter from which one sense can be got now and then another, depending upon how one turns it. He knows himself. The expression *gnothi seauton*[33] has been repeated often enough and in it has been seen the goal of all human endeavor. That is quite right, too, but it is equally certain that it cannot be the goal if it is not at the same time the beginning. The ethical individual knows himself, but this knowledge is not a mere contemplation (for with that the individual is determined by his necessity), it is a reflection upon himself which itself is an action, and therefore I have deliberately preferred to use the expression "choose oneself" instead of know oneself. So when the individual knows himself he is not through; on the contrary, this knowledge is in the highest degree fruitful, and from it proceeds the true individual. If I desired to be clever I might say at this point that the individual knew himself in such a way as Adam "knew" Eve in the Old Testament sense of the word. By the individual's intercourse with himself he impregnates himself and brings himself to birth. This self which the individual knows is at once the actual self and the ideal self which the individual has outside himself as the picture in likeness to which he has to form himself and which, on the other hand, he nevertheless has in him since it is the self. Only within him has the individual the goal after which he has to strive, and yet he has this goal outside him, inasmuch as he strives after it. For if the individual believes that the universal man is situated outside him, that from without it will come to him, then he is disoriented, then he has an abstract conception and his method is always an abstract annihilation of the original self. Only within him can the individual acquire information about himself. Hence, the ethical life has this duplex character, that the individual has his self outside himself and in himself. The typical self, however, is this yet imperfect self, for this is only a prophecy and therefore not the real self. Nevertheless, this typical self accompanies him constantly, but the more he realizes it, the more it vanishes within him, until at last, instead of being visible in front of him, it lies behind him like a pallid possibility. With this picture it is as with man's shadow: in the morning man casts his shadow before him, at midday it goes almost unobserved beside him, in the evening it falls behind him. When the individual knows himself and has chosen himself he is about to realize himself, but as he has to realize himself freely he must know what it is he would realize. What he would realize is in fact himself, but it is his ideal self which he acquires nowhere but in himself. If one does not hold fast to the fact that the individual has the ideal self in himself, his *Dichten und Trachten* [thought, aspirations, endeavors, studies] remain abstract. He who would copy another man and he who would copy the normal man become both of them, though in different ways, equally affected.

The aesthetic individual views himself in his concretion and then distinguishes *inter et inter*.[34] He regards some things as belonging to him accidentally, other things as belonging to him essentially. This distinction, however, is exceedingly relative, for so long as a man lives merely aesthetically one thing belongs to him as accidentally as another, and it is merely for lack of energy an aesthetic individual maintains this distinction. The ethical individual has learned this in despair, hence he has another distinction, for he, too, distinguishes between the essential and the accidental. Everything posited by his freedom belongs to him essentially, however accidental it may seem to be; everything else is for him accidental, however essential it may seem to be. In the case of the ethical individual, however, this distinction is not the fruit of his arbitrary determination and does not imply that he has plenary power to make himself what he would. The ethical individual, to be sure, may venture to use the expression that he is his own editor, but at the same time he is fully conscious that he is responsible—responsible to himself personally, inasmuch as what he chooses will have decisive influence upon him, responsible in view of the order of things in which he lives, and responsible in the sight of God. Thus regarded, the distinction, I believe, is correct; for only that belongs to me essentially which I ethically accept as my task. If I refuse to accept it, then what essentially belongs to me is that I have refused it. When a man views himself aesthetically he perhaps distinguishes as follows, saying, "I have a talent for painting, which I regard as accidental; but I have wit and cleverness of mind, which I regard as the essential thing, and it could not be taken away from me without my becoming another man." To this I would reply, "This whole distinction is an illusion, for if you do not accept this wit or cleverness ethically as a task, as something for which you are responsible, it does not belong to you essentially, and this principally for the reason that so long as you are merely living aesthetically your life totally is unessential." He who lives ethically abolishes to a certain degree the distinction between the accidental and the essential, for he accepts himself, every inch of him, as equally essential. But the distinction returns, for when he has done this he distinguishes again, yet in such a way that for the accidental which he excludes he accepts an essential responsibility for excluding it.

In case the aesthetic individual sets a task for his life with "aesthetic seriousness," it is properly nothing but the task of being more and more absorbed in his own accidentality, of becoming an individual whose irregularity and paradoxicality no one has seen the match of, a grimace of a man. The reason why one so seldom meets such a figure in real life is that people so seldom have a conception of what it is to live. On the other hand, since many have a positive predilection for chattering, one meets on the streets, in society and in books with a great deal of chatty nonsense which bears unmistakably the stamp of the rage for originality which being transferred to real life would enrich the world with a multitude of artifacts each one more ludicrous than the other. The task which the ethical individual sets himself is to transform himself into the universal man. Only the ethical individual seriously renders an account to himself and is therefore honest with himself, only he has the paradigmatic grace and decorum which is more beautiful than any other. But to transform oneself into the universal man is only possible if already *kata dunamin*[35] I have this in myself. For this universal can very well coexist with and in the particular without consuming it; it is like the fire which burned in the bush without consuming it. If the universal man is situated outside of me, only one method is possible, and that is to divest myself of my whole concretion. One often sees this striving after unbridled abstraction. Among the Hussites there was a sect of men who thought that the most obvious way to become the normal man was to go naked like Adam and Eve in paradise.[36] Often enough one encounters in our age people who in a spiritual sense teach the same thing, that one becomes the normal man by becoming utterly stark naked, as one can become by divesting oneself of one's whole concretion. But it is not so. In the act of despair the universal man comes forth and now is behind the concretion, breaking out through it. In a language there are many more paradigmatic verbs than the one which in the grammar is set forth as the paradigm. It is accidental that this one is presented, since all the others were equally suited for this use. So it is also with men. Every man can, if he will, become the paradigmatic man, not by wiping out his accidentality but by remaining in it and ennobling it. But he ennobles it by choosing it.

You now will have perceived that the ethical individual has gone through in the course of his life the stages which earlier we showed to be distinctive stages. In the course of his life he will develop the personal, the civic, the religious virtues, and his life and its progress consist in the fact that he constantly translates himself from one stage to another. So soon as a man thinks that one of these stages is sufficient and that a person may venture one-sidedly to concentrate upon it, that man has not chosen himself ethically but has overlooked the importance either of isolation or of continuity, and above all has not apprehended that the truth consists in the identity of the two.

He who has ethically chosen and found himself possesses himself as he is determined in his whole concretion. He has himself, then, as an individual who has these talents, these passions, these inclinations, these habits, who is under these influences, who in this direction is affected thus, in another thus. Here, then, he has himself as a task, in such a sort that the task is principally to order, cultivate, temper, enkindle, repress, in short, to bring about a proportionality in the soul, a harmony, which is the fruit of the personal virtues. Here the aim of his activity is himself, but not as arbitrarily determined, for he has himself as a task which is set for him, even though it has become his by the fact that he has chosen it. But although he himself is his aim, this aim is nevertheless another, for the self which is the aim is not an abstract self which fits everywhere and hence nowhere, but a concrete self which stands in reciprocal relations with these surroundings, these conditions of life, this natural order. This self which is the aim is not merely a personal self but a social, a civic self. He has, then, himself as a task for an activity wherewith as this definite personality he takes a hand in the affairs of life. Here his task is not to cultivate himself but to exert an influence, and yet at the same time he cultivates himself, for, as I remarked earlier, the ethical individual so lives that he is constantly passing from one stage to the other. If the individual has not originally understood himself as a concrete personality in continuity, neither will he acquire this subsequent continuity. If he thinks that the trick is to begin like a Robinson Crusoe, he remains a fanciful adventurer to the end of his days. On the other hand, when he perceives that if he does not begin concretely he will never get to the point of beginning, and that if he does not begin he will not end, then he will be at once in continuity with the past and with the future. From the personal life he translates himself into the civic, and from this into the personal. The personal life as such was an isolation and hence imperfect; in the fact that through the civic life he comes back into his personality the personal life manifests itself in a higher form. Personality manifests itself as the absolute which has its teleology in itself.

When the performance of duty has been represented as the task for a man's life people have often recalled that duty itself vacillates, that laws may change. You easily see that the latter expression has in view especially the fluctua-

tions to which the civic virtues are always exposed. Yet this
scepticism does not apply to negative morals, for they remain unchanged.²There is another scepticism, however,
which applies to all duty, namely, the consideration that I
am utterly unable to do duty. Duty is the universal, what
is required of me is the universal; what I am able to do is
the particular.³This scepticism, however, has great significance, inasmuch as it shows that personality is the absolute.
But this must be more closely defined. It is to be noted that
language itself emphasizes this scepticism. I never say of a
man that he does duty or duties, but I say that he does *his*
duty, I say, "I am doing *my* duty, do *yours*." This shows
that the individual is at once the universal and the particu-
lar.⁴Duty is the universal which is required of me; so if I
am not the universal, I am unable to perform duty. On the
other hand, my duty is the particular, something for me
alone, and yet it is duty and hence the universal. Here personality is displayed in its highest validity. It is not lawless,
neither does it make laws for itself, for the definition of
duty holds good, but personality reveals itself as the unity
of the universal and the particular. That such is the case
is clear, it can be made comprehensible to a child; for I
can do duty and yet not do *my* duty, and I can do *my*
duty and yet not do duty. I cannot see why for this cause
the world should sink into scepticism, for the difference between good and evil always remains, and so do responsibility and duty; even though it is impossible for another to
say what *my* duty is, it will always be possible for him to
say what is *his* duty, and this would not be the case if the
unity of the universal and the particular were not posited.
5 One may seem perhaps to have disposed of all scepticism
by getting duty turned into something external, something
fixed and definite, of which one can say simply, this is duty.
But that is a misunderstanding, for in this instance the
doubt lies not in the external but in the internal, in my relation to the universal. As a particular individual I am not
the universal, and to require that of me is absurd. So if I
am to be able to perform the universal, I must be the universal at the same time that I am the particular; but thus
the dialectic of duty is within me. As I have said, this doc-

trine involves no danger to the ethical, on the contrary it
upholds it. If one does not adopt this doctrine, personality
becomes abstract, its relation to duty abstract, its immortality abstract. The distinction between good and evil is not
abolished, for I doubt if there ever has been a man who
maintained that it is a duty to do evil. That he did evil is
another matter, but he tried at the same time to make himself and others believe that it was good. It is unthinkable
that he might be able to continue in this vain conceit, since
he himself is the universal and so has the enemy not outside
himself but within him. If, on the contrary, I assume that
duty is something external, the distinction between good
and evil is abolished, for if I am not myself the universal
I can come only into an abstract relationship with it; but
the distinction between good and evil is incommensurable
for an abstract relationship.

Precisely when one perceives that personality is the absolute, is its own end and purpose, is the unity of the universal and the particular, precisely then will all scepticism
which takes the historical as its point of departure be effectually overcome. Freethinkers have often sought to confuse
the concepts by remarking that sometimes one race of people has declared holy and lawful the very thing which in
the eyes of other peoples was an abomination and a crime.
Here they have allowed themselves to be dazzled by the
external; for in the ethical realm there is never any question
about the external but only about the internal. But however much the external may change, the moral content of
action may nevertheless remain the same. Thus, for example, there certainly has never been a race of men who
taught that children should hate their parents. However,
in order to nourish doubt, it has been recalled that, whereas
all civilized nations made it a duty for children to take
care of their parents, savages have the custom of putting
their aged parents to death. It is quite possible that such
is the case; but with this one has got no further, for the
question remains whether the savages mean thereby to do
anything evil. The ethical always consists in the consciousness of wanting to do the good, whereas it is another question whether the savages are not chargeable with defective

knowledge. The freethinker perceives very clearly that the easiest way to volatilize the ethical is by opening the door to the historical infinity. And yet there is something true in his position, for in the last resort, if the individual is not himself the absolute, empiricism is the only road open to him, and this road has with respect to its issue the same peculiarity as has the river Niger with respect to its source, that no one knows where it is. If finiteness is my lot, it is arbitrary to come to a stop at any particular point. On this road, therefore, one never gets to the point of beginning, for in order to begin one must have got to the end, but this is an impossibility. If personality is the absolute, then it is itself the Archimedean point from which one can lift the world. That this consciousness cannot mislead the individual to want to cast reality from him you can readily see, for if he would be the absolute in this sense, he is nothing at all, an abstraction. Only as the particular is he the absolute, and this consciousness will save him from all revolutionary radicalism.

Here I will bring my theorizing to an end. I feel keenly that I am not suited to this part, nor do I desire to be, but I should be completely satisfied if I might be regarded as a fairly practical fellow. Besides, all theorizing takes so much time. What I can do as an active agent in an instant, or can at once begin to do, requires much ado and difficulty before one can manage to express and describe it. Now it is not my intention to lecture you on the doctrine of duties and to talk in the usual way about duties towards God, towards oneself, and towards one's neighbor. Not at all as though I scorned this classification or as though what I have to teach were too profound to be associated with Balle's "Lesson-Book"[37] or might presuppose greater preliminary knowledge than that book presupposes; not at all for such reasons, but because I believe that in the matter of ethics it is not a question of the multifariousness of duty but of its intensity. When with all his energy a person has felt the intensity of duty he is then ethically mature, and in him duty will emerge of itself. The chief thing is, not whether one can count on one's fingers how many duties one has, but that a man has once felt the intensity of duty in such a way that the consciousness of it is for him the assurance of the eternal validity of his being. I, therefore, by no means extol a man for being a man of duty, any more than I would commend him for being a bookworm, and yet it is certain that the man before whom duty has never revealed itself in its whole significance is quite as poor a sort as is the scholar who thinks like the foolish inhabitants of the village of Mol that learning comes to one *mir nichts und dir nichts.*[38] Let the casuists be absorbed in discovering the multifariousness of duties, the chief thing, the only saving thing, is that in relation to his own life a man is not his uncle but his father.

Let me illustrate what I mean by an example. I choose for this purpose the impression I have retained from my earliest childhood.[39] When I was five years of age I was sent to school. It is natural that such an event always makes an impression upon a child, but the question is, what impression. Childish curiosity is engrossed by the various confusing conceptions as to what significance this may properly have. That this was the case with me too is quite likely; however, the chief impression I got was an entirely different one. I made my appearance at school, was introduced to the teacher, and then was given as my lesson for the following day the first ten lines of Balle's "Lesson-Book," which I was to learn by heart. Every other impression was then obliterated from my soul, only my task stood out vividly before it. As a child I had a very good memory, so I had soon learned my lesson. My sister had heard me recite it several times and affirmed that I knew it. I went to bed, and before I fell asleep I catechized myself once more; I fell asleep with the firm purpose of reading the lesson over the following morning. I awoke at five o'clock, got dressed, got hold of my lesson-book, and read it again. At this moment everything stands as vividly before my eyes as if it had occurred yesterday. To me it was as if heaven and earth might collapse if I did not learn my lesson, and on the other hand as if, even if heaven and earth were to collapse, this would not exempt me from doing what was assigned to me, from learning my lesson. At that age I knew so little about duties, I had not yet, as you see, learned to know them from Balle's "Lesson-Book," I had only one duty, that of learning my lesson, and yet I can trace my whole ethical view of life to this impression. I may smile at a little nipper of five years who takes hold of a thing so passionately, and yet I assure you I have no higher wish than that at every time of life I may take hold of my work with the same energy, with the same ethical earnestness as then. It is true that in later life one acquires a better conception of what one's work is, but still the chief thing is the energy. I owe it to my father's serious-mindedness that this event made such an impression upon me, and if I owed him nothing else, this would suffice to put me eternally in his debt. What is really important in education is not that the child learns this and that, but that the mind is matured, that energy is aroused. You often talk about how glorious a thing it is to have a good head. Who will deny that this is important? And yet I am nearly inclined to believe that one can make oneself that if one will. Give a man energy, passion, and with that he is everything. Take a young girl, let her be silly, high-flown, a perfectly foolish ninny, think of her as deeply and sincerely in love, and you will see that the good head comes of itself, you will see how shrewd and cunning she becomes in scenting out whether she is loved in return; let her become fortunate in love, and you will see how enthusiasm blossoms upon her lips; let her become unfortunate, and you will hear the cool reflections of wit and understanding.

I can say that in this respect my childhood has been fortunate because it has enriched me with ethical impressions. Permit me to dwell upon it a moment longer; it recalls to me my father, and that is the most precious recollection I possess, and being by no means a poor and unfruitful memory it gives me occasion to illustrate once again my dictum that the total impression of duty is the principal thing and not by any means the multifariousness of duties. If the latter is made prominent, the individual is reduced and ruined. Now in this respect I was fortunate as a child, for I never had many duties but generally only one, but that was a duty in earnest. When I was two years older I was sent to the Latin School. Here began a new life, but here again the principal impression was the ethical, al-

though I enjoyed the greatest freedom. I went amongst the
other pupils, heard with amazement their complaints of
their teachers, beheld the marvelous event of a pupil being
taken out of school because he could not get on with his
teacher. If from an earlier time I had not been so profoundly
influenced, an event such as this might have had an injurious effect upon me. Now such was not the case. I knew
it was my duty to go to school, to the school where for
good and all I had been sent. Even though everything else
were to be changed, this could not be changed. It was not
merely fear of my father's seriousness which instilled into
me this notion, but it was the lofty impression of what a
person's duty is. Even though my father were dead and I
placed under the supervision of another whom I might
have induced to take me out of the school, I never would
have ventured, or indeed, really wished to do it, it would
have been as though my father's shade had come following
me to school; for here again I would have had an infinite
impression of what my duty was, so that no lapse of time
would have obliterated the recollection that I had violated
his will. For the rest I enjoyed my freedom, I knew only
one duty, that of attending to my school, and in this respect
I was left entirely to my own responsibility.

When I was sent to this school and the prescribed school-
books had been bought, my father handed them to me with
the words, "William, when the month is up, you are the
third in your class." I was exempted from all parental
twaddle. He never asked me about my lessons, never heard
me recite them, never looked at my exercise book, never
reminded me that now it was time to read, now time to
leave off, never came to the aid of the pupil's conscience,
as one sees often enough when noble-minded fathers chuck
their children under the chin and say, "You had better be
doing your work." When I wanted to go out he asked me
first whether I had time. That I was to decide for myself,
not he, and his query never went into details. That nevertheless he was deeply concerned about what I was doing
I am perfectly certain, but he never let me observe it, in
order that my soul might be matured by responsibility.
Here again it was the same, I had not many duties—and

how many children are spoiled by being overwhelmed by
a regular ceremonial of duties! So I got a thoroughly deep
impression of the fact that there was something called duty
and that it had eternal validity. In my time we studied
Latin grammar with a thoroughness which in this age is
unknown. Through this instruction I received an impression
which in another way had a singular influence upon my
soul. In so far as I dare give myself credit for a capacity to
view things philosophically, I owe it to this impression of
my childhood. The unconditional respect with which I regarded the rule, the reverence I cherished for it, the contempt with which I looked down upon the miserable life
the exception led, the righteous way, so it seemed to me,
in which it was tracked down in my exercise book and
always stigmatized—what else is this but the distinction
which lies at the bottom of every philosophical way of
thinking? When under this influence I regarded my father,
he appeared to me an incarnation of the rule; what came
from any other source was the exception, in so far as it was
not in agreement with his command. When I regarded that
fellow pupil who was taken out of the school, I felt that he
must be an exception unworthy of my attention, and that
all the more because the fuss they made about him proved
sufficiently that he was an exception. The childish rigorism
with which I then distinguished between the rule and the
exception, in grammar as well as in life, has now indeed
become softened, but I still have that distinction within
me, I know how to call it forth, especially when I see you
and your like who seem to propound the doctrine that the
exception is the most important thing, yea, that the rule
only exists in order that the exception may show off to
advantage.

The energy with which I become ethically conscious is
therefore the thing that counts, or rather I cannot become
ethically conscious without energy. I can therefore never
become ethically conscious without becoming conscious of
my eternal nature. This is the true proof of the immortality
of the soul. It is, of course, not a full-grown proof unless the
task is congruous with duty, but what for eternity is my
duty is an eternal task. The circumstance that the first ten

lines of Balle's "Lesson-Book" were assigned to me as a
task from which nothing else in the world could ransom
me was in a certain sense the first proof presented to me
of the immortality of my soul. The imperfection of it consisted, not in any lack of energy on my part, but in the
casual character of the task.

It is not my intention to lead you into a consideration of
the multifariousness of duty. If I would express duty negatively, it would be easy; if I would express it positively, it
would be very difficult and prolix; indeed, upon reaching a
certain point it would be impossible. On the contrary, what
my purpose was, what to the best of my ability I have
endeavored to do, was to illuminate the absolute importance of duty, the eternal validity for personality of the
relationship of duty. For so soon as in despair a person has
found himself, has absolutely chosen himself, has repented
himself, he has himself as a task under an eternal responsibility, and thus duty is posited in its absoluteness. However, since this person has not created himself but chosen
himself, duty is the expression of his absolute dependence
and of his absolute freedom as identical with one another.
The particular duty he will teach himself, and in vain will
seek enlightenment upon it from any other man, and yet
he will again in this case be autodidact as well as theo-
didact,[40] and vice versa. His duty is in no case something
abstract, partly because for him it is not anything external
(for when this is the case it is always abstract), and partly
because he himself is concrete, for he has chosen himself
ethically, has chosen himself in all his concretion, and relinquished all claim to the abstractness of arbitrary will.

What remains is to show how life looks when it is regarded ethically. You and all aestheticists are very willing
to go halves, you concede that the ethical has its importance, you say that it is respectable for a man to live for
his duties, that it is worthy of all honor, indeed, you even
let fall some ambiguous words to the effect that it is quite
fitting that there are men who live for their duties, that it
is well the majority of people do so—and you meet with
men of duty who are good-natured enough to find that
there is sense in this talk, in spite of the fact that like all

scepticism it is, of course, nonsensical. On the other hand, you for your part are not willing to have anything to do with the ethical. That would deprive life of its significance and above all of its beauty. The ethical, you think, is something totally different from the aesthetical, and when it prevails it destroys the other entirely.

Now if this were so, I should nevertheless have no doubt what to choose. In despair there is an instant when it seems to be as you say, and if a man has not felt this, his despair has been deceitful and he has not ethically chosen himself. However, it is not so, and therefore the next instant despair reveals itself not as a breach but as a metamorphosis. Everything comes back, but comes back transfigured. Therefore, only when one regards life ethically does it acquire beauty, truth, significance, firm consistence; only when a man lives ethically does his life acquire beauty, truth, significance, security; and only in the ethical life view are the autopathetic doubt and the sympathetic doubt set at rest. For in fact the autopathetic and the sympathetic doubt only come to rest in one and the same thing, because both are essentially the same doubt. For the autopathetic doubt is not an expression of egoism but a claim [Fordring] of the self-love which promotes [fordre][41] its own self in the same sense that it promotes the self of everyone else. This observation, I think, is of great moment. Thus, supposing that every imaginable favor has fallen to his lot, an aestheticist who is not an egoist must be in despair over his happiness, because he must say, "What makes me happy is something which cannot be given in the same way to any other man and which no other man can himself acquire." He must, in fact, be fearful lest someone should ask him why he sought his happiness, for he had become happy in order that other men might feel that they could not become happy. If such a man had any sympathy, he would give himself no rest till he had found a higher principle of life. When he had found it he would not be afraid to talk about his happiness, for then, if he were to talk about it rightly, he would say something along with this which would absolutely reconcile him with every man, with humanity as a whole.

However, let us pause to consider the category which

aesthetics claims as its own, namely, beauty. Life loses its beauty, you say, so soon as the ethical prevails. "Instead of the happiness, beauty, and freedom from care which life has when we regard it aesthetically, we get conscientious activity, praiseworthy industry, indefatigable and unremitting zeal." In case you were present here with me I would beg you to give me a definition of the beautiful in order that I might make a beginning. Since you are not present I will take the liberty of attaching my argument to the definition you are accustomed to give: "The beautiful is that which has its teleology in itself." You take as illustration a young girl, you say, "She is beautiful, joyful, carefree, perfect harmony complete in itself, and it is stupid to ask why she exists, for she has her teleology in herself." I shall not annoy you by questioning whether the young girl is really profited by having her teleology only in herself, or whether you, being granted the opportunity of expounding to her your view of the divine character of her existence, would not flatter yourself that she might at last make a mistake and believe that she existed for the sake of listening to your insinuations. You regard nature and find it equally beautiful and are ready to anathematize every finite view of it. Nor shall I torment you here by inquiring whether it is not essentially characteristic of nature to exist for something else. You regard the works of art and of poetry, and you cry out with the poet, *Procul, o procul este profani!*[42] and by the *profani* you understand those who would degrade poetry and art by giving them a teleology which lies outside of them.

As for poetry and art, I would remind you again that they provide only an imperfect reconciliation with life, and also that when you fix your gaze upon poetry and art you are not beholding reality—and properly, it was of this we were supposed to be speaking. So we come back to reality, and since it is likely that in real life you will find very little that is beautiful if you strictly apply the requirements of art, you give another meaning to the beautiful. The beautiful about which you talk is the individually beautiful. You view every particular man as a tiny factor or moment of the whole, you view him precisely in his characteristic peculiarity, and thus even the accidental, the insignificant, acquires significance, and life has the impress of beauty. So then you regard every particular man as a moment. But in fact the beautiful according to your definition was that which has its teleology in itself, but when a man is merely a moment he has his teleology not in himself but outside himself. So even though the whole be beautiful, the parts in themselves are not. And now for your own life. Has that its teleology in itself? Whether a man is justified in leading such a life of mere contemplation I will not decide—but *eh bien* let us assume that the significance of your life is to contemplate others, then after all you would not have your teleology in yourself. Only when every particular man is a moment and at the same time the whole can he be regarded with a view to his beauty; but when he is regarded thus he is regarded ethically, and if he is regarded ethically, he is regarded in terms of his freedom. Let him be qualified as characteristically as you please, if this qualification is a necessity, he is merely a moment, and his life is not beautiful.

When you define the beautiful as that which has its teleology in itself and adduce by way of illustration a young girl or nature or a work of art, I can make nothing out of it but that the whole rant about all these things having their teleology in themselves is an illusion. If there is to be any question of teleology there must be a movement, for as soon as I think of a goal I think of a movement; even when I think of one who is at the goal I always think of a movement, for I reflect that he has reached it by a movement. What you call beautiful manifestly lacks movement; for the beautiful in nature simply *is*, and when I view a work of art and penetrate its thought with my thought, it is really in me the movement occurs, not in the work of art. It may be you are right in saying that the beautiful has its teleology in itself, but as you construe this definition and employ it, it is no more than a negative expression which signifies that the beautiful has not its teleology in anything else. Therefore, you will not be able to employ a seemingly synonymous expression to the effect that the beautiful about which you talk has inner teleology or immanent teleology. For so soon as you employ this expression you require movement, history, and with this you have passed beyond the spheres of nature and of art and are in the sphere of freedom and of ethics.

Now when I say that the individual has his teleology in himself this cannot be misunderstood, as though I meant by this that the individual is the central thing, or that the individual in an abstract sense ought to be sufficient unto himself; for if this is understood abstractly, I get no movement after all. The individual has his teleology in himself, has inner teleology, is himself his teleology. His self is thus the goal towards which he strives. This self of his, however, is not an abstraction but is absolutely concrete. In the movement towards himself the individual cannot relate himself negatively towards his environment, for if he were to do so his self is an abstraction and remains such. His self must be opened in due relation to his entire concretion; but to this concretion belong also the factors which are designed for taking an active part in the world. So his movement, then, is from himself through the world to himself. Here the movement is a real movement, for it is a work of freedom, but at the same time it is immanent teleology, and hence it is here only there can be any question of beauty. If this is the case, the individual is seen to be higher than every relationship in which he stands. But from this it by no means follows that he is not in this relationship, nor can anything tyrannical be discerned in this, inasmuch as the same thing is true of every individual. I am a married man, and you know that I have the profoundest respect for this relationship, and I know that I humble myself under it lovingly; and yet I know that in another sense I am higher than this relationship; but I know also that in exactly the same sense this is the case with my wife—and therefore, as you know, I would not love the young girl we spoke about, because she did not share this view.

Therefore, only when I regard life ethically do I see it with a view to its beauty, and only when I regard my own life ethically do I see it with a view to its beauty. And if you were to say that this beauty is invisible, I would make answer: in a certain sense it is, in another sense it is not;

that is to say, it is visible in the trace it leaves in history, visible in the sense in which it was said, *Loquere ut videam te.*[43] It is indeed true that I do not see the consummation but the struggle, but after all, I see the consummation every instant I will, if I have the courage for it, and without courage I see absolutely nothing eternal, and accordingly nothing beautiful.

When I regard life ethically I regard it with a view to its beauty; life then to me becomes rich in beauty, not poor in beauty as it really is for you. I do not need to travel all over the land to discover beauties, nor to follow them up in the streets, I do not need to appraise and reject. Well, that is natural, I haven't as much time for it as you, for when with joy but also with seriousness I see my life with a view to its beauty I always have enough to do. If sometimes I have an hour free, I stand at my window and regard men, and I see every one with a view to his beauty. Though he be ever so insignificant, ever so lowly, I see him with a view to his beauty; for I see him as this particular man who is yet at the same time the universal man, I see him as one who has this concrete task in life, he does not exist for the sake of any other person, even though he were a hired servant; he has his teleology in himself, he is victorious, he accomplishes this task, that I see; for the man of courage does not see spooks, but on the other hand he sees victorious heroes; the coward does not see heroes but only spooks. He must conquer, of that I am certain, therefore his strife is beautiful. As a rule I am not much inclined to strive, at least not with anybody but myself, but you may be sure that for this faith in the victory of the beautiful I will fight in deadly earnest, and nothing shall wrest it from me. Though with prayers one would wrest from me this faith, though one would wrest it from me by force, I should not let it be taken from me for anything in the world, nor for the whole world, since only by losing this faith would I lose the whole world. By means of this faith I see the beauty of life, and the beauty I see has not the trait of sadness and melancholy which is inseparable from all beauty of nature and of art, inseparable even from the eternal youth of the Greek gods. The beauty I see is joyful and victorious and

stronger than the whole world. And this beauty I see everywhere, even where your eye sees nothing.

Stand here by my window for once. A young girl is
going by. Do you remember that we once met her in the
street? She was not pretty, you remarked; but when you
had regarded her a little more closely you recognized her
and went on to say, "Several years ago she was charming
and was a great success at the balls, then she had a love
affair, and an unhappy one at that. The deuce only knows
how she stood it, she took the thing so much to heart that
her beauty faded away with grief, now she is no longer
beautiful, and there the story ends." Well, that can be
called regarding life with a view to its beauty! To my eyes,
however, she has lost nothing, and to me she seems more
beautiful than ever. Your way of regarding the beauty of
life appears to me therefore to have a great resemblance
to the *joie de vivre* which prevailed in the period when
drinking songs were in vogue, when men became merry
and gay by singing airs like this:[44]

> But for the grape's red juice
> Who would stay longer here?
> Only crime and abuse
> Are heard of far and near.
> Brothers, drink and forget
> That earth is a vale of tears.
> Drink then and do not let
> The soul be appalled by fears.

Let us now come a little closer to some of the situations
in real life, especially those where the aesthetical and the
ethical come into contact, in order to consider to what extent the ethical may deprive us of some beauty, or whether
it does not rather impart to everything a higher beauty. So
I think of a definite individual who in a certain sense is
"like most people are," in another sense is concrete in himself. Let us be quite prosaic. This man has to live, he has to
clothe himself, in short, he has to exist. Perhaps he addressed himself to an aestheticist to find out how he was
to manage, nor would he fail to get enlightenment. The
aestheticist would perhaps say to him, "When a man is

single he requires three thousand dollars a year to live comfortably, if he has four thousand dollars, he needs that too. If he would marry, he must have at least six thousand. Money, after all, is and remains the *nervus rerum gerendarum* [the power to get things done], the true *conditio sine qua non* for living; for of course it is beautiful to read about rural contentment, about idyllic frugality, and I am fond of reading such poetic fiction, but of such a mode of life one would soon tire, and those who live thus do not enjoy this life half so much as those who have money and then in repose and comfort read the songs of the poets. Money is and remains the absolute condition for living. If one has no money, he is and remains excluded from the list of patricians, he is and remains a plebeian. Money is the prime condition, but from this it by no means follows that every one who has money knows how to use it. Those who understand this are in turn the optimates among the patricians."

By this explanation our hero evidently was not profited, all this practical wisdom did not apply to him at all, and he must have felt like a sparrow at a dance of cranes. For suppose, for example, he were to say to the aestheticist, "That's all well enough, but I have neither three thousand dollars a year nor six thousand, either in capital or in interest, I have absolutely nothing at all, hardly a hat." Then his counselor would likely shrug his shoulders and say, "Well, that's another matter, then you must be content with going to the workhouse." If the aestheticist were very good-natured, he would perhaps call back the poor wretch and say to him, "I don't want to bring you to despair before I have tried my utmost. There are a few remedies for distress which one should not leave untried before bidding farewell to joy and taking the vow and putting on the straitjacket. Marry a rich girl, play the lottery, go to the colonies, spend some years scraping money together, worm yourself into the favor of an old bachelor that he may appoint you his heir. For the moment our ways separate, make money, and you will always find in me a friend who knows how to forget that there was a time when you had no money." After all, there is something dreadfully heartless in such a view of life—thus to murder in cold blood all joy in life for him who has no money. And that is what the moneyed man does, for at least it is his opinion that without money there is no joy in life. If I were to put you in comparison with that aestheticist, were to point to you as one who cherishes or utters such thoughts, I should be doing you a very great injustice. For on the one hand, your heart is too good to be the abode of such abominable baseness, and on the other hand, your soul is too sympathetic to utter such thoughts even if you had them. I do not say this as though I meant that he who is without money has need of such compassionate consideration, but because this, after all, is the least one might require of a man who imagined that he was specially favored: that he should not be proud of it nor take pleasure in wounding others not so favored. Let a man be proud, in God's name! It would be better if he were not, but let him be proud, only let him not be proud of money, for there is nothing that so degrades a man.

Now you are accustomed to having money and have sense enough to know what it implies. You insult no one (differing in this respect from the aestheticist we were talking about), you are glad to help when you can, indeed when you lay stress upon the misery of not having money it is done out of sympathy. Your mockery, therefore, is directed not against men but against existence where now things are simply so arranged that not all men can have money. "Prometheus and Epimetheus,"[45] you say, "were undeniably very wise, but all the same it is incomprehensible that when in other respects they endowed men so gloriously it did not occur to them to give them money also." If you had been present on this occasion and had known what you now know, you would have come forward and said, "Ye good gods, you deserve thanks for all you have done, but (pardon me for speaking to you so frankly) you have no knowledge of the world; for a man to be happy he needs one thing more, namely, money. What good does it do him to be created to rule over the world when he can't find time for this because of the necessity of making a living. What a way to act! thrusting out into the world a rational creature, and then letting him toil and moil! Is that the way to treat a human being?" On that topic you are inexhaustible. "Most men," you say, "live to get a living, when they have got that they live to get a good living, when they have got that they die. With genuine emotion, therefore, I read a while ago a notice in the newspaper in which a wife announced the death of her husband. Instead of commenting diffusely upon the pain of losing the best husband and most loving father, she said very briefly that this death was such an affliction because only a short time before it her husband had obtained a pretty good living.

"A good deal more is implied in this than the sorrowing widow and the ordinary reader of the obituary notice can see in it. This way of looking at things can be fashioned into a proof of the immortality of man. This proof might be formulated as follows: It is every man's destiny to get a good living. If a man dies before he got it, he has not attained his destiny, and everyone is free to surmise whether in another world he will attain his destiny. On the other hand, if he gets a good living, he has attained his destiny, but the destiny of getting a good living cannot mean that he shall die, but on the contrary that he shall live well on his good living, *ergo* man is immortal. This proof might be called the popular proof, or the proof from a living. If this proof were added to the previous proofs, every reasonable doubt concerning immortality must be regarded as overcome. This proof can perfectly well be associated with the previous proofs, indeed, it is precisely in this connection that it appears in its full glory, seeing that as the conclusion it refers back to the others and proves them. The other proofs start out with the consideration that man is a rational being; now inasmuch as someone might doubt this, the proof from a living is adjoined to prove this assumption by the following syllogism: to whom God gives a living He gives an understanding, to whom God gives a good living He gives a good understanding, *ergo*. That sorrowing widow had a presentiment of this, she felt the profound tragedy in life's contradictions."

So mockery and flippancy is what you have to contribute in the face of this situation. Presumably it never occurs to you that your view might be profitable and instructive to anybody. Nor presumably does it ever occur to you that by such a declamation you may do harm. For it is quite possible to think that a man who in himself harbored resentment enough at being forced into the labor of life might become still more impatient, still more fretful, by paying attention to the passionateness not devoid of wit with which you would think on his behalf and by giving heed to your sympathetic mockery. I advise you to proceed with caution.

So along the path our hero has taken he will seek in vain for enlightenment. Let us hear now what an ethicist would reply to him. He would say, "It is every man's duty to work in order to live." In case he had nothing more to say, you presumably would reply, "There we have again the old fudge about duty and duty, everywhere it is duty, it is not possible to think of anything more tiresome than this prudery which cows everybody and clips their wings." At this point be so kind as to remember that our hero had no money, that the heartless aestheticist had none to spare for him, and that you had not so much left over that you could assure him of his future. So if he didn't want to sit down and reflect what he would have done if he had had money, he must consider some other expedient. In the next place you will see that the ethicist addressed him with perfect courtesy, he did not treat him as an exception, he did not say to him, "Good Lord! You are simply so unfortunate that you must try to learn to put up with it." On the contrary, he made the aestheticist an exception, for he said, "It is every man's duty to work in order to live." In so far, then, as a man does not need to work he is an exception, but to be an exception is, as we agreed above, not great but little. Therefore, if a man will view the matter ethically he will see that to have money is a humiliation, for every special favor is a humiliation. When he views it thus he will not be enamored of any special favor. He will then humble himself under it, and when he has done that he will again be exalted by the thought that this favor is an expression for the fact that a great claim is made upon him.

If that ethicist from whom our hero sought advice is himself acquainted with what it means to work in order to live, his words will have still more weight. It is to be wished that in this respect people had more courage, and the reason why one often hears so loudly uttered this despicable talk about money being the principal thing is to be found partly in the fact that those who must work lack ethical energy to own up to the significance of work, lack conviction of its significance. Marriage is not harmed by seducers but by cowardly husbands. So it is in this case. The despicable talk we have listened to does no harm, but those people harm the good cause who, being compelled to work in order to live, desire one moment to have their life recognized as meritorious in comparison with that of idlers, the next moment they lament and sigh, and say that after all it is far more beautiful to be independent. What respect will younger people have for life when they hear such talk from older people? Here again you have done yourself much harm by your experimentation, for you have learned to know much which is not good and gladdening. You know very well how to tempt a man and coax from him the admission that he would prefer, after all, to be exempt from work, and so you triumph.

The question whether it might not be possible to imagine a world in which it was not necessary to work in order to live is really an idle question since it does not deal with the given reality but with a feigned situation. This, however, is always an attempt to belittle the ethical view. For if it were a perfection on the part of existence not to have to work, then that man's life would be the most perfect who didn't have to. Then one could say that it was a duty to work only by attaching to the word duty the sense of a dolorous necessity. Duty then would express, not the universal-human but the common, and in this case duty would not be the expression for the perfect. Therefore, I would reply quite aptly that it must be regarded as an imperfection on the part of existence that man did not need to work. The lower the scale of human life, the less evident is the necessity of working; the higher the scale, the more evident it is. The duty of working in order to live expresses the universal-human, and it expresses the universal also in another sense because it expresses freedom. It is precisely

by working that man makes himself free, by working he
becomes lord over nature, by working he shows that he is
higher than nature.

Or might life lose its beauty for the fact that a man must
work in order to live? We are back again at the same old
point: everything depends upon what one understands by
beauty. It is beautiful to see the lilies of the field (though
they sew not neither do they spin) so clothed that even
Solomon in all his glory was not so magnificent; it is beautiful to see the birds without anxiety finding their food; it is
beautiful to see Adam and Eve in Paradise where they could
get everything they pointed at; but it is still more beautiful
to see a man earning by his work what he has need of. It
is beautiful to see a providence satisfying all and caring
for all, but it is still more beautiful to see a man who is,
as it were, his own providence. Man is great, greater than
any other creature, for the fact that he can provide for
himself. It is beautiful to see a man possessing an affluence
which he himself has earned, but it is also beautiful to see
a man doing the still greater trick of transforming little into
much. It is an expression of man's perfection that he can
work, it is a still higher expression for it that he must.

In case our hero will adopt this view, he will not feel
tempted to wish for a fortune which comes to him while
he sleeps, he will not be in love with the prerequisites of
life, he will feel the beauty of working in order to live, he
will sense in this his human dignity; for it is not greatness
in the case of plants that they do not spin, but it is their
imperfection that they cannot. He will not desire to strike
up a friendship with that opulent aestheticist. With level-
headedness he will discern what is great, and will not let
himself be frightened by men of money. Strangely enough,
I have seen men who joyfully felt the significance of working, were satisfied with their work, happy in their frugal
competence, and yet had not courage as it were to admit
this. When they talked about what they needed they always made it seem as if they needed much more than they
really did, they did not want to seem industrious, although
they really were, just as though it were a greater thing to
need much than to need little, greater to be an idler than

to be industrious. How seldom one encounters a man who says calmly and with cheerful dignity, "I don't do this or that, I have not the means for it." It is as though a man had a bad conscience, as though he were afraid of getting the answer the raven got.[46] In this way all true virtue is destroyed or transformed into a phantom. For why should people be frugal who don't need to be? And those who are obliged to be frugal make a virtue of necessity. Just as though one could not be frugal unless one had at hand the possibility of affluence, just as though need were not just as great an enticement to frugality.

So presumably our hero would resolve to work, and yet he would find himself exempted to a certain extent from sordid cares about daily bread. Such sordid cares I have never known, for though in a way I must work in order to live I have always had a liberal competence and cannot therefore speak from experience, but I have always had an eye open to the hardship of this situation . . . and to its beauty also, its educating and ennobling effect, for I believe that there is no care which educates like this. I have known men whom I would not think of calling cowardly or effeminate, who were not in the least disposed to think that man's life ought to be without strife, who felt strength and courage and inclination to fight in a cause where others would lose heart, at the same time I have often heard them say, "God preserve me from care for daily bread. There is nothing which so stifles the higher aspirations in a man." Such utterances have often given me occasion to reflect (and my own life has given me occasion to verify it) that there is nothing so deceitful as the human heart. A man will have courage to venture out into the most dangerous conflicts, but is not willing to engage in a conflict for daily bread, and at the same time he would make out that it is a greater thing to engage in the other conflicts than in this latter one. Well, that's obviously convenient. One chooses an easier conflict which, nevertheless, in the eyes of the multitude seems more dangerous; one persuades oneself that this is the truth; one conquers and so of course is a hero, and a hero of a very different sort than if he had conquered in that other paltry conflict which is unworthy of a man. In-

deed, when besides care for daily bread one has within oneself such a hidden enemy to combat, it is no wonder one
wishes to be rid of this other conflict. Yet a man ought, at
least, to be honest enough with himself to admit that the
reason why he shunned this conflict was that it is far harder
than the other. But if it is harder, then the victory also is
far more beautiful. In case a man is not himself tried in
this conflict, he owes every combatant the admission that
his conflict is the most dangerous, he owes him this *amende
honorable*. If one looks at care for daily bread as an affair
of honor in a still stricter sense than any other combat, one
has already made some progress. Here as in every other
case the important thing is to be in the correct position, not
to be wasting one's time on wishes but to comprehend one's
task. If this task is apparently lowly and insignificant, petty
and disheartening, then one knows that this only makes the
strife more difficult and victory more beautiful. There are
men who are honored by the insignia of orders, and there
are men who shed honor upon the orders. Let that man
apply this to himself who while he feels strength and inclination to engage in glorious conflicts must be content
with the most lowly of all, the conflict for daily bread.

Then, too, the conflict for daily bread has the highly educative characteristic that the reward is so small, or rather
is nothing at all, the combatant striving merely to procure
the possibility of being able to continue to strive. The
greater the reward of battle and the more it is external to a
man, so much the more does the combatant dare to rely
also upon all the ambiguous passions which dwell in every man. Ambition, vanity, pride—these are powers which
possess a prodigious elasticity which is able to drive a man
far. He who strives for daily bread sees at once that these
passions fail him. For how could he suppose that such a
strife might interest others or arouse their admiration? If he
has no other powers, he is disarmed. The reward is so small;
for when he has drudged and toiled and moiled he has perhaps earned precisely what is needful—what is needful to
keep him alive, in order again to be able to toil and moil.
The conflict for daily bread is so ennobling and educative
because it does not permit a man to deceive himself with

regard to his own situation. If he sees nothing higher in this conflict, it is wretched, and he is right in regarding it as an affliction to have to strive to be able to eat his bread in the sweat of his brow. But this strife is so ennobling because it compels him to see something else in it, compels him, if he will not throw himself away entirely, to see in it a combat of honor, and to perceive that the reward is so small in order that the honor may be the greater. So he strives, indeed, to acquire a competence, but what after all he is striving for first and foremost is to acquire himself; and we who have not been subjected to this test but yet have preserved a feeling for the truly great will look on, and if he permits it we will honor him as an honorary member of society. He has, then, a double conflict; he may lose in the one conflict and yet at the same time conquer in the other. If I were to imagine the almost unimaginable, that all his efforts to earn a livelihood were to fail, then indeed he has lost, and yet at the same time he may have won the most beautiful victory it is possible to win. It is upon this I will fix my glance, not upon the reward he missed, for that is too trifling a thing. He who has a reward before his eyes forgets the other conflict; if he does not win the reward, he has lost all; if he wins it, it nevertheless always remains dubious how he won it.

Indeed, what conflict could be more educative than that for daily bread? How much of the spirit of childhood is required in order sometimes almost to smile at all the earthly trouble and travail an immortal spirit has to put up with in order to live, how much humility in order to be content with that little which is earned with difficulty, how much faith in order to see a guidance of providence in one's own life too; for it is easy enough to say that God is greatest in the least manifestations, but to see Him in them requires the strongest faith! What love for mankind to rejoice with the fortunate and to be able to cheer those who are alike in misfortune! What an intense and penetrating consciousness of oneself to make sure one is doing all one can, what perseverance and what vigilance! For what enemy is more crafty than this solicitude? A man does not get rid of it with a few stirring movements, does not frighten it away by noise and racket. What grace and distinction one must have to turn away from it and yet not shun it! How often the weapons must be changed: now one must work, now wait, now brave it out, now pray! And with what delight and joy and ease and dexterity the weapons must be changed, for otherwise the enemy has conquered!

And with this, time passes, a man is not granted opportunity to see his beautiful plans realized, the wishes of his youth fulfilled. He sees others who succeed in this. They gather the crowd around them and reap its applause, they take delight in its jubilation, while he stands as a solitary artist upon the stage of life, having no public and no one who has time to look at him—of course not, for it takes time, his exhibition is not a half hour of juggling, the tricks he performs are of a finer sort and require more than a "cultivated public" to understand them. But neither does he covet this applause. "When I was twenty years of age," he says perhaps, "I too dreamed of combat, I imagined myself in the lists, I looked up at the balcony, I saw the circle of maidens, saw them anxious on my behalf, saw them wave to me their applause, and I forgot the toil of the combat; now I have grown older, my combat is now a different one, but my soul is not less proud. I demand another umpire, a connoisseur, I demand an eye which seeth in secret, which doth not grow weary of seeing, which beholds the strife and perceives the danger; I demand an ear which hears the labor of thought, which divines how my better nature twists itself out of the torture of temptation. To that umpire I will look up, after His applause I will aspire, even though I am not able to deserve it. And when the cup of suffering is held out to me, I will not fix my glance upon the cup but upon Him who holds it, I will not stare at the bottom of the cup if at once I have not drained it, but will fix my gaze immovably upon Him from whom I receive it. Joyfully I will take the cup in my hand, not as when on a festive occasion I drain it to the health of another and am myself gladdened by the delicious taste of the beverage; no, I will taste its bitterness, and as I taste it I will cry out to myself, 'To my health!' because I know and am convinced that by this cup I am purchasing for myself an eternal health."

So it is, I believe, one must ethically conceive the combat fought for daily bread. I will not stand up so doggedly for my rights as to challenge you to indicate exactly at what point in your theory of aesthetics you deal with this subject, but I merely leave it to your own consideration whether by this conflict life loses its beauty if one does not will that it should, or whether it does not gain a higher beauty. To deny that such a conflict exists is indeed madness, to forget it because it bypasses one's own house is thoughtlessness, and, in case one lays claim to a reasoned view of life, it is heartlessness and cowardice.

The fact that many men do not regard the conflict for daily bread in this way is no valid objection, and it surely is a good and pious desire when for such people I wish that they might be magnanimous enough to regard it thus, be inspired not to see amiss like those men in the apocryphal story in Daniel who "did not look up to heaven but looked upon Susanna."

The ethical view that it is every man's duty to work in order to live has accordingly two advantages over the aesthetical view. In the first place, it is consonant with reality and explains something universal in it, whereas the aesthetical view propounds something accidental and explains nothing. In the second place, it construes man with a view to his perfection, sees him in his true beauty. This may be regarded as all that is necessary and more than is sufficient concerning this subject. If you wish to have a few empirical observations, I throw them into the bargain—not as though the ethical view stood in need of any such support, but because you perhaps may profit by them.

An old man whom I once knew always used to say that it was well for a man to learn to work for his living, that what applies to children applies to grown-ups: they've got to learn young. Now it is not my meaning that it would be good for a young man to be at once disheartened by the need of making a living. But only let him work in order to live. The financial independence so highly extolled is often a snare: every desire can be satisfied, every inclination followed, every whim gratified, until they all conspire against oneself. He who must work will remain unacquainted with the vain joy of being able to get everything, he will not learn to trust defiantly in his wealth, to remove with money every obstacle, to purchase for himself every liberty; but then neither will his mind be embittered, he will not be tempted to turn his back upon existence with proud disdain, as many a rich youth has done, and to say as Jugurtha said of Rome, "Here is a city which is for sale if it finds a purchaser,"[47] he will not in a brief space of time have acquired a wisdom whereby he does men an injustice and makes himself unhappy.

So when I often hear people complain that they are compelled to work, compelled to trouble themselves about such things, men whose souls' high flight ought not to be thus checked, then I cannot deny that I sometimes become impatient, that I could wish that Harun al Raschid still went about amongst us dealing out a bastinado to everyone who complained unseasonably.[48] Now you are not in the position of needing to work in order to live, and it is by no means my purpose to counsel you to throw away your fortune so that it may become a necessity for you to work; that is of no avail, and all experimentation is foolishness which comes to nothing. In another sense, however, I believe that you are in the position of needing to acquire the conditions requisite for living. In order to live you must acquire mastery over your innate melancholy. With a view to this situation I apply to you the words of that old acquaintance of mine, that you be taken in time. This melancholy has been your misfortune, but you will see the day when you yourself will admit that it has been your good fortune. So acquire the condition for being able to live. You are not one of those who will make me impatient by complaints, for I believe rather that you would do anything but complain, and you know exceedingly well how to bite back your sufferings within yourself. Beware, however, lest you fall into the opposite extreme, into a mad defiance which consumes one's strength in the effort to conceal pain, instead of using it to bear pain and to vanquish it.

Our hero, then, is willing to work, not because it is for him a *dura necessitas*,[49] but because he regards it as the most beautiful thing and the most perfect. (The notion that

he might not be able to regard it thus because, after all, he
is compelled to put up with it, is one of those foolish and
partly malicious misapprehensions which locate a man's
value outside of him in the accidental.) But precisely because he is willing to work, his occupation can be work
and not slave-labor. He requires, then, a higher expression
for his occupation, an expression which indicates the relation of his occupation to his own person and to that of other
men, an expression which is able to define it for him as
pleasure and at the same time to assert its importance.
Here a deliberation will again be necessary. With the wise
man of the three thousand dollars he counts it beneath his
dignity to have any dealings, but our hero is like most
people. To be sure, he learned young, but nevertheless,
he has acquired a taste for living aesthetically, he is like
most people, ungrateful. Although it was the ethicist who
helped him out of his former embarrassment, it is not to
him he first has recourse. Perhaps as a last resort he secretly
relies upon the ethicist to help him out of this fix, for our
hero is far from being so petty as not to be ready to admit
that the ethicist really helped him out of his embarrassment,
although he had no money to give him. He has recourse
then to a more humane aestheticist. So this man will also
know how to give him a dissertation about the importance
of working. Without work life at last becomes tiresome.
"One's work, however, ought not to be work in the strictest
sense but ought constantly to be a work which could be
defined as pleasure. One discovers in oneself some aristocratic talent or another whereby one distinguishes oneself
from the mob. This one cultivates—not frivolously, for then
one soon becomes tired of it, but with all possible aesthetic
seriousness. Life then has for one a new significance because one has one's work, a work which yet really is one's
pleasure. Being financially independent, one takes good
care of this talent in order that, unhampered by the neces-
sities of life, it may develop into its full vigor. This talent,
however, one does not treat as a plank whereby one is saved
in the shipwreck of life, but as a wing by means of which
one may soar over the world; one does not treat it as a
toiling nag but as a prancing steed." Our hero, however, has

no such aristocratic talent, he is like most people. So the aestheticist knows nothing better for him to do than "to put up with being classified by the mob's trivial definition of what it is to be a laboring man. But do not lose courage, this too has its importance, it is honest and respectable. Become a diligent and industrious man, a useful member of society. I already take delight in seeing you, for the more multifarious life is, the more interesting it is for the onlooker. Hence it is that I and all aesthetes hate a national costume because it would be so tiresome to look at people if all were dressed alike. So then let every individual pursue his own occupation in life, for with that, life becomes all the more beautiful for me and my kind who make it their profession to be onlookers." Our hero, I should hope, becomes a little impatient at this treatment, he is indignant at the insolence of such a classification of men. Moreover, independence played after all a considerable role in the aestheticist's view of life, and independent is simply what he is not.

Perhaps he cannot yet make up his mind to have recourse to the ethicist. He ventures to make one more attempt. He meets a man who says, "One must work in order to live, that's the way life is." Here he seems to have found the man he sought, for this is precisely what he thinks. So he is willing to pay attention to this discourse. "One must work in order to live, that's the way life is, it is the seamy side of existence. One sleeps seven hours every day, that is time wasted, but it has to be; one works five hours of the day, that is time wasted, it has to be. With five hours' work one has one's livelihood, and when one has that, then one begins to live. So one's work had better be as dull and meaningless as possible, so long as one gets one's livelihood from it. If one has a special talent, one must not commit against it the sin of making it one's means of livelihood. No, one's talent must be coddled, that is a thing one possesses for its own sake, one takes greater joy in it than a mother takes in her child, one cultivates and develops it in the twelve hours of the day, sleeps seven hours, is hardly human for five hours, and so life becomes after all pretty tolerable, yea, even rather beautiful; for the five hours' work is not so dreadful after all, for since one's thoughts are never on the work, one gathers strength for the avocation which is one's delight."

Our hero is again no nearer his goal than before. For in the first place he has no special talent with which to fill up the twelve hours at home, in the second place he has already got a more beautiful notion of what it is to work and he is not willing to give that up. So he will likely resolve to seek help again from the ethicist. The ethicist speaks briefly: "It is every man's duty to have a calling." More he cannot say, for the ethical as such is always abstract, and there is no such thing as an abstract calling for all men; he presupposes, on the contrary, that every man has a particular calling. What calling our hero should choose the ethicist cannot inform him, for this requires a detailed knowledge of the aesthetical components of his entire personality, and even if the ethicist had this knowledge, he would still refrain from choosing for him, since by doing so he would be renouncing his own view of life. What the ethicist can teach him is that there is a calling for every man, and when our hero has found his the ethicist can admonish him to choose it ethically. For what the aestheticist had to say about the aristocratic talents is a confused and sceptical discourse about the very thing which the ethicist clearly explains. The life views of the aestheticists always imply differences: some men have talents, others have not, and yet what distinguishes them is a more or a less, a quantitative determinant. Hence it is arbitrary on their part to draw the line at a particular point, and yet the nerve of their life view consists precisely in this arbitrary distinction. Their life view therefore posits a discord in existence which they find themselves unable to resolve, and so they frivolously and heartlessly arm themselves against it. The ethicist, on the other hand, reconciles man with life, for he says, "Every man has a calling." He does not do away with the differences, but he says, "In all the differences there is the common factor left that each is a calling. The most eminent talent is a calling, and the individual who is in possession of it cannot lose sight of reality, he does not stand outside of the universal-human, for his talent is a calling. The most insignificant individual has a calling, he shall not be cast out, not be reduced to living on a par with the beasts, he does not stand outside of the universal-human, he has a calling."

The ethical thesis that every man has a calling is the expression for the fact that there is a rational order of things in which every man, if he will, fills his place in such a way that he expresses at once the universal-human and the individual. With this way of regarding it has existence become less beautiful? One has no occasion to rejoice in an aristocracy which is founded upon an accident and accidentally founded upon it; no, one has a realm of gods.[50]

When the talent is not construed as a call (and when it is so construed every man has a call), then the talent is absolutely egoistic. Everyone, therefore, who founds his life upon a talent leads, so far as he can, a robber existence. He has no higher expression for the talent than that it is a talent. So this talent wants to come to the fore in its unique difference. Every talent has, therefore, a tendency to make itself the central factor, every condition must be present to promote it, for only in this wild bursting forth consists the real aesthetic enjoyment of the talent. If there is a simultaneous talent with another direction, the two collide in mortal conflict, for they have no concentric direction, no higher expression in common.

So our hero has got what he sought, a work whereby he might live; he has got at the same time a more significant expression for its relation to his personality: it is his calling, and so the accomplishment of it is associated with a satisfaction of his whole personality; he has got also a more significant expression for the relation of his work to other men, for since his work is his calling he is thereby put essentially on an equal footing with all other men, he is then doing by his work the same thing that every other man does, he is performing his calling. He claims recognition of this, more he does not claim, for this is the absolute. "If my calling is an insignificant one," says he, "I can be faithful to my calling and am essentially just as great as the greatest, without being for an instant so foolish as to forget the differences; that would do me no good, for were I to forget them there would be an abstract calling for all, but an abstract calling is no calling, and I would have lost again just as much as the greatest stands to lose. If my calling is insignificant, I can be unfaithful to my calling, and if I am, I commit just as great a sin as does the greatest. I shall not be so foolish as to want to forget the differences or to think that my unfaithfulness might have consequences just as dreadful for the whole as has the unfaithfulness of the greatest; that does me no good, I myself am the one who would lose most by it."

The ethical consideration that everyone has a calling possesses a double advantage over the aesthetic theory of talent. In the first place, it explains [*forklarer*] talent not as something accidental in existence but as the universal; in the second place, it exhibits the universal in its true beauty. For talent is beautiful only when it is transfigured [*forklaret*] as a call, and existence is beautiful only when everyone has a call. Such being the case, I beg you not to disdain a simple empirical observation which so far as concerns the principal theme of this discourse you will have the kindness to regard as a superfluity. When a man has a calling he generally has a norm outside himself which, without making him a slave, does nevertheless prescribe in a measure what he must do, apportions for him the time, often gives him occasion to begin. If for once he does not make a success of his business, he hopes to do it better next time, and this next time is not too far distant. On the other hand, the man who has no calling must generally work very much more *uno tenore*, in case he proposes a task for himself. There is no place for him to break off except as he does it of his own accord. If he fails in it, then the failure is complete, and he has great difficulty in beginning again since he lacks an occasion which prompts him to do so. So he is easily tempted to become a pedant, if he would not become an idler. It is such a common thing to accuse of pedantry people who have definite official duties. Generally such a man cannot become a pedant. He, on the other hand, who has no official duties is tempted to become a pedant in order to put up at least a little resistance to the too great freedom by reason of which he may easily be tempted to go astray. One therefore may very properly be inclined to forgive him for his pedantry, since it is a sign of something good in him. But on the other hand, it may be regarded as his punishment for wanting to emancipate himself from the universal.

Our hero found a more significant expression for the relation of his work to other men in the fact that it was a calling. Thus he has recognition, he has obtained his credentials. But now when he is discharging the duties of his calling he finds in that his personal satisfaction, but at the same time he requires an expression for the relation of this activity to other men, he requires to be *accomplishing* something. Here, perhaps, he will again go astray. The aestheticist will explain to him that this satisfaction of the talent is the highest thing, and that the question whether he is accomplishing anything or not is entirely secondary. He will, perhaps, adopt a practical bigotry which believes in its inept zeal that it is accomplishing everything, or he will assume an aesthetic air of importance which thinks that to accomplish anything in the world is something which falls to the lot of a few elect individuals, that there are certain eminent talents which accomplish something, the men left over are *numerus,* a superfluity in existence representing the prodigality of the Creator. But none of these explanations is of any use to our hero, for he is like most people.

Let us again have recourse to the ethicist. He says, "What every man accomplishes and can accomplish is to do *his* job in life. For in case it were true that certain men accomplish something and others do not, and the reason for this was an accidental difference, then scepticism has again obtained the upper hand." We must therefore say that looking at it essentially every man "accomplishes as much as another." I am by no means preaching indolence, but on the other hand one must be cautious in using the expression "accomplish." This has always been a theme for your derision, and, as you once expressed it, you have "studied profoundly integral and differential and infinitesimal calculus in order to reckon how much is accomplished on the whole by a clerk in the Admiralty who in the entire bureau is regarded as a smart worker." Use your talent for mockery only against persons who would make themselves important, but do not abuse it to confuse men's minds.

The expression "to accomplish" indicates a relation between my action and another man outside of me. Now it is easy to perceive that this relation is not subject to my control, and that in view of this one can say with as much justification of the most eminent talent that it accomplished nothing as this can be said of the most insignificant man. There is no distrust of life implied in this, on the contrary, it implies a recognition of my own unimportance and a respect for the importance of every other man. The man who possesses the most eminent talent is able to do his job, and the most insignificant man can do that too. Neither of them can do more. Whether they might accomplish something does not lie in their power, but it does lie in their power to hinder themselves from doing it. I therefore give up all the self-importance which often looks so big, I do my job, and I do not waste my time on calculating whether I am accomplishing anything. So what I accomplish follows upon my job as a piece of good luck in which I may well take delight but which I dare not impute absolutely to myself. A beech grows up, forms its crown of leaves, and men delight to sit in its shade. If it were to become impatient, if it were to say, "Here in this place where I stand there hardly ever comes a living being. What use is it for me to grow, to shoot out my branches, what do I accomplish by it?" it would with that only delay its growth, and perhaps there came a wayfarer who said, "If this tree instead of being stunted had been a leafy tree, I now might have taken rest in its shade." Imagine that the tree had been able to hear!

So every man can accomplish something, he can accomplish his job. The job may be of very various kinds, but we are always to hold fast to this, that every man has his job, and that all men are reconciled by the expression that each of them does his job. The relation of my job to the other man, or what I shall accomplish (taking this word in its usual sense), is not under my control. Even the man whose job in life is to develop himself, even he accomplishes, if we look at it essentially, just as much as every

other man. It might therefore seem as if that aestheticist
was right when he expressed the opinion that one should
not consider what one was accomplishing but merely enjoy the satisfaction of unfolding one's talent. However, his
mistake was that he stopped with the selfish definition of
talent. He accounted himself one of the elect and was unwilling to accomplish in his life the universal, to regard his
talent as his job. The person, however, of whom one could
say that his job in life consists simply and solely in developing himself belongs of course to the class of persons who
humanly speaking are the least talented. Take a young girl
for instance. She belongs to the class of people of whom
one is not tempted to say that they are able to accomplish
something. In addition, suppose that she has been unhappy
in love, that she has been deprived of the last prospect of
accomplishing anything; if nevertheless she does her job, if
she develops herself, she accomplishes, if we look at it essentially, just as much as the greatest.

Accomplishing, then, is identical with doing one's job.
Think of a man who is profoundly and sincerely moved;
to him it never occurs to question whether he will accomplish something or not; it is only that an idea is intent upon
realizing itself in him with all its might. Let him be an
orator, a priest, or whatever you will. He does not speak
to the multitude in order to accomplish something, but the
melody within him must ring out, only then does he feel
happy. Do you believe that he accomplished less than one
who became puffed up with the idea of what he will accomplish, who keeps himself going with the thought of
what he himself will accomplish? Think of an author; to
him it never occurs to question whether he will obtain a
reader or whether he will accomplish anything by his book;
he is only intent upon apprehending the truth. Do you believe that such a writer accomplishes less than one whose
pen is under the supervision and direction of the thought
that he will accomplish something?

Strangely enough, though neither you nor I nor our hero
himself nor that shrewd aestheticist has noticed it, it is
nevertheless true, our hero possesses an extraordinary talent. Thus it is that the spiritual quality in a man may lie

for a long time concealed till its quiet growth has reached a certain point and then it proclaims itself with all its power. The aestheticist will likely say, "Well, now it's too late, now he's botched once for all, poor man!" The ethicist, on the contrary, will say, "It was lucky for him, for now that he has come to realize the truth his talent will not become a snare unto his feet, he will perceive that a man needs neither financial independence nor five hours of slave-labor in order to conserve his talent, but that his talent is precisely his calling."

So our hero works in order to live; this work is at the same time his pleasure; he fulfills the duties of his calling, he accomplishes his job—to say it all in one word, and with a word which inspires you with dread . . . he has a living. Do not be impatient, let the poet say it, and it sounds prettier:[51]

> Instead of childhood's golden promise,
> He makes a living scant but honest.

And then what next? You will smile, you think I have something up my sleeve. You already shudder at my prosaic intention, for you say, "Now it comes to nothing less than getting him married; yes, do be so kind, you had better have his banns published, I shall have no objection to make against your and his godly resolution. It is incredible how rationally consistent everything is in existence: a living and a wife. Indeed, even that poet with his chime of bells struck a phrase which indicates not obscurely that with the living comes the wife. Against one thing only I must protest, that you call your client a hero. I have been tractable and compliant, I had no wish to condemn the man, I always had hopes of him, but really you must now excuse me if I go around by another street and no longer am inclined to hear a word about him. An office-seeker and a wife-seeker—I have all respect for him, but as for being a hero, surely he himself would not lay claim to that." You think then that in order to be called a hero one must do something extraordinary. In that case your prospects are really brilliant. Suppose now that it required much courage to do the extraordinary, and of course he who shows such courage is a hero. In calling a man a hero one must reflect not so much upon what he does as upon how he does it. One man may conquer kingdoms and lands without being a hero, another may show himself a hero by ruling his own spirit. One man may show courage by doing the extraordinary, another by doing the ordinary. The question in every case is, how he does it. You will not deny that in the foregoing recital our hero showed a disposition to do the extraordinary, indeed, I cannot yet entirely vouch for him that he will not try it. Presumably it was upon this you based your hope that he would become a real hero. Upon this I based my fear that he would become . . . a fool. So I have showed the same forbearance towards him that you have, from the beginning I had hopes of him, I have called him "hero," in spite of the fact that several times he seemed on the point of wanting to make himself unworthy of this title. Therefore if I get him married, I tranquilly get him off my hands and gladly deliver him into the hands of his wife. By reason of the refractory disposition he previously displayed he has qualified himself to be put under a more special supervision. This work his wife will undertake, and so all will go well, for whenever he is tempted to want to be an extraordinary man his wife will at once orient him again, and thus in all quietness he will earn the name of hero, and his life will not be without exploits. Then I have nothing more to do with him, unless he might feel himself drawn to me in the same way that I shall feel myself drawn to him if he continues his heroic course. He will then see in me a friend, and our relationship will not be without significance. He will know how to put up with the fact that at that juncture you withdrew from him, and all the more because he might easily become a little suspicious if it should please you to take an interest in him. With a view to this situation I wish him good fortune, and to every married man I wish the same good fortune.

However, we have not yet got so far along as that, not by a long shot. So for a long time you can still hope—as long, that is to say, as I need to fear. For our hero is like most people and consequently has a certain propensity for the extraordinary; he is also a little ungrateful, and hence

at this juncture he wants to try again his luck with the
aestheticists before turning for help to the ethicist. He
knows also how to gloss over his ingratitude, for he says,
"The ethicist really did help me out of my confusion; the
view of my activity which I owe to him still satisfies me
entirely, the seriousness of it uplifts me. However, so far as
my love is concerned, I surely might wish in this respect
to enjoy my freedom, to follow the promptings of my heart.
Love has no liking for this seriousness, it demands the lightness and grace of aesthetics."

You see, I still may have trouble enough with him. It
seems almost as though he had not entirely understood the
foregoing experiences. He still continues to believe that the
ethical lies outside the aesthetical, and this in spite of the
fact that he himself has to admit that by the ethical view
of it life acquired beauty. Well, we shall see. Just puff a
little, and then I can get out of this situation all the mis-
understandings I want.

Although you have never replied to my previous letter
either verbally or in writing, you presumably remember its
content, and will remember particularly how I there sought
to show that, by means of the ethical, marriage is the aesthetic expression of love. So presumably you will forgive
me for my self-confidence in believing that the thought I
there developed, seeing that I made it fairly comprehensible
to you, I shall easily be able, if need be, to explain to our
hero. He had recourse to the aestheticists and left them no
wiser as to what he should do, but rather as to what he
should not do. For a while he was witness to the craftiness
of a seducer, he listened to his indecent talk but has learned
to despise his art, has learned to see through him, to see
that he is a liar, a liar when he feigns love, when he pretends to feelings in which perhaps there once was truth
when by them he belonged to another, to see that he deceives doubly, both her whom he would make believe that
he cherishes such feelings, and her to whom they rightfully
belong, that he is a liar when he makes himself believe that
there is something beautiful in his lust. He has learned to
despise the clever mockery which would make love a childish prank at which one could only smile. He has seen your

favorite play, *The First Love,* by Scribe. He does not claim
to have culture enough to appraise the play aesthetically,
but he finds it unjust on the part of the poet to let Charles
sink so low in the course of eight years. He is ready to admit that such things may happen in real life, but he does
not think that this is what one should learn from a poet. He
finds that there is a contradiction in the play for the fact
that it represents Emmeline as at once a high-flown fool
and a really lovable girl—as Rinville at the first glance is at
once convinced that she is, in spite of his prejudice against
her. He finds that in view of this it is again an injustice to
let Charles in the course of eight years become a depraved
man. It seems to him that the play ought not to be a comedy but a tragedy. He finds that it is unjust of the poet to
let Emmeline yield so frivolously to her misapprehension,
forgive Rinville frivolously for deceiving her, forget Charles
frivolously and thus to mock frivolously her own feelings,
build frivolously her whole future upon her own frivolity,
upon Rinville's frivolity, and upon the frivolity of Charles.
He finds that the original Emmeline is indeed sentimental
and high-flown, but the reformed Emmeline, the shrewd
type, is a being far inferior in his eyes to the former notwithstanding all her imperfections.

He finds it inexcusable on the part of the poet to represent
love as a prank it takes a man eight years to live into and
half an hour to get out of, head over heels, without the
slightest impression being left by this change. He was glad
to observe that it was not exactly the men he most respects
who laugh especially at such plays. For an instant the
mockery made his blood run cold, but again he is sensible
of the flood of feelings which arises in his breast, he is convinced that this pulsation is the life-principle of the soul, and
that he who would suppress it is dead and doesn't need
to have himself buried. For a little while he let himself be
lulled by the mistrust of life which would teach him that
everything is transitory, that time changes everything, that
there is nothing one can venture to build upon and so conceive a plan for one's whole life. His indolence and cowardice found this talk thoroughly acceptable, it was a
comfortable costume to assume, and in men's eyes not un-

becoming. However, he has examined this talk sharply, he has seen the hypocrite, the pleasure-lover who came in humble dress, the wolf in sheep's clothing, and he has learned to despise this talk. He has perceived that it is an insult and consequently is unfair to want to love a person for the obscure and not for the conscious elements in her nature, to want to love in such a way that one could think of the possibility that this love might cease and that one might then dare to say, "I can't help it. Feeling is not under a man's control." He has perceived that it is an insult and consequently is unfair to want to love with one side of the soul but not with the whole soul, to treat one's love as fractional quantity and yet take the whole love of another, to want to be to a certain degree a riddle and a secret. He has perceived that it would be unfair for him to have a hundred arms so that he might embrace many, he has only one bosom and wishes only for one whom he may embrace. He has perceived that it is an insult to want to attach oneself to another person in the way one attaches oneself to a finite and casual thing, conditionally, so that if later difficulties were to arise one could change one's attachment again. He does not believe that for a man who loves it is possible to change, unless it be for the better. And were this to come to pass, he believes in the power of the relationship to make it all right again. He recognizes that what love requires is like the Temple tribute, a holy tax which is paid in its own peculiar coin, and that one does not accept all the riches of the world as quittance for the most insignificant claim if the impress of the coinage is counterfeit.

Our hero, you see, is on the right path, he has lost faith in the hardened common sense of the aestheticists and in their obscure feelings which are supposed to be too delicate to be expressed as duty. He has accepted the ethicist's declaration that it is the duty of every man to marry; he has understood this correctly, to the effect that he does not sin who fails to marry, except in so far as he himself is to blame for it, since in that case he offends against the universal-human which is set before him too as a task which must be realized, but that he who marries realizes the universal. Further than this the ethicist cannot bring him, for as we have said the ethical is always the abstract; it can only tell him what the universal is. So in this instance it cannot possibly tell him whom he ought to marry. For that would require a precise acquaintance with all his aesthetic qualifications; but this the ethicist does not possess, and even if he did possess it, he would nevertheless beware of demolishing his own theories by undertaking to make the choice for him. So when he himself has chosen, the ethical will consecrate the choice and ennoble his love; and to a certain degree it will also be helpful in choosing, since it will save him from a superstitious faith in the accidental, for a merely aesthetic choice is really an indefinite choice; and unconsciously the ethical helps every man, but since this assistance is unconscious it has the semblance of being a disparagement of life, reflecting its wretchedness, instead of which it is an enhancement of life, reflecting its divine character.

"A man with such excellent principles," you say, "one surely may trust to walk alone and may venture to expect great things of him." I am of the same opinion and hope that his principles are so firm that they will not be shaken by your derision. However, there is still a sharp corner we have to turn before we are safe in port. For our hero has heard a man for whose judgment he has great respect express the opinion that in tying oneself by a marriage to a person for one's whole life one must be cautious in making the choice; it must be an extraordinary girl who, precisely by reason of her extraordinary qualities, would provide security for his whole future. Might you not now feel inclined to hope a little while longer for our hero? At all events I fear for him.

Let us take up this question in a thorough way. You, in fact, believe that in the solitary stillness of the forest there dwells a nymph, a being, a maiden. Very well then, this nymph, being, maiden, leaves her solitude, makes her appearance in Copenhagen, or like Kaspar Hauser[52] in Nürnberg—the place makes no difference—suffice it to say, she makes her appearance. Believe me, there will be a wooing! I leave it to you to develop this theme in detail. You can write a romance entitled, "The Nymph, the Being, the Maiden in the Solitude of the Forest," *ad modum* the celebrated romance found in all lending libraries, "The Urn in the Solitary Dale."[53] She has made her appearance, and our hero has become the lucky man, she has bestowed her love upon him. Might we agree to this? I have no objection —I, in fact, am married. You, on the other hand, would perhaps feel offended that such a common everyday person was preferred before you. But since you are interested in my client, and since this is the only way left for him to become a hero in your eyes, do give your consent. Let us now see if his love and his marriage became beautiful. The gist of his love and of his marriage consisted in the fact that she was the one only girl of her kind in the whole world. So the point lay in her difference. For such good fortune no equal could be found in the whole world, and precisely in this his good fortune consisted. It is possible he may be unwilling to marry her. For would it not be a degradation of such a love to give expression to it in so common and vulgar a form as marriage? Would it not be presumptuous to require that two such lovers should enter the great company of wedded people, so that in a certain sense there would be nothing more to say about them than about every wedded couple, that they were married? This you will perhaps find quite right, and the only objection you would have to make would be that it is wrong for such a clown as my hero to run off with such a maiden. If on the other hand, he had been an extraordinary man, like you for example, or just as extraordinary a man as she was a girl, then it would be all right, and their love relationship the most perfect that could be imagined.

Our hero has got himself into a critical position. About the girl there is only one opinion, she is an extraordinary girl. I myself, married man that I am, say with Donna Clara, "In this case rumor has not said too much, she is a marvelous maiden, the beautiful Preciosa."[54] It is so tempting to lose sight of the ordinary and to float in the airy medium of the fairy tale. And yet he has himself perceived the beauty in marriage. What is it that marriage does? Does it deprive him of anything, does it take away from

her any beauty, does it abolish one single difference? By no
means. But it shows to him all these things as accidents so
long as marriage is external to him, and only when he gives
to the difference the universal expression is he in secure
possession of it. The ethical teaches him that this relationship is the absolute. For the relationship is the ordinary
and universal. It deprives him of the vain joy of being the
extraordinary in order to give him the true joy of being the
universal. It brings him into harmony with existence as a
whole, teaching him to rejoice in this; for as the exception,
as the extraordinary, he is in conflict, and since what constitutes the extraordinary is in this instance his good fortune,
he must be conscious of his existence as a vexation to the
ordinary or universal, provided there was truth in his good
fortune, and after all, it might be in truth a misfortune to
be fortunate in such a way that one's good fortune, viewed
essentially, was different from that of others. In this way he
wins the accidental beauty and loses the true beauty. This
he will perceive, and he will again return to the maxim of
the ethicist that it is the duty of every man to marry, and
he will see that he has not only truth but beauty too on
his side. Suppose, then, he gets that marvelous maiden. He
will not be enamored of the differences. He will rejoice
right heartily in her beauty, in her charm, in the wealth of
intelligence and the warmth of feeling she possesses, he will
count himself fortunate, but essentially he will say, "I am
not different from any other married man, for the relationship is the absolute." Suppose he gets a less gifted girl. He
will be joyful in his good fortune, for he will say, "Even
though she stands far beneath others, essentially she makes
me just as happy, for the relationship is the absolute." He
will not fail to appreciate the importance of the differences,
for just as he perceived that there was no abstract calling
but that every man has his, so he will perceive that there
is no abstract marriage. Ethics tells him merely that he
shall marry; it does not tell him with whom. Ethics explains
[*forklarer*] to him the universal in the difference, and he
transfigures [*forklarer*] the difference into the universal.

So the ethical view of marriage has several advantages
over every aesthetic interpretation of love. It elucidates the

universal, not the accidental. It does not show how a couple of very singular people with extraordinary traits might become happy, but how every married couple may become so. It regards the relationship as the absolute, and so does not apprehend the differences as guarantees but comprehends them as tasks. It regards the relationship as the absolute and hence beholds love with a view to its beauty, that is, its freedom; it understands historical beauty.

So our hero lives by his work, his work is at the same time his calling, hence he works with pleasure. The fact that it is his calling brings him into association with other men, and in performing his job he accomplishes what he could wish to accomplish in the world. He is married, contented with his home, and time passes swiftly for him, he cannot comprehend how time might be a burden to a man or be an enemy of his happiness; on the contrary, time appears to him a true blessing. He admits that in this respect he owes a great deal to his wife. It is true (I forgot to mention it) there was a misunderstanding about the nymph from the forest, he did not become the fortunate man, he had to content himself with a girl who was like most girls, in the same sense that he as a man is like most people. However, he is very joyous for all that; indeed, he once confided to me that he thought it pretty lucky he didn't get the marvelous maiden, the task would perhaps have been too great for him; when, before one begins, everything is so perfect, it is so easy to do harm. Now, on the contrary, he is full of courage and confidence and hope, he is perfectly enthusiastic, he says fervently, "The relationship after all is the absolute." More firmly than of anything else he is convinced that the relationship will have power to develop this ordinary girl into everything great and beautiful; his wife in all humility is of the same opinion. Yea, my young friend, the way of the world is strange; I did not in the least believe that there existed in the world a marvelous maiden such as you talk about, and now I am ashamed almost of my incredulity, for this ordinary girl with her great faith is a marvelous maiden, and her faith is more precious than gold or green forests. In one respect I remain in my old unbelief that such a marvelous maiden is to be found in the solitude of the forest.

My hero (or would you deny him the right to this appellation? A courage which dares to believe in transforming an ordinary girl into a marvelous maiden, does this not seem to you the true heroic courage?)—my hero thanks his wife particularly for the fact that time has acquired for him such a beautiful significance, and this he ascribes in a certain degree to marriage—and in that he and I, we two married men, are in perfect agreement. In case he had got that nymph from the forest and had not married, he then would have been apprehensive that their love would flare up in particular moments of singular beauty, which would leave behind them vapid intervals. They would then perhaps have wished to see one another only when the sight might be very significant; if several times they were disappointed in this expectation, he is then apprehensive that the whole relationship had gradually resolved itself into nothing. On the other hand, the humble marriage which made it a duty to see one another daily, for richer for poorer, had spread over the whole relationship an equality and evenness which made it so delicious to him. The prosaic marriage had in its lowly incognito concealed a poet which not only glorified life on particular occasions but was always at hand and with his music thrilled even the poorer hours.

In this respect I share completely my hero's opinion of marriage, and here it clearly shows its superiority, not only over the single life but over every merely erotic union. The latter consideration my new friend has this instant set forth, only the former, therefore, I will stress with a few words. One may be as intelligent as you please, one may be industrious, one may be enthusiastic for an idea, there come moments, nevertheless, when time becomes a bit long. You so often deride the other sex. I have often admonished you to desist. Regard, if you will, a young girl as an incomplete being; I should like to say to you, however, "My good wise man, go to the ant and become wise, learn from a girl how to make time pass, for in this she has an innate virtuosity." Perhaps she has no conception such as a man has of severe and persistent labor, but she is never idle, is always occupied, time is never long for her. I can speak of this from experience. It befalls me at times (more rarely now because I try to resist it, believing as I do that it is a husband's duty to be pretty much of an even age with his wife)—at times it befalls me that I sit and subside into myself. I have attended to my work, I have no desire for any diversion, something melancholy in my temperament acquires ascendency over me; I become very many years older than I really am, I become almost a stranger to my domestic life, I can see that it is beautiful, but I look at it with unaccustomed eyes, it seems to me as if I were an old man, my wife a younger sister happily married, in whose house I now sit. At such hours time naturally becomes long for me. Now if my wife were a man, it would perhaps be the same with her, and we would perhaps both of us come to a standstill; but she is a woman and stands on good terms with time. Is it a perfection on the part of a woman, this secret rapport with time? Is it an imperfection? Is it because she is a more earthly being than man? Or because she has more eternity within her? It is for you to make answer. You are a philosophic mind.

When I am sitting thus lost and abandoned and then look at my wife walking about the room lightly and beautifully, always occupied, always with something to attend to, my eye involuntarily follows her movements, I participate in all that she undertakes, and it ends with my being again reconciled with time, finding that again time acquires significance for me, that the instant again moves swiftly. What is it she has in hand? Well, with all the will in the world I cannot say, not if it were to cost me my life, it remains a riddle to me. What it is to work far into the night, to be so tired that I am almost unable to arise from my chair, what it is to think, what it is to be so completely empty of thoughts that it is not possible to get the least thing through my head, that I know; what it is to be lazy I know also, but this way of being occupied as my wife is remains a riddle to me. She is never tired and yet never inactive, it is as though her occupation were a game, a dance, as though to play were her occupation. What is it she fills up the time with? For you can well understand that it naturally is not with acquired dexterities, not with these tomfooleries in which bachelors generally excel. And speaking of bachelors, I see with my mind's eye that your youth is coming to an end; you ought to be prepared to fill in the idle moments, you should learn to handle the flute or try to invent an ingenious instrument for scraping your pipe. However, I don't like to think of such things, I soon tire of thinking of them, I return to my wife, I never grow tired of looking at her. What she has in hand I cannot explain, but she does it all with a charm, with a grace, with an indescribable ease, straight away, without ceremony, as a bird sings its aria, and I believe also that it is with a bird's labor her occupation can best be compared, and yet her arts seem to me true witchery. In this respect she is my absolute refuge. So when I sit in my study, when I become tired, when time becomes long for me, I steal into the parlor, I sit down in a corner, I say not a word for fear of disturbing her in her job, for though it looks like a game it is accomplished with a dignity, a decorum which inspires respect, and she is very far from being, as you say of Mrs. Hansen, a busybody who buzzes about and by her buzzing spreads abroad in the parlor the matrimonial music.

Yes, my good wise man, it is incredible what innate virtuosity a woman possesses; she explains in the most interesting and beautiful way the problem which has cost many a philosopher his reason, the problem of time. A problem upon which in vain one seeks enlightenment from many philosophers with all their prolixity, she explains without ado at any time of the day. As she explains this problem, so she explains many others in a way which arouses the profoundest admiration. Although I am not a husband of many years' standing I believe I could write a whole book about this. That I will not do, but I will recount to you a story which to me has been very suggestive. Somewhere in Holland there lived a learned man, he was an orientalist and was married. One day he did not come to the midday meal, although he was called. His wife waits longingly, looking at the food, and the longer this lasts the less she can explain his failure to appear. Finally she resolves to go

over to his room and exhort him to come. There he sits alone
in his work-room, there is nobody with him. He is absorbed
in his oriental studies. I can picture it to myself. She has
bent over him, laid her arm about his shoulders, peered
down at the book, thereupon looked at him and said, "Dear
friend, why do you not come over to eat?" The learned man
perhaps has hardly had time to take account of what was
said, but looking at his wife he presumably replied, "Well,
my girl, there can be no question of dinner, here is a vocalization I have never seen before, I have often seen the
passage quoted, but never like this, and yet my edition is
an excellent Dutch edition. Look at this dot here! It is
enough to drive one mad." I can imagine that his wife
looked at him, half-smiling, half-deprecating that such a
little dot should disturb the domestic order, and the report
recounts that she replied, "Is that anything to take so much
to heart? It is not worth wasting one's breath on it." No
sooner said than done. She blows, and behold the vocalization disappears, for this remarkable dot was a grain of snuff.
Joyfully the scholar hastens to the dinner table, joyful at
the fact that the vocalization had disappeared, still more
joyful in his wife.

Do I need to draw out the moral from this story? If that
scholar had not been married, he perhaps would have gone
crazy, perhaps he would have taken several orientalists with
him, for I doubt not that he would have raised a terrible
alarm in the literary organs. You see why I say that one
ought to live on good terms with the other sex, for (be it
said between us) a young girl explains everything and
doesn't give a fig for the whole consistory, and if a man is
on good terms with her he delights in her information, but
if not, she makes sport of him. But this story teaches also
in what way one is to live on good terms with her. If that
scholar had not been married, if he had been an aestheticist
who had in his power all the requisites, perhaps then he
would have become the lucky man to whom that marvelous
maiden wished to belong. He would not have married, their
sentiments were too superior for that. He would have built
her a palace and would have spared no refinement to make
her life rich in enjoyment, he would have visited her in her

castle, for so she wished it to be; with erotic coquetry he
would have made his way to her on foot while his valets
followed him in a carriage, bringing rich and costly gifts.
So, then, in the course of his oriental studies he stumbled
upon that remarkable vocalization. He would have stared
at it without being able to explain it. The moment, however,
was come when he should make his visit to the ladylove.
He would have cast this care aside, for how could he becomingly make a visit to a ladylove with thoughts of anything else but of her charms and of his own love? He would
have assumed an air of the utmost amiability, he would
have been more fascinating than ever, and would have
pleased her beyond all measure because in his voice there
was a distant resonance of many passions, because out of
despondency he had to contend for cheerfulness. But when
at dawn he left her, when he had thrown her the last kiss
and then sat in his carriage, his brow was darkened. He
arrived home, the shutters were closed in his study, the
lamps lit, he would not be undressed but sat and stared at
the dot he could not explain. He had indeed a girl whom
he loved, yea, perhaps adored, but he visited her only when
his soul was rich and strong, but he had no helpmeet who
came in and called him at midday, no wife who could blow
the dot away.

In general woman has an innate talent, a primitive gift
and an absolute virtuosity for explaining finiteness. When
man was created he stood there as the master and lord of
all nature; nature's pomp and splendor, the entire wealth of
finiteness awaited only his beck and call, but he did not
comprehend what he was to do with it all. He looked at
it, but it was as though at the glance of the spirit everything vanished, he felt as though if he were to move he
would with one step be beyond it all. Thus he stood, an
imposing figure, thoughtfully absorbed in himself, and yet
comic, for one must indeed smile at this rich man who did
not know how to use his wealth—but also tragic, for he
could not use it. Then was woman created. She was in no
embarrassment, she knew at once how one had to handle
this affair; without fuss, without preparation, she was ready
at once to begin. This was the first comfort bestowed upon

man. She drew near to him, humble as a child, joyful as a child, pensive as a child. She wanted only to be a comfort to him, to make up for his lack (a lack which she did not comprehend, having no suspicion that she was supplying it), to abbreviate for him the intervals. And, lo, her humble comfort became life's richest joy, her innocent pastimes life's most beautiful adornment, her childish play life's deepest meaning.

A woman comprehends finiteness, she understands it from the bottom up, therefore she is beauteous (essentially regarded, every woman is beauteous), therefore she is charming (and that no man is), therefore she is happy (happy as no man is or should be), therefore she is in harmony with existence (as no man is or should be). Therefore one may say that her life is happier than that of man; for finiteness can perhaps make a human being happy, infinitude as such can never do so. She is more perfect than man, for surely one who can explain something is more perfect than one who is in pursuit of an explanation. Woman explains finiteness, man is in chase of infinitude. So it should be, and each has one's own pain; for woman bears children with pain, but man conceives ideas with pain, and woman does not have to know the anguish of doubt or the torment of despair, she is not obliged to stand outside the idea, but she has it at secondhand. But because woman thus explains finiteness she is man's deepest life, but a life which should always be concealed and hidden as the root of life always is. For this reason I hate all talk about the emancipation of woman. God forbid that ever it may come to pass. I cannot tell you with what pain this thought is able to pierce my heart, nor what passionate exasperation, what hate I feel toward everyone who gives vent to such talk. It is my comfort that those who proclaim such wisdom are not as wise as serpents but are for the most part blockheads whose nonsense can do no harm. Yea, in case the serpent were able to make her believe this, able to tempt her with the apparently delectable fruit, in case this contagion were to spread, in case it were to penetrate also to her whom I love, my wife, my joy, my refuge, my life's very root, then indeed would my courage be broken, then the passion of freedom in my soul would be quenched, then I know well what I would do, I would sit down in the marketplace and weep, weep like that artist whose work had been destroyed and who did not even remember what he himself had painted.

But this will not come to pass; it must not and cannot. Let evil spirits attempt it, or stupid men who have no faintest notion of what it is to be a man, either of the greatness or the lowliness of it, no notion of the perfection of woman in her imperfection. Might there be one single woman simple and vain and pitiable enough to believe that in man's category she might be more perfect than man, and not to perceive that her loss would be irreparable? No base seducer could think out a more dangerous doctrine for woman, for once he has made her believe this she is entirely in his power, at the mercy of his will, she can be nothing for man except a prey to his whims, whereas as woman she can be everything for him. But the poor wretches know not what they do, they are not able to be men, and instead of learning to be that they would ruin woman and would be united with her on terms of remaining what they were, half-men, woman being promoted to the same paltry condition. I remember reading once a rather clever satire upon the emancipation of woman. The author dwelt especially upon the form of dress, which in this case he thought ought to be alike for men and women. Imagine such an abomination! It seemed to me that the author had not conceived his task profoundly enough, that the contrasts he dwelt upon were not essentially relevant to the idea. For an instant I will venture to think the unseemliness of this, knowing that in doing so the seemliness and beauty will be manifest in all their truth. What is more beautiful than a woman's plentiful hair, than her abundant tresses? And yet the Scripture says[55] that this is a token of her imperfection and adduces several reasons for this. And is it not so? Look at her when she bows her head toward the earth, when the luxuriant braids almost touch the ground, and it looks as though they were tendrils of a flowering plant by which she was firmly attached to the earth. Does she not stand there as a more imperfect being than man who looks up

to heaven[56] and barely touches the earth? And yet this
hair is her beauty, yea, it is her power too, for it is indeed
by this, as the poet says, she catches man, by this she takes
man prisoner and binds him to the earth. I should like to
say to such blockheads as preach emancipation, "Behold,
there she stands in all her imperfection, a lowlier being
than man; if you have the courage, clip the rich tresses,
sheer asunder these heavy chains—and let her run like a
crazy woman, like a criminal, a horror to men."

Let man give up the claim to be the lord and master of
nature, let him yield this place to woman, she is its mistress, it understands her, and she understands it, every hint
of hers it follows. For this reason she is everything to man,
for she bestows upon him finiteness, without her he is an
unstable spirit, an unhappy creature who cannot find rest,
has no abiding place. I have often had joy in viewing
woman in this light; to me she is a symbol of the congregation, and the spirit is in great embarrassment when it has
not a congregation to dwell in, and when it dwells in the
congregation it is the spirit of the congregation. Hence it
is, as I have already remarked, that the Scripture does not
say that a maiden shall leave father and mother and shall
cleave unto her husband (as might be expected, since the
woman is in fact the weaker who seeks refuge in man);
no, it says, "A man shall leave his father and mother and
shall cleave unto his wife," for in so far as she gives him
finiteness she is stronger than he. Therefore nothing can
provide so beautiful an image of the congregation as does
woman. If people would view the matter thus, I really believe that many prospects for the beautification of divine
worship would be opened up. What bad taste it is in our
churches that the congregation, when it does not represent
itself, is represented by the parish clerk or the bell ringer!
It ought always to be represented by a woman.

In our church services the congregation has always failed
to make upon me a truly salutary impression. And yet there
was one year of my life when I came pretty close to my
idealized conception. It was in one of our churches here in
the city. The church itself attracted me greatly, the clergy-
man whom I heard every Sunday was a right reverend

personality, a unique figure, who knew how to bring out old and new from the experiences of an eventful life; he was perfectly in place in the pulpit. As a priest he satisfied completely my soul's ideal demand, he satisfied it as a figure, satisfied it as an orator. I was glad every Sunday to think that I was to go to hear him. But what increased my joy and made perfect for me the impression of divine worship in this church was another figure, an elderly woman, who likewise attended every Sunday. She used to come a little before the service began, and I likewise. Her personality was for me an image of the congregation, and thinking of her I forgot the disturbing impression of the parish clerk at the church door. She was a woman of a certain age, apparently about sixty years old, but was still beautiful, her features noble, her look full of a certain humble dignity, her countenance expressive of deep, pure, feminine character. She looked as if she had experienced much, not precisely stormy events, but as a mother who had borne life's burdens and yet had preserved and attained the ability to rejoice over the world. So when I saw her coming far down the aisle, when the sexton had met her at the church door and now as a servant was deferentially escorting her to her seat, then I knew she would also pass the pew where I sat. So when she went by I always rose and bowed to her. For me there was so much implied in this bow, it was as though I would beg her to include me in her supplications. She entered her pew, giving a kindly greeting to the sexton, she remained an instant on her feet, she bowed her head, held a handkerchief an instant before her eyes as she prayed —it would take a pithy preacher to make so strong and salutary an impression as did the solemnity of that venerable woman.

It sometimes came into my mind that perhaps I, too, was included in her prayer, for to woman it belongs essentially to pray for others. Think of her in whatever position of life you will, at whatever age, think of her in prayer, and as a rule you will find her praying for others, for her parents, for her loved one, for her husband, for her children, always for others. To man it belongs essentially to pray for himself. He has his definite task, his definite place. The character of his resignation is therefore different; he strives even in prayer. He relinquishes the fulfillment of his wish, and what he prays for is strength to renounce it. Even when he wishes something this thought is constantly present. Woman's prayer is far more substantial, the character of her resignation is different. She prays for the fulfillment of her wish, she is resigned to the thought that she can do nothing about it, but for this reason she is also far more apt to pray for others than is man, for if he would pray for another, he essentially would pray that there might be granted him strength to bear and joyfully to triumph over the pain due to the fact that his wish was not fulfilled; but such a prayer of intercession is imperfect if regarded as intercession, though as a prayer for oneself it is true and right. In this respect man and woman march, as it were, in two ranks. First comes woman with her intercession, moving the Divinity, as it were, with her tears; then comes man with his prayer, bringing to a stop the first rank when it would fearfully betake itself to flight; he has a different tactic which always results in victory. This is due again to the fact that man is in pursuit of infinitude. If woman loses the fight, she must learn from man to pray, and yet intercession belongs to her so essentially that even in this case her intercession for man will be different from his own prayer. In a certain sense, therefore, woman is more believing than man, for woman believes that with God all things are possible; man believes that for God there is something impossible. Woman becomes more and more intense in her humble craving; man gives up more and more, until he finds the immovable point from which he cannot be expelled. This is due to the fact that it belongs essentially to man to have doubted, and all his wisdom will bear an impress of this.

The joy I derived from the beauty of divine worship in that church was, however, of short duration. In the course of the year that priest was transferred, the venerable matron, my pious mother I might almost call her, I saw no more. I often thought of her however. Later when I was married she often hovered before my mind. If the Church paid attention to such matters, our worship would surely gain in beauty and solemnity. Imagine yourself at a baptism where such a venerable woman stood beside the priest and said the Amen, instead of having the bell ringer bleat it out as he now does. Imagine yourself at a wedding where she assisted—would not this be beautiful? For who can give one so lofty an impression of the beauty of a prayer of intercession as such a woman?

But here I sit and preach, forgetting what I properly have to talk about, forgetting that it is to you I have to speak. This is due to the fact that my new friend has put you quite out of my mind. With him, you see, I would gladly talk about such things, for in the first place he is no mocker, and in the second place he is a married man, and only one who has an eye for the beauty of marriage will also be able to see the truth in my remarks.

So I return to our hero. This title he certainly deserves, but for all that I will not continue to use it henceforth, for I prefer another designation which is dearer to me, and with a sincere heart will call him my friend, as with joy I call myself his friend. You see then that life has provided him with "the article of luxury called a friend." You thought perhaps that I would pass over in silence the subject of friendship and its ethical validity, or rather that it would be impossible for me to introduce this subject, seeing that it has no ethical significance at all but falls entirely under aesthetical categories. You are perhaps surprised that wanting to mention this subject I mention it in this place; for friendship is in fact the first dream of youth, it is precisely in early youth the soul is so soft and romantic that it seeks friendship. It would have been more in place, you think, to speak about friendship before I let my friend enter into the holy estate of matrimony. I might reply that as far as this goes it happened, strangely enough, to my friend that before he was married he had not felt himself drawn so strongly to any person that he could venture to characterize the relation as friendship. I might add that I am glad of this because I wanted to deal with friendship last, believing as I do that the ethical factor in it has not the same degree of validity as it has in marriage, and that in this fact precisely is to be seen its imperfection. This reply might appear inadequate in view of the fact that this situation on the part of my friend might be thought abnormal, and for this reason I am disposed to treat this subject a little more carefully.

You are an observer, you will therefore concede the justice of my observation that marked individual difference in character is indicated by considering whether the season of friendship falls in the period of very early youth or emerges only at a later age. Volatile natures have no difficulty in adjusting themselves to themselves, their self is from the very beginning current coin; so then trade begins at once. It is not so easy for the deeper natures to find themselves, and until they have found their self they cannot wish that anyone should offer them a friendship they cannot requite. Such natures are commonly absorbed in themselves, and they are observers—but an observer is no friend. So the situation might be explained if such were the case with my friend. However, he has been married. Now the question is whether there is something abnormal in the fact that friendship only appeared after this—for in the foregoing discussion we agreed that it was proper for friendship to come about in later years, but we did not speak of its relation to marriage. Let us here make use again of our common observation. We must now take into consideration a man's relation to the other sex. To those who at a very early age seek the relation of friendship it not rarely happens that when love begins to assert itself friendship fades completely. They discover that friendship was an imperfect form, break off the earlier relationship and concentrate their whole soul exclusively upon love. Others have the opposite experience. Those who too early tasted the sweetness of love, relishing its joys in the intoxication of youth, acquired perhaps an erroneous impression of the other sex. They became perhaps unjust towards the other sex. By their frivolity they purchased perhaps costly experiences, perhaps believed in feelings within themselves which proved not to be durable, or they believed in feelings on the part of others which vanished like a dream. So they gave up love; it was both too little and too much for them, for they had encountered the dialectical difficulty in love without being able to solve it. They then chose friendship. Both of these formations may be regarded as abnormal. My friend is in

neither of these situations. He had not made a youthful
trial of friendship before he learned to know love, but neither had he harmed himself by enjoying too early the un-
ripe fruit of love. In his love he found the deepest and most
complete satisfaction, but precisely because he was thus
absolutely set at rest, there now was opened up to him the
possibility of a different relationship which in another way
might acquire for him a profound and beautiful significance, for whosoever hath, to him shall be given, and he
shall have more abundance. A *propos* of this he often remembers that there are trees which bear flowers after the
fruit, so that both flowers and fruit are contemporary. With
such a tree he compares his life.

But precisely because it was by and with his marriage
he learned to see the beauty in having a friend or friends,
he has not been for an instant perplexed as to how he ought
to regard friendship, or in doubt that it loses its significance
if one does not regard it ethically. The many experiences
of his life had pretty much destroyed his faith in the aestheticists, but marriage had entirely eradicated every trace
of this from his soul. So he felt no inclination to let himself
be infatuated by aesthetical jugglery but acquiesced in the
view of the ethicists.

In case my friend had not been of such a mind I might
have found pleasure in referring him to you, for what you
have to say on this topic is confused to such a degree that
presumably he would have become completely perplexed
at listening to you. You treat friendship as you do everything else. Your soul lacks ethical concentration to such a
degree that one can get from you opposite explanations
about the same thing, and you are in the highest degree a
proof of the thesis that sentimentality and heartlessness
are one and the same. Your view of friendship can best be
likened to a witch's letter, and he who is willing to adopt
this view must become crazy, as to a certain degree the one
who propounds it must be assumed to be. If when you are
incited to it one hears you propounding the divinity of love
for young men, the beauty of encountering a kindred soul,
one may be almost tempted to fear that your sentimentality
will cost you your young life. At other times you talk in

such a way that one would almost think you were an old practitioner who had become sufficiently acquainted with the emptiness and inanity of the world. "A friend," you say, "is an enigmatical thing; like fog he can be seen only at a distance, for only when one has become unfortunate does one remark that one *has had* a friend." It is easy to see that at the bottom of such a judgment upon friendship there lies a different requirement from that which you previously made. Previously you were talking about intellectual friendship, about the beauty of a spiritual erotic with a common enthusiasm for ideas; now you talk about a practical friendship on a business basis, about mutual assistance in the difficulties of earthly life. There is something true in both requirements, but if one cannot find for them a point of unity, it is doubtless best to conclude with your final result, that friendship is nonsense, a result which you deduce from each of your theses and from both in their reciprocal contradiction.

The absolute condition for friendship is agreement in a life view. If one has that, one will not be tempted to found one's friendship upon obscure feelings or upon inexplicable sympathies. Consequently, one will not experience these ludicrous reversals of one day having a friend and the next day having none. One will not fail to appreciate the importance of the inexplicable sympathies, for one is not in a stricter sense a friend of everybody who shares the same life view, but it is not alone upon the enigmatic factor of sympathy one has to count. A true friendship always requires consciousness of its motives and is thereby saved from being a vain enthusiasm.

The moral view in which friends are united must be a positive view. Thus my friend and I have a positive view in common. Therefore, when we look at one another we do not laugh like those augurs of the Roman story, on the contrary, we become serious. It was quite natural for the augurs to laugh, for their view of life was a negative one. You understand that very well, for it is one of your romantic wishes "to find a kindred soul with whom one could laugh at the whole thing." And you say that "the dreadful thing about life, the thing that almost terrifies one, is that hardly anybody notices how miserable it is, and of these few there is only a rare exception who knows how to retain his good humor and laugh at it all." If this longing of yours for a kindred soul is not satisfied, you know how to make the best of it, "for it is in conformity with the idea that there can only be one who laughs; such a one is the true pessimist; if there were more of that kind, it would be proof in fact that the world was not entirely miserable." Now your thought is in full swing and knows no limit. So you express the opinion that "even laughter is only an imperfect expression of the derision the world deserves. If it is to be perfect, one ought properly to be serious. It would be the most perfect mockery of the world if one who propounded the deepest truth was not an enthusiastic believer but a doubter. And this would not be unthinkable, for no one can propound positive truth so admirably as a doubter, the only drawback is that he doesn't believe it. If he were a hypocrite, the mockery would rebound upon him; if he were a doubter, wishing perhaps to believe what he propounded, the mockery would be entirely objective, existence would be mocking itself through him; he propounded a doctrine which could explain everything, the whole race could repose in it securely, but this doctrine could not explain the founder of it. If a man were so shrewd as to be able to conceal the fact that he was mad, he would be able to make the whole world mad." Having such a notion of life, it is difficult to find a friend with a common moral view. Or have you perhaps found such a friend in the mystical society of Symparanekromenoi you sometimes talk about?[57] Are you perhaps an association of friends who mutually regard one another as so shrewd that you know how to conceal your madness?

There lived in Greece a wise man; he enjoys the singular honor of being reckoned among the seven wise men if it is assumed that this number was fourteen. If my memory is not very much at fault, his name was Myson. An ancient author relates that he was a misanthrope. This author tells his story very briefly: "It is related of Myson that he was a misanthrope and that he laughed when he was alone. When someone asked why he did so, he replied, 'Just because I am alone.'" You see that you have a predecessor; you will aspire in vain to be admitted into the number of the seven wise men, even though this were defined as twenty-one, for Myson stands in your way. This, however, is of minor importance; but you yourself will perceive that he who laughs when he is alone cannot possibly have a friend, and that for two reasons: first, because he doesn't get a chance to laugh so long as the friend is present; secondly, because the friend must be afraid that he is only waiting for him to go in order that he may have a chance to laugh at him. Therefore, behold, the devil must be your friend! I might almost be tempted to beg you to take this literally, for it is said also of the devil that he laughs when he is alone. It appears to me that there is something very disconsolate in such an isolation, and I cannot help thinking how dreadful it is when a man awakes to another life on the Day of Judgment and again stands there quite alone.

So then friendship requires a positive view of life. But a positive life view cannot be conceived unless it has in it an ethical factor. To be sure, in our age one often enough encounters people who have a system in which there is no place for the ethical.[58] Let them have ten times a system, a life view they have not. In our age such a phenomenon can be explained readily; for as our age is preposterous in so many ways, so it is also in the fact that one is initiated into the greater mysteries before being initiated into the lesser ones. The ethical factor in the life view is thus the starting-point for friendship, and only when one regards friendship in this way does it acquire significance and beauty. If one stops with the sympathetic, the mysterious, then friendship will find its most perfect expression in the relation which exists between the social birds, the so-called lovebirds, whose solidarity is so heartfelt that the death of one is also the death of the other. Although in nature such a relation is beautiful, it is unseemly in the world of spirit. Agreement in a moral view is the constituent factor in friendship. If this is present, the friendship endures even though the friend dies, for the transfigured friend lives on in the other; if this ceases to be, friendship is over even though the friend goes on living.

If one regards friendship thus, one regards it ethically and therefore with a view to its beauty. It thus acquires both significance and beauty. Do I have to cite an authority on my side against you? Very well, then! How did Aristotle interpret friendship? Did he not make this the starting-point for his whole ethical view of life? For with friendship, he says, the concepts of justice are so broadened that they coalesce with it. He bases the concept of justice upon the idea of friendship.[59] His category is thus in a certain sense more perfect than the modern view which bases justice upon duty, the abstract categorical—he bases it upon the social sense. One easily sees from this that for Aristotle the idea of the state becomes the highest idea—but this in turn is the imperfection in his category.

However, I shall not venture to enter into such investigations as the relation between the Aristotelian and the Kantian interpretation of the ethical. I cited Aristotle only to remind you that he too perceived that friendship contributes to help one ethically in gaining reality.

He who regards friendship ethically sees it as a duty. I might therefore say that it is every man's duty to have a friend. However, I prefer to use another expression which exhibits the ethical element in friendship and in everything else which was dealt with in the foregoing discussion, and at the same time emphasizes sharply the difference between the ethical and the aesthetical: I say that it is every man's duty to become revealed. The Scripture teaches that every man must die, and then comes the Judgment when everything shall be revealed. Ethics says that it is the significance of life and of reality that every man become revealed. So if he is not, the revelation will appear as a punishment. The aestheticist, on the contrary, will not attribute significance to reality, he remains constantly concealed, because, however frequently and however much he gives himself up to the world, he never does it totally, there always remains something that he keeps back; if he were to do it totally, he would be doing it ethically. But this thing of playing hide and seek always avenges itself, and of course it does so by the fact that one becomes enigmatical to oneself. Hence it is that all mystics, when they do not recognize the claim

of reality upon every man that he become revealed, stumble
upon difficulties and terrors which no one else knows of.
It is as though they discovered an entirely different world,
as though their nature was reduplicated in itself. He who
will not contend with realities gets phantoms to fight with.

Herewith I am through for the present. To propound a
doctrine of morals was never my intention. What I wanted
to do was to show how the ethical, in the regions which
border on the aesthetical, is so far from depriving life of
its beauty that it bestows beauty upon it. It affords peace,
assurance, and security, for it calls to us constantly: *quod
petis, hic est.*[60] It saves from every vain enthusiasm which
would enfeeble the soul and bestows upon it health and
strength. It teaches one not to overvalue the adventitious
or to deify fortune. It teaches one to be joyful in good fortune (and even this the aestheticist is not able to do), for
good fortune merely as such is an endless relativity; it
teaches one to be joyful in misfortune.

Regard what I have written as of no importance, regard
it as notes appended to Balle's "Lesson-Book"—that is of no
consequence; what I have said nevertheless has an authority which I hope you will respect. Or might it seem to you
perhaps that I have wrongfully wished to usurp authority,
that I have improperly confounded my official station with
this litigation, behaving as a judge, not as a party to it? I
cheerfully relinquish every pretension, I am not even a
party in this dispute with you; for while I willingly admit
that aesthetics might well give you power of attorney to
appear in its behalf, I am far from ascribing to myself
enough importance to appear with power of attorney for
ethics. I am nothing more than a witness, and it was only
in this sense I expressed the opinion that this letter has a
certain authority, for he who speaks of what he has experienced always speaks with authority. I am only a witness,
and here you have my declaration *in optima forma.*

I perform my duties as judge assessor, I am glad to have
such a calling, I believe it is in keeping with my faculties
and with my whole personality, I know that it makes demands upon my powers. I seek to fit myself for it more
and more, and in doing so I feel that I am developing my-

self more and more. I love my wife and am happy in my home; I hear my wife's lullaby, and it appears to me more beautiful than any other song—without my having to believe that she is a singer. I hear the cry of the little one, and to my ear it is not inharmonious; I see his elder brother growing up and being promoted in school, I contemplate his future joyfully and confidently—not impatiently, for I have plenty of time to wait, and this waiting is in itself a joy to me. My work has importance for me, and I believe that to a certain degree it has also for others, even though I cannot define and exactly measure its importance. I feel joy in the fact that the personal life of others has importance for me, and I desire and hope that mine also may have importance for those with whom in my whole view of life I am in sympathy. I love my fatherland, and I cannot well imagine that I could thrive in any other land. I love my mother tongue which liberates my thought, I find that what I have to say in the world I can capitally express in this tongue. Thus my life has significance for me, so much so that I feel joyful and content with it. With all that, I live at the same time a higher life, and when sometimes it occurs that I inhale and infuse this higher life in the respiration of my earthly and domestic life, I count myself blessed, and art and grace coalesce before me. Thus I love existence because it is beautiful and hope for an existence still more beautiful.

Here you have my declaration as a witness. If I could be dubious whether it was proper to make this deposition, it would be out of consideration for you, for I am almost afraid that it may hurt you to hear that life in its simplicity may be so beautiful. Accept, nevertheless, my testimony; let it cause you a little pain, but may it also have a joyful effect upon you; it has one quality which your life unfortunately lacks—trustworthiness. You can build upon it securely.

Lately I have often talked with my wife about you. She is really very much attached to you. I hardly need to say this, however, for you have many gifts for pleasing when you want to, but you have still more eyes for observing whether you succeed. Her feeling for you has my entire

approval. I do not readily become jealous, and in my case
this would be inexcusable—not because I am too proud (as
you think a man ought to be, proud enough, as you say,
"to be able to be quit at once with thanks"), but because
my wife is too lovable for that. I am not afraid. I believe
that in this respect I dare say that even Scribe would despair over our prosaic marriage, for I believe that even for
him it would be impossible to make it poetic. That he has
extraordinary powers and talents I do not deny; that according to my notion he abuses them I do not deny either.
Does he not do everything to make young women believe
that the assured love of marriage is not enough to make
life poetic, that marriage would be intolerable if one could
not count upon little love affairs alongside of it?[61] Does he
not represent that a woman even though she defiles herself
and her marriage by a culpable love still continues to be
lovable? Does he not hint obscurely that, since generally it
is by an accident such a relationship is discovered, a person
in real life may hope that when she has added her own
slyness to what she has learned from the heroine in his
plays she will succeed in remaining concealed all her life?
Does he not seek in every way to alarm husbands, does he
not take the most respected women against whom no one
would dare to harbor the least suspicion and represent that
they are defiled by a secret guilt? Does he not show over
and over again how vain the best means of defending marriage really are, how vain it is for a man to repose infinite
confidence in his wife and trust her above all things? And
in spite of this Scribe is pleased to say that every husband
is only a sluggish and drowsy marmot, an imperfect being
who is himself to blame for his wife going astray. I wonder
if Scribe is so modest as to assume that nobody learns anything from his plays, for otherwise he must perceive that
every married man must learn at once to discover that his
position is anything but secure and peaceful, indeed that
no police spy can lead such a restless and sleepless life as
he is compelled to lead—unless he will be reassured by
Scribe's consolation and himself seek a diversion like that
of his wife, concluding that marriage exists for the sake of

divesting the union with others of every tiresome appearance of innocence and making it quite interesting.

However, I leave Scribe alone, I am not capable of contending with him, but all the same I sometimes think with a certain pride that I, a humble and insignificant man, give the lie to the great writer Scribe by my marriage. Perhaps this pride is only beggar's pride, perhaps I am so fortunate because I am an ordinary man, an outsider to poetry.

So my wife is attached to you, and in this respect I am in sympathy with her feelings, all the more because I believe that her liking for you is due in part to the fact that she sees your weaknesses. She sees very clearly that what you lack is a certain degree of womanliness. You are too proud to be able to devote yourself to anyone. This pride does not tempt her in the least, for she regards the ability to devote oneself as the sign of true greatness. You perhaps will not believe it, but I assure you that I actually have to plead your cause against her. She affirms that in your pride you appraise all men and reject them. I try to explain that perhaps it is not quite as she thinks, that you reject men in an infinite sense, that the restlessness with which your soul aspires after the infinite makes you unfair to men. *That* she will not understand, and I can well comprehend it, for when one is so easily contented as she is (and how easily contented she is you can see from this fact among others, that she feels herself indescribably fortunate in being united to me) it is difficult to avoid condemning you. So my marriage too has its conflict, and in a way you are responsible for it. We shall get through that all right, and I have only to wish that to a married couple you may never become an occasion of a different sort of strife. You might, however, contribute a little to settle this strife between my wife and me. Do not think that I want to insinuate myself into your secrets, but I have just one question I would put to you, which I believe you can answer without encroaching on your rights. Answer me honestly and without circumlocution: do you really laugh when you are alone? You know what I mean. I do not ask whether it sometimes or even frequently occurs to you to laugh when you are alone, but whether you take satisfaction in this lonely laughter. For if not, then I have won and I shall surely be able to convince my wife.

Now whether you really do spend your time when you are alone by laughing I do not know, but at all events that appears to me a way of wanting to be a little more than queer; for it may be that your life has developed in a way which prompts you to feel the need of solitude, but not, so far as I can judge, in order to laugh. Even the most cursory observation shows that your life is planned on an uncommon scale. You do not seem by any means to find satisfaction in following the highways but rather in going your own gait. One can easily forgive a young man for a certain romanticism; it is another matter when it gets the upper hand to such a degree that it would pass itself off as the normal and the real. One owes it to a man who has thus gone astray to cry out to him, *"Respice finem"* [consider the end], and to explain that the word *finem* does not mean death (for even that is not the hardest problem for a man), but that it means life, that there comes an instant when it is a question of really beginning to live, and that it is a perilous thing to have so dispersed oneself that it becomes a matter of the greatest difficulty to collect oneself, yea, that this has to be done with such speed and haste that one cannot get everything together and consequently, instead of being an extraordinary man, one ends by being a defective specimen of humanity.

In the Middle Ages one went about it another way: one abruptly broke off life's regular development and went into a monastery. The faultiness of this step did not, of course, consist in the fact of entering the monastery but in the erroneous conceptions associated with it. For my part, I can very well reconcile myself to the fact that a man forms this resolution, indeed, I am able to regard it as very pretty; but on the other hand I require of him that he be clear about what this means. In the Middle Ages they thought that in choosing the cloister a man chose the extraordinary and himself became an extraordinary man; from the elevation of the monastery one looked down proudly, almost compassionately, upon the ordinary men. So it was no wonder that people entered the monasteries in droves when at

so cheap a price one could become an extraordinary man!
But the gods do not sell the extraordinary at a bargain
price. If the men who retired from active life had been
honest and sincere with themselves and with others, above
all if they had loved the thing of being a man, if they had
felt with enthusiasm all the beauty implied in this, if their
heart had not been unacquainted with a genuine and profound feeling for humanity, they too would perhaps have
retired to the solitude of the cloister, but they would not
have prided themselves foolishly upon being extraordinary
men, except in the sense that they were less perfect than
others; they would not have looked down condescendingly
upon the ordinary men but would have contemplated them
sympathetically, feeling a melancholy joy in the fact that
these men had succeeded in performing the beautiful and
the great things of which they were not capable.

In our age the monastic life has fallen considerably in
price, so one rarely sees a man who breaks with the whole
of existence, with the whole universal-human. On the other
hand, if one has a fairly close acquaintance with men, one
will sometimes encounter in a particular individual an erroneous doctrine which vividly recalls the monastic theory.
For the sake of regularity I will here pronounce at once my
view of what an extraordinary man is. The truly extraordinary man is the truly ordinary man. The more of the
universal-human an individual is able to realize in his life,
the more extraordinary he is. The less of the universal he
is able to take up into his life, the more imperfect he is.
He is then an extraordinary man to be sure, but not in a
good sense.

If, then, a man who is desirous of realizing the task
which is assigned to every man, the task of expressing the
universal-human in his individual life, were to stumble
upon difficulties, if it seems that there is something of the
universal which he is not able to take up into his life[62]—
what then does he do? In case his head is haunted by the
monastic theories, or by an aesthetic view which is quite
analogous to them, he is then joyful, from the first instant
he feels haughtily that he is an exception, an extraordinary
man, he is proud of it—just as childishly as if a nightingale

which had acquired a red feather in its wing were to rejoice in the fact that no other nightingale had the like of it. If, on the other hand, his soul is ennobled by love for the universal, if he loves the life of men in this world—what then does he do?

He deliberates whether and in how far this is true. A man may be to blame for this imperfection, or he may have it without blame, but it may be true that he is unable to realize the universal. If men in general were more conscious of themselves, many more perhaps would come to this conclusion. He will know also that indolence and cowardice may make a man believe such a thing, and that he can reduce the pain to an insignificance by transforming the universal into the particular and conserving an abstract possibility in relation to the universal. For in fact the universal exists nowhere as such, and it depends upon me, upon my energy of consciousness, whether in the particular I will see the universal or merely the particular.

Perhaps such a deliberation will not seem to him sufficient, he will venture to make an experiment. He will easily perceive that in case the experiment leads him to the same result, the truth will be impressed upon him all the more emphatically, and, if he would coddle himself, it would be best perhaps for him to desist, since he will have to wince more than ever. He will know that no particular is the universal. So if he would not delude himself, he will transform the particular into the universal. He will see in the particular much more than is contained in it as such: for him it is the universal. He will assist the particular by giving it the importance of the universal. If he notices that the experiment is not succeeding, he will have arranged everything in such a way that it is not the particular which wounds him but the universal. He will be on his guard not to let any confusion take place, lest he be wounded by the particular, for its wound will be too light for him and he will love himself too earnestly to count it of the greatest consequence to him that he get a light wound; he will love the universal too sincerely to wish to substitute the particular for it with the aim of escaping unscathed. He will be on his guard not to smile at the impotent reaction of the particular, will take care not to view the situation light-mindedly, even if the particular as such tempts him to do so; he will not allow himself to be disturbed by the strange misunderstanding that the particular has in him a greater friend than it has in itself. When he has done this he will calmly advance to meet the pain—although his mind is shaken, he does not waver.

Now if it happens that the universal which he is unable to realize is precisely that for which he was desirous, then if he is a magnanimous man he will in a sense rejoice at this. He will then say, "I have fought under the most un-favorable conditions. I have fought against the particular, I have set my desire upon the side of the enemy; to make the thing complete I have transformed the particular into the universal. It is true that all this will make the defeat harder for me, but it will also strengthen my consciousness, it will give it energy and clarity."

So at this point he has emancipated himself from the universal. He will not for an instant be in any obscurity about what such a step signifies, for it was really he himself who made the defeat complete and gave it significance; for he knew where he was vulnerable and how, and he inflicted upon himself the wound which the particular, as such, was not capable of inflicting. So he will be convinced that there is something of the universal which he is not able to realize. With this conviction, however, he is not through with the thing, for it will engender a profound sorrow in his soul. He will rejoice over the others to whom it was granted to accomplish this thing, he will perhaps perceive better than they how beautiful it is, but he himself will sorrow, not in a cowardly and despondent spirit, but deeply and frankly, for he will say, "I love the universal, nevertheless. *by sorrow* If it was the happy lot of the others to bear witness to the *became* universal by the fact that they realized it, well then, I bear *reconciled* witness to it by my sorrow." And this sorrow is beautiful, is itself an expression of the universal-human, a movement of its heart within him, and it will bring about his reconciliation with it.

With this conviction which he won he is not through with the matter, for he will feel that he has laid upon himself a great responsibility. "At this point," he says, "I have put myself outside the universal, I have deprived myself of the guidance, the security and tranquility which the universal gives, I stand alone, without sympathy, I am an exception." But he will not become cowardly and disconsolate, he will go his lonely way with confidence, he has indeed produced the proof of the rightness of what he did, he has his pain. He will not be in any obscurity with regard to this step, he possesses a deposition which he can produce any moment; no alarm can confuse it for him, no absence of mind; though he were to wake up in the middle of the night, he will instantly be able to render an account of everything. He will feel that the upbringing he is subjected to is hard, for the universal is a severe master when one has it outside of him, it constantly holds over him the sword of justice and says, "Why wilt thou be outside?" And even though a man says, "It is not my fault," it ascribes the blame to him nevertheless, and requires itself of him. So he will sometimes return to the same point, producing the proof again and again, and will then cheerfully go further. He reposes in the conviction he has fought for, and he will say, "What I rely upon, nevertheless, in the last resort is this, that there exists a righteous rationality, and I put my trust in its compassion, believing that it is compassionate enough to be just; for it would not be so dreadful if I were to suffer punishment which I had deserved because I had done wrong, but it would be dreadful if I should be able to do wrong in such a way that no one punished it; and it would not be so dreadful if in the infatuation of my heart I were to awaken with anguish and horror, but this is the dreadful thing, that I might so infatuate my heart that no one could awaken it."

However, this whole conflict is a purgatorial fire of which I can at least form a conception. People therefore should not be desirous of becoming extraordinary men, for that means something different from the capricious satisfaction of one's wilful lust.

He, on the other hand, who with pain was convinced that he was an extraordinary man is by his sorrow over it reconciled again with the universal; he will perhaps some day experience the joy that what caused him pain and made him lowly in his own eyes proves to be an occasion for his being lifted up again and becoming in a nobler sense an extraordinary man. What he lost in compass he gained perhaps in intensive inwardness. For not every man whose life is a mediocre expression of the universal is for this reason an extraordinary man, for this would be to idolize triviality: before he can truthfully be called such, one must ask also with what intensive strength he does this. Now that other man will be in possession of that strength at the points where he is able to realize the universal. His sorrow will thus vanish again, it will be resolved into harmony; for he will perceive that he had reached the confines of his individuality. He knows indeed that every man develops himself with freedom, but he knows too that a man does not create himself out of nothing, that he has his self in its concretion as his task; he will again be reconciled with existence, perceiving that in a certain sense every man is an exception, and that it is equally true that every man is the universal-human and at the same time an exception.

Here you have my notion of what it is to be an extraordinary man. I have too much love for existence and for what it is to be a man to be willing to believe that the path by which one becomes an extraordinary man is easy or without temptations. But even though a man be thus in a nobler sense an extraordinary man, he will nevertheless constantly admit that it would be still more perfect to take into himself the universal as a whole.

So receive my greeting, accept my friendship; for though I dare not in the strictest sense characterize our relation as friendship, yet I hope that my young friend will one day become so much older that I may truthfully use this word. Be assured of my sympathy. Receive a greeting from her whom I love, whose thoughts are hidden in my thoughts, receive a greeting which is inseparable from mine, but receive also a special greeting from her, a greeting friendly and sincere as hers always is.

When some days ago you were at our house you perhaps had no idea that again I had so big a letter ready. I know that you do not like to have people talk to you about your inner history, therefore I have chosen to write, and I will never talk to you about it. That you receive such a letter remains a secret, and I should be very sorry if it might have the effect of altering your relationship to me and my family. I know that you have enough virtuosity to hinder this, if you will, and therefore I beg you to do so for your sake and for mine. I have never wished to intrude upon your personal affairs, and I can well love you at a distance even though we often see one another. Your nature is too closely reserved to permit me to believe that it would be profitable to talk to you, but on the other hand I hope that my letter may not be without significance. So when you set to work upon yourself within the closed machinery of your personality, I put in my pleas and am convinced that they will have a part in the motion.

Since our epistolary relationship is thus to remain a secret, I observe all the formalities: I say farewell, as though we were far remote from one another, although I hope to see you at my house just as often as before.

ULTIMATUM

Perhaps with the letters I wrote you a while ago you have had the same experience as I, that much has been forgotten. If that be so, I would that in your case it might also be the same as in mine, that at any season, in spite of changing moods, you may be able to render an account to yourself of the thought and the movements. The expression, the form of presentation in which the thoughts are clothed, resembles the flowers which from one year to another are the same and yet not the same; but the attitude, the movement, the position are unchanged. If I were to write to you now, I might perhaps express myself differently. Perhaps in my letters I might even succeed here and there in being eloquent, although this is a grace to which I certainly make no claim and which my profession in life does not require of me. If I were to write now, I might perhaps succeed better; I do not know, for expression is a gift. "And every age, like every season, is with its special flowers bedecked."[1] The thought, on the other hand, is and remains, and I hope that in the course of time the movements may become easier and more natural, unaltered even when they are dumb because the flowers of expression have faded.

However, it is not to write a new letter I now grasp my pen, but because you have been vividly recalled to me by a letter I have received from an older friend who is a pastor in Jutland. So far as I know, you are unacquainted with him. My friendship with him began in my student days, and although there was a difference of five or six years between us, our relationship was rather intimate. He was a little man with a squarely built figure, merry, light-hearted and uncommonly jovial. Although in the depths his soul was serious, his outward life seemed gaily inconsequent. Learning enthralled him, but he was only a "pass" man, and in his final theological examination he managed to get no more than *haud illaudabilis* [not unpraiseworthy]. About four years ago he was thrust into a little parish on the Jutland heath. Outwardly he had a stentorian voice, and intellectually he had an originality which always distinguished him in the small circle with which I was acquainted. No wonder, then, that at the beginning he did not find himself thoroughly content, and that his post seemed to him unimportant. Now, however, he has regained his contentment, and it has had a very cheering effect upon me to read the letter I lately received from him. "The Jutland heath," he says, "is after all a good exercise ground for me and an incomparable study room for a parson. There I go on Saturdays to prepare my sermon, and everything widens out before me. I forget every actual auditor and gain an ideal one, gain complete self-forgetfulness, so that when I mount the pulpit it is as though I were still standing upon the heath where my eye discovers not a single soul, where my voice lifts itself with all its strength to outdo the violence of the storm."

I am not writing, however, in order to tell you this, but to send you a sermon of his which he inclosed with the letter. I did not wish to show it to you in person for fear of inciting your criticism, but I send the manuscript in order that it may make its impression upon you in a quiet hour. My friend has not yet delivered this sermon but expects to do so next year and is confident he will make every peasant understand it. You should not despise it on this account, for the beauty of the universal consists precisely in the fact that all can understand it. In this sermon he has apprehended what I said to you and also what I was desirous of saying. He has expressed it more felicitously than I find myself capable of doing. Take it then, read it, I have nothing to add, except that I have read it and thought of myself—read it then and think of yourself.

THE EDIFICATION IMPLIED IN THE
THOUGHT THAT AS AGAINST GOD
WE ARE ALWAYS IN THE WRONG

PRAYER

Our Father in heaven, teach us to pray aright, that our hearts may disclose themselves to Thee in prayer and supplication, and may conceal no hidden thought which we know is not well-pleasing to Thee, nor any secret fear that Thou wilt deny us anything which is truly to our advantage; so that the laboring thoughts, the restless mind, the fearful heart may there find rest where alone it is to be found, as we rejoice always in giving thanks to Thee, and gladly confess that as against Thee we are always in the wrong. Amen.

The Holy Gospel is written in the nineteenth Chapter of St. Luke, beginning at the forty-first Verse.

"And when he drew nigh, he saw the city and wept over it, saying, If thou hadst known in this thy day, even thou, the things which belong unto thy peace! but now they are hid from thine eyes. For the days shall come upon thee, when thine enemies shall cast up a bank about thee, and compass thee round, and keep thee in on every side, and shall dash thee to the ground, and thy children within thee; and they shall not leave in thee one stone upon another; because thou knewest not the time of thy visitation.

"And he entered into the temple, and began to cast out them that sold, saying unto them, It is written, And my house shall be a house of prayer: but ye have made it a den of robbers.

"And he was teaching daily in the temple. But the chief priests and the scribes and the principal men of the people sought to destroy him: and they could not find what they might do; for the people all hung upon him, listening."

What the Spirit through visions and dreams had revealed to the prophets, what they in a premonitory voice had proclaimed to one generation after another, the rejection of the elect people, the dreadful destruction of proud Jeru-

salem—that was drawing nearer and nearer. Christ goes up
to Jerusalem. He is not a prophet who proclaims future
events, His speech does not awaken anxiety and alarm, for
what still is hidden He sees directly before His eyes. He
does not prophesy, since the time for that is past—He weeps
over Jerusalem. And yet the city was still standing in its
glory, and the temple still held its head high, higher than
any structure in the world, and Christ Himself says, "If
thou hadst known in this thy day the things which are for
thy good!" But to this he adds, "Now they are hid from
thine eyes." In God's eternal counsel its destruction is determined, and salvation is hid from the eyes of its inhabitants.
Was the generation then living more wicked than the foregoing generations to which it owed its life? Was the whole
nation corrupt, was there none righteous in Jerusalem, not
a single one who could check God's wrath? Among all those
from whom salvation was hid was there no pious man?
And if there was one, then was no gate opened for him in
the time of anguish and distress when the enemy besieged
the city round about and pressed it upon every side? Did
no angel descend and save him when all the gates were
still shut, was no miracle wrought for his sake? No, its
destruction was determined; in vain the besieged city
looked in anguish for a way out, the army of the enemy
crushed it in its mighty embrace, and no one escaped, and
heaven remained shut and sent forth no angel except the
angel of death which brandished its sword over the city.
For the sin of the people this generation must suffer, for
the sin of this generation every individual in it must suffer.
Shall then the righteous suffer with the unrighteous? Is
this the jealousy of God, that He visits the sins of the fathers
upon the children unto the third and fourth generation—
in such a way that He does not punish the fathers but
the children? What answer should we make? Should we
say, "There have elapsed now nearly two thousand years
since those days; such a horror the world never saw before
and never again will see; we thank God that we live in
peace and security, that the scream of anguish from those
days reaches us only very faintly; we will hope and believe
that our days and those of our children may pass in quiet-

ness, unaffected by the storms of existence? We do not feel strong enough to reflect upon such things, but we are ready to thank God that we are not subjected to such trials."

Can anything be imagined more cowardly and more disconsolate than such talk? Is then the inexplicable explained by saying that it has occurred only once in the world? Or is not this the inexplicable, that it did occur? And has not this fact, the fact that it did occur, the power to make everything inexplicable, even the most explicable events? If once it occurred in the world that man's lot was essentially different from what it ordinarily is, what assurance is there that this will not recur, what assurance that this is not the true thing, and what ordinarily occurs is the untrue? Or is the true proved to be such by the fact that it most often occurs? And does not that really often occur which those ages witnessed? Is it not what we all of us in so many ways have experienced, that what occurs on a great scale is experienced also in a minor degree? "Think ye," said Christ, "that those Galileans whose blood Pilate commanded to be shed were sinners above all the Galileans because they suffered these things? Or the eighteen on whom the tower in Siloam fell and killed them, think ye that they were offenders above all the men that dwelt in Jerusalem?" So then those Galileans were not sinners above other men, those eighteen were not offenders above all the men that dwelt in Jerusalem—and yet the innocent shared the same lot as the guilty. It was a providential dispensation, perhaps you will say, not a punishment. But the destruction of Jerusalem was a punishment, and it fell with equal severity upon the innocent and the guilty. Hence you will not alarm yourselves by pondering such things. For that a man may have adversity and suffering, that these things as well as the rain may fall upon the just and upon the unjust, that you can comprehend, but that it should be a punishment!—and yet the Scripture so represents it. Is then the lot of the righteous like that of the unrighteous, has godly fear no promise for the life which now is, is then every uplifting thought which once made you so rich in courage and confidence only an illusion, a juggler's trick in which the child believes, the youth still hopes, but in which one who is a little older finds no blessing but only mockery and offense?

This thought shocks you, but yet it cannot and shall not acquire power to beguile you, it shall not be able to dull your soul. Righteousness you will love, righteousness you will practice early and late, though it have no reward, you still will practice it, you feel that it advances a claim which must in the end be satisfied; you will not sink back languidly and conclude that righteousness has promises but that you had forfeited them by not doing righteousness. You will not strive with men, but with God you will strive, and will not let Him go until He has blessed you. Yet the Scripture saith, "Thou shalt not contend with God."[2] Is it not this you are doing? Is this then again a disconsolate speech, is the Holy Scripture only given to man to humiliate him, to annihilate him? By no manner of means! When it is said, "Thou shalt not contend with God," the meaning of this is that you shall not wish to prove yourself in the right before Him. There is only one way of supporting the claim that you are in the right before God—by learning that you are in the wrong. Yea, this is what you yourselves ought to wish. So when you are forbidden to contend against God, this is an indication of your lofty station and by no means affirms that you are a lowly being which has no importance for Him. The sparrow falls to the ground—in a way it is in the right before God. The lily fades—in a way it is in the right before God. Only man is in the wrong, for to him alone is reserved that which to all other creatures was denied . . . to be in the wrong before God.

Ought I to speak differently, ought I to remind you of a wisdom which knows how to explain everything easily enough without doing injustice either to God or man? "Man is a frail creature," it says, "and it would be unreasonable of God to require of him the impossible. One does what one can, and if a person is once in a while a little remiss, God will never forget that we are weak and imperfect men." Ought I to admire most the lofty conception of the Deity which this shrewd saying betrays, or the deep insight into the human heart, the searching consciousness which scrutinizes itself and then comes to the comfortable conclusion that one does what one can? Would it be so easy a thing for you, my hearer, to determine how much it is one can? Were you never in such danger that almost in despair you exerted your strength to the utmost and yet ardently wished you could do more? And perhaps another man was watching you with a dubious and beseeching look, wondering if you might not do more. Or were you never alarmed about yourself, so much alarmed that it seemed to you as if there were no sin so black, no selfishness so odious, that it might not sneak into you and as a foreign power gain mastery over you? Did you never sense this dread? For if you never sensed it, then do not open your mouth to reply, for you are unable to answer the question here put to you. But if you have sensed this dread, then, my hearer, I ask you, Did you find repose in that saying: One does what one can? Or were you never in dread for others, have you not seen those men tottering to whom you were wont to look up with trust and confidence, and did you not hear a low voice whispering to you, "If even these men cannot accomplish the great, what then is life but vain toil and trouble, and what is faith but a snare which drags us out into the infinity in which we are unable to live? Far better, then, to forget, to relinquish every such pretension"? Did you not hear this voice? If you did not hear it, then do not open your mouth to reply, for you are unable to answer the question here put to you. But if you have heard it, my hearer, I ask you, Was this your consolation that you said: One does what one can? Was not this precisely the reason for your disquietude, that you did not know within yourself how much it is a man can do, that at one moment it seemed to you so infinitely much, at another so very little? Was it not for this reason your anxiety was so painful, that your soul could not penetrate your consciousness, that the more earnestly you desired to act, the more heartily you wished to, so much the more dreadful became the duplicity in which you found yourself involved, wondering whether you may not have done what you could, or whether you had done what you could, but no one came to your aid?

Therefore, no earnest doubt, no really deep concern, is

put to rest by the saying that one does what one can. If a man is sometimes in the right, sometimes in the wrong, to a certain degree in the right, to a certain degree in the wrong, who, then, is to decide this except man; but in deciding it may he not be to a certain degree in the right, to a certain degree in the wrong? Or is he when he judges his action a different man from the man who acted? Must doubt then prevail, constantly discovering new difficulties, and must concern walk alongside of the alarmed soul and imprint upon it the experiences it has had? Or might we prefer to be constantly in the right, in the sense that the irrational creatures are? We have, then, only the choice of being nothing before God, or the eternal torture of beginning over again every instant, but without being able to begin. For if we are to be able to determine definitely whether at the present instant we are in the right, this question must be definitely determined with a view to the preceding instant, and then further and further back.

Doubt is again stirred up, concern is again aroused; so let us strive to set them at rest by meditating upon

THE EDIFICATION IMPLIED IN THE THOUGHT THAT
AS AGAINST GOD WE ARE ALWAYS IN THE WRONG.

Being in the wrong—can any feeling be thought of more painful than this? And do we not see that men would rather suffer anything than admit that they are in the wrong? We do not approve of such stiff-necked pride either in ourselves or in others. We think it would be wiser and better to admit it when we really are in the wrong, and accordingly we say that the pain attendant upon this admission is like a bitter medicine which will prove to be healing; but we do not attempt to conceal the fact that it is painful to be in the wrong and painful to admit it. So we endure the pain because we know that it is for our good, we trust that some day we shall succeed in opposing a stronger resistance; perhaps we may carry it so far that we very seldom are really in the wrong. This way of thinking is so natural, so obvious to everybody. There is something edifying in being in the wrong, for when we admit it, we build ourselves up with prospects of its occurring more and more rarely. And yet it was not by this consideration we proposed to set doubt at rest, it was rather by meditating upon the fact that we are always in the wrong. But if the former way of looking at it was edifying for the hope it held out that in time we might no longer be in the wrong, how can the opposite consideration also be edifying which teaches us that with respect to the future as well as the past we are always in the wrong?

Your life brings you into manifold relationships with other people, some of whom love right and justice, while others do not seem willing to practice them. They do you a wrong. Your soul is not callous to the suffering they inflict upon you, but you search and examine yourself and are convinced that you are in the right. You repose quietly and staunchly in this conviction. However much they injure me, you say, they shall not be able to deprive me of the peace of knowing that I am in the right and suffer wrong. There is a satisfaction, a joy, in this reflection which surely every one of us has tasted, and when you continue to suffer wrong, you are edified by the thought that you are in the right. This consideration is so natural, so comprehensible, so often put to the test, and yet it is not by this we would quiet doubt and allay concern, but by reflecting upon the edification implied in the thought that we are always in the wrong. Can, then, this opposite consideration have the same effect?

Your life brings you into manifold relationships with other people, to some of whom you are drawn by a more heartfelt love than you feel for others. Now if such a man who was the object of your love were to do you a wrong, it would pain you deeply, would it not? You would carefully rehearse everything that had occurred—but then would you say, I know of myself that I am in the right, this thought shall tranquilize me? Oh, if you loved him, this thought would not tranquilize you, you would explore anew every possibility. You would not be able to come to any other conclusion but that he was in the wrong, and yet this certainty would disquiet you, you would wish that you might be in the wrong, you would try to find something which might speak in his defense, and if you did not find

it, you would first find comfort in the thought that you
were in the wrong. Or if the responsibility were laid upon
you of caring for the welfare of such a person, you would
do everything in your power, and if in spite of that the
other showed no appreciation and only caused you sorrow,
would you cast up the account and say, I know that I have
done right by him? Oh, no! If you loved him, this thought
would only distress you, you would grasp at every probability, and if you found none, you would tear up the reck-
oning in order to be able to forget it, and you would endeavor to edify yourself with the thought that you were in
the wrong.

So it is painful to be in the wrong, and the more painful
the more frequently it occurs; it is edifying to be in the
wrong, and the more edifying the more frequently it occurs!
That is clearly a contradiction. How can it be explained
except by the fact that in the one case you are compelled
to recognize that which in the other case you wish to recognize? But was not the recognition the same in both cases,
and does the consideration that one wishes or does not wish
exert any influence upon it? How is this to be explained,
except by the consideration that in the one case you loved
and in the other you did not, in other words, that in the
one case you found yourself in an infinite relationship to a
person, in another case in a finite relationship? Hence, to
wish to be in the wrong is the expression for an infinite
relationship; to wish to be in the right or to find it painful
to be in the wrong is the expression for a finite relationship!
So, then, it is edifying always to be in the wrong, for only
the infinite edifies, not the finite!

If, then, there was a man whom you loved, and in favor
of him you succeeded in deceiving your thought and yourself, you would still be in a perpetual contradiction, because you knew that you were in the right but wished that
you were in the wrong and wished to believe it. On the
other hand, if it was God you loved, could there be any
question of such a contradiction, could you then have
knowledge of anything else but what you wished to believe? Might He who is in heaven not be greater than you
who dwell on the earth? Might His riches not be more

abundant than your scant measure? His wisdom no deeper
than your shrewdness? His holiness no greater than your
righteousness? Must you not recognize this necessarily? But
if you must recognize it, then there is no contradiction between your knowledge and your wish. And yet if you necessarily must recognize it, then there is no edification in the
thought that you are always in the wrong, for we have
said that the reason why at one time it could prove so
painful to be in the wrong, and at another time edifying,
was because in the one case you were compelled to recognize that which in the other case you wished to recognize.
So in your relationship to God you would, it is true, be
freed from the contradiction, but you would have lost the
edification—and yet what we wished to ponder was precisely this: the edification in the fact that as against God
we are always in the wrong.

Might it really be thus? Why was it you wished to be in
the wrong with respect to a person? Because you loved.
Why did you find this edifying? Because you loved. The
more you loved, the less time you had to deliberate
whether you were in the right or not; your love had only
one wish, that you might constantly be in the wrong. So
also in your relation to God. You loved God, and hence
your soul could find repose and joy only in the thought
that you must always be in the wrong. It was not by the
toil of thought you attained this recognition, neither was
it forced upon you, for it is in love that you find yourself
in freedom. So if thought convinced you that such was the
case, that it could not be otherwise than that you must
always be in the wrong, or that God must always be in the
right, then this recognition followed as a logical consequence—but in fact you did not attain the certainty that
you were in the wrong as a deduction from the knowledge
that God was always in the right; but from love's dearest
and only wish, that you might always be in the wrong,
you reached the apprehension that God was always in the
right. But this wish is the affair of love, hence, of freedom,
and you were not in any way compelled to recognize that
you were always in the wrong. So it was not by reflection
you became certain that you were always in the wrong,

but the certainty was due to the fact that you were edified by this thought.

So it is an edifying thought that against God we are always in the wrong. If this were not the case, if this conviction did not have its source in your whole being, that is, did not spring from the love within you, then your reflection also would have taken a different turn; you would have recognized that God is always in the right, this you are compelled to recognize, and as a consequence of this you are compelled to recognize that you are always in the wrong. This conclusion would, in fact, be rather difficult, for you may well be compelled to recognize that God is always in the right, but to make application of this to yourself, to take up this perception into your whole being, is a thing you really cannot be compelled to do. So you recognize that God is always in the right, and, as a consequence of this, that you are always in the wrong; but this recognition does not edify you. There is no edification in recognizing that God is always in the right, and so, too, there is none in any thought which follows from this by necessity. When you recognize that God is always in the right you stand aloof from God, and so, too, when you recognize as a consequence of this that you are always in the wrong. On the other hand, if in virtue of no foregoing recognition you claim and are convinced that you are always in the wrong, then you are hidden in God. This is your divine worship, your religious devotion, your godly fear.

You loved a person, you wished that with respect to him you might always be in the wrong; but, alas, he was unfaithful to you, and however reluctantly you admitted it, however much it pained you, you nevertheless would have to recognize that you were in the right in your behavior towards him, and in the wrong for loving him so dearly. And yet your soul insisted upon loving him thus, only in this could you find peace and rest and happiness. Then your soul turned away from the finite to the infinite; there it found its object, there your love became a happy love. God I will love, you said; He bestows upon the lover all things, He fulfills my dearest, my only wish, that against Him I must be always in the wrong. Never shall any alarm-

ing doubt tear me away from Him, never shall I be terrified
by the thought that I could ever find myself in the right
against Him, against God I am always in the wrong.

Or is this not true, was not this your only wish, your
dearest wish, and were you not seized by a terrible dread
when for an instant the thought could enter into your mind
that you might be in the right, that God's governance was
not wisdom, but that your plans were; that God's thoughts
were not righteousness, but that your pursuits were; that
God's heart was not love, but that your sentiments were?
And was it not your bliss that you never could love as you
were loved? So, then, this thought that against God you
are always in the wrong is not a truth you are compelled
to recognize, not a comfort which assuages your pain, not
a compensation for the loss of something better, but it is a
joy in which you triumph over yourself and over the world,
it is your delight, your anthem of praise, your divine worship, a demonstration that your love is a happy one, as
only that love can be wherewith one loves God.

So, then, the thought that against God we are always
in the wrong is an edifying thought. It is edifying that we
are in the wrong, edifying that we always are. It proves its
edifying power in a double way: partly by the fact that
it checks doubt and allays the solicitude of doubt; partly
by the fact that it animates to action.

Surely, my hearer, you will still bear in mind the wisdom
which I described above. It appeared to be so trustworthy
and reliable, it explained everything so easily, it was willing
to conduct every man safely through life, unaffected by
the storms of doubt. "One does what one can," it called
out to the man who stood perplexed. And indeed it is undeniable that when one has done what one can, one is the
better for it. It had nothing more to say, it vanished like a
dream, or it remained as a monotonous repetition in the
ear of the doubter. Then when he would put it to use, it
appeared that he could not use it, it entangled him in a
mesh of difficulties. He could not find time to deliberate
how much he could do, for at the same time he had to be
doing what he could. Or if he found time to deliberate, the
test resulted in a more or less, an approximation, but never

anything exhaustive of his possibilities. How might a man
be able to depict his relationship to God by a more or a
less, or by an approximate definition? He then convinced
himself that this wisdom was a treacherous friend, who,
under the pretext of helping him, involved him in doubt,
drew him alarmingly into a perpetual circle of confusion.
What before had been obscure to him, but had not troubled him, became now, not any clearer, but alarming to
his mind and troubling. Only by an infinite relationship to
God could the doubt be calmed, only by an infinitely free
relationship to God could his anxiety be transformed into
joy. He is in an infinite relationship to God when he recognizes that God is always in the right, in an infinitely free
relationship to God when he recognizes that he himself is
always in the wrong. In this way, therefore, doubt is
checked, for the movement of doubt consists precisely in
the fact that at one instant he might be in the right, at
another in the wrong, to a certain degree in the right, to a
certain degree in the wrong, and this was supposed to characterize his relationship to God. But such a relationship to
God is no relationship, and it was the nutriment of doubt.
In his relationship to another man it was quite possible that
he might be partly in the wrong, partly in the right, to a
certain degree in the wrong, to a certain degree in the right,
because he, like every other man, is a finite being, and his
relation to other men is a finite relation which consists in a
more or a less. Therefore, so long as doubt would make the
infinite relationship finite, and so long as wisdom would fill
up the infinite relationship with finiteness, just so long
would he remain in doubt. So whenever doubt would alarm
him by the particular instance, would teach him that he
suffers too much, that he is tried beyond his powers, he
thereupon forgets the finite in the infinite thought that he
is always in the wrong. Whenever the affliction of doubt
would make him sad, he thereupon raises himself above
the finite into the infinite; for the thought that he is always
in the wrong is the wing whereby he soars above finitude,
it is the longing wherewith he seeks God, it is the love
wherein he finds God.

Against God we are always in the wrong. But does not

this thought produce anaesthesia? Edifying as it may be, is it not dangerous to a person, does it not lull him into a slumber in which he dreams of a relationship to God which yet is not a real relationship, docs it not consume the power of a man's will and the strength of his resolution? Not by any means! Or the man who wished to be always in the wrong with respect to another, was he dull and inactive, did he not do everything in his power to be in the right? And yet he wished only to be in the wrong. And how could the thought that as against God we are always in the wrong be anything but an animating thought? For what else does it express but that God's love is greater than our love? Does not this thought make a man glad to act? For when he is in doubt he has no power to act. Does it not make him fervent in spirit? For when he reckons finitely the fire of the Spirit is quenched. So when your only wish is denied to you, my hearer, you are joyful nevertheless; you do not say, "God is always in the right," for in that there is no joy; you say, "Against God I am always in the wrong." Though it were you, you yourself,[3] that had to deny yourself your dearest wish, you are joyful nevertheless, my hearer; you do not say, "God is always in the right," for in that there is no jubilation; you say, "Against God I am always in the wrong." Though that which was your wish were what others, and you yourself in a certain sense, might call your duty, though you must not only forego your wish but in a way be unfaithful to your duty, though you were to lose not only your joy but even your honor, you are joyful nevertheless; "Against God," you say, "I am always in the wrong." Though you were to knock but it was not opened unto you, though you were to seek but you did not find, though you were to labor but acquired nothing, though you were to plant and water but saw no blessing, though heaven were to remain closed and the witness failed to appear, you are joyful in your work nevertheless; though the punishment which the iniquity of the fathers had called down were to fall upon you, you are joyful nevertheless, for against God we are always in the wrong.

Against God we are always in the wrong. This thought

then checks doubt and calms its distress, it encourages and inspires to action.

Your thought has now followed the course of this exposition, perhaps hurrying swiftly ahead when it was along familiar paths it led you, slowly and perhaps reluctantly when the way was strange to you. But nevertheless you must admit that the case is as it was set forth, and your thought had no objection to raise against it. Before we separate, one question more, my hearer: Did you wish, could you wish, that the case might be different? Could you wish that you might be in the right? Could you wish that that beautiful law which for thousands of years has supported the race and every generation in the race, that beautiful law, more glorious than the law which supports the stars in their courses upon the vault of heaven, could you wish that this law might burst, with more dreadful effect than if that law of nature were to lose its force and everything were to be resolved into appalling chaos? Could you wish this? I have no word of wrath with which to terrify you; your wish must not proceed from dread of the presumptuous thought of willing to be in the right against God; I ask only, could you wish that it might be otherwise? Perhaps my voice does not possess enough strength and heartiness to penetrate into your inmost thought—O, but ask yourself, ask with the solemn uncertainty with which you would address yourself to a man who was able, you knew, by a single word to decide your happiness in life, ask yourself still more seriously, for verily it is a question of salvation. Do not check your soul's flight, do not grieve the better promptings within you, do not dull your spirit with half wishes and half thoughts. Ask yourself, and continue to ask until you find the answer. For one may have known a thing many times and acknowledged it, one may have willed a thing many times and attempted it; and yet it is only by the deep inward movements, only by the indescribable emotions of the heart, that for the first time you are convinced that what you have known belongs to you, that no power can take it from you; for only the truth which edifies is truth for you.[4]

NOTES AND INDEX

NOTES

1. Like the motto to Volume I, this one too speaks of the passions. Whereas A's motto is a defense of the passions, the motto chosen by B points out their dangers. The quotation is from Chateaubriand's short novel, *Atala* (1801). Atala is a young Indian woman. In order to rescue Chactas, who is under sentence of death, she flees with him to the desert. They fall passionately in love with each other. But since she has promised her dying mother perpetual chastity, she takes poison so as not to be overcome by her passion. As an old man, Chactas, telling this story to a melancholy young Frenchman, says: "René, if you fear the perturbation of the heart, you must beware of solitude in the wilds of nature. The great passions are hermits, and to transport them to the desert is to hand over to them their proper domain." With this motto Judge William answers the question posed by A's motto by saying in effect: Not until passion is brought out of isolation in the solitary individual and brought into communal life with the marriage partner and children is it sanctified, baptized.

"AESTHETIC VALIDITY OF MARRIAGE"

1. "Like the Page in Figaro," as S.K. said in the first draft.
2. Alluding to the many amours of Zeus.
3. For altar and hearth, i.e., house and home.
4. *Peter Schlemihl's wundersame Geschichte*, by A. von Chamisso, Chap. 1. *Werke*, IV, p. 276.
5. In part 6 of Vol. I.—too long drawn out and desperately tedious.

6. "To Eliza"—"Though women are angels, yet wedlock's the devil."

7. *Papirer* III, p. 129, shows that the reference is to *Gabrielle de Belle-Isle* by A. Dumas.

8. "Upon whom the gods bestowed beauty, wealth, and the power of enjoyment." Horace's *Letters* I, 4, 6.

9. Cf. *Repetition,* pp. 11 ff.

10. According to some reports the truce between Saladin and Richard Coeur de Lion was to last for three years, three months, three days, and three hours.

11. *Volksmährchen der Deutschen,* Gotha, 1787–89, III, p. 219.

12. *The Marriage of Figaro* by Mozart was translated into Danish by R. T. Bruun. Act i, scene 7.

13. As a cloud upon Semele, as rain upon Danae.

14. A poem entitled *The First Licking,* by Chr. Wilster, Copenhagen, 1827.

15. "The First Kiss of Love."

16. In Scandinavian mythology the goddess Frigga required everything in nature to promise not to harm Balder—but she forgot the mistletoe, which became his destruction.

17. One of Æsop's fables tells of a braggart who boasted of a prodigious leap he had made at Rhodes. One of the bystanders challenged him: here is Rhodes, now leap. *Salta* also means to dance.

18. *Skolemesteren i Alferne,* scene 4. J. L. Heiberg's *Poetiske Skrifter,* II, p. 57.

19. Really it is Troels in Holberg's *Barselstuen,* act i, scene 1, who says, "I would pledge myself to make half a hundred such children a year—that's no great miracle."

20. The words of the song were: "Tell me, Annette, why we have missed you so long in our meadow where you used to come among us with pipe and dancing? Why do you shun the joys of youth and seek out lonely places? Tell me why." It figured in a lyric comedy by Theaulon, translated into Danish in 1821.

21. In Ecclesiasticus 36:24–26.

22. Hagar. Genesis 21:9 ff.

23. Nehemiah 4:23.

24. An allusion to the remark about Nehemiah on p. 83.

25. "It is an old story." Quoted from Heine, *Lyrisches Intermezzo*, No. 39.

26. A few years later S.K. began but left unfinished a book with this title (One must doubt everything) in opposition to the followers of Descartes who made this their slogan. He frequently refers to this doctrine, but he lauds Descartes in the Preface to *Fear and Trembling*. The unfinished book in a translation by T. H. Croxall has been published.

27. Divide and conquer—an old Roman motto adopted by Louis XI of France.

28. This was S.K.'s own case.

29. I Timothy 4:4. Quoted from memory—and somewhat inexactly.

30. Oehlenschläger, *Skattegraveren*. "But if you utter one word, it vanishes again."

31. Caligula wished that the heads of all the Romans were on one neck so that with one stroke he could cut them off.

32. The Emperor Domitian. Suetonius, *Domitianus* 3.

33. The minister of Catherine II of Russia, who in order to make her believe that the money entrusted to him had been wisely spent improvised what appeared to be flourishing villages within sight of the road on which she traveled with him to inspect the province.

34. It was precisely his own case.

35. Horace, *Ars poetica* 323. The phrase means "round mouth," i.e., the ability to express oneself easily and fluently.

36. *Nouveaux Essais* II, Chap. 27.

37. Leviticus 24:9.

38. *Ueber das Verhältniss der bildenden Künste zu der Natur* (1807). *Sämmtliche Werke*, 1860, VII, pp. 289 ff.

39. Cf. *Papirer*, I C 80.

40. Fr. Schlegel's *Lucinde*.

41. Oehlenschläger's *Valravnen*. For "the imperishable nature, etc.," cf. I Peter 3:3, 4.

42. "When ten times repeated they please." Horace's *Ars poetica* 365.

43. *Nordens Guder,* "Freiers Sang ved Kilden."

44. A decorated birch rod with which Danish children wake up their parents on Shrove Monday.

45. Self-tormentor. It is the title of a Greek comedy translated by Terence.

46. "I have spoken and freed my mind." Roman orators sometimes concluded their speeches with these words.

47. *Erzählungen und Mährchen,* Prenzlau, 1826, II, pp. 323 ff.

"EQUILIBRIUM BETWEEN THE AESTHETICAL AND THE ETHICAL IN THE COMPOSITION OF PERSONALITY"

1. *Parmenides,* Chap. 19, defines the "now" as the border between the "before" and the "after."

2. Wolff, *Mythologie der Feen und Elfen,* Weimar, 1828. Translated from an English work—by what author I do not know.

3. Goethe, *West-östlicher Divan,* "Freiheit." The meaning of the couplet may be suggested by a free translation:

> "I give myself up to infinite space,
> And nothing but the stars are above my head."

4. "Light breathing"—distinguished by grammarians from a more definite aspiration of a Greek vowel. While this sign is used in certain Greek words, it has no effect on the manner of pronunciation. The reference to Cato in the next sentence recalls the persistence with which he insisted that "Carthage must be destroyed."

5. This was Hegel's claim. What follows here is an attack, not upon philosophy in general, but upon the Hegelian system, which was then the prevailing philosophy.

6. I have to confess that I do not know what is meant by this Spanish "s." But two possibilities have been suggested to me. First, it is notorious that in Spanish the letter "s" is often elided. Second, S.K. may have been thinking

of the cedilla, the little wiggle sometimes written under the letter "c," which in older type fonts was kept in a separate compartment.

7. *Papirer*, II A 484, shows that he was thinking of the reprobation of *acedia*. Cf. Dru, *The Journals of Søren Kierkegaard*, No. 292.

8. No man knew melancholy from his own experience better than S.K. He applied himself zealously to the anatomy of this disease of the spirit. This is the theme of two of his most notable works: *The Concept of Dread*, and *The Sickness unto Death*.

9. This term was derived from Plato's *Phaedrus* 22 and 37.

10. "Rolands Knappen," in *Volksmährchen der Deutschen*, Gotha, 1787, I, pp. 164 ff.

11. "Fleeing from poverty, over the sea, across rocky wastes, through fire." Horace's *Letters*, I, 1, 46.

12. A creative effort.

13. As Alcibiades says of Socrates in Plato's *Symposium*, 33.

14. S.K. constantly refers to Hegel's philosophy as "the System," condemning it because so long as it is unfinished it cannot properly claim to be a system. What follows is S.K.'s first open criticism of this philosophy.

15. Again and again S.K. quotes Matthew 16:26 in this form, the form which he found in the Danish Bible—instead of "lose" or "forfeit" one's soul. Where I can I have used the phrase familiar in English, but here I cannot.

16. "Philosophy" here means Hegelianism, which pretended to abolish the principle of contradiction.

17. It seems that at an earlier period S.K. frequently had this phrase in his mouth; for Hans Christian Andersen (mindful of the days when they ate at the same boarding house) put it into the mouth of the parrot which in one of his tales, *The Lucky Galoshes*, figures satirically as S.K.

18. The Danish Editors suggest that S.K. has in mind Ludvig Thostrup, in the play *Østergade og Vestergade* (*Kgl. Theaters Repertoire*, No. 12), Copenhagen, 1828.

19. Equable temperament.

20. Like the burning bush, Exodus 3:2.

21. A reference to part 5 of Vol. I, "The Unhappiest Man."

22. From Frankenau, *Samlede Digte*, p. 283, Copenhagen, 1815.

23. Quoted (somewhat inexactly) from Kruse's rendering.

24. Especially in "The Inconsolable."

25. Like Kronos.

26. This describes the Cynics and, to some extent, the Stoics.

27. Inner sanctuary.

28. It was a curious trait in S.K. that he somehow associated with himself the name Ludvig. This is no exception, for he was several times on the point of committing suicide, and the letter ascribed here to Ludvig is just such as he might have written to his brother Peter.

29. The Socratic ignorance.

30. The Church hard-pressed.

31. Cf. note 17 to the first letter: *Hic Rhodus, hic saltus.*

32. Presumably in "Aurelia."

33. Know thyself. This was the motto inscribed above the portal of the temple at Delphi upon which Socrates laid so much stress. It is highly important to note that S.K.'s term, "to choose oneself," is his rendering of the Socratic maxim.

In the preceding sentence is the term "witch's letter." Not one of the six publishers I consulted could tell me what to call it in English, although all of them immediately recognized a witch's letter (*Heksebrev*) when I described it. It is a book containing pictures, cut in two, of men or animals. The top halves and the bottom halves can be united in many different combinations to form all manner of fantastic figures.

34. Literally, "between and between," i.e., the distinction between one thing and another. This power to distinguish is the critical faculty. Hence *Inter et inter* was chosen by S.K. as the pseudonym for a little book which was a critical appreciation of a famous actress.

35. "In terms of possibility"—a *terminus technicus* in Aristotle's philosophy.

36. The Adamites.

37. A primer of morals for the young, written by Bishop Balle and in Denmark everywhere used in primary schools. S.K. frequently refers to it.

38. The simple inhabitants of the small island of Mol were a proverbial object of ridicule to the sophisticated citizens of Copenhagen. The German phrase means "without further ado."

39. Although the following account is put into the mouth of Judge William, there can be no doubt that it recounts S.K.'s own story.

40. Taught by God.

41. Evidently a play on words which uses the Danish *fordre* with the double meaning of the German *fordern*.

42. Virgil's *Aeneid* VI, 258: "Hence! keep far away, ye uninitiated!"

43. St. Augustine's prayer: "Speak, that I may behold Thee."

44. "Jordens Lethe," a drinking song by Baggesen. *Danske Værker* II, p. 218, Copenhagen, 1845.

45. According to the Greek myth Prometheus was the creator and benefactor of men. Etymologically interpreted, his name means forward-wise; that of his brother Epimetheus means backward-wise.

46. In the fable of the raven and the serviceberry.

47. Sallust, *Jugurtha* 35.

48. As in *The Arabian Nights*.

49. Hard necessity. Horace's *Odes* III, 24, 6.

50. The expression occurs in Vol. I, where the enthusiastic youth, early in his essay on "The Musical Erotic," ascribes to Mozart the first place in "the realm of gods."

51. Baggesen's poem "Appropriation," *Danske Værker* VI, p. 21. Copenhagen, 1845.

52. An enigmatical figure who cropped up in Nürnberg on May 26, 1828, and aroused a great sensation by the mystery surrounding his origin and his fate.

53. By L. F. Freiherren von Bilderbek, translated into Danish by Dean Horrebow in 1804.

54. *Preciosa,* a lyrical drama by Wolff, with music by C. M. von Weber, translated into Danish in 1822.

55. I Corinthians 11:5 ff.

56. At that time it was commonly thought that the Greek word for man, *anthropos,* meant etymologically one who looks up.

57. Part 3 of Vol. I is an essay on tragedy delivered before this society fantastically named "All-dead-together."

58. This was S.K.'s constant complaint against the Hegelian system.

59. *Nicomachean Ethics* VIII, 9 and 11.

60. Horace, *Letters,* I, 11, 29: "What you seek is here."

61. For example, in "Two Years after the Wedding," "The Riqueburg Family," "Aurelia," and "Either be Loved or Die."

62. This was S.K.'s case: he was unable to accomplish the universal by marrying. The pathos of the following passage is evident when we recognize that "the particular" was Regina Olsen. In *Fear and Trembling* this situation is regarded as the "teleological suspension of the ethical."

"ULTIMATUM"

1. Oehlenschläger's *Ludlams Hule* (*Samlede Værker,* XVII, p. 176).

2. Cf. Job 40:2.

3. Really this is the experience of S.K. himself.

4. This note on which *Either/Or* ends is heard again and again in S.K.'s works. In the *Postscript* it is heard in the assertion that "Subjectivity is the truth." Cf. the famous "Gilleleje-entry" in the Journal for 1835 (Dru's *Selections from the Journals,* No. 22).

INDEX

This book is written with such strict regard for topical coherence that the subjects listed in the index generally run through two or more or many pages; and because the exceptions to this rule are rare it is not necessary to note this fact by the customary signs, *seq.* or f. In many cases, of course, it is only a significant use of a word which is noted here.